"*Welcome to College* has been my go-to book for helping students prepare to succeed spiritually, relationally, and academically in college. No other book has such depth and balance. And I am thrilled that Jonathan has written a timely and helpful update, incorporating many of the biggest issues students face today. This book is a must-read for all Christian students who hope to have a vibrant faith in college."

—SEAN MCDOWELL, best-selling author, speaker, and professor at Biola University

"I know of no other book that has the breadth and depth of *Welcome to College* to help us equip the next generation with the truth. . . . My own kids will certainly have a copy in their hands as they step onto the college campus."

—BRETT KUNKLE, student impact director at Stand to Reason (str.org)

"In this updated second edition, Jonathan has improved an already excellent resource by adding the latest evidence for theism and Christianity and including critical discussions of controversial social and moral issues. If you're a student, don't you dare enter college until you've allowed Jonathan Morrow to prepare you. *Welcome to College: A Christ-Follower's Guide for the Journey* is essential to your success at university."

—J. WARNER WALLACE, cold-case detective, author of *Cold-Case Christianity*, and adjunct professor at Biola University

"If I could give just one apologetics book to a Christian going off to college, it is this one. Jonathan Morrow goes well beyond providing evidence for Christianity (as most such books do)—he provides succinct and sound answers to the kinds of moral and emotional issues that often trip up Christian college students. Highly recommended!"

—FRANK TUREK, broadcaster and author of *I Don't Have Enough Faith to Be an Atheist* and *Correct, Not Politically Correct*

"*Welcome to College* is easily the best resource for any Christian student who wants not just to survive college but to thrive on campus as an ambassador for Christ. No other book better equips young people for the challenges that lie ahead. I cannot recommend it enough!"

—SCOTT KLUSENDORF, president of Life Training Institute and author of *The Case for Life: Equipping Christians to Engage the Culture*

Praise for the First Edition

"*Welcome to College* addresses the most significant issues college students encounter with intelligent, practical wisdom. It will be of immense value to anyone making the adjustment to the exciting challenges these fast-paced years present."

—K. ERIK THOENNES, professor at Biola University and pastor at Grace Evangelical Free Church

"Wow! What a book! Quite frankly, this is the book I've been waiting for the last forty years to give to college students. It is the single best volume I have ever read for preparing students to follow Jesus and flourish as His disciples in college."

—J. P. MORELAND, author and distinguished professor of philosophy at Talbot School of Theology, Biola University

"Unpacking biblical truths, *Welcome to College* is a treasure book of wisdom that will literally save lives and help build a culture of life."

—KELLY MONROE KULLBERG, founder of The Veritas Forum and author of *Finding God Beyond Harvard*

"Jonathan Morrow has both the intellectual resources and the practical experience to provide an effective students' survival guide to university life. I'm impressed with the wide array of issues he discusses, from intellectual challenges to financial problems to sexual snares to getting enough sleep! All this is done in easily digestible bits for the student on the run.

This is a book I wish I could have given to my two kids when they went off to college!"

—WILLIAM LANE CRAIG, theologian, professor of philosophy, and author of *Reasonable Faith*

"Jonathan Morrow has written an extremely practical, insightful guide for navigating the challenges of college life. It is wide-ranging and wise. I enthusiastically recommend it!"

—PAUL COPAN, Pledger Family Chair of Philosophy and Ethics at Palm Beach Atlantic University

"Whether you are an incoming freshman or upperclassman, Jonathan provides straightforward, practical insight for dealing with current issues regarding living the Christian life on campuses everywhere. Not only is this a great read but you will find a place to turn to when questions or struggles show their face."

—TAYLOR MCCABE, film and digital media student at Baylor University

"This book will prepare anyone who is either enrolled in college or is planning to go to college for the daily challenges Christians deal with on campus. Jonathan Morrow is aware of the real college world and is dead-on with his excellent insight."

—BLAKE SMITH, construction engineering technology student at Texas Tech University

"Reading this book is like having your own personal mentor and friend to guide you through the rough rapids of college life. College is a great experience, but it can also be faith-shattering if you are not adequately prepared. This book is perfect for the high school senior who is curious about what college life will be like. It is also helpful for the college student who is dealing with the day-to-day challenges and questions faced both in and out of the classroom."

—MARK SCHMAHL, pastor of student ministries at Believers' Chapel

"With a refreshing mix of good humor and common sense, Jonathan Morrow guides the reader through the practical, intellectual, and moral thickets of beginning college. He writes as an older brother whose knowledge of the territory is recent and realistic. In short, readable chapters he covers all the expected issues and a good number of unexpected ones as well. Here is wisdom, not legalism. I highly recommend this book!"

—GARRETT DEWEESE, professor at large at Talbot School of Theology, Biola University

"Jonathan Morrow has provided a solid resource to Christian college students across the country. *Welcome to College* touches on many, if not all, of the major issues believers face on campus. The resources concluding each chapter are invaluable."

—B. J. WALTON, former men's discipleship coordinator at Biola University

"Christian students will be able to pick this up year after year and learn something new each time. It has the ability to connect with you no matter where you're at on your journey."

—KIM BOIKO, Biola University graduate

Also by Jonathan Morrow

*Is God Just a Human Invention? And Seventeen Other
Questions Raised by New Atheists*
Think Christianly: Looking at the Intersection of Faith and Culture
Questioning the Bible: 11 Major Challenges to the Bible's Authority

WELCOME TO COLLEGE

SECOND EDITION

**A CHRIST-FOLLOWER'S
GUIDE FOR THE JOURNEY**

JONATHAN MORROW

Kregel
Publications

Welcome to College: A Christ-Follower's Guide for the Journey
© 2008, 2017 by Jonathan Morrow
Second edition 2017

Published by Kregel Publications, a division of Kregel, Inc., 2450 Oak Industrial Dr. NE, Grand Rapids, MI 49505.

*For Mandi: There is no one I would rather be
on the journey with than you.*

*For Austin, Sarah Beth, and Madison:
My prayer for you is that you would love and follow
Jesus with courage and confidence all the days of your life,
and that the words and ideas in this book may
encourage you on this journey. I love you.*

*And for Brandon Garcia—a recent graduate—
who wanted to write a book for college students one day.
While he never got the opportunity to be formally published,
the text of his life remains with the many who knew him.
I dedicate this book to his memory, and celebrate his
passion for God, life, thinking well, and pursuing authentic
manhood. Brandon is now home, but is still missed.*

Contents

Foreword

MANY STUDENTS TEND TO APPROACH THE COLLEGE SELECTION PROCESS as if they were choosing a vacation spot. Other than confirming a chosen field of study, the questions they ask are somewhat shortsighted. Are the accommodations nice? How's the food? Is there on-campus entertainment? What about the football team?

These questions matter, of course. After all, it's no small commitment to spend a semester or two—or eight—at a particular place. In a very real sense, students are choosing where they are going to live. But going to college is less like choosing a vacation spot than it is committing to a four-year brain and heart surgery.

Many students simply are not prepared for the ideas, experiences, and relationships that will challenge their faith and shape their future. They will be stretched in unexpected ways, form habits of study and thinking, and embrace some vision of life that will lead them to either flourish or flounder. Away from the security of home, they will be forced to handle money, philosophies, roommates, temptation, and (at times) failure, all on their own.

That's why we worry about them. College is supposed to be something good, but we've seen too many casualties of campus life. We've read the headlines about rape culture, binge drinking, ideological indoctrination, and discrimination against students and faculty with Christian convictions. And we've heard the statistics, some of which are exaggerated, of how many students walk away from their Christian faith at college.

Well, I've got good news for the parents, youth pastors, mentors, and influencers who want to see the next generation successfully navigate the challenges of college. Students can tackle this new stage of life and emerge on the other side ready to make the most of the talents God has gifted to them and build a meaningful and faithful life. They don't have to be casualties.

Students can emerge smarter, sharper, and better followers of Christ after college.

In fact, I've met many who have, and so has Jonathan Morrow. As you will see in the pages ahead, *Welcome to College* is a clear, practical, and comprehensive guide to college life. I know of no better book you can put into the hands of a young Christian headed to college. Jonathan's many years of working with high school and college students is on full display here. He's what the author of Proverbs calls "a wise counselor," in everything from dealing with the intellectual assaults on Christianity and cultivating time-management skills to resolving relational conflict with peers and professors.

I've recommended *Welcome to College* for years and am happy to recommend it now to you and to the student you love.

John Stonestreet, 2017
President, Colson Center
for Christian Worldview

Preface to the Second Edition

I have no greater joy than to hear that my children are
walking in the truth.

—3 JOHN 4 (ESV)

IT'S HARD TO BELIEVE THAT EIGHT YEARS HAVE PASSED SINCE THE INItial publication of *Welcome to College*. Nearly 25,000 copies have been sold to date and I've been so encouraged by the response of readers who have shared how this material has helped equip them to follow Jesus in their college years with more confidence. I am grateful to God for the impact this book has had because my heart and passion is for students to walk in the truth. But as I talked with the publisher it became clear it was time to update this book for the young adults now heading into college. I am thankful that the majority of the first edition's content is as relevant today as when I first wrote it. But some updating of illustrations, evidence, and resources was needed. Also, there are questions students now wrestle with that weren't as much of an issue a decade ago, so I included some new material on topics such as how social media is affecting us as individuals and as a culture, how to think about Christianity and homosexuality, and how Christians should deal with marijuana even when it's legal.

After twelve years of speaking to and working with thousands of students at camps and conferences, in churches, and on campuses, I am more convinced than ever of the importance of the high school and college years in setting the trajectory for a life of following Jesus. There are real intellectual, moral, spiritual, and relational challenges. Students need to know what they believe as Christians, why they believe it, and how to live it out. Just because a student goes to church or attends youth group does not mean they are ready to follow Christ in today's culture. Mere attendance isn't cutting it; training is needed. Knowledge of the truth matters more than ever. And students need to know that they are not alone on this journey. They need encouragement to stand firm in a confused culture.

Some people are critical of this generation and believe students will not think about tough questions. My experience has shown the opposite to be true. Today's students are rejecting a cotton-candy Christianity filled with empty clichés and slogans. They are eager to be challenged and to engage the big questions of life, and they long for their lives to matter. It is my hope and prayer that the chapters in this book will help young adults build a lasting faith and will prepare them for a lifetime of following Jesus.

For today's generation,
Jonathan Morrow, 2017

Along the Way

COLLEGE IS AN INTERESTING PLACE.

I mean this both sarcastically and literally. You will see things in college that you never thought you'd see. You will also see stuff you would have rather not seen! You will meet lots of different kinds of people—some you'll like, some you won't. You will learn new things while in college (your parents will be glad to know this, even though much of it will happen outside the classroom), and you will be exposed to the wonderful world of ideas—for better or for worse. There will be good times, awkward moments, ups and downs, late nights and early mornings . . . a lot like your life already.

These four or five years will arguably be the most significant years of your life when it comes to determining the kind of person you'll be in the future and what kind of life you will lead. It is during these years that you lay the tracks your life will run along. No curfews . . . no parents . . . this is a whole new ball game (and for some—like me—a fresh start). So, what are you going to make of it? You are part of the privileged few who get the opportunity to go to college. While there has been an increase over the last decade, only about 7 percent of the world's population has the opportunity you have at this moment. How will you spend it? And if you are a Christian, what does it look like to spend it Christianly? (More on this later.)

We will cover many topics that will be important for you to think about during your college experience. To whet your appetite, here is just a sample of some of the issues and questions we will be talking about together:

- How do you grow spiritually?
- How can you discover what you are supposed to do with your life?
- How do you build and share your faith in a hostile environment?
- How do you manage your time so that you can study and have fun?

- Is all truth relative?
- Are there good reasons to be a Christian?
- What should you think about alcohol?
- How should you think about dating and sex as a Christian?
- How do you wisely navigate social media and protect your digital footprint?

Here's my disclaimer: I don't have all the answers. College in some ways will be experienced differently depending on the university you choose to attend, yet there are universal experiences and situations *all* collegians face. Although I don't have all the answers, by God's grace and His Word, together with the wisdom of mentors, friends, and some helpful books, I feel like I was able to do college right. I have no major regrets, and that had a lot to do with the people who walked, laughed, and prayed with me through those years.

So as a fellow traveler who just happens to be a few years further down the road than you are, the pages that follow will attempt to offer you some of the timeless principles and wisdom I picked up along the way . . . as well as some things I would have done a little differently if I had known then what I know now. As we explore these important issues together, I look forward to sharing some of my story with you. Even though it was not all good times, I had a blast in college.

I have tried to keep the chapters short and sweet since this won't be the only thing you will be reading this semester. Some of what we cover will challenge you, and that's a good thing. Be sure to check out the appendixes in the back of the book and the suggestions for further discovery at the end of each chapter. They might contain just what you need on a bad day or in a particularly challenging situation. In addition to those, there will always be resources available at my website, JonathanMorrow.org. And finally, I hope to challenge you as a follower of Jesus Christ to consider what your college experience would look like if it were spent in a distinctly Christian manner (Luke 10:27).

So if you haven't packed yet, that's OK—there's still some time. Thanks for inviting me along for the ride. My prayer is that you have the best college experience possible and that your relationship with Jesus Christ thrives like never before. *Welcome to college!*

Preparing for Campus Life

THERE I WAS, STANDING IN THE PARKING LOT LOOKING UP AT MY DORM. I had finally arrived . . . at college that is. And after filling out a pile of paperwork, I was the proud owner of a key that would cost me $15 to replace if lost—but it was to my *own* room. I walked in and was greeted by the sweet smell of industrial-strength disinfectant, cinderblock walls painted pale blue, a metallic bunk bed, and a yellowing bathroom that four sets of roommates would share. Along with my roommate, Dave, this was home my first year of college.

My first week of school was kind of a blur. Everything was new and I was nervous! Not only did I have to find out where to eat (and quickly learn what not to eat), I had to find my mailbox and sign up for a parking sticker. (My conspiracy theory is that universities fund their budgets by the revenue from all of the parking fines they make students pay—so be careful where and in which direction you park.)

Every kind of club and organization imaginable had tables set up all over campus. There were banners, fliers, welcome parties, and lots of free food. There were signs for rush week (for fraternities and sororities) and progressive dinners at local churches and ministries. It was a buffet of activity.

Within a couple of weeks, Dave and I had met a great group of Christian friends; we all ended up walking through college together. Within another couple of weeks, I had pledged and "de-pledged" a fraternity. God had other plans in that area that would unfold in my junior year.

Looking back now, I clearly see God's providence at work from the first day. An example: I was helping a friend from my home church in Knoxville move into an apartment. This divine appointment changed my life. In the course of unloading a moving truck with some other people, I met Rich—a guy who just happened to be the newly appointed campus director of Campus Crusade for Christ (now called Cru) at my school. We hit it off right away, and he invited me to a cookout at his house the following night. Several of us went, and the rest is history.

From that small group of students and staff we launched Cru on our campus. Rich became a mentor to me throughout college and one of my best friends. He taught me how to study God's Word for myself; we studied 2 Timothy and it is still my favorite book of the Bible. God used Cru more than anything else in college to shape my life and provide me with opportunities to serve, lead, and grow. It was through this experience that I discovered I wanted to spend my life investing in the lives of others (2 Tim. 2:2). And my training in Cru inspired me to pledge a fraternity my junior year and be a part of launching a ministry to fraternities and sororities. This by itself was incredibly rewarding, but it was also through this Greek ministry that I met my future wife.

I could go on. But my main point is this: you may think and feel at times that college is a random series of classes, events, and relationships. You may not even be at the college you wanted to attend. Regardless of the situation, I assure you that God is at work. If you yield to His will, you can be confident that He will lead you in the way you should go. Remember, He has good plans for you (Eph. 2:10).

Three Pieces of Wisdom

There are many important lessons to learn during college, but I think these three will be especially helpful in the beginning.

1. *You are not alone.* It will be tempting to think that you are the only one who has ever felt "this way" or struggled with a particular fear or insecurity in college. Not true! College can be lonely and overwhelming at times, but this is the reason that life is a team sport: we need each other. Good friends are essential in college. Moreover, as a son or daughter of God, you have the sure promise that your heavenly Father will never leave or forsake you (Matt. 28:20). Hang in there and stay faithful by leaning on God and the solid friends in your life.

2. *With freedom comes responsibility.* College is great! Finally you are not under the all-seeing eyes of parents. There are no curfews, and no one will make you do your homework or eat your vegetables. You don't even have to scrub the toilet or wash dishes if you don't want to (though I'd advise against this particular expression of liberty). What will you do with this newfound freedom? Will you define freedom as living any way you want, or will you define it as the opportunity to live how you ought to live? College is not like golf; there are no mulligans. Your free choices have real consequences. If you don't study or go to class, you'll fail. If you don't take care of your body, you will be sick much of the time. If you break the law, you will have to deal with the consequences. So enjoy your newfound freedom—I sure did—but be responsible in your decisions. What you sow now, you reap later.

3. *Don't take yourself too seriously.* Take college seriously, but don't take yourself too seriously. Like everyone else, you will have your moments of wanting to go crawl under a rock and hide out of embarrassment and awkwardness. Many situations will feel like they are the end of the world; they aren't. You are going to have some bad days. It's kind of like a rite of passage. If you can't laugh in the moment, you will definitely laugh later!

Two Survival Tips

Here are two other survival tips—free of charge. First, pick your roommates carefully. I was blessed with great roommates in college. They were Christians who encouraged me and held me accountable. We hung out together all the time and laughed *a lot*. I wouldn't have made it without them. Sure, we got on each other's nerves at times, but that's par for the course when you spend that much time with the same people. If you can help it, make sure you are in a good roommate situation; you want an encouraging and safe place to come home to at the end of the day.

Second, find your academic advisor and the financial aid office ASAP. This is critical. You want to graduate someday, right? Well, to ensure that, make certain you are taking the right classes in the right order. There are few worse feelings than heading into your last semester and finding out you still have twenty-four credits left to take! Also, make sure that your advisor is knowledgeable in your program's course requirements. I have heard numerous stories of advisors who didn't have a clue about the academic programs—they were assigned the job of advising because they lacked seniority within the department. If they look uncertain, seek out a second opinion!

As far as financial aid, you'll figure out soon enough how expensive college is. You might qualify for some financial aid. So find the financial aid office early and turn in your paperwork *on time*. I have known several people who lost out on thousands of dollars in financial aid because they forgot to turn in a form by the deadline.

Owning Your Faith

Now that you have successfully survived high school, it's time to embark on the challenging process of owning your faith in college. Up until now, your parents and youth pastor have probably played a significant role in shaping your Christian convictions—and this is a good thing. But your dad, mom, and youth pastor aren't here to tell you what to believe anymore. You will have to discover what you really believe. There will be growing pains, frustrating days, and some disillusionment along the way. This is a natural part of transitioning from a teenager to a responsible adult. There will be many voices offering their opinions.[4] You will have to decide which ones to listen to and why.

While we will spend plenty of time dealing with "practical college stuff," we also need to invest some time and effort in becoming grounded in what is true about you, God, the world in which you live, and the really big questions in life. Take it from one who has been where you are, this is time well spent.

Part of owning your faith in college means putting down roots and becoming established in your faith (Col. 2:6–7). God's Word calls us all to "grow in the grace and knowledge of our Lord and Savior Jesus Christ" (2 Peter 3:18). This means not only understanding what you believe and why you believe it but also growing in your ability and confidence to talk about it with others (1 Peter 3:15).

THE BIG IDEAS

- No matter how it looks at the moment, God is providentially at work in the everyday details of your college experience.
- Three important pieces of wisdom to remember are (1) you are not alone, (2) with freedom comes responsibility, and (3) don't take yourself too seriously.
- Two survival tips are (1) pick your roommates carefully and (2) find your academic advisor and the financial aid office ASAP.
- Owning your Christian faith is a necessary part of growing up and living well.

For Further Discovery

Fant, Gene C., Jr. *The Liberal Arts: A Student's Guide*. Reclaiming the Christian Intellectual Tradition. Wheaton, IL: Crossway, 2012.

Kullberg, Kelly Monroe. *Finding God Beyond Harvard: The Quest for Veritas*. Downers Grove, IL: InterVarsity Press, 2009.

———

JonathanMorrow.org. My personal website with videos, podcast, blog, and other helpful resources.

WelcomeToCollege.tv. *Welcome to College* online resources.

02

Think Christianly
Cultivating a Christian Worldview

*All truth, no matter where it be found or by whom it be
discovered, is still God's truth.*
—ARTHUR F. HOLMES[1]

*I believe in Christianity as I believe the Sun has risen, not
only because I see it, but because by it I see everything else.*
—C. S. LEWIS[2]

*So whether you eat or drink or whatever you do, do it all
for the glory of God.*
—1 CORINTHIANS 10:31

MOST CHRISTIANS HAVE BOUGHT INTO A LIE. THE LIE IS THAT RELIGIOUS
beliefs are to be kept private and should not impact who you are—and what
you say—in public. It's easy to fall into this way of thinking, but I want to help
you avoid this trap because it will weaken your faith. Popular culture teaches
that it doesn't matter if you are a Supreme Court Justice, doctor, lawyer, sales
representative, or college student, you must keep your spiritual beliefs to
yourself and out of everyone else's business. Often this is referred to as keeping the "sacred" and "secular" separate. Today's culture teaches that what is
sacred—personal religious beliefs about God or worship practices—should
be kept separate from what is *secular*—the public sphere of activity and what
the hard sciences can tell us. It's a long story, but this is an artificial distinction, resulting from ways of thinking inherited from the Enlightenment and
overflowing from the current misunderstanding of the relationship between
church and state (more on that later). Not only is the distinction artificial,
it's false! In reality, there is no separation between one's personal beliefs and

public life—especially for the Christian (1 Cor. 10:31)[3]—because our commitment to Jesus Christ should permeate *every* part of our lives.

Everyone Has a Worldview

Images and information constantly wash over us via high-definition TVs, high-speed Internet, smartphones, and social-media updates. All of these are mediums for constant messages, which necessarily flow out of different worldviews that, for good or ill, have a huge influence on us individually and culturally.

A worldview is a web of habit-forming beliefs about the biggest questions of life that helps you make sense of all your experiences. I like how Wheaton College president Philip Ryken puts it, "Whenever we bump into the world, our worldview has a way of spilling out. It comes out in what we think and love, say and do, praise and choose."[4]

Everyone has a worldview. It makes no difference whether someone is a Buddhist, Muslim, Christian, atheist, agnostic, humanist, or skeptic—they all have a worldview. Now, all these worldviews can't be true because that would mean there is no objective reality—no way things really are. Reality is *discovered* by human beings, not *created* by them. And only a little examination shows that different worldviews make contradictory claims—they can't all be true! So, one can test a worldview by examining how well the worldview's set of ideals and beliefs fit together and explain reality. Here are three helpful questions you can ask: Is it rational? Is it livable? And who says so?

What do these questions look like in action? As an example, I'll summarize some points I have developed in more detail elsewhere.[5] First, naturalism (the worldview behind much of atheism today, which claims that all phenomena can be adequately explained by scientific laws) is at its core irrational. Why? Because if the universe is just purely physical—molecules in motion—then where do nonphysical things like souls, reason, truth, logic, consciousness, and free will come from? In the naturalist story, if we are "lucky" enough to somehow find ourselves in a life-permitting universe and cross the gaping chasm between random chemicals and biological life without any supernatural activities along the way, then why think that we can trust our thinking? After all, the standard view from evolutionary biology of natural selection through genetic mutation is concerned with selective advantage for the species, not truth.[6] There are a lot of false beliefs I could hold that could also help me survive.

Next, atheism is unlivable because it fails to adequately deal with the problem of evil. According to atheism, there is no evil (or good for that matter). Why? Because there is no way the world is "supposed" to be. Where would an objective standard of good and evil come from? The six million Jews killed in the Holocaust at the hands of Nazi Germany can't truly be called evil; that's just what happened. And the wheels on the evolutionary bus go round and round, indifferent to human suffering, tears, and loss. Ultimately if someone is cunning or powerful enough—no matter how heinous his or her actions may be—they will get away with it in the end because there is no ultimate standard and no ultimate judge of human behavior. So a worldview that not only fails to account for evil but also provides no meaningful hope rooted in reality fails the livability test.

Lastly, when it comes to naturalism—who says so? Where does ultimate authority rest? The ever-changing opinions and evolving morality of *Homo sapiens*? Christianity, on the other hand, is rooted in the claims of Jesus of Nazareth who predicted his own death and rose from the dead to authenticate his claims. If true—and I discuss the powerful evidence to support this in chapter 17—then this man would have the authority to speak to the biggest questions of life.

People may not ask these three questions of their own beliefs or think carefully about the way they view the world, but they still have a worldview. And it affects every area of their lives. Every person—knowingly or not—filters the information that enters their minds through their worldview. They then make sense of that information based on their worldview. This process is automatic, and the filtered information shapes their beliefs and influences how they function in society, including the smallest decisions they make.

A good illustration of how this works is commercials. If I asked why you want Beats headphones, the odds are very good that you wouldn't respond with the scientific specs of how the noise cancelation feature works. You buy Beats to feel cool, empowered, unique, and untethered. Listen to how an advertising account manager, aka "consumer anthropologist," described working for Porsche: "My task was to hijack your imagination, brand your brain with our logo, and then feed you opinions you thought were your own. . . . An effective ad tries to tap viewers' most intense and emotional experiences, the trigger for all consumer impulses. My job was to save people from feeling impotent, unattractive, or powerless by offering them a Porsche, which promised to fix those problems."[7] It's only a commercial, right? The same thing happens with the shows and movies we stream on Netflix or Hulu (see chapter 40 for more on this). Our assumptions about questions of human worth or what happiness is and how to achieve it are subtly shaped without realizing it.

As Christians we must learn how to think Christianly in a world that is anything but Christian. Jesus of Nazareth, the smartest man who ever lived, has given this charge to His followers: "Love the Lord your God with all your heart and with all your soul and with all your strength and with all your mind" (Luke 10:27). This command covers our mental life, emotions, and actions. As a result, there should be a difference in the way a Christian student and a non-Christian student journey through high school and college. Christians are not to accept uncritically what the world tells us is true, good, and real because God has already spoken regarding these through creation (Ps. 19:1–4), the Scriptures (2 Tim. 3:16–17), and ultimately His one and only Son—Jesus Christ (Heb. 1:1–3).

If the Christian worldview is true—and there are many good reasons to think it is—then it's true for *all* of life. Let me rephrase this: if the Christian worldview best answers the most profound human questions (where we came from, who we are, how we should live, why the world is such a mess, and what our ultimate destiny is, to name a few), then it is true for more than just two hours on Sunday morning. Christianity has implications for every day of the week. There should be no separation between our private religious life and our public life. If we keep "the spiritual" segregated from the rest of our life, we live an unhealthy, fragmented life, which will keep us from maturing as Christ-followers.

Christians are not to withdraw from society and hide until Jesus returns; we are called to engage culture. Jesus uses salt and light as metaphors, challenging us to permeate the world around us (Matt. 5:13–16). We are not to be *of* the world, but we are to be *in* it (John 17:15–23; 1 John 2:15–16). So whether we are watching a movie, voting, studying for class, serving in a public or government office,[8] shopping for groceries, talking with a neighbor, watching the news, feeding the poor, working in a laboratory, creating art, composing literature, building houses, designing architecture, playing golf, or any other activity you can think of—we should strive to approach these activities *Christianly*. It is sometimes a challenge to figure out exactly what this looks like in each situation, but God will show us if we will seek Him.[9]

Worldviews in Conflict

I want to briefly point out, in case you haven't noticed, that there is a worldview struggle going on around us. Think of it like a spiritual tug-of-war for the hearts and minds of your generation. Generally speaking, in America there are three dominant worldviews: scientific naturalism, postmodernism, and Christian theism. If you pay attention, you can see this struggle play out in the media, at the movies, and in your classrooms. At the core of each of these worldviews is something incompatible with the other. Though many try to marry the three, it is impossible to do so without sacrificing something essential to each view.

Scientific naturalism[10] is the view that "the physical cosmos science studies is all that exists."[11] This worldview assumes that only material stuff exists and that science is the only source of knowledge concerning the world; everything else is mere conjecture. The implication of this view is that there can be no human soul or immaterial beings like angels or God. The supernatural is excluded by definition. Plainly stated: there is no spiritual reality in this world or the next. The grave is all there is.

Postmodernism[12] is a slippery worldview that by its nature resists a definition. But philosopher J. P. Moreland offers a helpful general description: "We may safely say that postmodernism is a form of cultural relativism. According to postmodernism, truth/falsehood, real/unreal, right/wrong, rational/irrational, good/bad are dichotomies relative to different linguistic communities. What is true, real and so forth, for one community may not be so for another."[13] Postmodernism says that there can be no "one way" to view the world, because reality is constructed through my community's perspective and linguistic practices. In other words, reality is something I create based on the way I view things. Popular postmodern slogans are "everything is interpretation" (reality is how I interpret it to be) and "incredulity toward metanarratives" (rejecting a universal story, explanation, or belief).

To illustrate the effects of postmodernism, take this example: a moral claim such as "rape is wrong" is no longer universally true with a capital *T*;

however, it can be true with a lowercase *t*. Confusing, I know. This means that rape is only wrong if a particular community *interprets* rape to be wrong. Postmodernism is a fundamental redefinition of truth, language, and reality.

In stark contrast to scientific naturalism and postmodernism, Christian theism[14] maintains that the God of the Bible exists and has revealed Himself ultimately in Jesus Christ. Christian theism values both the physical and nonphysical components of reality. Truth that transcends culture and language, objective morality, and spirituality are real features of our world, and we are able to discover them through rational investigation and experience. The grave is *not* all there is. Christian theism recognizes the actual existence of evil and understands this world to be broken, lost, and desperately in need of redemption.

As Christ-followers, we hold to a Christian worldview. We believe that all truth is God's truth. As my friend John Stonestreet likes to say, the true story of the world can be told in four parts: creation, fall, redemption, and restoration.[15] If we believe this, we must live it every day. We must not live fragmented lives leading to Christian schizophrenia. We should not *mindlessly* absorb the ideas of our culture.[16] God has already defined reality; it is our job to respond thoughtfully and engage it appropriately. Don't buy the lie that you need to keep your Christian faith to yourself. It is personal but *not* private. As a college student you have the opportunity to establish the biblical habit of living an integrated life for God's glory. In other words, *think Christianly!*

THE BIG IDEAS

- A worldview is a web of habit-forming beliefs about the biggest questions of life that helps you make sense of all your experiences. Everyone has a worldview.

- All worldviews can't be true because that would mean there is no objective reality. People *discover* reality, they don't *create* it by means of their culture's perspective or use of language.

- If Christianity is true, *then it is true for more than just two hours on Sunday morning.*

- The three worldviews competing for preeminence in America are scientific naturalism, postmodernism, and Christian theism.

- Since all truth is God's truth, we are not to live fragmented lives. Instead, we are to live integrated lives for God's glory (1 Cor. 10:31).

For Further Discovery

Challies, Tim. *The Next Story: Faith, Friends, and the Digital World.* Grand Rapids: Zondervan, 2015.

Copan, Paul. *True for You, but Not for Me: Overcoming Objections to Christian Faith.* Rev. ed. Minneapolis: Bethany House, 2009.

Morrow, Jonathan. *Think Christianly: Looking at the Intersection of Faith and Culture.* Grand Rapids: Zondervan, 2011.

Pearcey, Nancy R. *Finding Truth: 5 Principles for Unmasking Atheism, Secularism, and Other God Substitutes.* Colorado Springs: David C. Cook, 2015.

Smith, Warren Cole, and John Stonestreet. *Restoring All Things: God's Audacious Plan to Save the World Through Everyday People.* Grand Rapids: Baker, 2015.

Sunshine, Glenn S. *Why You Think the Way You Do: The Story of Western Worldviews from Rome to Home.* Grand Rapids: Zondervan, 2009.

ExploreWorldview.tv. An eight-video online worldview study taught by Jonathan Morrow and powered by Impact 360 Institute.

Impact360.org. Impact 360 Institute specializes in creating transformational worldview, apologetics, and servant-leadership experiences for high school (two-week Immersion experience) and college students (nine-month Gap Year experience).

JonathanMorrow.org. More resources for helping you build a Christian worldview and think Christianly about all of life.

03

Getting Theological
Knowing and Loving God

Disregard the study of God and you sentence yourself to stumble and blunder throughout life, blindfolded, as it were, with no sense of direction and no understanding of what surrounds you.
—J. I. PACKER[1]

You may not think of yourself as a theologian. . . . But everyone who thinks is a theologian, for at times, we all ponder God and the big questions of truth, life, and reality.
—RICK CORNISH[2]

> "Let not the wise boast of their wisdom
>   or the strong boast of their strength
>   or the rich boast of their riches,
> but let the one who boasts boast about this:
>   that they have the understanding to know me,
> that I am the LORD, who exercises kindness,
>   justice and righteousness on earth,
>   for in these I delight,"
> declares the LORD.
>   —JEREMIAH 9:23–24

THEOLOGY HAS TO BE ONE OF THE MOST INTIMIDATING AND MISUNDER-stood words in the English language. Most think that the only ones qualified to do it—whatever *it* is—are "professional Christians" who are cooped up in an ivory tower somewhere. This couldn't be further from the truth. In a way, everyone who has ever thought about God is a theologian. And while theology certainly requires thinking hard, it is far more than an abstract pursuit for the intellectually curious.

Theology involves the whole person, and it involves knowing and loving God. The authoritative source of Christian theology is the Bible: these sixty-six ancient documents reveal truths concerning who God is, who we are, and what life is all about. While the Scriptures are the final arbiter of truth about God, Christians today need to examine how Christians over the past two thousand years have understood theology. So tradition, which has been handed down from the community of believers preceding us, should be considered when we think about theology today. For example, if we come up with a teaching that no one has mentioned for two thousand years of church history, odds are we have taken a wrong turn in our thinking.

In addition, Christians ought to take reason and experience into account when doing theology. If we arrive at an interpretation of the Bible that says God is good *and* God is evil, then *reason* tells us that this is a contradiction—both statements can't be true at the same time. Likewise, the way someone personally *experiences* God's power and grace should also be taken into account. For example, some may claim that God does not heal people anymore, but a woman who has been miraculously healed from a disease would assimilate her experience of healing into her perception of God, thus affecting her theology.

In what follows, we will embark on an expedition to explore the broad strokes of what Christians believe. It won't be exhaustive, but it will give you a solid foundation to build upon as you engage God through His Word.

God Has Spoken

It is sometimes said that God has written two books: creation and the Bible. God has first revealed Himself through and in what He has made. This is His *general revelation* to all people, in that everyone has equal access to it simply by watching a sunset at the beach, standing on a mountaintop, or observing the night sky.

But God has also spoken through people in history and this is known as *special revelation*. In special revelation, God reveals information that could not have been discovered any other way (e.g., people can't deduce from a sunset that Jesus Christ has provided salvation for any who would place their trust in Him). As they were led by the Holy Spirit, the authors of Scripture communicated God's words to His people (from 1405 BC to AD 95). The books we possess, from Genesis to Revelation, are God's final and authoritative revelation to the world. No clearer word is needed and no higher authority can be appealed to.

An important corollary to this discussion is the Bible's status of being "without error," known as the doctrine of inerrancy. Because of God's perfect character and the fact that He cannot lie, it follows that His revelation to us would be without error. But, you might ask, didn't flawed and sinful human beings pen Scripture? Yes. But that is why the Holy Spirit guarded the original writings from error.

Theologian David Dockery offers a good summary of this doctrine: "When all the facts are known, the Bible (in its original writings) properly interpreted in light of which culture and communication means had developed by the time of its composition will be shown to be completely true (and therefore not false) in all that it affirms, to the degree of precision intended by the author, in all matters relating to God and his creation."[3] And even though none of the original manuscripts exist today, biblical scholars have sufficiently demonstrated that the Bible has been accurately and reliably preserved for us. Therefore, the Bible you can buy today in a bookstore or download from the app store is essentially the Word of God. Indeed, "All Scripture is God-breathed and is useful for teaching, rebuking, correcting and training in righteousness, so that the servant of God may be thoroughly equipped for every good work" (2 Tim. 3:16–17). Passages to explore: Psalm 19:1–4; Matthew 5:18; John 10:35; 17:17; Romans 1:18–25; 2:14–16; 1 Thessalonians 2:13; Titus 1:2; Hebrews 1:1–2; 6:18; 2 Peter 1:16–21.[4]

God Is Trinity

A distinctive of Christianity is its teaching concerning God as Trinity. Wayne Grudem offers a succinct summary of this doctrine: "*God eternally exists as three persons, Father, Son, and Holy Spirit, and each person is fully God, and there is one God.*"[5] Even though one will never find the word *trinity* in the Bible, this "tri-unity" is the picture of God revealed in its pages. A beautiful illustration of this is Jesus's prayer to the Father recorded in John 17. And while it is a revealed truth *beyond* reason—and we as finite creatures are unable to fully comprehend the mysterious depths of an infinite God—no logical contradiction exists in the doctrine of the Trinity. In short, it's not *against* reason.

But if this doctrine is impossible to fully comprehend, is it irrelevant?

Certainly not! The Trinity deeply informs all of reality. It means that God is essentially relational and therefore provides the framework for understanding community, the church, marital and familial relationships, and ultimately love. Moreover, the Trinity explains how creation and salvation were accomplished (i.e., the roles the Father, Son, and Holy Spirit played in each). One cannot be Christian and knowingly deny this essential doctrine.

What is God like? The Bible reveals that we are like God in some ways and unlike Him in others. The following are attributes that humans can exemplify at times, though imperfectly, whereas God exemplifies them perfectly and infinitely.[6]

- *God is loving.* The triune God is the perfect expression of self-giving love. His is not a selfish love that uses or manipulates; His kind of love seeks another's highest good and drives out all fear. It is this kind of love that He invites us into and that Jesus prayed we might experience (John 17).

- *God is just.* Corruption abounds in our world. So much so that we can't trust those in authority to act justly and do what is right. In stark contrast, God is just, true, and fair. He will always do right. Because of this, God will not allow sin and injustice to go unpunished.

- *God is merciful.* Mercy is when we don't get what we deserve (while grace is when we are given something we don't deserve). An offended king has the right to punish and exact judgment, yet He refrains because He chooses to extend mercy. Scripture repeatedly speaks of God's mercy toward us. God's justice demanded that atonement be made for sin, and His mercy provided us with a savior.

- *God is good.* God is the ultimate expression of goodness, moral perfection, and virtue. There is no defect, deficiency, or blemish in Him. A being with perfect knowledge and perfect power without perfect goodness would be a terrifying dictator. But thankfully God is good and always acts according to His nature. Because of God's goodness, we can trust in His absolute sovereignty no matter what happens.

In contrast, there are some significant ways in which God is radically different from us. Here are some of the most striking attributes:

- *God is holy.* He is set apart from everything that exists—no one is like Him. He is absolutely pure. Imagine brilliant rays of sunlight shining on an unspoiled blanket of snow on a crisp morning in the mountains—and this is still an utterly inadequate picture, for He dwells in unapproachable light.[7]

- *God is eternal.* God has always existed. There never was a time when He was not and there never will be a time when He will not be.

- *God is immutable.* God's character is constant and unchangeable. He is the same yesterday, today, and forever. God cannot lie; everything He has said He will do, He will certainly do.

- *God is omnipresent.* God is able to be fully present anywhere and at any time (though He is not identical with space because He transcends it). A child of God can never escape God's presence and providential care.

- *God is omniscient.* God is all-knowing. He knows everything possible and actual. He possesses complete knowledge of the past, present, and future. Knowing all truths and believing no falsehoods, He is perfect in knowledge. God is never caught off guard.

- *God is omnipotent.* God is perfect in power. Being untamed and completely free, God possesses the power to do anything He desires. God cannot do the logically impossible and cannot act contrary to His nature—but these are hardly limitations.[8]

While our knowledge of God is limited, we are confident that what has been revealed in Scripture is true of Him. There will be plenty of unanswered questions this side of heaven, but God has given us all we need for a relationship with Him and each other. Passages to explore: 2 Chronicles 16:9; Job 42:2; Psalms 86:5; 90:2; 115:3; 119:68; 139; Isaiah 6:3; Malachi 3:6; John 3:16; Romans 3:26; 1 Timothy 6:15–16; Titus 3:5–7; Hebrews 13:8; James 1:17; 1 Peter 1:2; 1 John 4:8, 18; Jude 25; Revelation 15:3.

Humanity in God's Image

Only humans bear God's image. As a result, all of humanity is endowed with inherent dignity and value. Theologian Bruce Ware summarizes how we bear the image of God:

God made human beings, both male and female, to be created and finite *representations* (images *of* God) of God's own nature, that in *relationship* with Him and each other they might be His *representatives* (imaging God) in carrying out the *responsibilities* He has given to them. In this sense, we are *images of God* in order *to image God* and His purposes in the ordering of our lives and the carrying out of our God-given responsibilities.[9]

We were created in the image of God in order to experience a vibrant relationship with our triune God and authentic relationships in community with one another.

Furthermore, humans possess intellect, emotions, moral capacities, and free will, and we are composed of a body (material substance) and a soul (immaterial substance).[10] God created us to be a unified, functional whole. However, sin made it possible to separate the body from the soul in death (i.e., the soul of the believer goes to be with the Lord until the final resurrection when the soul will be reunited with a new body to enter into the new heaven and the new earth). Passages to explore: Genesis 1:26–27; Matthew 10:28; Luke 10:27; 2 Corinthians 4:16; 5:1–9; 7:1; Philippians 1:21–24; James 3:9.

The Corruption of Humanity

What was created good in the beginning has been corrupted due to the disobedience of Adam and Eve. Everyone born after Adam validates his initial act of disobedience through sins of commission (doing what we should not do) and sins of omission (not doing what we ought to do). We are deluding ourselves if we think we would have acted differently in the garden.

Consequently, we now live in a world wracked with pain, suffering, evil, and death. Things were not supposed to be this way.[11] The effects of sin have corrupted every aspect of our nature (intellect, emotions, morality, and will), fractured our relationships with our fellow humans and nature, and defaced the image of God within us. What we all deserve on account of our sinful rebellion against a holy God is death and eternal separation from Him. Passages to explore: Genesis 3; Jeremiah 17:9; Romans 3; 5:12–21; 6:23; 8:19–23.

The Incarnation, Death, and Resurrection of Jesus Christ

God, being great in mercy and love, did not abandon us in our helpless state. The Father sent His Son, Jesus Christ, to become our legal substitute. Jesus, who became like us in every respect but without sin, lived the perfect life we could not live and died the death that was ours to die, so that we might be reconciled to God. Jesus as fully human identified with our offense against God, and Jesus as fully God could satisfy the Father's wrath (a human being *should* have died for sin, but only God *could* have).

As a result of Christ's work at the cross, the wrath of God has been satisfied (i.e., propitiation). Moreover, Jesus Christ made atonement (i.e., covering) for the sins of the whole world so that whoever places their trust in Him can be redeemed, forgiven, declared righteous (i.e., justified), and adopted into the family of God forever.

The resurrection of Christ and His subsequent ascension into heaven is God the Father's vindication (or amen) that Jesus accomplished salvation once and for all. It is finished. Passages to explore: John 1:1–14, 29; 3:16; Romans 4:24–25; 5:1–11; 1 Corinthians 15; 2 Corinthians 5:17–21; Philippians 2:5–11; 1 Timothy 2:3–6; Hebrews 4:15; 1 Peter 2:24; 1 John 2:2.[12]

A Restored Relationship with God and Each Other

The work of Christ makes it possible for people to be reconciled with God. We become innocent and righteous children of God by grace through faith. There is nothing that anyone can do to earn salvation; it is the gift of God so that no one may boast. No one is good enough; we are all sinners before God. We are merely beggars who have accepted bread—all the glory goes to God for our salvation. Once we accept Christ, God gives us His Holy Spirit to guide and comfort us, to make us more like Christ, to seal us for the day of redemption, and to provide us with assurance of our relationship with God.

The collective group of Christians around the world is known as the body of Christ, or the church. We are now family—adopted brothers and sisters in Christ. The church exists to worship God, proclaim the good news of Jesus to the world, be the pillar and support of the truth, edify and build up believers, do good works, and be salt and light. Biblical images of the church include the people of God, the body of Christ, the temple of the Spirit, a royal priesthood, the bride of Christ, and God's flock of sheep.[13] Passages to explore: Matthew 28:19–20; John 1:12; 3:16; Acts 1:8; Romans 6:23; 1 Corinthians 12:13; Ephesians 1:13–14; 2:1–10; 1 Timothy 3:15; Titus 3:3–7.

How It All Ends, and Then Begins Anew

One day, Jesus Christ will interrupt history and return bodily and visibly to the earth. No one knows the day or the hour; we are just called to be ready. Christians are to live each day as if Christ could return today. On account of God's patience toward humanity, each day He waits allows more and more people to embrace Jesus as their savior. But the opportunity for reconciliation with our Creator will not go on forever.

The crucified Messiah will return one day to reign as King and Lord. In that day, God will judge all the inhabitants of the earth—past and present—because of humanity's universal rebellion. Everyone deserves hell, which is eternal separation from the presence of God. Everyone will be judged according to either their own righteousness and deeds or Christ's righteousness and deeds. Those who have a relationship with God through Jesus Christ will be ushered into the joy of their master and experience eternal life in a new heaven and new earth where God will dwell forever among them. Every tear will have been wiped away and evil and death will finally be vanquished. God will completely and decisively redeem and restore that which was originally corrupted by sin. Passages to explore: Daniel 12:1–2; Matthew 24:36; 25:1–46; 2 Peter 3:9–10; Revelation 20:11–15; 21:3–5.

That's a lot to take in and we've only begun to scratch the surface. But we need to remember that the goal of theology is not to accumulate data about God. Rather, it should deeply affect us. David Clark paints a compelling picture: "When . . . theology reaches full bloom, it blossoms into . . . the wisdom of God. This leads us to passionate love for God, genuine worship of the Trinity, true community with fellow Christians, and loving service in personal evangelism and social compassion—all to the glory of God. That is what it means to know and love the true and living God. Absolutely nothing matters more."[14]

Why Don't Christians All Believe the Same Things?

It doesn't take long to discover that other Christians do not believe the same things as you. Your parents and friends may not share your beliefs and vice versa. What are you to make of this? It is crucial to understand that all beliefs are not created equal. To see what I mean by this, let's divide various Christian beliefs into three categories: convictions, persuasions, and opinions.[15]

1. *Convictions* are "central beliefs, crucial to salvation, over which we should be willing to denounce someone in serious disagreement and (if there is no repentance) eventually divide fellowship."[16] Some examples of these are the Trinity, deity of Christ, and salvation by faith through grace. This category most closely resembles what people sometimes call "mere Christianity." If someone doesn't affirm the beliefs in this area, then it is difficult to see how they can be called a Christian in any meaningful or historical sense. Likewise, if people with comprehension of this set of beliefs willingly deny them, then it seems that they cannot call themselves Christians. Ultimately, these are matters for God's perfect knowledge to decide, for only He knows the heart of each person (1 Sam. 16:7).

2. *Persuasions* are "beliefs about which we are personally certain but which are not crucial to salvation. We must accept believers with differing persuasions as members in good standing of God's family, even though we are certain they are wrong on these points."[17] Some examples would be whether a Christian should be baptized by immersion or sprinkling, whether the spiritual gifts of speaking in tongues and prophecy are available today, how old the universe and earth are, or how one understands God's sovereignty and human freedom in relationship to each other. For instance, even though eighteenth-century evangelists John Wesley and George Whitefield passionately differed on their views of predestination, they remained friends and partners in ministry. These questions mattered, of course, but were not core questions.

3. *Opinions* are "beliefs about subjects on which either we have no preference but acknowledge that others may be right in holding a different view, or . . . we do not have any confidence that we yet know the truth of the matter."[18] The Bible is usually silent or ambiguous on these types of issues. Some examples are which Bible translation is best, what the dress code should be in church, or whether Christians should see R-rated movies.

It is important to emphasize that these categories are not determined according to how firmly or passionately one believes something. Rather they concern *what is central* to the Christian faith and gospel and what is less so.[19] Augustine, the great theologian of the early church, put it this way: "In essentials, unity; in nonessentials, liberty; and in all things, charity."[20]

Having confidence and conviction in our carefully considered beliefs is a praiseworthy pursuit, but achieving unity amidst a mosaic of beliefs requires grace, maturity, and most of all love. When we are tempted to separate or slander over nonessentials, we would do well to heed the apostle John's reminder that Christ's disciples are to be known by their love for one another (John 13:35).

THE BIG IDEAS

- The goal of theology is to know and love God.
- While the Bible is the ultimate source and authority for Christian theology, tradition, reason, and experience are valuable contributors to the process.
- In explaining why so many Christians disagree, it is helpful to use the categories of convictions, persuasions, and opinions.

For Further Discovery

Cornish, Rick. *5 Minute Theologian: Maximum Truth in Minimum Time.* Nashville: Tyndale House, 2014.

Erickson, Millard J., and L. Arnold Hustad. *Introducing Christian Doctrine.* 3rd ed. Grand Rapids: Baker, 2015.

Morris, Thomas V. *Our Idea of God: An Introduction to Philosophical Theology.* Vancouver: Regent College Publishing, 2002.

Morrow, Jonathan. *Questioning the Bible: 11 Major Challenges to the Bible's Authority.* Chicago: Moody Publishers, 2014.

Thoennes, Erik. *Life's Biggest Questions: What the Bible Says About the Things That Matter Most.* Wheaton, IL: Crossway, 2011.

and mind. As minimal Christian truth initially sinks in and is intellectually acknowledged, the Holy Spirit persuades a person to respond to the Person the truth reveals. When response comes, understanding is deepened. Another step of deeper reliance is possible. And the process of growth continues.[15]

Walking by Faith

As important as an act of faith is at a point in time, the Christian life is a walk of faith—continuing acts of obedience. Sometimes the notion of "blind faith" creeps into our understanding of walking by faith as well. Didn't Paul say, "We live by faith, not by sight" (2 Cor. 5:7)? He did, but as Clark explains, "This means only that at times a Christian may rightly allow faith, in the sense of trust in God, to guide his thinking even though he has *no direct* evidence. For instance, if I trust my friend and he says he will do something for me, I may rightly believe he will do it, even when I lack direct evidence that he will fulfill his promise. . . . Loyalty and allegiance, based partly on past experience, may rightly guide my thinking and acting."[16]

This same sentiment is expressed in Hebrews 11 where these courageous men and women did not allow their circumstances to have the final word.[17] Rather, they continued to look forward to what had been promised with hope and trust. Faith in this context is a confident expectation in the promises and faithfulness of God. In the everyday circumstances of life, biblical faith is active trust that God is who He says He is and will do all that He has promised to do (Ps. 9:10; Heb. 10:19–23; 11:1).

This is what it means for the righteous to live by faith (Rom. 1:17). We trust God even in the midst of difficult times *because He is faithful.* We trust Him even when the fog of life rolls in, making it difficult to see the way forward. This is the kind of faith God is pleased with (Heb. 11:6).

THE BIG IDEAS

- "Christian faith is not blind in the least; rather it is dependent upon a historical event that can be thoroughly investigated with eyes wide open." —Craig Hazen

- Faith is active trust in what we have good reason to believe is true.
- Sincerity is not enough; the object of faith must be reliable and trustworthy.
- The act of saving faith includes three essential elements: understanding, assent, and trust. Christian faith involves the *whole* person, and the biblical term that best captures this is the "heart."
- Walking by faith means living in light of the promises and faithfulness of God.

For Further Discovery

Howe, Thomas A., and Richard G. Howe. "Knowing Christianity Is True: The Relationship Between Faith and Reason." In *To Everyone an Answer: A Case for the Christian Worldview*. Edited by Francis J. Beckwith, William Lane Craig, and J. P. Moreland. Downers Grove, IL: InterVarsity Press, 2009.

Kreeft, Peter, and Ronald K. Tacelli. "Faith and Reason." In *Handbook of Christian Apologetics: Hundreds of Answers to Crucial Questions*. Downers Grove, IL: InterVarsity Press, 1994.

Lewis, C. S. *Mere Christianity*. New York: HarperCollins, 2015.

Moreland, J. P., and Klaus Issler. *In Search of a Confident Faith: Overcoming Barriers to Trusting in God*. Downers Grove, IL: InterVarsity Press, 2008.

Moreland, J. P., and Mark Matlock. *Smart Faith: Loving Your God with All Your Mind*. Colorado Springs: NavPress, 2005.

Can We Know Anything at All?

THE GREAT PHILOSOPHER ARISTOTLE ONCE OBSERVED, "ALL MEN BY nature desire to know." One of the most important and frequently asked questions throughout the history of thought is, "Can we know anything at all?" At first glance, it seems obvious that we can. But after looking a bit closer, this question is not quite as easy to answer as one might think.

Consider these examples of things you might know: You had bacon and eggs for breakfast yesterday. Jamestown was settled in 1607. Your girlfriend (or boyfriend) likes you. For every action, there is an equal and opposite reaction. Racism is wrong. You are hungry right now. God exists. When you were three, you really liked to play with Legos. Three plus four equals seven. There is a book in front of you. You are feeling anxious about an upcoming decision.

Would you say that you *know* these things? If so, *how* do you know? If not, why not? Do you have to be one-hundred-percent certain before you can say that you know something? Most, if not all, of the items in this list we would claim to know (or at least think we know). But do we really?

What is knowledge and how does it work? (The fancy name for the study of knowledge is *epistemology*.) These are not just abstract questions that philosophers get paid to think about. Knowledge plays a crucial part in our everyday lives—we can't help believing and claiming to know things. And most would agree that it is better to hold more true beliefs than false ones. If knowledge is important in everyday affairs then how much more so is it for those in college? After all, one of the goals of college is for students to acquire knowledge in particular areas of thought. So in what follows, we will briefly explore knowledge in general and then discuss why it is important to Christianity in particular.

In our culture, one common way of thinking about knowledge is empiricism. Empiricism is the view that knowledge can *only* be attained (either directly or indirectly) through sensory experience. In other words, if you can't see, smell, touch, taste, or hear it, then it doesn't count as knowledge.

This may be a good start, but a little reflection reveals that this approach is ill-equipped to account for everyday things that we know. Think about love. How much does love weigh? What does love taste like? Love doesn't seem to fit into any sensory category. On strict empiricism, I can't *know* that I love my wife. But I do know that I love my wife. Moreover, I know—independent of any lab experiment—that it is wrong to torture babies for fun, that Alexander the Great actually lived, and that I am anxious about a test. Yet none of these are known by way of my five senses. So clearly there have to be *nonempirical* (i.e., not based on sense experience) sources of knowledge as well.

A quick observation about science: the fact that empiricism is such a powerful undercurrent in our culture explains why many people think that science *alone* gives us knowledge of fact, whereas anything discovered by something other than "the scientific method" yields only opinion. Now don't misunderstand me, science is *an important* way that we gain knowledge, but it is not the *only* way. (We'll talk about this more in chapter 18, "Science Rules!")

Sources of Knowledge

Generally speaking, knowledge can be defined as "true belief based upon adequate reasons."[3] For the sake of clarity, I will be using "adequate reasons" synonymously with "justification." For something to count as knowledge (1) you must believe it, (2) the belief you hold must be true (i.e., it accurately describes the way things actually are), and (3) this true belief must be justified.

Evidence comes in a variety of forms, and the amount of evidence necessary to satisfy the "adequate reasons" condition for knowledge will be situation specific. This seems clear enough. Before applying this definition to a concrete example, we need to examine what provides us with knowledge. Here are six widely recognized sources of knowledge:[4]

1. *Perception.* This involves knowledge of our immediate environment (e.g., the person in front of me is wearing a blue T-shirt, or the surface of a table feels smooth).

2. *Memory.* This involves our knowledge of the past and the things we have learned before (e.g., I know I had spaghetti for dinner last night, or I remember rattlesnakes are poisonous and I should stay away from them).

3. *Testimony.* This includes knowledge gained by means of what people tell us (e.g., my third-grade teacher told me that Columbus sailed the ocean blue in 1492, or CNN reported that planes crashed into the World Trade Center).

4. *Introspection.* If perception deals with our awareness of things external to us, then introspection accounts for our knowledge of our internal states (e.g., I am feeling anxious about a test that I just took, or I am excited about my date this weekend).

5. *Reasoning.* This involves our knowledge based on inferences from other things we observe—connecting the dots if you will (e.g., my iPhone is an electrical device, and since electrical devices tend to short out when they get wet, I should keep it away from water).

6. *Rational insight.* This involves knowledge of the things we can just "see" are true without having to observe them—we don't seem to *reason to* these things, we *reason with* them (e.g., basic laws of logic like the law of noncontradiction—a statement can't be true and false at the same time and in the same way—elementary mathematics, concepts like "larger than" or "to the left of").

Consider this example: I wake up in the morning and find myself with the belief that my keys are on the kitchen table. I remember putting them there the night before. Also, out of habit, I usually leave my keys on the table when I get home each day, so they are probably there. They are in fact on the kitchen table. I walk into the kitchen and see them there (my senses are generally reliable).[5] According to this scenario, I am justified in my claim to know my keys are on the kitchen table. Can you pick out the different elements of the definition of knowledge and identify which sources of knowledge were used?

However, just because we can gain knowledge from these sources doesn't mean that they're infallible or that our beliefs are indefeasible. In fact, we can be mistaken from time to time about our beliefs based on these sources, and this leads us to the issues of skepticism and certainty.

Skepticism and Certainty

Must we have bombproof certainty (i.e., it's impossible that I am wrong) before we can say that we know something? Is it all or nothing, one-hundred-percent certainty or utter skepticism?

I don't think so, because this is a false dilemma. A skeptical approach to knowledge maintains that knowledge itself is impossible or that no beliefs can be justified evewn if they happen to be true. Not only is this view unlivable, but it also seems self-contradictory. Even the radical skeptic thinks he knows enough to claim you're mistaken. Even still, skepticism is not all bad. A healthy bit of skepticism can be a good thing, since we don't want to be gullible.[6] The bottom line is this: just because it's possible that I am mistaken about something, it doesn't follow that I am mistaken about it. In order for my skeptical friend to show that, they must give me reasons that dislodge me from that belief.

Concerning certainty, there is precious little—if anything—that we are one-hundred-percent certain of. But that shouldn't worry us, because beliefs and knowledge don't work this way. Depending on the issue at hand, an individual's strength of belief can and does vary. For example, though it is possible I am mistaken, I have a high degree of confidence that I exist. However, I have a lower degree of confidence in the local weather station's prediction that it will rain tomorrow or that the plane will actually arrive on time. Admitting degrees of certainty does not eliminate the possibility of knowledge. And realizing we could possibly be wrong fosters an appropriate posture of humility concerning knowledge.

Two Main Views

Rejecting skepticism as an approach to knowledge, there are two main views as to how people arrive at knowledge. The first approach is *methodism* (not the Protestant denomination), which holds that people can only know things if they have followed the appropriate method or satisfied the right set of criteria. This may be helpful down the line, but initially it raises the question of how we know a particular method is correct. This then leads to an infinite regress (e.g., Criteria X would need Criteria Y to explain X, and then Criteria Z would have to be invoked to justify Y, and so on).[7]

The alternative to methodism is *particularism*, which maintains that we should take knowledge on a case-by-case basis. One should carefully evaluate whether or not there is good reason to be skeptical. If no reason seems forthcoming or plausible, then it is entirely reasonable to recognize the item under consideration as an item of knowledge. Or as Garry DeWeese and J. P. Moreland put it, "We start with clear instances of knowledge, formulate criteria based on those clear instances and extend our knowledge by using those criteria in borderline, unclear cases."[8] In my view, particularism seems the best answer to the problem of how we come to know things, and it also stops the skeptic's endless barrage of "how do you know that's . . . ?"

By way of illustration, a skeptic might pose this question to a particularist: How do you know you are not living in a dream world and are really hooked up to a machine controlled by a mad scientist? The particularist would try to establish whether or not there are valid reasons why he should think he is being deceived. In the absence of any valid reasons, true existence is more plausible than the mad-scientist theory. But—here's the catch—the particularist does not have a free pass to rationalize any piece of knowledge. The point is that *appropriate reasons or justification* must be provided in order for a particularist to renounce a belief that was held with a high degree of confidence.

Inference to the Best Explanation

When given some range of facts that must be explained, a method known as IBE finds an explanation to fit all of the facts. IBE—this extremely helpful form of reasoning—means "inference to the best explanation." Lawyers and judges use this approach in the court of law. Doctors use it when diagnosing a patient. Scientists use it when seeking to explain an unusual phenomenon. And historians use it when trying to decide whether it is reasonable to believe that Jesus Christ rose from the dead. IBE is particularly useful when seeking to evaluate belief systems or worldviews (e.g., naturalism, Islam, or Christianity). The question is the same, "What explanation best accounts for all of the data?"[9] For example, when considering the problem of evil, any worldview that fails to recognize the existence and reality of evil will not adequately explain people's all-too-real encounters with it. Employing IBE, one would reject such a worldview.

Intellectual Virtues

One of the ways that we can increase the chances of forming true beliefs and arriving at knowledge is by pursuing intellectual virtues. An intellectual virtue is "a characteristic of a person who acts in a praiseworthy manner in the process of forming beliefs."[10] For example, James Beilby and David Clark describe the intellectual virtues of honesty and courage: "Being intellectually honest means making a fair appraisal of the evidence at hand, dedicating effort to reach valid conclusions, admitting personal biases that affect beliefs, and seeking to reduce those biases. In an intellectual context, courage involves, among other things, being willing to take the minority position when the evidence points in that direction. It also means investigating personally held beliefs with rigor."[11] These virtues do not happen by accident; they are the result of forming healthy intellectual habits over time.

We have looked at a definition of knowledge, examined how we come to know things, and explored various sources of knowledge. But the goal of knowledge is not just to accumulate data. The acquisition of knowledge should help us along the path of becoming virtuous people and flourishing as followers of Jesus Christ. Knowledge, over time and with effort, becomes understanding. Understanding then describes the growing integration of our fragmented knowledge into an increasingly coherent picture of God and our world. And as we grow in understanding, we have the opportunity to grow in wisdom as well, which is the skillful application of knowledge and understanding to life.[12]

Solomon speaks of the blessing that accompanies this dynamic pursuit: "Blessed are those who find wisdom, those who gain understanding" (Prov. 3:13; see also 2:6). Knowledge is the crucial first step in this process. And as Christ-followers, we should remember that our actions flow out of what we truly believe (Rom. 12:1–2).

Christianity as a Knowledge Tradition

Unfortunately, many people today think that you can't know religious or moral truths.[13] Why? Because if physics, chemistry, biology, or genetics doesn't deal with a topic, then it can't be known. In other words, it's fine for you to say you *believe* that Jesus is God but not that you *know* Jesus is God. However, if this were the case, then Christianity would consist of mere opinion and no substantive knowledge. This might seem reasonable if empirical knowledge were the only epistemological game in town. But since there are clear examples of nonempirical knowledge in the world (like we have already seen), then there is the legitimate possibility of religious knowledge.

In principle then, there appears no good reason to exclude the knowledge claims of Christianity simply because they are "religious." If they do not hold up to scrutiny, that is one thing. But Christianity, which is rooted in history, makes many claims, some of which are empirically testable, while others appeal for verification by nonempirical means. The crucial point to grasp is that Christianity (and religion in general) rises to the level of being either true or false, and it can be known to be true or false (Luke 1:1–4; 1 John 5:13). If Christianity is relegated to the realm of fairy tales, which may provide personal significance or meaning but not knowledge, then people will continue to not take the claims of Jesus or the Christian worldview very seriously. This will also reduce the confidence that Christians have in everyday life. If, however, people are invited to consider the claims of Christianity as a knowledge tradition then there is a good chance that they might come to know the living God and live life according to the knowledge provided in His Word.

THE BIG IDEAS

- *Empirical* knowledge is gained only through the five senses. *Nonempirical* knowledge is acquired without using the five senses.
- Knowledge can be defined as "true belief based upon adequate reasons." Widely accepted sources of knowledge are *perception, memory, testimony, introspection, reasoning,* and *rational insight.*

- Knowledge doesn't require one-hundred-percent, bombproof certainty—it comes in degrees of confidence.

- The two primary approaches to how we know things are (1) *methodism*, which holds that people can only know things if they have followed the appropriate method or satisfied the right set of criteria, and (2) *particularism*, which suggests we begin with what we clearly seem to know, come up with how we come to know these things, and then use that criterion when we run into more controversial instances.

- Since we don't want to be gullible, a healthy bit of skepticism can be good at times. And since we don't want the acquisition of knowledge to lead to arrogance or manipulation, cultivating a posture of intellectual humility is a virtue.

- An intellectual virtue is "a characteristic of a person who acts in a praiseworthy manner in the process of forming beliefs." —JAMES BEILBY AND DAVID CLARK

- Christianity rises to the level of being either true or false, and it can be known to be true or false (Luke 1:1–4; 1 John 5:13). If Christianity is viewed as a fairy tale, it may provide personal significance or meaning, but not knowledge; then people will continue not taking the claims of Jesus very seriously.

For Further Discovery

Beilby, James, and David K. Clark. *Why Bother with Truth?* The RZIM Critical Questions Booklet Series. Norcross, GA: RZIM, 2000.

Copan, Paul. "How Do You Know You're Not Wrong?" In *How Do You Know You're Not Wrong? Responding to Objections That Leave Christians Speechless.* Grand Rapids: Baker, 2005.

———. "Whatever Works for You." In *How Do You Know You're Not Wrong? Responding to Objections That Leave Christians Speechless.* Grand Rapids: Baker, 2005.

DeWeese, Garrett J., and J. P. Moreland. "How Do I Know?" In *Philosophy Made*

Slightly Less Difficult: A Beginner's Guide to Life's Big Questions. Downers
Grove, IL: InterVarsity Press, 2009.

Pearcey, Nancy. *Total Truth: Liberating Christianity from Its Cultural Captivity.*
Wheaton, IL: Crossway, 2008.

Wood, W. Jay. *Epistemology: Becoming Intellectually Virtuous.* Downers Grove, IL:
InterVarsity Press, 1998.

Truth Matters

To say of what is that it is not, or of what is not that it is, is false, while to say of what is that it is, and of what it is not that it is not, is true.

—ARISTOTLE[1]

If you look for truth, you may find comfort in the end: if you look for comfort you will not get either comfort or truth—only soft soap and wishful thinking to begin with and, in the end, despair.

—C. S. LEWIS[2]

You will know the truth, and the truth will set you free.

—JESUS (JOHN 8:32)

SEEKING THE TRUTH IS A POWERFUL FORCE THAT DRIVES US TO FIND answers to questions that matter. Just think of the passion with which Harry Potter seeks answers for why he is so connected to Lord Voldemort. Or think of *Captain America: Civil War* in which "Cap" is trying to prove the innocence of Bucky (aka the Winter Soldier). He wants the truth because the truth is valuable. The truth is liberating. Truth matters because reality is involved.

A Basic Fact of Existence

Truth is a basic fact of existence. Even though people seem confused about what truth is these days—or skeptical about the possibility of truth—deep down they have an awareness of truth. Here is a common-sense definition of truth: "Truth *corresponds* or *relates* to reality (the real world) as it actually is. . . . [Therefore,] if something is true, it is true for *all people,* at *all times,* and in *all places* regardless of a person's awareness or beliefs."[3] Truth is simply telling it like it is, or describing the way things actually are.

The Truth Is Out There

Do you remember the TV show *The X-Files*? (If not you can look it up on Netflix.) The theme that drove this show was "the truth is out there." The writers of that show were more profound than they probably realized. Despite fashionable postmodern murmurings, the truth is *out there*. By that I mean *truth is discovered, not created*.[4]

Most people are willing to accept this idea of truth when dealing with issues of science, but if the conversation turns to religion or ethics and morality—all bets are off. You may have heard the following slogans or objections at some point:

Christianity (or Islam, or Buddhism, or insert whatever) *can be true for you but not for me* (relativism). But is this statement true for both of us?

Truth is what works for me (pragmatism). But just because something works—or is useful—does that make it true?

Since so many people disagree about the truth, there must not be any. But if we apply this approach to life then that would mean that because my wife and I disagree over where the car keys are at this moment that they don't exist—an absurd conclusion to be sure.

It doesn't matter what you believe as long as you are sincere. But the problem with that is someone can be sincerely wrong. For example, I am not a fan of heights. So if I were about to jump out of a perfectly good airplane, I can assure you that I would have all the sincerity in the world when I pulled the parachute cord! But guess what? If someone packed the parachute incorrectly, then I am going to have a very bad day regardless of how sincere I am.

A fundamental fact of reality is that two things can't be true at the same time and in the same way (this is called the law of noncontradiction). Either I ate my peanut butter and jelly sandwich or I didn't. Either God exists or He doesn't. It can be either-or . . . but not both. Either rape is right, or it's wrong. Either Jesus is the Son of God (Christianity), or Jesus was only a great prophet (Islam)—but not both. You get the picture.

Now truth may be hard to discover, but just because the quest proves difficult doesn't mean the treasure doesn't exist. You need to be aware that many of your fellow students and professors will be more interested in creating their own truth based on how they feel than working hard to discover the truth. This will make your conversations about the big questions of life—and especially Christianity—interesting indeed. The truth is valuable treasure, just waiting to be discovered.

Why Truth Matters for Christians

So why does truth matter for you as a Christian? The Bible repeatedly talks about truth and makes numerous claims about truth (i.e., statements about reality).[5] Listen to what Isaiah records about God: "I, the LORD, speak the truth" (Isa. 45:19). Jesus, in His prayer, asked God the Father to sanctify us (His disciples) by the truth, and said that His word is truth (John 17:17). In short, what God reveals in His Word accurately describes reality.[6] As C. S. Lewis put it in *God in the Dock*, "Christianity claims to give an account of *facts*—to tell you what the real universe is like. Its account of the universe may be true, or it may not, and once the question is really before you, then your natural inquisitiveness must make you want to know the answer. If Christianity is untrue, then no honest man will want to believe it, however helpful it might be: if it is true, every honest man will want to believe it, even if it gives him no help at all."[7]

Most important to our discussion of truth is the fact that God passionately wants His image-bearers to find it. Take a look at this insightful passage written by the apostle Paul: "God our Savior . . . wants all people to be saved and *to come to a knowledge of the truth*. For there is one God and one mediator between God and mankind, the man Christ Jesus, who gave himself as a ransom for all people" (1 Tim. 2:3–6, italics added). God desires everyone to come to know the truth. "The truth about what?" you might ask. The reality that Christ Jesus is the one and only mediator between God and humanity, and that He gave His life for everyone so that they could be reconciled to God (John 14:6; Acts 4:12). God wants people to embrace the reality that they are desperately in need of a savior, and then He desires that they embrace the reality of forgiveness and restored relationship with Him through Jesus. In 1 Timothy 2:7 Paul goes on to say that he is telling the truth and is not lying.

As Christians, we ought to be passionate about knowing the truth because God is passionate about making it known. God's Word calls the church to be "the pillar and foundation of the truth" (1 Tim. 3:15). Part of maturing as an individual and follower of Christ is seeking to increase in our knowledge[8] of the truth while decreasing the amount of falsehoods we believe. This is no easy task. Yet God desires truth in our innermost being (Ps. 51:6 NIV 1984). Perhaps if God were posting an advertisement on Google today, it might read "Wanted—Seekers of Truth."

THE BIG IDEAS

- Truth "*corresponds* or *relates* to reality (the real world) as it actually is. . . . [Therefore,] if something is true, it is true for *all people*, at *all times*, and in *all places* regardless of a person's awareness or beliefs." —NORMAN GEISLER AND JOSEPH HOLDEN

- Despite fashionable postmodern murmurings, the truth is *out there*. By that I mean *truth is discovered, not created.*

- The Bible claims to tell the truth about reality.

- As Christians, we ought to be passionate about knowing the truth because God is passionate about making it known.

For Further Discovery

Copan, Paul. *True for You, but Not for Me: Overcoming Objections to Christian Faith*. Rev. ed. Minneapolis: Bethany House, 2009.

Moreland, J. P. *Love Your God with All Your Mind: The Role of Reason in the Life of the Soul*. Rev. ed. Colorado Springs: NavPress, 2012.

Morrow, Jonathan. *Think Christianly: Looking at the Intersection of Faith and Culture*. Grand Rapids: Zondervan, 2011.

Pearcey, Nancy. *Saving Leonardo: A Call to Resist the Secular Assault on Mind, Morals, and Meaning*. Nashville: B&H Publishing, 2010.

Smith, R. Scott. *Truth and the New Kind of Christian: The Emerging Effects of Postmodernism in the Church.* Wheaton, IL: Crossway, 2007.

ExploreTruth.tv. A seven-session online study taught by Jonathan Morrow that will help you break free from the riptide of relativism (powered by Impact 360 Institute).

A Moral Disaster
Why Moral Relativism Is a Bad Idea

There is one thing a professor can be absolutely certain of: almost every student entering the university believes, or says he believes, that truth is relative. . . . The students, of course, cannot defend their opinion. It is something with which they have been indoctrinated.

—ALLAN BLOOM[1]

Ethical relativism is the doctrine that the moral rightness and wrongness of actions varies from society to society and that there are no absolute moral standards binding on all men at all times. Accordingly, it holds that whether or not it is right for an individual to act in a certain way depends on or is relative to the society to which he belongs.

—JOHN LADD[2]

In those days there was no king in Israel; everyone did what was right in his own eyes.

—JUDGES 21:25 NASB

EVERYTHING IS RELATIVE. (IS THIS STATEMENT RELATIVE?) THAT'S JUST true for you, not for me. (Is this statement true for both of us?) Who are you to judge? (Who are you to ask?)

The list of slogan banter could go on and on. Unfortunately, these self-refuting one-liners are enough to stop many Christians in their tracks when it comes to talking about the existence of objective moral values (i.e., some things are right or wrong independent of how I feel about them). These slogans fall under the category of *moral relativism*, which is alive and well as "47 percent of American emerging adults agreed that 'morals are relative,

59

there are not definite rights and wrongs for everybody."[3] Professor Louis Pojman tells a funny story concerning relativism that brings the critical issues into sharp relief:

> In the opening days of my philosophy classes, I often find students vehemently defending subjective relativism: "Who are you to judge?" they ask. I then give them their first test. In the next class period, I return all the tests, marked "F," even though my comments show that most of them are of a very high caliber. When the students express outrage at this . . . I answer that I have accepted subjectivism for marking the exams. "But that's unjust!" they typically insist—and then they realize that they are no longer being merely subjectivist about ethics.[4]

This anecdote testifies to the reality that people are relativists when it affects *everyone else*, but when it affects *them personally*, they quickly become objectivists.

The Argument from Disagreement Is Overrated

Sometimes when I am speaking to students on truth, I will do an exercise where we explore different moral claims to see if they are objective or subjective. For example, I will make the claim "premarital sex is morally wrong" and ask how many think this statement is objectively wrong. Some of the Christians will then hedge their bets by saying for them it's objective, but for those who disagree it's subjective. The mistaken (but very common) underlying assumption is that since so many individuals and cultures disagree regarding moral issues, then the obvious conclusion is that there must be no objective moral values. But as Francis Beckwith points out, "Relativism does not follow from disagreement."[5] Simply because people disagree doesn't mean there is no fact of the matter. Suppose you run into a member of the "flat earth society" and find yourself in a heated discussion about whether the earth is indeed flat. At the end of the debate, you still disagree. Does that mean that there is no objective fact of the matter concerning the earth? If anything, disagreement ought to motivate us to understand why we disagree, not to give up on the conversation altogether.

Another misconception is that if we admit there are objective moral values, then this will automatically lead to oppression and violence. Now it certainly could (and unfortunately it has at times in the past), but this no more follows than the conclusion that money is evil because it has been used inappropriately in the past.

Some Things Are Obviously Right and Wrong

Contrary to popular opinion, people intuitively know that some things are right and wrong. For example: kindness is a virtue; compassion is a good thing; the Holocaust was deeply evil; child abuse is always wrong. So while there may be some gray areas when it comes to certain moral discussions, all moral issues are not up for grabs. And all it takes to undermine moral relativism is to admit the existence of *one* universal moral fact.[6]

The Reformer's Dilemma

Who doesn't admire someone who stands up for what's right—even in the midst of passionate opposition?[7] Figures like Jesus, Gandhi, and Martin Luther King Jr. come to mind. They were all countercultural. And most of us would agree that they affected change for the better. However, if moral relativism is true, then what is "right" is determined by whatever the majority of the culture believes. But this leads to the absurd consequence that those seeking to reform the immoral practices of society (e.g., eliminating racism) are the immoral ones because they are acting against the cultural majority. This is a powerful reason to reject moral relativism.

The Impossibility of Moral Progress

Most of us have a strong intuition that moral progress is not only possible but beneficial. However, if moral relativism is true, then moral progress becomes, by definition, impossible. According to a consistent moral relativist, not only was someone like Martin Luther King Jr. wrong for challenging the deeply held moral beliefs of his culture, but the change he affected did not technically improve the morals of society—*it just changed them.* As Francis Beckwith and Gregory Koukl put it, "Morals can change, but they can never improve."[8] But this seems patently false! We want to say that holding the belief that racism is wrong is a moral *improvement* over holding that it is acceptable.

Moral Relativism Leads to Absurd Conclusions

In addition to the counterintuitive consequences mentioned above, moral relativism would leave us in the frustrating position of not being able to say that there is a moral difference between Adolf Hitler and Mother Teresa. The only way to do so would be to appeal to an *external* standard of morality. Yet, this is precisely what moral relativism denies. But surely such a conclusion is absurd. Mother Teresa lived to save lives; Hitler lived to destroy them.

Reaping What We Sow

When you're a kid, playing make-believe is innocent. When individuals and cultures play make-believe with reality there are disastrous consequences. People will believe ridiculous things in the name of "freedom of expression." You will hear things like "Pornography isn't wrong . . . it's just a business." Yeah, right. The global hunger for porn is not unrelated to the horrors of human trafficking and the objectification of women. It's simply naive to think otherwise.

As Christians we have a moral obligation to think clearly and stand courageously for truth because it's impossible to love our neighbors as ourselves if we don't. As Dallas Willard puts it, "Bluntly, to serve God well we must think straight; and crooked thinking, unintentional or not, always favors evil. And when the crooked thinking gets elevated into group orthodoxy, whether religious or secular, there is always, quite literally, 'hell to pay.'"[9] Bad ideas are not harmless.

Michael Novak doesn't mince words:

> During the next hundred years, the question for those who love liberty is whether we can survive the most insidious and duplicitous attacks from within, from those who undermine the virtues of our people, doing in advance the work of the Father of Lies. "There is no such thing as truth," they teach even the little ones. "Truth is bondage. Believe what seems right to you. There are as many truths as there are individuals. Follow

your feelings. Do as you please. Get in touch with your self. Do what feels comfortable." This is how they speak, those who prepare the jails of the twenty-first century. . . . [They] do the work of tyrants.[10]

Too strong? Honestly, not strong enough. We may think we are free because we live in a democracy and therefore are immune from tyranny. Not if we lose moral truth.

As a society, the ideas that we sow in this generation will be reaped by the next. Ideas and attitudes that seem benign enough in the confines of a classroom, song, or movie lead to horrific consequences when lived out in everyday life. When you lose objective moral truth, the most vulnerable in our society are at the greatest risk. Are the human rights of the unborn nullified for the personal convenience of having abortion on demand? (Especially the horrors of partial-birth abortion when the baby is already viable outside the womb?)[11] Or think of the elderly whose care now appears to them as burdensome to their family or society in states where physician-assisted suicide is now law.[12] Only time will tell if our culture will continue to plant toxic ideas in the name of freedom, only to eat its poisonous fruit in the years ahead. What is crystal clear is that you and I as followers of Jesus can't sit back and do nothing.

THE BIG IDEAS

- We have looked at five reasons why moral relativism is a bad idea: (1) disagreement is overrated, (2) people know *at least some things* are right and wrong, (3) the reformer's dilemma shows morality can lie with the cultural minority (e.g., Martin Luther King Jr. working for equal rights), (4) moral progress is impossible if moral relativism is true, and (5) moral relativism leads to absurd conclusions (e.g., Mother Teresa is not morally different than Adolf Hitler).

- All it takes to undermine relativism is admitting the existence of one universal moral fact.

- Ideas that seem benign enough in the confines of a classroom lead to horrific consequences when lived out in everyday life.

For Further Discovery

Beckwith, Francis J. "Why I Am Not a Moral Relativist." In *Why I Am a Christian: Leading Thinkers Explain Why They Believe*. Edited by Norman L. Geisler and Paul K. Hoffman. Grand Rapids: Baker, 2006.

Beckwith, Francis, and Gregory Koukl. *Relativism: Feet Firmly Planted in Mid-Air*. Grand Rapids: Baker, 1998.

Copan, Paul. "The Moral Argument." In *The Rationality of Theism*. Edited by Paul Copan and Paul K. Moser. London: Routledge, 2003.

———. *True for You, but Not for Me: Overcoming Objections to Christian Faith*. Rev. ed. Minneapolis: Bethany House, 2009.

McDowell, Sean, and Jonathan Morrow. *Is God Just a Human Invention? And Seventeen Other Questions Raised by the New Atheists*. Grand Rapids: Kregel, 2010.

ExploreTruth.tv. A seven-session online study taught by Jonathan Morrow that will help you break free from the riptide of relativism (powered by Impact 360 Institute).

True Tolerance
Tolerance Just Ain't What It Used to Be!

Truth is not bigoted. People can surely be bigots. . . . How we approach and communicate truth is what determines bigotry and narrow-mindedness.

—CHAD MEISTER[1]

Answer a fool according to his folly,
or he will be wise in his own eyes.
—PROVERBS 26:5

Therefore each of you must put off falsehood and speak truthfully to your neighbor, for we are all members of one body.
—EPHESIANS 4:25

IN A PREVIOUS CHAPTER WE LEARNED THAT "TRUTH *CORRESPONDS* OR *relates* to reality (the real world) as it actually is. . . . [Therefore,] if something is true, it is true for *all people*, at *all times*, and in *all places* regardless of a person's awareness or beliefs."[2] That means that while everyone could be wrong about what the truth concerning something actually is, *everyone can't be right!* This is where tolerance comes in, or at least it used to before our society became confused about its meaning.

The *Encarta* dictionary offers these two definitions for *tolerance*: "(1) the acceptance of the *differing views* of other people, for example, in religious or political matters, *and fairness toward the people who hold these different views*, (2) the act of putting up with something or somebody irritating or otherwise unpleasant."[3] However, the idea of tolerance in today's culture means agreeing that everyone's moral and spiritual views are equally true. If you disagree or don't accept another's beliefs, then you're being intolerant. Tolerance just ain't what it used to be! (Being from Tennessee, I can say "ain't.") Paul Copan couldn't be more right when he says, "If disagreement didn't exist, then tolerance would be unneeded. It's the existence of real differences between people that makes tolerance necessary and virtuous."[4] The following observation by Dallas Willard hits the nail on the head:

> Tolerance has suffered a great deal recently in our religious and political and educational areas. And tolerance, because truth has been pulled away from it, has slipped over into the idea that everything is equally right. No longer is tolerance a matter of saying, "I disagree with you and I believe you're wrong, but I accept you and I extend to you the right to be wrong." That's not enough. We're now in the situation where everyone must be equally right, where you cannot say that people are wrong and still claim to love them.[5]

Well, that pretty well sums up our situation. As one Harvard graduate put it in a commencement address, "The freedom of our day, is the freedom to devote ourselves to any values we please, *on the mere condition that we do not believe them to be true.*"[6] The message being heralded from our society is clear: "Believe whatever you want, but don't think you actually have the truth because that's intolerant." I experienced this attitude firsthand in college.

University 101

It was in the middle of the first semester of my freshman year, and I was sitting in University 101 (this is where they offer such helpful information as "this is college, the library is over there, you need to study"). Thankfully, most classes usually came and went without much excitement. But one day was different—*controversial topic day*. Here's what happened. First, the teacher described a controversial topic or complicated ethical dilemma and then asked the students to get up and go to one side of the room if they agreed or the other side if they disagreed with the statement or view. She started with easier statements like "cheating is wrong" and then worked her way up to more volatile issues like euthanasia and abortion.

I knew it was coming eventually. The teacher threw out, "As a Christian you believe all non-Christians are going to hell." This was a *Matrix*

The Bible—Divine and Human

The Bible is a *unique* book—but it is still a book. Yet, many think they have to read the Bible differently than any other book they read, like it is a book of magic. At the other end of the spectrum, some people read Scripture as an academic book of literature or history only—discounting the miraculous part of it—and miss the heart of its message. Biblical scholar Roy Zuck offers good advice: "The Bible then . . . is a human book and is also a divine book. Neither can be denied. If we look on the book as only human, then we approach the Bible rationally. If we look on the book as only divine while ignoring its human elements, we approach the Bible as a mystical book. Seeing that the Bible is both human and divine, we seek to interpret it as we would any other book while at the same time affirming its uniqueness as a book of divine truth from the hand of God."[3]

Read the Bible Christianly

As you read the Bible, do so with a desire to hear from the living God. God will honor your teachability, humility, and openness. Pray for God's help as you read the Bible. David models the kind of expectancy we want in Psalm 119:18, "Open my eyes, that I may behold wonderful things from Your law" (NASB).

Also, reading the Bible Christianly means reading it with certain presuppositions (see David's approach in Ps. 119).[4] Scott Duvall and Daniel Hays in their excellent book *Grasping God's Word: A Hands-On Approach to Reading, Interpreting, and Applying the Bible* offer the following four important Christian presuppositions:

1. The Bible is the Word of God. Although God worked through people to produce it, it is nonetheless inspired by the Holy Spirit and is God's Word to us.

2. The Bible is trustworthy and true.

3. God has entered into human history; thus the supernatural (e.g., miracles) does occur.

4. The Bible is not contradictory; it is unified, yet diverse. Nevertheless, God is bigger than we are, and he is not always easy to comprehend. Thus the Bible also has tension and mystery to it.[5]

This does not mean that we read the Bible blindly or carelessly or that we can't ask the hard questions (see my book *Questioning the Bible* for more on this). Nor does reading it with these presuppositions guarantee the accuracy of our interpretation of individual passages. Rather these commitments have to do with the general posture of our hearts toward the God of the Bible. We stand under the authority of Scripture, not vice versa.

Don't Disregard the Past

Sometimes well-meaning Christians have uninformed interpretations; they haven't really studied the commentary of the Christians who have preceded us. Throughout church history, theologians have clarified doctrine and made creedal statements at various councils. And while not everything they believed was correct, we have the opportunity to dialogue with the voices of the past. We should never hold to the mistaken notion that God has revealed truth to this generation only. We deprive ourselves of a wonderful resource by not appreciating and utilizing our godly heritage.

The Basic Story Line of the Bible

One of the reasons we find the Bible so difficult to read is that we only understand fragments of the bigger story—we don't have the big picture. I think that once you understand the bigger themes and events in the Bible, you will enjoy your time in God's Word much more richly.

The central person of the biblical story is Jesus Christ—every theme either anticipates His coming or is explained by His coming. A helpful way to understand the broad strokes on the biblical canvas is to view the Bible in four movements:

1. *Creation.* God, the creator of all that is, created humanity to have an intimate relationship with Himself (Gen. 1–2).
2. *Fall.* The first humans, Adam and Eve, disobeyed God. As a result, sin, death, and separation from God spread to every human born after them. The Old Testament is the anticipation of a Messiah (savior) who is to come through the lineage of Abraham and David to the nation of Israel. God chose Israel to be His witness to the world and to be

His vehicle of blessing to the world. The Israelites were given special promises and entrusted with the very words of God through the patriarchs and prophets. Unfortunately, much of the Old Testament reveals their utter failure to obey God and their idolatrous pursuit of other gods (Gen. 3–Malachi).

3. *Redemption.* In spite of the faithlessness and disobedience of Israel, God did not reject them or relinquish His desire to redeem humanity. So in the city of David, the Savior Jesus Christ—the long-awaited Messiah— was born. This is the good news that will be for all the peoples of the world. Christ lived a sinless life, was crucified, buried, and raised again, all to forgive the sins of whoever would trust in Him—no matter what their status in life, race, gender, or ethnicity. This good news must be proclaimed to the ends of the earth by Christ-followers, and the primary way God will accomplish this task is through the body of Christ—the church (Matthew–Jude).

4. *Restoration.* The church lives in light of the imminent second coming of Jesus Christ, after which God will judge the world and make all things new. Sin and death were initially judged and conquered at the cross, but they will be finally eradicated when Christ returns. Those who are not in Christ will be judged and eternally separated from God. Those who are in Christ will enter into joy, rest, and bliss—living in the presence of God for all eternity on a new heaven and new earth (Revelation).

Three Basics Steps to Reading the Bible

God intended for us to understand His Word. One indicator of this is the amount of Scripture we are told to obey or listen to; understanding is a prerequisite for obedience. When it comes to reading the Bible, there are three basic steps: (1) observation, (2) interpretation, and (3) application.[6] Let's take them each in turn.

Observation: What do I see?

It is a common occurrence when Christians gather for Bible study or small group to hear the question, "What does this passage mean to you?" Sounds harmless enough. However, it has skipped two essential steps in the process. Before we can determine what implications a particular text has for our lives, we must first discover what the text means. It is important for our generation to understand that the meaning of a Bible passage is determined by the *author* (the Holy Spirit through the prophet Jeremiah, for example), not the reader (you or me). As a reader, I no more control the meaning of a passage of Scripture than I control the meaning of my income tax statement from the IRS. (Somehow, I don't think they would be very sympathetic to *my* interpretation of my tax statement, which is that they owe me money rather than vice versa.)

Stating this principle of biblical interpretation succinctly, *a text cannot mean what it never meant.* So how do we discover what it meant?

Observation—here we ask and answer the question, *What do I see?* We are not interpreting anything yet—that's step two. We are just making observations of the scene . . . like a good CSI detective. A key to getting the most out of reading God's Word is learning the art of asking good questions of the passage. Ask the five *W*'s and an *H* and then jot down your findings in a notebook or journal:

- *Who.* Who is the author? Who is the intended audience?
- *What.* What is going on in this passage? What are the facts/details?
- *Where.* Where are the events of this passage taking place (geographically)?
- *When.* When did these events take place? When was this book/letter written?
- *Why.* Why does the author say what he says? Are there any clues in the text?
- *How.* How does the writer communicate the message of this passage?

Asking these questions will point you in the right direction as you seek to understand a passage.

Here are just some of the things to be aware of as you observe the passage:

- Look for words/themes that are repeated. If the word *faith* shows up several times in the span of a chapter, take note. Repetition is significant because it indicates the author's desire to emphasize certain ideas or details.

- Look for comparisons/contrasts. These will be signaled by the words *but*, *like*, and *as* (e.g., the righteous will be like . . . *but* the wicked will . . .). Comparisons/contrasts show up a bunch in Psalms and Proverbs.
- Watch for the word *therefore*. Whenever you come across it, ask, "What is the *therefore* there for?" Know that the word *therefore* will always point to what has come just before it. Take Romans 12:1 as an example. The *therefore* culminates Paul's argument of Romans 1–11 (in light of all that I have taught you . . . present your bodies as a living sacrifice).

Sometimes we grow impatient with the observation stage and prematurely rush on to interpretation because we think that is where the real action is! But this is a mistake, because the observation stage is critical for good interpretation. Heed the sage advice of Howard Hendricks: "Observation will give you the basic building blocks out of which you will construct the meaning of a passage. The answers to your questions will come directly from your observation process. That is why I say, the more time you spend in observation, the less time you will need to spend in interpretation, and the more accurate will be your results. The less time you spend in observation, the more time you will need to spend in interpretation, and the less accurate will be your results."[7]

Interpretation: What does it mean?

Some passages of Scripture are easy to interpret because the meaning is plain (e.g., John 11:35). But often we will come across passages that aren't as clear as we would like them to be. So with humility, we must do the careful work of interpretation (2 Tim. 2:15). We can grow in our ability to interpret the Bible with practice, similar to becoming increasingly more skilled at playing a musical instrument over time. The first rule of interpretation is that we must remember that "God chose specific times, places, situations, tools, and people through which to communicate the truth."[8] So we need to increase in our appreciation and understanding of the historical setting in which these writings were composed and delivered. The books I suggest at the end of the chapter will equip you in more detail, but here are some important things to keep in mind as you seek to discover the meaning of a text:

1. *A culture/time/geography/language gap exists between biblical times and the twenty-first century.* America is much different than Judea/Palestine

was two millennia ago. We should do our best not to read our modern expectations or biases into a passage; rather, we need to immerse ourselves in the culture of the ancient world and allow the text to speak for itself. Commentaries, Bible dictionaries, and Bible handbooks greatly help in this process.

2. *Different kinds of literature and figures of speech are being used in the Bible.* In the same way that we read text messages differently than online journal articles, so do we read the Bible according to its genres. Psalms is poetry; if we try to interpret a psalm like one of Paul's letters, we will misinterpret the text. Gospels are interpreted differently than the Wisdom Literature found in Proverbs. Also, the authors of the Bible use figures of speech to clearly and compellingly communicate God's Word to us. Our approach to the text should not be so woodenly literal as to not allow for normal conventions of language.

3. *Context is king.* Many errors in interpretation can be avoided by carefully reading the paragraphs before and after the passage being studied. When we are able to see the author's full flow of thought, we can better understand what he is intending to say or not say in a given text. Always read a passage in context.

4. *Pay attention to the words, grammar, and syntax used.* Over time, words can change in meaning. A word written in 585 BC will most likely not carry the exact meaning as that same word used in AD 90. So we must examine how other writers and literature used that word during that time period. Also of importance are the parts of speech and their relationship within the sentence. Take for example the notion of forgiveness. If the Bible uses a past tense verb to say that my sin debt has been paid for, I can interpret this to mean that I do not need to keep trying to atone for my own sin (Col. 2:14).

5. *Scripture helps interpret Scripture.* When all is said and done, Scripture will not contradict Scripture. If we are reading one of Paul's letters, we should ask if our interpretation fits with what we know about the rest of Paul's writings. And if our conclusion fits with the general tenor of the New Testament, then we know that we have arrived at a good interpretation of the passage.

Once we feel confident about what the text means,[9] then we can move to the crucial—yet often neglected—task of application.

Application: What does it mean for my life?

Unfortunately, many of us stop the process at understanding what a text means. But Christianity is not about acquiring Bible trivia; it is about our lives being conformed to the image of Jesus Christ.[10] And this occurs when we apply the truth discovered in Scripture to our lives. As you read the text, here are some questions you should ask that will help you discover how to apply God's Word:

- Is there an example for me to follow?
- Is there a sin to avoid?
- Is there a promise to claim?
- Is there a prayer to repeat?
- Is there a verse to memorize?
- Is there a command to obey?
- Is there a condition to meet?
- Is there an error to mark?
- Is there a challenge to face?[11]

While the meaning of a text will never change, the ways to apply the text are endless. As Hendricks and Hendricks put it, "There is only one ultimate interpretation of a passage of Scripture. The text doesn't mean one thing today and something else tomorrow. Whatever it means, it means forever. But you will never cease the process of applying that truth to your life."[12]

The Role of the Holy Spirit in Interpreting the Bible

Can an unbeliever grasp the content of the Bible? Yes and no. Yes, if we mean the text can be understood by employing a sound approach to literature—to the basic grammar, context, and content of a passage. But an unbeliever cannot *fully appreciate* and take to heart the truth of the Bible. God's Spirit helps Christians discern the spiritual realities of the text and then apply them to their lives (1 Cor. 2:14). Duvall and Hays offer a helpful summary:

When it comes to biblical interpretation, having the Holy Spirit does not mean that the Spirit is all we need, since he will not make biblical interpretation automatic. He expects us to use our minds, valid inter-pretive methods, and good study helps. The Spirit does not create new meaning or provide new information, but he does enable us to accept the Bible as God's Word and grasp its meaning. The Spirit will not change the Bible to suit our purposes or match our circumstances, but he will work in our lives as interpreters. He restores us to our senses and helps us grow up spiritually so we can hear his voice in the Scriptures more clearly.[13]

The Words of God Are Your Life

The author of Hebrews reminds us that "the word of God is alive and active. Sharper than any double-edged sword, it penetrates even to dividing soul and spirit, joints and marrow; it judges the thoughts and attitudes of the heart" (Heb. 4:12). We should not treat Scripture like a frog we are dissecting for biology class. It is God who is doing the restorative surgery in our soul. We want to use the minds God has given us—in addition to study tools—and the guidance of the Holy Spirit to humbly seek God's revealed truth in Scrip-ture. Whether you are a new believer or have a few years under your belt of walking with Christ, commit to seeking the God of the Word during your college years. For as Moses reminded the people of Israel, "They are not just idle words for you—they are your life" (Deut. 32:47).

THE BIG IDEAS

- The Bible is both a divine and human book; we should approach it as such.
- We need to read the Bible Christianly with an open heart toward God.
- We can learn a lot from Christians of the past.
- The four major themes of the Bible are creation, fall, redemption, and restoration.
- There are three basic steps to studying the Bible: observation, interpretation, and application.
- While the presence of the Holy Spirit in our lives does not eliminate the need for good interpretive skills, He is essential for us to understand and apply Scripture.

For Further Discovery

Bartholomew, Craig G., and Michael W. Goheen. *The Drama of Scripture: Finding Our Place in the Biblical Story*. Grand Rapids: Baker, 2014.

Duvall, J. Scott, and J. Daniel Hays. *Grasping God's Word: A Hands-On Approach to Reading, Interpreting, and Applying the Bible*. 3rd ed. Grand Rapids: Zondervan, 2012.

Hendricks, Howard G., and William D. Hendricks. *Living by the Book: The Art and Science of Reading the Bible*. Chicago: Moody Publishers, 2007.

Morrow, Jonathan. *Questioning the Bible: 11 Major Challenges to the Bible's Authority*. Chicago: Moody Publishers, 2014.

Radmacher, Earl D., Ronald B. Allen, and H. Wayne House, eds. *Nelson's New Illustrated Bible Commentary: Spreading the Light of God's Word into Your Life*. Nashville: Thomas Nelson, 1999.

Can I Trust the Bible?

The Bible is not a book like any other. It makes a claim that God spoke and speaks through its message. It argues that as his creatures, we are accountable to him for what he has revealed. The trustworthiness of Scripture points to its authority as well. Scripture is far more than a history book, as good and trustworthy as that history is. It is a book that calls us to examine our lives and relationship to God. Beyond the fascinating history, it contains vital and life-transforming truths about God and us.

—DARRELL BOCK[1]

The Bible consists of the writings of more than forty people. From all walks of life—including kings, herdsmen, poets, philosophers, statesmen, legislators, fishermen, priests, and prophets—these people wrote over a span of more than fifteen hundred years. They lived in diverse cultures, and wrote in a variety of literary styles. But the message of the Bible is one great drama in which all the parts fit together.

—ROBERT SAUCY[2]

When all the facts are known, the Bible (in its original writings) properly interpreted in light of which culture and communication means had developed by the time of its composition will be shown to be completely true (and therefore not false) in all that it affirms, to the degree of precision intended by the author, in all matters relating to God and his creation.

—DAVID DOCKERY[3]

WHERE DID THE BIBLE COME FROM? WHO WROTE IT? DID JESUS WALK around speaking King James English? How do I know that what I was reading in the Bible before I went to sleep was what was originally written down?

I became a Christian as a junior in high school at the age of seventeen. But it wasn't until I arrived at college that I began to experience doubts about whether the Bible was reliable. I hadn't really given it much thought. But upon further reflection I decided that if I trusted my life to the God revealed in the pages of the Bible, I needed to know if I could trust the Bible itself. So I started doing some homework. I bought books, read articles, and checked out websites. The more I studied, the more excited and encouraged I became. My conclusion? There is considerable evidence supporting the Bible's reliability. I could—with eyes wide open—trust it. Do I still have questions about difficult passages every now and then? Sure. But I investigate them, and there are always reasonable options and plausible explanations available.

So why do I say all this? It will be hard for you to sustain a desire to read and study God's Word if you have genuine intellectual doubts about whether or not you can trust it. The solution to your doubt is not just to muster up more faith by sheer willpower. This is kind of like trying to hold your breath for ten minutes—eventually you will have to take another breath. You need to investigate whether or not the Bible is reliable. I want to assist you in that investigation by sharing with you some of my discoveries on the reliability of the Old and New Testaments. In most cases, I will only have room to give you my conclusions, but you can follow my research trail in the endnotes and the resources I recommend. Also, I encourage you to pick up a copy of my book *Questioning the Bible: 11 Major Challenges to the Bible's Authority* for a deeper look at the toughest objections to the Bible.

How Ancient Documents Work

To begin with, you need to know that *none* of the original manuscripts of either the Old or New Testaments are still in existence—all that remain are imperfect copies.[4] But this is exactly the same situation of *all* the other ancient works of literature as well. No one has the originals. For example, even though we don't have the original writings of Plato or Socrates, this doesn't make us doubt their existence. Even with all the power and wealth of Rome, we don't possess the original documents that the historian Tacitus penned. While this may come as a surprise, this fact should not turn us into skeptics regarding ancient texts. But we do need to recognize how the composition and transmission of ancient documents worked.

Two quick illustrations might help restore your confidence in reliable copies. First, how do we know how long a yard is? There is a "standard" yard at the Smithsonian Institute. But what if it were stolen and melted in a vat of boiling lava? Could we never measure anything again? Is all hope lost for football referees? Of course not. Why? We have reliable copies that are extremely accurate. We know essentially how long a yard is even if we don't possess the original.[5]

Another illustration: What time is it? Look at your smartphone and then compare it with a clock around you. Most likely, they don't show the same time. Are you thrown into fits of despair because you don't know what time it *really* is? The official time for the United States is kept by the Time Service Department at the US Naval Observatory.[6] If it were somehow destroyed, would no one know what time it is? Again, no, because we have lots of reliable copies. We know essentially what time it is even if we don't live at the US Naval Observatory!

Copies of the Old and New Testaments work the same way. The more copies we have to examine and the closer they are to when the documents were originally written, the better. And you should also know that no other ancient work even comes close to the number and quality of ancient manuscripts we have of the Old and New Testaments. As a classical studies minor in college, I didn't hear any of my professors call into question the textual reliability of any of the works that we were studying.[7] And yet when it came to my Bible as literature class, it was open season for all manner of objections about reliability. In my experience, the texts of the Bible are often perceived to be guilty until proven innocent while other works of antiquity are typically presumed innocent until proven guilty.

Old Testament linguist and scholar Gleason Archer observes, "It is highly significant that these nonbiblical texts are so cheerfully accepted even though, for example, works of Tacitus, Lucretius, Catullus, and Aristotle have fewer than five extant copies each and largely bear much later datings than many biblical texts."[8]

The complete Bible didn't descend from heaven on a cloud neatly bound in Italian leather with the apostle's or prophet's name embossed on the front.

Rather, God was pleased to use ordinary people—with whatever language and materials were available to them—to write down His revelation to humanity and pass it on from generation to generation. Since we live in the information age we sometimes forget that the printing press wasn't invented until the fifteenth century. Up until that time, *everything* was written by hand. The writers of the Old Testament had to hand copy these texts on whatever materials were available (stone, clay tablets, papyrus, parchment, or leather—all of which deteriorate over time). So in order for an ancient document to be considered reliable, it is not reasonable for us to expect Moses to have typed up the book of Deuteronomy, run spell-check, and then printed it off on acid-free paper.

On the Reliability of the Old Testament

The Old Testament was originally written in Hebrew (with a few chapters in Aramaic), and it contains thirty-nine books written from about 1400–400 BC. The following paragraphs offer some good reasons to believe we possess an accurate Old Testament text.

First, the scribes who copied and preserved the text were careful and meticulous.[9] They developed numerical systems to ensure an accurate copy. They counted the number of lines, words, and letters per page of the new copy and then checked them with the count of the original. If they didn't match up, then the copy was destroyed and they started over.[10]

Next, archaeological discoveries shed light on many of the people, places, and events recorded in the Bible. While archaeology doesn't prove that the Bible is true, it certainly does confirm the historical reliability of the text.[11] I don't have room to tell you about all of these exciting discoveries, but you can see pictures and descriptions of many of them in the full-color *Archaeological Study Bible*. There is cause for continued optimism because only about 10 percent of the biblical sites in Israel have been excavated. Who knows what other biblical treasures lie buried in the sand?

Perhaps the strongest evidence for the reliability of the Old Testament is the discovery of the Dead Sea Scrolls in 1947 at Qumran. (During my graduate studies, I had the privilege of visiting the site where they were discovered. I saw a copy of the famous Isaiah scroll at the Shrine of the Book in

Israel.) The significance of this discovery cannot be overstated. Up until the time of the discovery, we had known how carefully scribes had passed down the text. But critics of the Bible continually claimed that if we ever found earlier documents, proof could be shown for how much the text had been changed and corrupted. So when a shepherd boy who was tending his goats stumbled upon pottery in a cave containing ancient texts, it sent shock waves through the biblical world. Eight hundred scrolls, containing fragments from every book of the Old Testament except Esther, were discovered dating from 250 BC to AD 50. But most significant was that an entire manuscript of Isaiah was found dating to circa 75 BC. Old Testament scholars were then able to compare this text of Isaiah with the earliest existing copy of Isaiah in the Masoretic text (the Hebrew text of the Jewish Bible) dating to AD 1008–1009. Their conclusion? Ninety-five percent word-for-word copying accuracy over almost 1,100 years! And the 5 percent of variations consisted of nothing more significant than omitted letters or misspelled words—slips of the pen.[12] In light of the discovery of the Dead Sea Scrolls at Qumran, it is fair to say that the burden of proof is on the critic who claims that the Old Testament has not been reliably preserved.

The oldest Old Testament manuscript discovered so far is a fragment of the priestly blessing from Numbers 6:24–27 found in a silver amulet near Jerusalem dating to the seventh century BC (2,600 years old). Now, you might be wondering why we don't have more Old Testament documents. Here are several reasons: (1) old manuscripts written on papyrus or leather aged and deteriorated over time; (2) much of Israel's history is marked by war, and Jerusalem was destroyed and burned at least twice during the time the Old Testament was written; and (3) "when manuscripts began to show signs of wear, the Jewish scribes reverently disposed of them because they bore the sacred name of God. Disposing of the manuscripts avoided defilement by pagans. Since scribes were meticulous in copying biblical manuscripts, there was little reason to keep old manuscripts. When scrolls became worn, they were placed in a storage room called a *genizah* . . . until there were enough to perform a ritual burial ceremony."[13] Once all of these factors are considered, we shouldn't be surprised that we have not found more.

One last question needs answering before we leave the Old Testament:

How were the books of the Old Testament canon chosen? While I can't get into all the details here, the key point to remember is that "the books did not *receive* their authority because they were placed into the canon [i.e., standard]; rather, they were *recognized* by the nation of Israel as having divine authority and were therefore included in the canon. These books were used to determine beliefs and conduct long before ecclesiastical councils recognized their authority."[14]

After a lifetime of studying the text of the Old Testament, Bruce Waltke concludes that "95 percent of the Old Testament is . . . textually sound."[15] The remaining 5 percent does not affect any key Christian doctrine, and as more texts are discovered and existing ones translated, that percentage should continue to decrease. As strong as the case is for the reliability of the Old Testament, the New Testament case is even stronger! And as Darrell Bock notes, "The case is strongest where it matters most—in its portrayal of Jesus."[16]

On the Reliability of the New Testament

The New Testament was originally written in Greek from AD 49 to AD 95, and it consists of twenty-seven books. The following paragraphs tell a few of the many reasons we have a reliable New Testament text.

First, the New Testament has an incredible amount of manuscript evidence supporting it. Most ancient documents have only a handful of copies left. For example, we have 109 copies of the Greek historian Herodotus, thirty-one copies of Tacitus's *Annals,* and 150 of Livy's *History of Rome.* Next to the New Testament, Homer's *Illiad* has about 2,300 copies. But we have more than 5,700 ancient manuscripts of the Greek New Testament alone (and this number is growing). That doesn't even include the 10,000 Latin manuscripts and almost one million New Testament quotations from the early church fathers. We truly possess an embarrassment of riches—no other ancient document even comes close![17]

Second, not only do we have an abundance of manuscripts to work with, we also have early texts for the New Testament. The earliest fragment of the New Testament is from the John Rylands papyri that were found in Egypt. It contains a portion of John 18 and dates to AD 117–134. If John wrote his gospel around AD 95—allowing for the time to be translated and circulated down to Egypt—you will find this date fairly close to the time when John actually wrote it. Moreover, copies of almost the entire New Testament were already established by AD 250 (the Bodmer papyri and Chester Beatty papyri).[18] Because of the number and quality of the existing manuscripts, New Testament scholar Dan Wallace concludes that "we are now certain of over 99 percent of the original New Testament, and of the remaining 1 percent there are finite options . . . and not one of [the variant readings] . . . that has any claim to authenticity affects any cardinal truth of Scripture."[19]

Third, the New Testament is historically accurate. For example, Luke—the author of Luke and Acts—was a first-rate historian. He was careful to do his homework (Luke 1:1–4) and it shows because he accurately describes people, places, and events of the ancient world.[20]

Fourth, multiple witnesses exist, and these writers have proven trustworthy. It is not insignificant that several of them died for what they knew to be either true or false.[21] One of the most striking examples of a New Testament writer's honesty is found in Matthew 16:23, where we see Jesus calling Peter "Satan." Why would Matthew record the story of Peter being rebuked by Jesus if it didn't actually happen?[22] Also, the independent writings in the New Testament weren't compiled into a single volume until later. When seeking to establish historical reliability, it is significant when you have agreement from independent sources (this is known as the criterion of multiple attestation). Our judicial system calls this corroborating evidence.

Fifth, the New Testament has received archaeological confirmation. Just as many aspects of the Old Testament have been archaeologically confirmed, so too has the New Testament. One recent discovery confirming the reliability of the gospel accounts was the Pool of Siloam referred to in John 9. Admittedly, all the evidence is not in, and some things may never be known. But what has been unearthed has provided additional warrant in our belief that the text of the New Testament has been accurately composed and passed down.

How do we know that the right books were included in the New Testament? Paul Copan summarizes, "The books of the New Testament—like those of the Old Testament—had an authority that was *recognized* rather than *bestowed*."[23] In other words, the people who formed the biblical canon did not invest certain writings with authority. Rather, they affirmed *what was already authoritative within the community* and organized it. The selection process (known as canonization) generally followed four criteria: (1) *apostolicity* (written by an apostle or under the authority of one), (2) *orthodoxy* (not contradicting previously revealed truth), (3) *antiquity* (from the time of the apostles), and (4) *universality* (being widely accepted as authoritative).[24] In light of these facts, Christians possess sufficient reason to trust that we have the books of the Bible that God—through the apostles and prophets—intended us to have.

Summing It All Up

I have chosen to focus primarily on external reasons the Bible is reliable because that is usually where the strongest challenges come. But I don't want to leave you with the impression that only what is confirmed by sources outside of the Bible can be considered reliable. It's a nice bonus when a new discovery is made, but the Bible—like any historical document—should be viewed as reliable unless for internal or external reasons it is shown not to be.

By way of summary, Douglas Stuart concludes concerning the reliability of the Old Testament and New Testament texts that "99 percent of the original words in the New Testament are recoverable with a very high degree of certainty. In the case of the Old Testament the figure might be more like 95 percent. When the words that are recoverable with a fairly high degree of certainty are added, we may be confident that we are able to read, reflect upon, and act upon what is practically equivalent to the original itself. There is no area of Christian faith or practice that actually stands or falls on textual studies."[25]

I want to close with a final reason you can trust the Bible. Jesus did. He affirmed the writings of the Old Testament[26] (Matt. 5:17–18; Luke 24:25–32; John 10:34–36) and promised what would become the New Testament (John 14:26; 16:12–14). And if Jesus is who He claimed to be, and God did in fact raise Him from the dead, then His testimony is powerful evidence that the Bible is truly God's Word to us (2 Tim. 3:16–17; 2 Peter 1:20–21). Trusting the Bible is not a blind leap of faith; it is an entirely reasonable thing to do.

THE BIG IDEAS

- The Bible did not magically fall from heaven, leather bound; its composition was a divine and human process consistent with the natural limitations associated with writing documents in the ancient world.

- Reasons supporting the reliability of the Old Testament are (1) the scribes who copied and preserved the text were careful and meticulous; (2) archaeological discoveries shed light on many of the people, places, and events recorded in the Old Testament; and (3) the discovery of the Dead Sea Scrolls in 1947 at Qumran confirms the accuracy of Old Testament writings—most importantly the book of Isaiah.

- Reasons supporting the reliability of the New Testament are (1) the incredible amount of manuscript evidence, (2) the early texts for the New Testament, (3) the historical accuracy of the New Testament, (4) the multiple trustworthy witnesses who testify to its message, and (5) archaeological confirmation.

- The books included in the Old and New Testaments were *recognized* as authoritative by the community; they weren't *bestowed* with authority. As it became necessary to list the authoritative books of Scripture, they did so. Jesus affirmed writings from the Old Testament and promised what would become the New Testament.

For Further Discovery

Blomberg, Craig. *The Historical Reliability of John's Gospel*. Downers Grove, IL: InterVarsity Press, 2014.

Bock, Darrell L. *The Missing Gospels: Unearthing the Truth Behind Alternative Christianities*. Nashville: Thomas Nelson, 2007.

Bock, Darrell L., and Daniel B. Wallace. *Dethroning Jesus: Exposing Popular Culture's Quest to Unseat the Biblical Christ*. Nashville: Thomas Nelson, 2010.

Bruce, F. F. *The Canon of Scripture*. Downers Grove, IL: InterVarsity Press, 1988.

Hoffmeier, James K. *The Archaeology of the Bible*. Oxford: Lion Hudson, 2015.

Kaiser, Walter C., Jr. *The Old Testament Documents: Are They Reliable and Relevant?* Downers Grove, IL: InterVarsity Press, 2001.

Kruger, Michael J. *Canon Revisited: Establishing the Origins and Authority of the New Testament Books.* Wheaton, IL: Crossway, 2012.

Morrow, Jonathan. *Questioning the Bible: 11 Major Challenges to the Bible's Authority.* Chicago: Moody Publishers, 2014.

Wegner, Paul D. *The Journey from Texts to Translations: The Origin and Development of the Bible.* Grand Rapids: Baker, 2004.

BiblePlaces.com. This helpful site "features photographs and information on sites in Israel, Jordan, Egypt, Turkey, and Greece with an emphasis on biblical geography, history, and archaeology."

Knowing Versus
Showing Your Faith

The Spirit himself testifies with our spirit that we are God's children.

—ROMANS 8:16

Because you are his sons, God sent the Spirit of his Son into our hearts, the Spirit who calls out, "Abba, Father."

—GALATIANS 4:6

Reason in the form of rational arguments and evidence plays an essential role in our showing Christianity to be true, whereas reason in this form plays a contingent and secondary role in our personally knowing Christianity to be true. The proper ground of our knowing Christianity to be true is the inner work of the Holy Spirit in our individual selves; and in our showing Christianity to be true, it is his role to open the hearts of unbelievers to assent and respond to the reasons we present.

—WILLIAM LANE CRAIG[1]

THERE YOU ARE IN A FRESHMAN PHILOSOPHY CLASS. YOU ARE A NEW Christian. And the professor asks for a show of hands to see how many Christians are in his class this semester. You enthusiastically raise your hand—two others in the class of about thirty-five join in. Expecting the professor to respect your religious beliefs, he surprises you by announcing with a sarcastic grin that each year he has students just like you who have naively bought into Christianity only to give it up by the end of the semester. Over the course of the semester your professor raises objections against

Christianity that you have never heard before, and this causes you to really doubt your faith. Maybe Christianity isn't true. After all, this guy is really smart and knows a lot more than you.

This scenario raises an important question: *How does a person know that Christianity is true?* If someone presents me with an argument I've never heard before—or that I don't know how to answer—is my knowledge of Christianity completely undermined? If it is, then we are all in trouble, because this would mean that every Christian seeking confidence in the Christian faith would require a PhD in Christian apologetics. I grappled with this insecurity for a while: How did I know that Christianity is true? Then I discovered a book by Christian philosopher William Lane Craig; his book really helped me make sense of this question.[2] Craig drew a distinction between *knowing* Christianity to be true and *showing* Christianity to be true.

Knowing Christianity to Be True

The Bible teaches that a believer knows Christianity is true on the basis of the internal witness of the Holy Spirit (Rom. 8:16; Gal. 4:6; 1 John 3:24; 4:13). When a person trusts Jesus Christ for salvation, a lot of really incredible stuff happens. One is that God sends His Holy Spirit to live within each of us (John 14:16–17, 20; 2 Cor. 1:22; Eph. 1:13–14). God's Spirit then testifies to our spirit that we are His children. In other words, God lets us know directly—without spoken or written words—that we belong to Him, that Jesus Christ has forgiven our sins, and that we have been reconciled to God. This is how you *know* that Christianity is true.

Imagine that you are back in the classroom. Let's say that in the middle of a lecture your philosophy professor pronounces that some scholars think that Jesus of Nazareth never actually existed—the New Testament completely made Him up. As a Christian, you have the belief that Jesus was a person of history. If you didn't, then you wouldn't be a Christian! But today you hear for the first time that some people (probably intelligent people or your professor wouldn't have quoted them) doubt that Jesus was real, and this initially troubles you. Up until now, you've never had reason to doubt that Jesus was a real (living and breathing) historical person.

Your professor's claim is aimed at "defeating" your confidence in Jesus.

Philosophers have creatively called this kind of claim a "defeater." So your professor throws this potential defeater for Christianity at you. But even though you can't explain *how* you know, you *just know* deep down that your professor must be wrong—Jesus is real. So how do you know this? Answer: by the internal witness of the Holy Spirit we just talked about. Even if you didn't have any other reason or evidence for believing, you are still justified and rational in believing that Jesus was a historical figure.

To illustrate how this works, prominent Christian philosopher Alvin Plantinga tells a story of a person charged with committing a crime.[3] All of the circumstantial evidence was stacked against him—think CSI. It didn't look good. Yet, even if this guy is unable to refute any of this evidence against him, he is still within his rights to believe that he is innocent. Why? Because he knows he did not commit the crime! And this knowledge defeats even the most powerful evidence against his innocence. The internal testimony of the Holy Spirit in your life as a Christian works the same way. The Holy Spirit living within you overpowers the evidence stacked up against Christianity. Because of the Holy Spirit, your reason to believe that Jesus was real is simply more powerful than believing He was not. To put it another way: the Holy Spirit is a defeater of the defeater that was raised against Christianity by your professor! . . . Got that?

Does this mean that you shouldn't examine the historical evidence about Jesus? No. Go for it! God in His wisdom has given us His Spirit to let us know that we are His children, but He also revealed Himself in history, which everyone can freely explore and investigate. By the way, if you researched Jesus as a historical figure, you would not only discover that New Testament documents repeatedly affirm Him as a historical person, but Roman historians Tacitus and Suetonius, Roman governor Pliny, and Jewish historian Josephus (just to name a few) all write about the life and ministry of Jesus.[4] Jesus was an authentic historical figure—but this moves us beyond how we *know* Christianity to be true to how we *show* Christianity to be true.

Showing Christianity to Be True

Showing Christianity to be true involves giving reasons or evidences that are publicly available to everyone. For example, a friend can take you at your word about your assurance that Christianity is true, but they can't get inside of you to experience it for themselves. The task of showing Christianity to be true is often called apologetics. While the Bible doesn't require all Christians to be scholars, it does command us to do all that we can to always be ready to give a defense (literally, an apologetic) for the hope within us (1 Peter 3:15; Jude 3). Showing others that Christianity is true can come in many forms: by living a virtuous and attractive life; by giving reasons why it is reasonable that God exists, that Jesus was who He claimed to be, and that Jesus's resurrection actually happened; by sharing how God has changed your life; or by showing that the Christian worldview makes the best sense of our biggest questions and life experiences. These are all publicly available ways by which we can show the truthfulness of Christianity, with the *primary* purpose of bringing evidence to others.[5]

On a practical note, the combination of pressure from both peers and authority (like a professor) regarding Christianity *might* make it very difficult for someone to experience the assurance of the Holy Spirit. So doing some investigation as to how other Christians have successfully defended the faith might boost your confidence to defend the truth of Christianity. While your knowing Christianity to be true is not based on evidence or arguments *alone*, evidence and arguments can add to or reinforce your confidence that Christianity is true. By the way, after two thousand years there are no new major arguments against Christianity. The objections to God's existence or the reliability of the Bible you encounter today have been raised before, just with minor variations and by different people. Christians throughout church history have been defending the faith.[6] And today we are experiencing a renaissance in Christian apologetics when the arguments for Christianity are even stronger and more precise than ever. I have included resources in this book that will give you reasonable answers to almost anything you'll come up against in college.

Now I want to be clear about what I am *not* saying. Christianity isn't true for you because you happen to believe it and false for your professor because he doesn't believe it. This is a form of relativism. If Christianity is true, then that means it accurately describes *all* of reality *for* everyone *whether* they believe or not (see chapter 6, "Truth Matters"). Our question addresses how *you personally* know that Christianity is true.

I am also *not* saying that if you ever experience any emotional or intellectual doubt, then you are not a Christian (see chapter 20, "Dealing with

Doubt"). Far from it! Ours is a faith seeking understanding. Pursue your honest questions and doubts; God is big enough to handle them. But also remember that it is possible for you to grieve the Holy Spirit by sin and willful disobedience to God in your life (Eph. 4:30). This makes the Holy Spirit's witness hard to hear in those moments you need Him most. So it is important that you confess your sins as you become aware of them (1 John 1:9) in order to maintain a spiritually healthy relationship with God. Also pray that God would fill you with His Spirit daily (Eph. 5:17–18).

College is a time when ideas can dramatically affect your spiritual life, and you need to learn how to take every thought captive to the obedience of Christ (2 Cor. 10:3–5). As we grow and mature as Christians we learn to love God with our minds as well as our hearts. The good news is that you don't have to be ashamed about what you believe or squeamish about what you don't know yet—there are many solid reasons why Christianity is true. There is no need to check your brain at the door or commit intellectual suicide simply because you have chosen to follow Jesus. Remembering the distinction between how you *know* and how you *show* Christianity to be true will better prepare you for times of doubt or times when your faith is under fire.

THE BIG IDEAS

- The believer knows Christianity is true on the basis of the internal witness of the Holy Spirit (Rom. 8:16; Gal. 4:6; 1 John 3:24; 4:13).

- Showing Christianity to be true involves giving reasons or evidences that are publicly available; these evidences are called apologetics (1 Peter 3:15).

- *Knowing* Christianity to be true is *primarily for your own personal assurance* (though this as part of your testimony can be a powerful way you can testify that Christianity is true).

- *Showing* Christianity to be true is *primarily for the benefit of others* (though it does reinforce your confidence as well).

- Maintaining a healthy spiritual life will help you combat nagging doubts or outright attacks on your faith.

For Further Discovery

Copan, Paul. *How Do You Know You're Not Wrong? Responding to Objections That Leave Christians Speechless.* Grand Rapids: Baker, 2005.

Craig, William Lane. *Reasonable Faith: Christian Truth and Apologetics.* 3rd ed. Wheaton, IL: Crossway, 2008.

Habermas, Gary R. "The Testimony of the Holy Spirit and Evidence." In *The Risen Jesus and Future Hope.* Oxford: Rowman & Littlefield, 2003.

Moreland, J. P., and William Lane Craig. *Philosophical Foundations for a Christian Worldview.* Downers Grove, IL: InterVarsity Press, 2009.

Plantinga, Alvin. *Knowledge and Christian Belief.* Grand Rapids: Eerdmans, 2015.

No Apologies Needed

The crushing weight of the secular outlook ... permeates or pressures every thought we have today. Sometimes it even forces those who self-identify as Christian teachers to set aside Jesus' plain statements about the reality and total relevance of the kingdom of God and replace them. ... The powerful though vague and unsubstantiated presumption is that something has been found out that renders a spiritual understanding of reality in the manner of Jesus simply foolish to those who are "in the know." But when it comes time to say exactly what it is that has been found out, nothing of substance is forthcoming.

—DALLAS WILLARD[1]

Success in evangelism is simply communicating Christ in the power of the Holy Spirit and leaving the results to God. Similarly, effectiveness in apologetics is presenting cogent and persuasive arguments for the Gospel in the power of the Holy Spirit and leaving the results to God.

—WILLIAM LANE CRAIG[2]

Dear friends, although I was very eager to write to you about the salvation we share, I felt compelled to write and urge you to contend for the faith that was once for all entrusted to God's holy people.

—JUDE 3

HAVE YOU EVER BEEN EMBARRASSED? I MEAN REALLY EMBARRASSED. We're talking "I don't want to go to school the next day" kind of stuff. Maybe you had a bad haircut, didn't have the latest clothes, or had a blemish on your face. While I experienced numerous embarrassing moments in college, one in particular stands out. As I mentioned before, our dorm room shared a bathroom with four other rooms. But the door leading from each room into the bathroom could be locked. Well, my roommate was leaving for class one day and forgot that I was in the shower, locked the door, and went off to class. So after my nice hot shower, I was greeted by a locked door! I was locked in the bathroom with no way to get out. No one else was in their dorms, so I waited and kept knocking. Finally, another person came to the door. So I walked through his room, out his door (remember, these dorms all had outside entrances), onto the open walkway, and all the way around the building with nothing but a towel on! I knew my roommates would have a fun time with this one.

When we are embarrassed, we don't want to look anyone in the eye; instead we try to fade into the background. Let me ask you a question: Are you embarrassed to be a Christian? Do you view your relationship with God like a bad haircut—kind of hoping no one will notice? Are you timid about mentioning the name of Jesus?

Jesus's earliest followers wrestled with being ashamed of Jesus. Peter, for example, denied three times that he even knew Christ to people he had never met (Luke 22:57–61). Yet it is this same Peter—transformed by the reality of Jesus's resurrection from the dead and the indwelling power of the Holy Spirit—who calls Christians to "always be prepared to give an answer to everyone who asks you to give the reason for the hope that you have. But do this with gentleness and respect" (1 Peter 3:15).[3]

You and I have God's Spirit living inside of us, and we have God's promise that He is with us even to the end of the age (Matt. 28:20). We also have the charge to always be ready to give an answer for the hope that we have. Now this "giving an answer" may not always mean giving a detailed, rational argument for the existence of God . . . though it might. What it also could mean is responding in love to someone who doesn't deserve love, or sharing how God has changed your life. Regardless, there will be times when you and I will be called to give an answer. Engaging in this process is known as apologetics.

Why Apologetics Is Important

Apologetics has been defined various ways, but here is how I would summarize it: for a Christian, apologetics is about knowing *why* you believe what you believe and then being able to give reasons for faith with gentleness and respect as opportunities arise. Learning what you believe and why you believe it takes time and effort. But it's so worth it. Learning about God is also part of loving God—loving Him with our minds. We are not supposed to have all the answers, but as maturing believers in Christ, we ought to be able to handle common objections to the Christian faith (we will look at some of these in the next few chapters). It is beneficial for Christians to engage in the study of apologetics for several reasons.

First, exploring what you believe and why you believe it increases your confidence as a Christian. Christians are constantly bombarded (both actively and passively) with reasons that Christianity is not true or real. Just watching a movie or the evening news can discourage you. Yet, I have found that the more I explore what I believe and why, the more confidence I have that the God of the Bible is who He claims to be. When I investigate the historical evidence for who Jesus is, and how He rose from the dead, a refreshing breeze blows through my soul. Even though I am inundated each day by the claim that truth and morality are relative, I return to why I know objective morality exists and how some things are right and some things are wrong.

When people tell me that life is an accident, I reflect on the beauty and intricate design in our world. In chapter 20 we will explore how to deal with honest doubts, but one of the most powerful things you can do in times of doubt is to remind yourself of what you have investigated and know to be true. Being able to remind yourself of what is true and why it is true is one of the fruits of studying apologetics.

Another benefit of apologetics is that it helps clear away barriers people have that are keeping them from considering the claims of Christianity. Now don't become discouraged by those who want to play stump-the-Christian. Some people use argumentative questions as a smoke screen to hide the fact that they just don't want to become a Christian. But others have legitimate and sincere questions that are hindering them from trusting Jesus Christ. You and I can be helpful in this situation if we are available to the Spirit's leading in our life . . . and we've done our homework.

Let's say Joanne comes to you and honestly wants to know how someone can trust the validity of the Bible since it has been copied so many times.

Good question. In your response you could summarize some of the key points from chapter 10, "Can I Trust the Bible?" Perhaps it will make sense to her. If so, she is now a step closer to encountering the Jesus of the New Testament. Part of being ready to give an answer for the hope within you is doing your homework.

While it is true that you can't argue someone into the kingdom of heaven, this statement misses the point.[4] One of the mysteries of conversion is that people seem to come to faith for lots of different reasons. But the constant is that the Holy Spirit is at work in the world (John 16:8–11) and is pleased to use *any* means at His disposal—including good arguments—to draw people to Christ. We are called to be the best ambassador for Jesus Christ we can be and then leave the results to God (2 Cor. 5:20).

A Preserving Agent

Not only is apologetics beneficial for believers and unbelievers, but it also helps preserve culture. Ideas matter and have consequences. In fact, Paul tells us that we are to destroy strongholds and high-minded things raised up against the knowledge of God (2 Cor. 10:3–5). Listen to the advice of William Lane Craig:

> The gospel is never heard in isolation. It is always heard against the background of the cultural milieu in which one lives. A person reared in a cultural milieu in which Christianity is still seen as an intellectually viable option will display an openness to the gospel that a person who is secularized will not. . . . It is for that reason that Christians who depreciate the value of apologetics because "no one comes to Christ through arguments" are so shortsighted. For the value of apologetics extends far beyond one's immediate evangelistic contact. It is a broader task of Christian apologetics to help create and sustain a cultural milieu in which the gospel can be heard as an intellectually viable option for thinking men and women. It is not implausible that robust apologetics is a necessary ingredient in fostering a milieu in which evangelization can be most effectively pursued in contemporary Western society and those societies increasingly influenced by it.[5]

If a culture no longer believes in concepts like truth and knowledge or good and evil, then it is extremely difficult to help people understand the message of the gospel. Engaging in the discipline of apologetics (as opposed to appealing to a private, blind leap of faith) will help Christians be a preserving agent in our culture—salt.

You need to know that there are strong reasons supporting the Christian faith: God's Word, changed lives, archaeological and scientific discoveries, philosophical arguments, historical evidence, love, goodness, and the Holy Spirit—just to name a few. Don't worry, no one has found out that Christianity is false and you are the only one who still doesn't know. As Christians, we don't need to walk around as if we are afraid we have something hanging out of our noses that everyone can see but us. You don't have to check your brains at the door. Your mind and heart are *both* valued as a follower of Jesus (Luke 10:27). Let us pray that we would have the courage in this generation to contend for the faith and *always* be ready to give an answer for the hope we have in Christ. Listen to Paul's challenge: "Do not be ashamed of the testimony about our Lord or of me his prisoner. Rather, join with me in suffering for the gospel, by the power of God" (2 Tim. 1:8). God is real, Christianity is true, and we have no reason to be ashamed.

THE BIG IDEAS

- Apologetics is about knowing *why* you believe what you believe and then being able to give reasons for faith with gentleness and respect as opportunities arise (1 Peter 3:15).

- Exploring what you believe and why increases your confidence as a Christian.

- Apologetics helps clear away barriers people have that are keeping them from considering the claims of Christianity.

- The study of apologetics is important in preserving a cultural environment that allows the gospel to make sense to unbelievers.

- We have no reason to be ashamed to testify about our Lord, Jesus Christ (2 Tim. 1:8).

For Further Discovery

Geisler, Norman L., and Frank Turek. *I Don't Have Enough Faith to Be an Atheist*. Wheaton, IL: Crossway, 2004.

Groothuis, Douglas R. *Christian Apologetics: A Comprehensive Case for Biblical Faith*. Downers Grove, IL: InterVarsity Press, 2011.

McDowell, Sean, ed. *The Apologetics Study Bible for Students: Hard Questions, Straight Answers*. Nashville: B&H Publishing, 2010.

———. *A New Kind of Apologist*. Eugene, OR: Harvest House, 2016.

McDowell, Sean, and Jonathan Morrow. *Is God Just a Human Invention? And Seventeen Other Questions Raised by the New Atheists*. Grand Rapids: Kregel, 2010.

Morrow, Jonathan. *Questioning the Bible: 11 Major Challenges to the Bible's Authority*. Chicago: Moody Publishers, 2014.

Impact 360 Institute at www.impact360.org.

Jonathan Morrow at www.JonathanMorrow.org. My personal website with apologetics and worldview resources.

Reasonable Faith with William Lane Craig at www.reasonablefaith.org.

Stand to Reason at www.str.org.

The Existence of God
God Is There and Is Not Silent

*I want atheism to be true and am made uneasy by
the fact that some of the most intelligent and well-
informed people I know are religious believers. It isn't
just that I don't believe in God and, naturally, hope
that I am right in my belief. It's that I hope there is
no God! . . . I don't want the universe to be like that.*

—THOMAS NAGEL[1]

*You have made us for yourself, and our hearts are
restless until they find rest in you.*

—AUGUSTINE[2]

Why is there something and not nothing?

—G. W. LEIBNIZ[3]

I DIDN'T CHOOSE TO FOLLOW JESUS CHRIST UNTIL MY JUNIOR YEAR OF
high school. Honestly, my problem was not that I didn't believe God existed
but that I didn't think He was really involved in the world or interested in
me. I suspect I am not alone in my experience. Since the beginning of time,
history reveals that the vast majority of people—regardless of geography—
have believed that some sort of god or higher power exists. According to a
Pew study, four out of five people in the world believe in God, and by their
projections this isn't going to change any time soon.[4] Atheism, the belief that
there is no god, is a minority view, albeit a vocal one (especially the New
Atheists like Richard Dawkins, Christopher Hitchens, and Sam Harris). A
little more common is the belief that no one can know if God exists. This is
agnosticism. Even still, the fact is that many people in different locations and
under varying circumstances have believed in a god.

While arguments for God's existence didn't play a role in my conversion to Christianity, I have found them to be very encouraging in my spiritual life, especially in times of doubt. I have also found reasons for God's existence to be useful in interacting with unbelievers because it will cause them to stop and think. And thinking about God is important because "what people perceive as real, true, right, valuable, and meaningful is dramatically influenced by their view of whether God is real or not."[5]

You may have been told that there are no good arguments for God's existence. Now, if you mean by "good argument" one that compels someone into belief (kind of like making them say "uncle"), then the answer is no. But there are very few things in life that work this way (if any). And for a number of reasons, people will vary in what they find persuasive (this depends on certain background beliefs or assumptions about reality). But that being said, I think there are good arguments available that make belief in God more plausible than not.

The following are just a handful of reasons why believing that God exists makes good sense. All of these could be put in logical form, but in order to keep it simple, I will just describe them, leaving you to do more reading as you are interested. (I would encourage you to start with the book my friend Sean McDowell and I wrote together on the evidence for God called *Is God Just a Human Invention?*)

The Argument from Existence

I like big questions, and they don't come much bigger than, "Why is there something and not nothing?" Think about it. It is quite easy for us to take existence for granted (we are busy people after all). People generally agree that things don't just exist without a good explanation. It really isn't an explanation to say, "That's just the way things are, pass the popcorn." Let me illustrate. Our family likes to go to the movies. Suppose we show up at the theater to watch the latest Marvel superhero movie, but stop and ponder why there is a movie theater here. "It just is" (like a brute fact or something) isn't very satisfying. On the other hand, suppose we learn that this is the fastest-growing area in the city and Carmike wanted to build a movie theater here to accommodate all the people moving to town. That is a plausible explanation—certainly more plausible than "It just is." Well, think of existence like a gigantic movie theater (this includes stuff like the physical universe and the fact that you are conscious and able to read these words). There is nothing about the physical universe and the people within it that is—strictly speaking—*necessary* (i.e., it had to be this way).

So why does *anything* exist at all? I think the best explanation for the existence of everything is God. Now you might say that there are other *possible* explanations, and I agree. But here is an important point to remember. Just because someone can dream up an alternative scenario or utter some words that might be logically possible—that's not enough. You are after what is *reasonable* and *plausible*. After careful inquiry, I think you will find that other reasons are pretty flimsy, make some pretty big assumptions (i.e., that the universe has always existed and is somehow metaphysically necessary), and are not nearly as plausible as God. The apostle Paul offers the Christian answer. "For in him all things were created: things in heaven and on earth, visible and invisible . . . all things have been created through him and for him . . . and in him all things hold together" (Col. 1:16–17).

The Argument from Cause and Effect

The argument that we just looked at sought an explanation for why anything exists at all. A similar argument is the argument of cause and effect.[6] Cause and effect is one of the most basic laws of the universe. Every effect must have an adequate cause. If a ball is moving, there must have been a "mover." So an argument could be formulated like this: (1) whatever begins to exist has a cause; (2) the universe began to exist; therefore (3) the universe has a cause.

In order to deny this argument, someone would have to deny either (1) or (2). Though people have tried to deny both, most people intuitively think (1) is true. So what about (2), that the universe began to exist? I will leave most of the details for your homework, but the best scientific theory states the universe began to exist 13.7 billion years ago in an event called the "big bang"—that is when time, space, matter, and energy came into being. Before then there was nothing—not empty outer space—nothing whatsoever! For a long time people thought that the universe was eternal. But through the work of Albert Einstein and discoveries by Edwin Hubble, the eternal universe theory was rejected. So if the universe had a cause, and this cause needs to be *beyond* space, time, matter, and energy, then this looks like a good candidate for an intelligent agent of considerable power—which we could call God. Incidentally, the first sentence of the Bible fits well with this conclusion: "*In the beginning God created the heavens and the earth*" (Gen. 1:1, italics added).

The Argument from Design

Have you heard of Anthony Flew? He was arguably the most famous atheistic philosopher of the twentieth century (if you are in a philosophy class you might come across his famous article "The Presumption of Atheism"). In December of 2004 at age eighty-one, Flew became convinced of the design argument (which is based in part on evidence marshaled by intelligent design theorists) and rejected atheism. He came to believe in some sort of god—though it is unclear if he ever became a Christian. In one interview he admitted, "A super-intelligence is the only good explanation for the origin of life and the complexity of nature."[7] I share this to illustrate how powerful the argument for design is.

In short, the design argument is that the complexity of life (at the molecular and cosmological levels) is best explained by an intelligent agent, not a random, purposeless process. I won't talk about all of the scientific data here, but the more scientists discover about the fascinating world of molecular biology—and the amount of design in the universe—the more implausible is the appeal to random selection. The complex machinery at the molecular level is incredible; one such machine has been made famous by Michael Behe: the bacterial flagellum.

Information is the hallmark of design, and we know that information is always the product of a mind, not a random process. A feeling of awe is generated when we look at the immensity and elegance of the genetic information contained in DNA. Design is evident from the smallest molecule to the most sublime galaxy. But not only is it finely tuned, it also seems designed for discovery. In other words, the only place that complex life is known to be able to thrive in the universe—earth—is also the best place to discover things about our universe. Ours is a privileged planet.[8] Our universe has been literally designed for discovery. David, the shepherd-king, records a similar inference in one of his psalms:

The heavens declare the glory of God;
> the skies proclaim the work of his hands.

Day after day they pour forth speech;
> night after night they reveal knowledge.

They have no speech, they use no words;
> no sound is heard from them.

Yet their voice goes out into all the earth,
> their words to the ends of the world.

(PS. 19:1–4)

The Argument from Morality

Confusion abounds about what is right and wrong these days (refer to chapter 7 for a refresher on moral relativism). Admittedly, there are plenty of moral gray areas and sometimes it isn't easy to figure out what the right thing to do is in a given situation. But let's leave the ambiguous cases aside for the moment. Are there some things that are *always* and *everywhere* wrong (i.e., objective moral facts about the world)? I think there are. Here are three examples of objective moral truths: (1) the atrocities the Nazis committed in the Holocaust during World War II were wrong; (2) rape is always wrong; and (3) torturing babies for fun is always wrong. Now hopefully these are beyond dispute. The question we need to ask is this: If there are objective moral facts, what makes the best sense for the reason objective morality exists?

The government is certainly not the reason objective morality exists. Even if a government passed a law justifying these, we would still want to say they are wrong. Another popular view says that objective morality exists because humans have evolved to a higher level of moral reasoning because it is a biologically useful adaptation (a kind of herd morality). A significant problem with this view is that, by the nature of naturalistic evolution, species adapt without an ultimate purpose or end goal in mind (i.e., no *telos*). Strictly speaking, evolution is not trying to "go" anywhere. At best all evolution can describe is how things have occurred up until this point in history, but it cannot provide any basis for how we ought to act tomorrow. We could have just as easily evolved to accept different moral facts. Also, this concept seems contradictory. Given that Darwinian evolution has the principle of survival of the fittest at its core, it would not make sense that we evolved to be more sensitive to injustice, believing that racism is wrong or that the diseased, handicapped, and elderly *ought* to be cared for. The eugenics movements in America and Germany were scientifically efficient but morally reprehensible.[9]

So if humans didn't create moral facts, and Darwinian evolution can't adequately account for them,[10] what's left? In my opinion, the most compelling answer is that God, a moral lawgiver, exists and has created humans with inherent dignity and the ability to discern right from wrong at a fundamental level. Again, this inference harmonizes well with the picture we find in the Bible:

> Even Gentiles, who do not have God's written law, show that they know his law when they instinctively obey it, even without having heard it. They demonstrate that God's law is written in their hearts, for their own conscience and thoughts either accuse them or tell them they are doing right. (Rom. 2:14–15 NLT)

The Argument from Desire

One of the most powerful arguments I know of for God's existence appeals not to the head but to the heart. And the most eloquent presentation of it I have found comes from C. S. Lewis in *Mere Christianity*:

> Creatures are not born with desires unless satisfaction for those desires exists. A baby feels hunger: well, there is such a thing as food. A duckling wants to swim: well, there is such a thing as water. Men feel sexual desire: well, there is such a thing as sex. If I find in myself a desire which no experience in this world can satisfy, the most probable explanation is that I was made for another world. Probably earthly pleasures were never meant to satisfy it, but only arouse it, to suggest the real thing.[11]

Which one of us has not felt both the exhilaration and heartache that accompanies a sunset? It is beautiful, but then the sun fades into the deep and darkness falls. Having had the opportunity to live in southern California for a couple of years, I have experienced amazing sunsets numerous times.

Perhaps one of the reasons I love sunsets so much is that they remind me of the hope that one day the beauty will not fade away.

The point that Lewis is making is that the intense desire we feel is not a desire to acquire things such as sports cars or more money. Rather, this kind of desire arises from within us; longing for something more is a universal human experience. And if these longings arise from within us, then there is something out there that was meant to ultimately satisfy us.

History and experience have taught us that nothing in this life completely satisfies. Every wonderful pleasure or achievement still leaves us wanting more. Like scooping up a handful of water, ultimate satisfaction dribbles between our fingers no matter how hard we squeeze. French philosopher and mathematician Blaise Pascal accounts for this feeling by suggesting that humans all possess a God-shaped vacuum that nothing in this life will fill. The thought that this life is all there is leaves us cold and depressed. There has to be life beyond this life, something that will truly satisfy! Three thousand years ago, Solomon arrived at the same conclusion: "[God] has made everything beautiful in its time. He has also set eternity in the human heart" (Eccl. 3:11).

THE ULTIMATE ARGUMENT: Jesus

More could be said, but I think we have *at least* established that belief in God is not for the intellectually naive. There are good reasons to believe that God exists. But as a Christian, I want to say that the point is not simply to believe *that* God exists—even the demons believe that (James 2:19)! And while these arguments for God's existence—if successful—don't lead us to the *Christian* God, they certainly point in that direction. Moreover, these arguments fit well with biblical teaching.

Yet, of all that has been covered, the most compelling argument for God's existence is the person of Jesus of Nazareth. If Jesus is who He claimed to be, then God not only exists, but He desires a relationship with His creation. So much so that God has sent His only Son, Jesus, to become one of us, live a perfect life, and die a criminal's death so that He could bring anyone who would trust in Him into relationship with God (John 1:12; 3:16; 5:24). Jesus is the ultimate testimony that God is there and is not silent.

THE BIG IDEAS

- It is significant that far more people throughout history have believed that God or some higher power exists, while atheism has always been a minority view.

- The existence of God better accounts for (1) why anything exists at all, (2) the beginning of the universe, (3) the intricate and complex design of the universe, (4) the fact of objective moral values, and (5) the "longing for more" common to all humans.

- Believing in God does not make someone intellectually naive. On the contrary, there are many good reasons that make belief in God *at least* as plausible as any other answer.

- The life of Jesus is the ultimate testimony to God's existence and His desire to enter into relationship with His creation.

For Further Discovery

Craig, William Lane. *Reasonable Faith: Christian Truth and Apologetics*. 3rd ed. Wheaton, IL: Crossway, 2008.

Craig, William Lane, and J. P. Moreland. *The Blackwell Companion to Natural Theology*. Malden, MA: Wiley-Blackwell, 2009.

Keller, Timothy. *Making Sense of God: An Invitation to the Skeptical*. New York: Viking, 2016.

Lewis, C. S. *Mere Christianity*. New York: HarperCollins, 2015.

McDowell, Sean, and Jonathan Morrow. *Is God Just a Human Invention? And Seventeen Other Questions Raised by the New Atheists*. Grand Rapids: Kregel, 2010.

Meyer, Stephen C. *Signature in the Cell: DNA and the Evidence for Intelligent Design*. New York: HarperOne, 2009.

Wallace, J. Warner. *God's Crime Scene: A Cold-Case Detective Examines the Evidence for a Divinely Created Universe*. Colorado Springs: David C. Cook, 2015.

Williams, Clifford. *Existential Reasons for Belief in God: A Defense of Desires and Emotions for Faith*. Downers Grove, IL: InterVarsity Press, 2011.

Do All Roads Lead to God?

The truth is that all religions are not the same. All religions do not point to God. All religions do not say that all religions are the same. In fact, some religions do not even believe in God. At the heart of every religion is an uncompromising commitment to a particular way of defining who God is or is not. Buddhism, for example, was based on Buddha's rejection of two of Hinduism's fundamental doctrines. Islam rejects both Buddhism and Hinduism. So it does no good to put a halo on the notion of tolerance and act as if everything is equally true. In fact, even all-inclusive religions such as Bahaism end up being exclusivistic by excluding the exclusivists!

—RAVI ZACHARIAS[1]

I am the way and the truth and the life. No one comes to the Father except through me.

—JESUS (JOHN 14:6)

The God who made the world and everything in it is the Lord of heaven and earth and . . . gives everyone life and breath and everything else. From one man he made all the nations, that they should inhabit the whole earth; and he marked out their appointed times in history and the boundaries of their lands. God did this so that they would seek him and perhaps reach out for him and find him, though he is not far from any one of us.

—ACTS 17:24–27

"SO LONG AS YOU'RE SINCERE, IT DOES NOT MATTER WHAT YOU BELIEVE in the end—*all roads lead to God.*" According to the Pew Research Center, most Americans "agree with the statement that many religions—not just their own—can lead to eternal life" (including a stunning 57 percent of evangelical protestant Christians!).[2] This is a common way of thinking today, but is it correct? Are the contents of our beliefs really unimportant? Sincerity is a virtue, but it doesn't make things true or false. I've held many sincere beliefs that teachers felt obliged to count wrong throughout the years. Even in spite of our common intuitions that what we believe actually matters, this view persists in our culture; actually, it's gaining ground. I think this has to do with the fact that our generation, through the Internet and global media, has been exposed to how religiously diverse the world really is. And since all of these religions are historically and geographically limited, is it reasonable to believe that one of them could be universally true? Moreover, think of how much blood has been shed in the name of religion throughout history. Couldn't all this needless loss of life disappear if people would stop being so religiously imperialistic?

Pluralism Versus Particularism

There are diverse opinions concerning how to address the issue of pluralism versus particularism, but for the sake of simplicity they can be boiled down to two alternatives: *religious particularists* believe that a universally true religion exists, while *religious pluralists* maintain that no universally true religion exists. Biblical Christianity would fall into the religious particularist camp.[3] But this raises some difficult issues that need to be dealt with, and next to the problem of evil, I think this is the most powerful objection to Christianity.[4] In order to keep us from getting lost in the weeds of a difficult discussion, we will use a question/answer format.

Are all religions basically the same?

In answering this question, it will be helpful to distinguish between *unsophisticated religious pluralism* (URP) and *sophisticated religious pluralism* (SRP). Now URP maintains that all of the religions are true and that they basically teach the same thing. I am not trying to be mean here, but this is a view that people haven't thought through or are parroting as a slogan they picked up from the media, the classroom, or somewhere along the way. Ask anyone who has studied comparative religion and they will quickly list major differences between them.

For example, philosopher of religion William Lane Craig highlights the essential differences between Islam and Buddhism: "Islam believes that there is a personal God who is omnipotent, omniscient, and holy, and who created the world. It believes that people are sinful and in need of God's forgiveness, that everlasting heaven and hell awaits us after death, and that we must earn our salvation by faith and righteous deeds. Buddhism denies all these things. For the classical Buddhist ultimate reality is impersonal, the world is uncreated, there is no enduring self, life's ultimate goal is not personal immortality but annihilation, and the ideas of sin and salvation play no role at all."[5] Essential differences could be pointed out in Christianity, Judaism, and Hinduism as well as others. URP is plainly false.

Now SRP makes a surprising claim—*none* of the world's religions (strictly speaking) are true; *they're all false!* Craig summarizes: "They are all culturally relative ways of misconstruing reality. Ultimate reality, which you cannot accurately call 'God,' should be given some nondescript name like 'the Real' or 'the Absolute.' Nothing can be known about it, but the world's religions all picture it in different ways. Though literally false, all the world's religions are effective in transforming people's lives."[6] While this view is growing in support (except by the devout adherents of the various world religions), you are less likely to encounter it at this stage of college. So I won't address it here, but if you do come across it, there are several books in which SRP has been sufficiently critiqued.[7]

Isn't it arrogant to believe that one religion is true, and others are not?

A common tactic used to silence religious particularists is to claim they are arrogant and immoral for believing that there is only one way to God. In response to this charge, philosopher Alvin Plantinga asks, "Suppose I think the matter over, consider the objections as carefully as I can, realize that I am finite and furthermore a sinner, certainly no better than those with whom I disagree, and indeed inferior both morally and intellectually to many who do not believe what I do; but suppose it *still* seems clear to me that the proposition in question is true [e.g., that Jesus Christ is the only way to God]: can I really be behaving immorally in continuing to believe it?"[8] It seems not. Moreover, the charge of arrogance and immorality cuts both ways because implicit in the SRP view is the claim that everyone else but them has it wrong! All of the devout adherents of the world's major religions—billions of people—have it wrong. If that doesn't count as arrogance, I am not sure what does.[9]

If I had been born in India, would I have been a Hindu?

The short answer to this question is that nothing really follows (with logical necessity) from where I happen to be born; the truth or falsity of a religion is not determined by where someone is born. Plantinga responds that the same reasoning applies to pluralists themselves: "If the pluralist had been born in Madagascar, or medieval France, he probably wouldn't have been a pluralist."[10] Furthermore, this question seems to imply that people can't escape the cultural views they were born into. Also, the reality of conversions from within closed countries to a different belief system undercuts the weight of this objection.[11] Finally, the notion of the Christian God's providential ordering of the world rules out people being born somewhere by historical accident (Acts 17:24–28).

Are people condemned to hell simply because they have never heard about Jesus?

This gets to the heart of the objection against Christianity. I think the best way to answer this question—if we are using the Bible as our authority—is to demarcate the boundaries of the discussion.[12] This will help us see where the appropriate place to admit tension and mystery is. Any distinctively Christian answer to this challenging question must account for (at least) the following passages and revealed truths as we reason from the Scriptures:

1. God is compassionate and just (Gen. 18:25; Deut. 32:4; Pss. 7:9; 85:11; 89:14; 145:8–9; Rev. 16:7).

2. All are sinners in need of a savior (Rom. 3:10–18, 23; 5:12–21; 6:23; Eph. 2:1–3).

3. Jesus Christ is the *only* means of salvation (John 14:6; Acts 4:12; 1 Tim. 2:5; 1 John 2:2) and the only way to God.

4. Since the time following the resurrection of Jesus, no one can be saved apart from the knowledge of Christ (Acts 16:31; 17:30–31; Rom. 10:14).

5. God genuinely desires all to be saved (Ezek. 18:23; John 3:16; 1 Tim. 2:3–6; 2 Peter 3:9).

6. God has revealed Himself to the whole world both in creation (Ps. 19:1–2; Acts 14:15–17; Rom. 1:19–20) and human conscience (Eccl. 3:11; Rom. 2:14–16), so that people are without excuse.

7. God's Spirit is at work convicting the world of sin, righteousness, and judgment (John 16:8–11).

8. Christians are commanded to take the gospel to the whole world (Matt. 28:19–20; Acts 1:8).[13]

9. God has providentially arranged the world so that people might seek Him and everyone who seeks Him will find Him (Acts 17:24–28).

10. There will be people from every tribe, tongue, and nation in heaven (Rev. 7:9).

11. The awful reality of hell indicates that not everyone is saved in the end (Matt. 10:28; 25:31–46; 2 Thess. 1:7–9).

12. There does not seem to be a second chance after death to accept the gospel (Heb. 9:27).[14]

It is crucial to highlight a few things. First, people are judged for their sins—*not what they don't know*. The Bible clearly teaches that people are judged for their willful sins (Isa. 64:6–7; Matt. 5:48; 12:36; 2 Tim. 4:14; James 2:10–11; Rev. 20:12–15) according to the standard of revelation they have received (Rom. 2:4–16; James 4:17).[15] They are not condemned because a missionary never made it to them and they never heard the name of Jesus.

Second, they are *already condemned* and actively choosing life away from God (though this will look different for all of us). Humanity's universal problem is that we suppress the truth available to everyone that God exists (Rom. 1), mute our conscience and fail to live up to even our own standards (Rom. 2), and ultimately want to go our own way (Rom. 3).

Finally, God has many ways to get the message of the gospel to those who seek Him (through missionaries, dreams, visions, radio, Bibles, Internet, TV, tracts, etc.).

At the end of the day, God doesn't specifically answer this question to our (emotional) satisfaction in the Bible. We are left with some mystery when it comes to saying exactly how God will work out His plan of salvation among the nations. Therefore we trust ultimately in His goodness and justice. Will not the judge of the earth do right?

Biblical Compassion and a Word to the One Asking the Question

After thinking about the questions we've discussed above, Christians should be moved to compassion and action. We need to respect people from other faiths and religions—we are not enemies. Craig summarizes a biblically expressed compassion to this issue, "No orthodox Christian *likes* the doctrine of hell or delights in anyone's condemnation. I truly wish universalism were true, but it is not. My compassion toward those in other world religions is therefore expressed, not in pretending that they are not lost and dying without Christ, but by supporting and making every effort myself to communicate to them the life-giving message of salvation through Christ."[16]

One final thought. People who ask the question, "Do all roads lead to God?" are either asking out of sincerity or using it as a smoke screen.[17] James Sire is frequently asked this question when speaking on college campuses. Here is my summary of his basic response (after talking about the things I mentioned above): Whatever might be said of the person who has never heard of Jesus Christ, you have understood the seriousness of the question and the offer of salvation in Jesus Christ alone. You have now heard the gospel and are responsible for it; what are *you* going to do with Jesus's offer?[18]

THE BIG IDEAS

- *Religious particularists* believe that a universally true religion exists; *religious pluralists* maintain that no universally true religion exists.

- There is a difference between *unsophisticated religious pluralism* and *sophisticated religious pluralism*.

- If the religious particularist can be charged with arrogance, then so can the religious pluralist.

- People are not condemned to hell because they don't believe in Jesus. They are ultimately condemned based on their works (Isa. 64:6; Matt. 5:48; 12:36; 2 Tim. 4:14; James 2:10–11; Rev. 20:12–15) and according to the standard of revelation they have received (Rom. 2:4–16; James 4:17).

For Further Discovery

Copan, Paul. *True for You, but Not for Me: Overcoming Objections to Christian Faith*. Rev. ed. Minneapolis: Bethany House, 2009.

Corduan, Winfried. *Pocket Guide to World Religions*. Downers Grove, IL: InterVarsity Press, 2010.

Craig, William Lane. "Christ, the Only Way." In *Hard Questions, Real Answers*. Wheaton, IL: Crossway, 2003.

Garrison, David. *A Wind in the House of Islam: How God Is Drawing Muslims Around the World to Faith in Jesus Christ*. Monument, CO: WIGTake Resources, 2014.

Qureshi, Nabeel. *Seeking Allah, Finding Jesus: A Devout Muslim Encounters Christianity*. Grand Rapids: Zondervan, 2014.

ExploreTruth.tv. A seven-session online study taught by Jonathan Morrow that will help you break free from the riptide of relativism (powered by Impact 360 Institute).

ExploreWorldview.tv. An eight-session online study taught by Jonathan Morrow that will help you understand and test competing worldviews (powered by Impact 360 Institute).

15

The Problem of Evil and Suffering

Is he [God] willing to prevent evil, but not able? then is he impotent. Is he able, but not willing? then is he malevolent. Is he both able and willing? whence then is evil?

—DAVID HUME[1]

Paradoxically, then, even though the problem of evil is the greatest objection to the existence of God, at the end of the day God is the only solution to the problem of evil. If God does not exist, then we are lost without hope in a life filled with gratuitous and unredeemed suffering. God is the final answer to the problem of evil, for He redeems evil and takes us into the everlasting joy of an incommensurable good: fellowship with Him.

—WILLIAM LANE CRAIG[2]

Therefore we do not lose heart, but though our outer man is decaying, yet our inner man is being renewed day by day. For momentary, light affliction is producing for us an eternal weight of glory far beyond all comparison, while we look not at the things which are seen, but at the things which are not seen; for the things which are seen are temporal, but the things which are not seen are eternal.

—2 CORINTHIANS 4:16-18 NASB

THINGS ARE CLEARLY NOT HOW THEY OUGHT TO BE.[3] EVEN AS I SIT AND write this at a coffee shop, I watch an elderly woman, hunched over and racked by disease, eating with her daughters. The effects of sin have corrupted health and life. You and I will also suffer the indignity of deteriorating physically. I have held my brother's hand as he took his last breath after losing his battle with cancer. We live in a world where death and tragedy are commonplace. Wars, genocide, disease, famine, abuse, torture, and earthquakes are reported constantly in our never-ending news cycle of updates, YouTube clips, and what's trending on social media. In the twentieth century alone, Hitler killed six million Jews, and Stalin was responsible for the deaths of millions upon millions of his own countrymen.[4] If we sit and reflect on the atrocities of this world in numb silence long enough, we can formulate but one question: Why? This question—known as the problem of evil—has become the major objection to belief in God. So how do we respond? What do we say to others? What do we tell ourselves?

There have been tons of pages written on this subject, so I won't be able to address all of the suggested answers in detail (I will simply refer you to the suggested reading). But know this ahead of time: the problem of evil is not like a tricky math problem—there is no solving it; it is not that easy. My aim is to help set the context for this discussion in a way that deals honestly with evil yet provides genuine hope in the midst of it.

Preliminaries for Our Discussion

Given the magnitude of this discussion, you just have to dive into it and sort out terms and approaches as you go along. But I want to say two things at the outset. First, there is a difference between the so-called *intellectual problem of evil* and the *personal/existential problem of evil*. When ministering to someone, it is important to know which of these is the question at hand.

To know how God and evil can coexist without contradiction is an intellectual question and should be addressed as such. A hug and a Bible verse is not the way to satisfy this intellectual struggle. On the other hand, many times people wrestle with the personal/existential problem of evil and thus have different needs. Sophisticated philosophical answers and rigorous analysis will come across as cold, sterile, and unhelpful to this person. What this person needs is the ministry of presence by others, prayer, community, love, and hope. There may be a time when they desire more explanation, but now is not the time.

Second, when dealing with the problem of evil, it is helpful to distinguish between a *theodicy* and a *defense*. A *defense* merely attempts to show that there is a logical reason behind why a good, all-powerful God would allow evil—the goal being to show that God and evil are not logically contradictory.

A *theodicy* is more ambitious in that it seeks to say what God's reasons *actually are* for allowing evil.

There Is a Problem of Evil—Right?

One of the things for us to remember is that Christianity is not the only worldview that has to deal with evil—everyone must account for evil. In light of this fact, let's examine the three most prominent worldviews: pantheism, atheism, and Christian theism.[5]

Pantheism

Pantheism is a monistic worldview in that it claims all reality is one and that physical reality is an illusion—*in the end all is god*. Most eastern religions like Buddhism and Hinduism would fall into this category. Pantheism generally regards evil as an illusion. It appears real, but it isn't. While this escapes the bite of the problem of evil, it completely disregards our strong intuitions that evil is real, despicable, and painful. Many find this solution unsatisfying.

Atheism

Atheism is the view that God does not exist. And depending on the variety of atheism we look at, we will discover that if there is no God, there is no good. And if there is no good, then there is no evil. All that is left is valueless and amoral stuff—that's it. To put it in Darwinian terms, we are left with words like *beneficial* and *nonbeneficial, conducive* and *nonconducive*—but vanished are the words *good* and *evil*. It is not surprising that few find this answer livable and satisfying.

Another atheistic option is admitting the reality of good and evil (presumably borrowing these categories from a theistic worldview), but then admitting that there is no explanation of what they are and where they came from—and more to our issue—no solution as to how to eliminate evil. Atheism kind of offers a "tough luck" response to evil—an unlucky hand, what else can be said?[6]

Christian Theism

Christian theism affirms the existence of a good and all-powerful God and the reality of evil in the world.[7] Evil was not God's intention for the world. According to Genesis 1 everything that God created was good; evil entered the world through sin. Evil is not an illusion, but neither is it a "thing." Evil is a departure from the way things ought to be. It is a corruption of good; in other words, it is a parasite.[8] Just as rust cannot exist without iron, and adultery is impossible without the good of marriage, so evil is what it is in virtue of what it steals and corrupts from good.

It is here where the intellectual problems of evil come in. If God is all-good, all-knowing, and all-powerful, then He would want to get rid of evil. He would be powerful enough to get rid of evil, yet evil exists. There seems to be a contradiction in the Christian conception of God and the reality of evil.[9]

INTELLECTUAL PROBLEMS OF EVIL:
The Logical and the Probabilistic Arguments

Given space constraints, I will only be able to recount what I take to be plausible and persuasive Christian theist responses[10] to the two intellectual problems of evil: (1) it is logically contradictory for the Christian God and evil to coexist; and (2) given the magnitude, duration, and intensity of evil in the world, it is highly improbable that God exists.

All that is needed to dispose of the charge of logical incoherence is to supply a logically possible, morally sufficient reason that a good God would allow evil (i.e., a defense). In response to (1), Alvin Plantinga describes such a possible reason in his famous free will defense:

> A world containing creatures who are significantly free (and freely perform more good than evil actions) is more valuable, all else being equal, than a world containing no free creatures at all. Now God can create free creatures, but He can't *cause* or *determine* them to do only what is right. For if He does so, then they aren't significantly free after all; they do not do what is right *freely*. To create creatures capable of *moral good*, therefore, He must create creatures capable of moral evil; and He can't give these creatures the freedom to perform evil and at the same time prevent them from doing so. As it turned out, sadly enough, some of the free creatures God created went wrong in the exercise of their freedom; this is the source of moral evil. The fact that free creatures sometimes go wrong, however, counts neither against God's omnipotence nor against His goodness; for He could have forestalled the occurrence of moral evil only by removing the possibility of moral good.[11]

Concerning the amount and intensity of evil in the world making it improbable that God exists, Christians can admit this might be true *if only the evidence from evil is factored into the equation.* But if other evidence is factored in as well, then this objection fails. As William Lane Craig states concerning (2):

> [The Christian] will insist that we consider, not just the evil in the world, but all the evidence relevant to God's existence, including the ontological argument for a maximally great being, the cosmological argument for a Creator of the universe, the teleological argument for an intelligent Designer of the cosmos, the noological argument for an ultimate Mind, the axiological argument for an ultimate, personally embodied Good, as well as evidence concerning the person of Christ, the historicity of the resurrection, the existence of miracles, plus existential and religious experience. When we take into account the full scope of the evidence, the existence of God becomes quite probable. . . . Indeed, if he includes the self-authenticating witness of the Holy Spirit as part of his total warrant, then he can rightly assert that he knows that God exists, even if he has no solution to the problem of evil.[12]

As to the extent of evil, humans are simply in no position to judge how much would be necessary were we to know God's reasons for allowing it. This is not a cop-out, just an honest assessment of our limited cognitive abilities and perspective. Given that God is infinitely wiser than we are, we would expect His reasons for allowing evil to be beyond our grasp.

While both of these answers are plausible and helpful so far as they go, we are still left wanting more. And I will readily admit that there is not a detailed, specific, and fully satisfying answer to the problem of evil. But I think Christianity has the best answer out there.[13]

Evil, the Cross, and the Redemption of Jesus

The incarnation of Jesus demonstrates that God is not aloof or uninvolved in our world. He stepped into our existence, experienced all that we have ever experienced and more, and was crucified in our place to conquer death and evil. An innocent man went through an unjust trial so that we would not have to go through a just one. It was the evil in our hearts that nailed Christ to that cross. But God took our evil and redeemed it for good, the salvation of all who would trust Him. The Bible says that God made Him who knew no sin to become sin on our behalf (2 Cor. 5:21). And on that dark day, Jesus cried out, "My God, my God, why have you forsaken me?" (Matt. 27:46). His cry of desperation was met with the silence of the Father.

As Ravi Zacharias says, "Jesus did not conquer death in spite of pain and suffering; He conquered through it."[14] Christianity boasts the only God who has wounds. Jesus—a real flesh-and-blood human being—was publicly crucified.[15] Evil and sin have been conquered at the cross and await final destruction at Christ's return; evil will not have the final word. Alister McGrath reminds us that "experience cannot be allowed to have the final word—it must be judged and shown up as deceptive and misleading. The theology of the cross draws our attention to the sheer unreliability of experience as a guide to the presence and activity of God. God *is* active and present in His world, quite independently of whether we experience Him as being so. Experience declared that God was absent from Calvary, only to have its verdict humiliatingly overturned on the third day."[16]

Of the worldviews we looked at earlier in the chapter, Christianity is the only one that treats evil as being real *and* offers reasons it will be overcome. It is almost as if the entire story of the Bible is God telling us what He is doing about evil, and the culminating of that story is Jesus Christ.

Lessons from Joseph, Job, and Lazarus

In addition to the testimony of the cross, I have found the stories of three men to be both instructive and encouraging. These are the stories of Joseph, Job, and Lazarus.[17]

Joseph, whose story is told in Genesis 37–50, encountered evil and betrayal at the hands of his brothers. Injustice after injustice continued to afflict Joseph at every turn. Yet, he trusted God in the midst of it all. In the end, God gave him the grace to be able to say, "As for you, you meant evil against me, but God meant it for good in order to bring about this present result, to preserve many people alive" (Gen. 50:20 NASB; see also Rom. 8:28). *God's providence may be mysterious—even inscrutable—but it is not without purpose.*

Few have suffered like Job. He lost everything—family, wealth, and finally his health. He challenged God and wanted to know why—what had he done to deserve this? God responded with no answers but lots of questions (Job 38–42). The point was clear: God is God and Job is not. Yet there is a more subtle and pastoral point to this. These questions interrogated all of the mysteries of Job's world, and yet he could not answer them. Job was asking God why evil and suffering had been allowed in his life. But if Job could not make sense of natural events, then how would God's answer of why evil exists make any sense at all? God was in essence saying, "I am God and you are just going to have to trust me." So the lesson here is, *I don't know why, but I know God . . . and He is good!*

The story of Lazarus is remarkable at many levels (John 11). But I want to highlight one aspect of this story as it relates to how Jesus interacted with Lazarus and his family. The gist of the story is that Lazarus, who was loved by Jesus, died before Jesus arrived. Jesus could have arrived before Lazarus's death, but He didn't. This is what Martha and Mary criticized Him for. Jesus's interaction with evil, suffering, and death in this passage is instructive: *Jesus was able to prevent Lazarus's death, allowed it to happen anyway, was grieved by what He allowed, and did something about it in the end (i.e., raise him from the dead).*

When dark days hit, remember that God is always with you in the midst of whatever evil you encounter; He will never leave you or forsake you. Also, God will redeem the evil He allows in your life for good, even if you don't see it immediately or at all (Rom. 8:28). Finally, suffering is temporary and leads to increased faith now and glory in the future (2 Cor. 4:16–18; 1 Peter 1:6–7). God is good. Even when it feels like He is not there, you can trust Him completely because He is faithful and true (2 Tim. 1:12).

The Patience of God

So why hasn't God rid the universe of evil by now? I think Peter helps us answer some of that question:

> But by the same word the present heavens and earth have been reserved for fire, by being kept for the day of judgment and destruction of the ungodly. . . . Do not let this one thing escape your notice, that a single day is like a thousand years with the Lord and a thousand years are like a single day. The Lord is not slow concerning his promise, as some regard

slowness, *but is being patient toward you, because he does not wish for any to perish but for all to come to repentance.* But the day of the Lord will come like a thief; when it comes, the heavens will disappear with a horrific noise, and the celestial bodies will melt away in a blaze, and the earth and every deed done on it will be laid bare. (2 Peter 3:7–10 NET, italics added)

Evil, whatever may be said of it, does awaken people to their mortality and need for a savior. C. S. Lewis observes that "God whispers to us in our pleasures, speaks in our conscience, but shouts in our pain: it is His megaphone to rouse a deaf world."[18] Humanity's greatest good is not the absence of temporal pain; it is to know God. And God, being a good God, patiently waits for all who would turn to Him in faith. But the passage in Peter shows us that the patience of God will run out someday as the time of salvation passes and the time of reckoning evil will commence.

THE BIG IDEAS

- The reality of evil in our world is undeniable. Everyone, not only the Christian, has to answer the problem of evil.

- Next to Christian theism, the two other major worldviews do not offer plausible solutions to the problem of evil. Pantheism regards evil as illusory. Atheism either asserts that evil does not exist at all or concedes that it does but provides no explanation for it . . . and no hope of conquering it.

- God conquered evil at the cross and redeemed it for good, thus providing salvation to all who would place their trust in Jesus.

- The reason that God has not yet finally and completely judged evil is that He is patiently allowing people to turn to Him in faith.

For Further Discovery

Craig, William Lane. "Suffering and Evil (I)." In *Hard Questions, Real Answers.* Wheaton, IL: Crossway, 2003.

———. "Suffering and Evil (II)." In *Hard Questions, Real Answers*. Wheaton, IL: Crossway, 2003.

Keller, Timothy. *Walking with God Through Pain and Suffering*. New York: Dutton, 2013.

Lewis, C. S. *A Grief Observed*. New York: HarperSanFrancisco, 2001.

———. *The Problem of Pain*. New York: HarperCollins, 2009.

McDowell, Sean, and Jonathan Morrow. *Is God Just a Human Invention? And Seventeen Other Questions Raised by the New Atheists*. Grand Rapids: Kregel, 2010.

Meister, Chad, and James K. Dew, eds. *God and Evil: The Case for God in a World Filled with Pain*. Downers Grove, IL: InterVarsity Press, 2013.

Thirty-One Flavors
of Jesus

Western culture is a Jesus-haunted culture, and yet one that is largely biblically illiterate. Almost anything can pass for knowledge of Jesus and early Christianity in such a culture.

—BEN WITHERINGTON[1]

Students of Jesus today are faced with a multitude of options, ranging from the traditional Jesus who was Savior, Lord, and founder of the church, to a Jesus who was considerably different—a Jesus who was a sage, a religious genius or social revolutionary. These latter three portraits, though clearly drawing their energies from live wires in the Gospels, leave us with a Jesus who is not big enough to explain his crucifixion, his following, or the development of the Church. If we today are going to be honest about Jesus, we have to choose a Jesus who satisfies all the evidence historians have observed and who will also explain why it is that so many people have found him to be so wonderful that they attend churches every week to worship him.

—SCOT MCKNIGHT[2]

Jesus went out, along with His disciples, to the villages of Caesarea Philippi; and on the way He questioned His disciples, saying to them, "Who do people say that I am?" They told Him, saying, "John the Baptist; and others say Elijah; but others, one of the prophets." And He continued by questioning them, "But who do you say that I am?" Peter answered and said to Him, "You are the Christ."

—MARK 8:27–29 NASB

We LIVE IN A JESUS-HAUNTED CULTURE. PEOPLE ARE VAGUELY FAMILIAR with the name Jesus, but His identity is left up to the individual to determine. It's kind of like flavors of ice cream—Jesus is cookies and cream to some or coffee mocha fudge to another. To some Jesus is a moral example to follow. Others will say Jesus just loved people as they were and never judged them. Still others will say He was a wise sage or guru who was in touch with the spiritual world. If we take the ice-cream approach, there is a flavor of Jesus for each person. One thing is clear: confusion abounds today about who Jesus really is.

For example, some scholars (like those in the radical Jesus Seminar[3]) claim that Jesus didn't say or do most of what is recorded in the Gospels. These scholars believe that the early church invented the idea that Jesus was God, that it was not spoken by Jesus Himself. Therefore, in order to get back to the "historical Jesus," we must strip away all the mythology and speculation that has followed Him throughout history.

On top of the headlines that pop up every Christmas and Easter discounting the person of Christ, there are also the claims found within books trying to debunk the historical Jesus.[4] Take for example the blockbuster novel *The Da Vinci Code*, written by Dan Brown (it has now sold almost eighty million copies worldwide). This book states (among other things) that Jesus didn't really die on the cross but instead was married to Mary Magdalene and had children.[5] The book also claimed that this truth had been covered up by the church for two thousand years!

But there's more—now archaeologists have discovered "missing gospels" excluded from the Bible that supposedly give us new information of Jesus.[6] Two of the most popular recently discovered documents are the Gospel of Thomas and the Gospel of Judas. In light of all this, are we left with endless speculations about the identity of Jesus, or is there a fact of the matter? Wouldn't it be a reasonable approach for us to let Jesus speak for Himself and then allow people to decide whether to accept or reject His self-portrait? If Christianity is true, then there is no more important question anyone can ask than "who is Jesus?"

It would take more than one book to thoroughly respond to all of the claims mentioned above, but you can be confident that much has been written responding to these creative speculations. (These sources can be found at the end of the chapter.) In the next few pages, I just want to say a little about these "missing gospels" and then allow Jesus to speak for Himself.

Missing Gospels?

You may have heard of these so-called missing gospels, but odds are you have never read them. I remember the first time I heard about them—*it made me nervous*. What would I find? Would my faith turn out to be in a lie? Then I read them and felt *much* better! Not only did I laugh out loud in places, but I also realized how different, both in style and content, these writings were from those of the New Testament. I want to give you a taste of some of what you will find in these missing gospels. The following quotations all come from Bart Ehrman's *Lost Scriptures: Books That Did Not Make It into the New Testament*.[7] (Just so you know, Ehrman is not a Christian.)

Have you ever wondered what Jesus was like as a little boy? The New Testament covers Jesus's birth but then skips ahead to when He is twelve years old in the temple sitting with the teachers (Luke 2:42–51). What about all the years in between? Here are two passages from the Infancy Gospel of Thomas:

> Now the son of Annas the scribe was standing there with Joseph; and he took a willow branch and scattered the water that Jesus had gathered. Jesus was irritated when he saw what had happened, and said to him: "You unrighteous, irreverent idiot! What did the pools of water do to harm you? See, now you also will be withered like a tree, and you will never bear leaves or root or fruit." Immediately that child was completely withered. Jesus left and returned to Joseph's house. But the parents of the withered child carried him away, mourning his lost youth. They brought him to Joseph and began to accuse him, "What kind of child do you have who does such things?"[8]

Evidently Jesus didn't play nice with the other children! Here is another interesting snapshot of Jesus's childhood:

> Somewhat later he has going through the village, and a child ran up and banged into his shoulder. *Jesus was aggravated and said to him, "You will go no further on your way." And right away the child fell down and died....* The parents of the dead child came to Joseph and blamed him, saying

"Since you have such a child you cannot live with us in the village. Or teach him to bless and not curse—for he is killing our children!"[9]

One thing is clear—*Don't mess with Jesus!*

But what about Jesus's grown-up life and ministry? Do we learn anything new from these missing gospels? You ladies will be especially interested in this next recently discovered pearl of wisdom from Jesus:

> His disciples said to him, "When will the kingdom come?"
>
> [Jesus said,] "It will not come by waiting for it. It will not be a matter of saying 'here it is' or 'there it is.' Rather, the kingdom of the father is spread out upon the earth, and men do not see it."
>
> Simon Peter said to them, "Let Mary leave us, for women are not worthy of life."
>
> *Jesus said, "I myself shall lead her in order to make her male, so that she too may become a living spirit resembling you males. For every woman who will make herself male will enter the kingdom of heaven."*[10]

Ironically, it is often claimed that Gnosticism and these new gospels are more woman-friendly or politically correct than all of those patriarchal Judeo-Christian Gospels because of their inclusive view of God as mother.[11] Yeah, sure, I can see that. One thing you need to realize is that *all* of these writings come from *at least* one hundred and twenty years after Jesus's crucifixion and reveal people's speculations about what Jesus might have been like.[12] But in contrast to these anonymous writers, the New Testament writer Luke—a competent historian—interviewed eyewitnesses within a thirty-year window of Jesus's public execution (Luke 1:1–4 and Acts 1:1–2).

Well, enough about the new gospels. Let's turn our attention to the good old Gospels that we've had all along and see what they show us about Jesus.

Jesus Speaks

New Testament scholar Darrell Bock often likes to point out that when Jesus was asked who He was, He responded not with a lot of words or speeches but with what He was doing.[13] When John the Baptist's disciples came to Jesus and asked Him if He was the one Israel was expecting or not, Jesus answered,

"Go back and report to John what you have seen and heard: The blind receive sight, the lame walk, those who have leprosy are cleansed, the deaf hear, the dead are raised, and the good news is proclaimed to the poor" (Luke 7:22). His actions, many times, spoke louder than His words. In this case, Jesus was doing all the things the promised Messiah would do according to the prophet Isaiah (Isa. 35:5–6; 61:1). Most scholars today—except the most skeptical—accept that Jesus did some pretty amazing things. But do Jesus's actions tell us more than that?

There is a great passage in Mark 2:1–12 in which Jesus is teaching to a packed house at Capernaum. There is a paralytic man there and his friends are trying to get him to Jesus, but they can't because of the crowds. So they boldly lower him down through the roof to see if Jesus will heal him. How does Jesus respond? "Your sins are forgiven." This surprised both the religious leaders in the crowd and the paralytic. The paralytic was probably thinking, "Hey, I asked to be healed, not forgiven!" And the religious leaders responded, "Why does this fellow talk like that? He's blaspheming! Who can forgive sins but God alone?" (v. 7). But Jesus wanted to make a point, so He said, "Which is easier: to say to this paralyzed man, 'Your sins are forgiven,' or to say, 'Get up, take your mat and walk'? But I want you to know that the Son of Man has authority on earth to forgive sins" (vv. 9–10). He said to the paralytic, "I tell you, get up, take your mat and go home" (v. 11). So the paralytic was healed *and* forgiven. The point was this: anyone could have said that the paralytic's sins were forgiven, but how would anyone have known that it really happened? Jesus gave a visible demonstration of His authority, proving by the miracle that He could also forgive sins. According to the Old Testament, only God could forgive sins, so this miracle was a clear audio-visual illustration of Jesus claiming to be God.

Another important passage describes Jesus's trial before the Jewish leadership (Mark 14:60–64). They asked Him point-blank, "Are you the Messiah, the Son of the Blessed One?" Jesus's response is powerful: "I am. . . . And you will see the Son of Man sitting at the right hand of the Mighty One and coming on the clouds of heaven." Now there is a lot here. But the most important point is this: Jesus is quoting Daniel 7:13–14 and refers to Himself as the "Son of Man." If you go back and read the Daniel passage, you will see that the Son of Man is in the presence of the Ancient of Days (God Himself) and is given authority by Him (see Ps. 110). The Jewish leadership—who knew their Hebrew Scriptures well—got the message loud and clear. Hearing Jesus's claim, they were indignant, declaring it blasphemy. They began scheming to condemn Jesus to death for claiming to be God (Mark 14:63–64).

People don't get crucified for spouting off moral platitudes or loving everybody (though Jesus certainly loved people and was not promoting immorality). Something more is needed. And as we will see in the next chapter—on whether or not Jesus rose from the dead—*no reputable New Testament scholar* denies that Jesus died by Roman crucifixion. So even though you might find some Internet skeptics who deny this, the fact of Jesus's public execution by Rome is historical bedrock.[14] So why was He crucified? This passage in Mark is your answer. The Jewish leadership clearly understood who Jesus claimed to be—God—and they conspired with the Romans to have Him crucified because of it. Contrary to what critics like Bart Ehrman say today, the early church did *not* turn Jesus into a God four hundred years later at a church council. Jesus was extremely clear about His claim to deity, and it got Him crucified![15]

Much more could certainly be said about what Jesus said and did, but I would encourage you to read the Gospels for yourself with an open mind—you won't be disappointed. If Jesus really is who He claimed to be, then that means His message is true as well: *forgiveness and an eternal relationship with God in His kingdom are available through Him alone.* And that eternal relationship begins the moment a person takes Jesus at His word (John 1:12; 17:3). The choice is clear: the new and improved Jesus, or the historical Jesus of the New Testament? C. S. Lewis put it best:

> A man who was merely a man and said the sort of things Jesus said would not be a great moral teacher. He would either be a lunatic—on the level of a man who says he is a poached egg—or else he would be the Devil of Hell. You must make your choice. Either this man was, and is, the Son of God: or else a madman or something worse. You can shut Him up for a fool, you can spit at Him and kill Him as a demon; or you can fall at His feet and call Him Lord and God. But let us not come with any patronizing nonsense about His being a great human teacher. He has not left that open to us.[16]

THE BIG IDEAS

- Since we live in a Jesus-haunted culture, there are as many different flavors of Jesus as there are people. The question is: What did He claim about Himself?

- The so-called missing gospels were written anonymously as well as significantly later than the writings of the New Testament. While they are sometimes comical to read, and may offer *some* new historical information about what certain groups of people were saying about Jesus, they do not give us anything new about Jesus Himself. Christians should not fear the claims of these missing gospels.

- Jesus wasn't crucified for being a wise sage or spiritual guru. He was crucified because He claimed by His words and deeds to be God. We can either take Him at His word or reject Him, but we are not free to create our own personal flavor of Jesus. As C. S. Lewis put it, "He has not left that open to us."

For Further Discovery

Bauckham, Richard. *Jesus and the Eyewitnesses: The Gospels as Eyewitness Testimony*. Grand Rapids: Eerdmans, 2008.

Bock, Darrell L. *The Missing Gospels: Unearthing the Truth Behind Alternative Christianities*. Nashville: Thomas Nelson, 2007.

Bowman, Robert M., and J. Ed Komoszewski. *Putting Jesus in His Place: The Case for the Deity of Christ*. Grand Rapids: Kregel, 2007.

Keener, Craig S. *The Historical Jesus of the Gospels*. Grand Rapids: Eerdmans, 2009.

Morrow, Jonathan. *Questioning the Bible: 11 Major Challenges to the Bible's Authority*. Chicago: Moody Publishers, 2014.

Strauss, Mark L. *Four Portraits, One Jesus: A Survey of Jesus and the Gospels*. Grand Rapids: Zondervan, 2011.

Wilkins, Michael J., and J. P. Moreland. *Jesus Under Fire: Modern Scholarship Reinvents the Historical Jesus*. Grand Rapids: Zondervan, 2010.

Did Jesus Rise
from the Dead?

> *The uniqueness and the scandal of the Christian religion rests on the mediation of revelation through historical events. Christianity is not just a code for living or a philosophy of religion. It is rooted in real events of history. To some people this is scandalous because it means that the truth of Christianity is inexplicably bound up with the truth of certain historical facts. And if those facts should be disproved, Christianity would be false. This, however, is what makes Christianity unique because, unlike other world religions, modern man has a means of actually verifying Christianity's truth by historical evidence.*
>
> —GEORGE LADD[1]

> *The disciples had nothing to gain by lying and starting a new religion. They faced hardship, ridicule, hostility, and martyrs' deaths. In light of this, they could never have sustained such unwavering motivation if they knew what they were preaching was a lie. The disciples were not fools and Paul was a cool-headed intellectual of the first rank. There would have been several opportunities over three to four decades of ministry to reconsider and renounce the lie.*
>
> —J. P. MORELAND[2]

> *Fortunately, the Christian faith does not call for us to put our minds on the shelf, to fly in the face of common sense and history, or to make a leap of faith into the dark. The rational person, fully apprised of the evidence, can confidently believe that on that first Easter morning a divine miracle took place.*
>
> —WILLIAM LANE CRAIG[3]

THE RESURRECTION IS AT THE HEART OF CHRISTIANITY. IF IT DID NOT happen then Christianity is false and is perhaps the most horrible lie in history. But don't take my word for it; listen to what the apostle Paul says:

> Now if Christ is preached, that He has been raised from the dead, how do some among you say that there is no resurrection of the dead? But if there is no resurrection of the dead, not even Christ has been raised; and *if Christ has not been raised, then our preaching is vain, your faith also is vain.* Moreover we are even found *to be* false witnesses of God, because we testified against God that He raised Christ, whom He did not raise, if in fact the dead are not raised. For if the dead are not raised, not even Christ has been raised; *and if Christ has not been raised, your faith is worthless; you are still in your sins.* Then those also who have fallen asleep in Christ have perished. *If we have hoped in Christ in this life only, we are of all men most to be pitied.* (1 Cor. 15:12–19 NASB, italics added)

There are people who say that it doesn't ultimately matter whether or not Jesus was raised from the dead in space-time history. Don't buy it! Because if Jesus never rose from the dead, you need to find a new religion!

In the passage we just read from Paul, he could have said that people should put their faith in Jesus no matter what the historical evidence shows—just have blind faith. But he didn't. Instead he "locks together the resurrection of Christ, a knowable historical event—the truth of which can be determined through evidence and reason—with saving faith," which means that the "Christian faith is not blind in the least; rather it is dependent upon a historical event that can be thoroughly investigated with eyes wide open."[4] In this chapter, we are going to investigate the evidence *for* the resurrection. We won't have the time to discuss all of the evidence for the resurrection or deal with many of the alternate theories people have come up with through the years, though at the end of the chapter I list some good books you can read if you are interested.

My approach to this topic may not be what you are expecting. I am not going to say "just believe the Bible" or "just have more faith." Instead, we will build a case for the resurrection of Jesus that does not appeal to the Bible as the inspired ("God-breathed") and inerrant (without error in the original manuscripts) Word of God. Just so we are clear, *I do believe* the Bible is both inspired and inerrant (2 Tim. 3:16–17), but a compelling case for the resurrection of Jesus of Nazareth can be built without appealing to the Bible (at least in the way that many people think of the Bible). If you or someone you come across is skeptical about the Bible, then the approach we are going to take is a powerful way to investigate just what—if anything—happened that Sunday morning two thousand years ago.

Minimal Facts Approach

We are going to use the "minimal facts approach" developed in the excellent book *The Case for the Resurrection of Jesus* by Gary Habermas and Michael Licona.[5] It is called a minimal facts approach because the historical facts they appeal to "are backed by so much evidence that nearly every scholar who studies the subject, even the rather skeptical ones, accepts them."[6] This even includes atheistic scholars. There are five facts[7] that *must* be accounted for by anyone who investigates the historical evidence for the resurrection of Jesus:

1. Jesus died by crucifixion.
2. Jesus's disciples believed that He rose and appeared to them.
3. The church persecutor Paul was suddenly changed.
4. The skeptic James, brother of Jesus, was suddenly changed.
5. The tomb was empty.

It is not enough to say something happened and leave it at that. The facts demand an explanation.

Using the Bible to Prove the Bible?

Before we dive in, I want to address a common objection people raise against the Bible. It goes something like this: "You can't use one book of the Bible to support what another book of the Bible says, because you're just arguing in a circle." While this is a common objection, it is false for several reasons. First, I have already mentioned that I am not treating the Bible (for our purposes here) as a divinely inspired book. I am treating the New Testament as a work of ancient literature just like the works of Herodotus, Livy, or Aristotle.

Next, because the Bible can be found at Barnes & Noble as just one book, many people think it was initially written as one book. The reality of the situation is that while some "holy" books, like the Qur'an (the holy book of Islam), are the product of one author, the New Testament "is a collection of twenty-seven separate texts, written in Greek by nine authors expressed in distinctive styles and with varying emphases" over the span of sixty years.[8] These writers just didn't sit down in a room somewhere and decide that they needed to get their story straight. They were themselves eyewitnesses to the events, or they interviewed eyewitnesses (Luke 1:1–4).

It is significant when multiple authors or sources, writing independently of one another, agree on the same historical facts. This is known as the criterion of multiple attestation. Therefore, a Christian can use one book of the Bible to argue for another and not be guilty of circular reasoning.

Now to the five facts.

1. Jesus died by crucifixion. This fact is recorded in all four gospels as well as being referred to by other New Testament writers. In addition to these Christian sources, there are several non-Christian sources that report Jesus's crucifixion. For example, in AD 115 the Roman historian Tacitus describes how Christians were blamed for the burning of Rome: "Nero fastened the guilt and inflicted the most exquisite tortures on a class hated for their abominations called Christians by the populace. Christus, from whom the name had its origin, suffered the extreme penalty during the reign of Tiberius at the hands of one of our procurators, Pontius Pilatus [see Matt. 27:2]."[9] Due to passages like this from outside of the New Testament, and the strong witness in the New Testament, there is no doubt that Jesus of Nazareth was executed by Roman crucifixion around AD 30–33.

2. Jesus's disciples believed that He rose and appeared to them. First, the disciples *claimed* to have seen the risen Jesus. In addition to their own testimony recorded in the Gospels, we also have the testimony of the apostle Paul (1 Cor. 15:3–11), the oral tradition that would become the basis of the New Testament writings,[10] and the written works of the early church. The disciples' claim that they had seen the risen Jesus cannot be disputed.

Second, following the death of Jesus, something powerful happened to the disciples that transformed them "from fearful cowering individuals who denied and abandoned him [Jesus] at his arrest and execution into bold proclaimers of the gospel of the risen Lord [see Mark 14:66–72 and Acts 4:18–20]."[11] Not only did they *claim* the resurrection of Christ, they really *believed* it. So firm was their commitment that they were willing to be imprisoned, tortured, or even martyred for it. The historical record is clear on this point. Habermas and Licona observe that "the apostles died for holding to their own testimony that they had *personally* seen the risen Jesus. Contemporary martyrs die for what they *believe* to be true. The disciples died for what they knew to be either true or false."[12]

3. The church persecutor Paul was suddenly changed. Saul of Tarsus thought that he was doing God's will by persecuting Christians. He held the coats of those who stoned the first Christian martyr (Acts 7:58). Then suddenly, Saul became Paul on the road to Damascus. Paul became the *chief* proclaimer and defender of the gospel of Jesus Christ in the early church. How did this happen? Paul claimed throughout his letters (and Luke corroborated this in the book of Acts) that the risen Jesus appeared to him. Nothing else makes good sense of this radical transformation.

4. The skeptic James, brother of Jesus, was suddenly changed. James was not a big fan of his brother Jesus while Jesus was alive. But shortly after his brother's death, James became one of the leaders of the early church (Acts 15:12–21; Gal. 1:19), having converted to Christianity. Not only was he a follower of Christ for the rest of his life, but both Christian and secular sources report that James was martyred for his belief in the risen Jesus. Again, this powerful transformation is another testimony of the resurrection of Jesus.

5. The tomb was empty. Three of the strongest pieces of evidence that support the empty tomb are (a) the Jerusalem factor, (b) enemy attestation, and (c) the testimony of women.

   a. The Jerusalem factor. Where was Jesus executed? Jerusalem. Where did
      His disciples proclaim His resurrection fifty days later? Jerusalem. This
      is an important point because "it would have been virtually impossible
      for the disciples to proclaim the resurrection in Jerusalem had the
      tomb not been empty."[13] Why? Because if you were going to start telling
      people that the guy who was publicly executed and buried just fifty days
      ago has been raised from the dead (and you know this is a lie), then you

certainly don't start announcing it in the one place they can walk over to the tomb and bring out His body! That is . . . unless it is true.

b. Enemy attestation. It makes sense that the disciples said that Jesus rose from the dead—they were His friends. But it is an entirely different thing that Jesus's enemies—those who had Him crucified—admitted the tomb was empty. That is what we have recorded in Matthew 28:11–15. The Jewish leadership initiated a cover-up by telling the guards to say that the disciples had come in the night and stolen Jesus's body. If there was a body in the tomb, then there would be no need to create a cover story.

c. The testimony of women. In the ancient world, the legal testimony of women was not taken seriously . . . if it was even considered at all— sorry, ladies. The theory that the gospel writers made up the story of Jesus's resurrection makes no cultural sense! No fiction writer in the first century AD would have ever placed women at the climax of the story, when the hero rises again. This would have made no sense because— sadly—no one would have believed a woman! So the only reason you would mention women finding the tomb first is because that is what actually happened . . . and all four gospels mention this fact.

These are the facts. What hypothesis explains all of these the best? After careful examination, only the theory of Jesus's rising from the dead has the power and scope to explain these minimal facts (plus ones we didn't even mention).[14] Every other theory has way too many difficulties. And unless you assume that naturalism is true and that miracles can't happen, then the most reasonable thing to do is to investigate miracle claims on a case-by-case basis. And in the case of Jesus of Nazareth and the resurrection, the historical evidence is very strong.

I had the great privilege of visiting the garden tomb in Jerusalem recently (it is one of the two sites that tradition considers to be where Jesus was crucified and buried). It is owned and operated by a group of British Christians.

Now it could be that Jesus was not crucified and buried at the garden tomb site. Maybe it happened where the Church of the Holy Sepulcher is now. Either way, the thousands of people who visit the garden tomb each week are reminded of an important fact—He is risen! The grave could not hold Christ! Every time a tour is given of the garden tomb, faithful Christians proclaim the same message that the disciples began to proclaim two thousand years ago. And each week pilgrims travel to visit the sites in the Holy Land where they meet the risen Jesus and begin a relationship with Him. The resurrection is no secondary issue; it is the heart of Christianity. It is only because Jesus is risen that you and I can experience forgiveness, hope, and eternal life.

THE BIG IDEAS

- The resurrection of Jesus Christ is at the heart of Christianity—if it did not happen, then Christianity is a lie and you need to find another religion!

- Christianity does not separate faith from history (1 Cor. 15:12–19).

- The five minimal facts are (1) Jesus died by crucifixion; (2) Jesus's disciples believed that He rose and appeared to them; (3) the church persecutor Paul was suddenly changed; (4) the skeptic James, brother of Jesus, was suddenly changed; and (5) the tomb was empty.

- The three strongest reasons to think that the tomb was empty are (1) the Jerusalem factor, (2) enemy attestation, and (3) the testimony of women.

- Something powerful and literally life-changing happened to lots of people after Jesus's death. What was it? Other explanations fall short. Nothing less than God raising Jesus from the dead accounts for these five facts.

For Further Discovery

Craig, William Lane. *Reasonable Faith: Christian Truth and Apologetics*. 3rd ed. Wheaton, IL: Crossway Books, 2008.

Geivett, R. Douglas, and Gary R. Habermas. *In Defense of Miracles: A Comprehensive Case for God's Action in History*. Downers Grove, IL: InterVarsity Press, 1997.

Habermas, Gary R. *The Risen Jesus and Future Hope*. Oxford: Rowman & Littlefield, 2003.

Habermas, Gary R., and Michael R. Licona. *The Case for the Resurrection of Jesus*. Grand Rapids: Kregel, 2004.

Licona, Michael R. *The Resurrection of Jesus: A New Historiographical Approach*. Downers Grove, IL: InterVarsity Press, 2010.

Wright, N. T. *The Resurrection of the Son of God*. Minneapolis: Augsburg Fortress, 2003.

ExploreTheResurrection.tv. A nine-session online study taught by Jonathan Morrow that will help you make the historical case for the resurrection of Jesus (powered by Impact 360 Institute).

Science Rules!

At the outset it should be stated that there is no "scientific method," no formula with five easy steps guaranteed to lead to discoveries. There are many methods, used at different stages of inquiry, and in widely varying circumstances.

—IAN BARBOUR[1]

If the direction in which science carries philosophy is a one-way street towards physicalism, determinism, atheism, and perhaps even nihilism, then the intellectual obligation of those who wrestle with philosophical questions would be unavoidable. We must understand the substantive claims of physical science . . . and we must understand the strengths and limitations of science as a source of answers to these questions.

—ALEXANDER ROSENBERG[2]

Nonbelievers may hear all the notes of science, but without a theistic context and perspective they will not hear the song.

—GEORGE MARSDEN[3]

SCIENCE RULES IN OUR CULTURE. IF YOU'RE A SCIENTIST PEOPLE HAVE TO listen to you, and if you're not—well, "no one wants to be dismissed as 'unscientific.'"[4] Scientific discovery is the crown jewel of human progress. Our society's position is this: science can tell us everything we need to know; or if it can't right now, just give it some time and it will eventually solve all our problems. If you've ever played spades, you know that the ace of spades trumps everything; in our culture science is the ace of spades. Science has become so exalted that any person wearing a white lab coat can talk about almost anything—without being an expert—and be treated as authoritative on a topic.[5]

Now before you jump to conclusions, I am not denigrating scientists or

141

science in general. I merely want to suggest that the deification of science as the end-all and be-all of existence should be rejected and replaced with a more humble view of scientific inquiry. We need to remember that the latest theory in science is only years—maybe months—away from being redefined or replaced by a better theory. Also, I am not "attacking science" because I'm afraid science will disprove the Bible. On the contrary, I think God's two books—nature and the Bible—will be found to be in complete harmony when all is said and done. Let's make a few observations about science and how it works; our goal is to have a healthier view of science and then examine how theology and science should relate to one another.

Science Is a Lot Harder to Define Than You Would Think

In middle school we all learned that science equals (or is equivalent to) the scientific method. Oh how easy life would be if this were all there was to it. Don't get me wrong; the scientific method is helpful . . . so far as it goes. But in reality there is not *one* scientific method; there are *many* methods. Some of them are significantly dissimilar. It may come as a surprise to you, but it is very difficult (and often controversial) to distinguish what counts as a scientific explanation from a nonscientific one. This difficulty has become known as the "demarcation problem" (i.e., finding the line or criterion that separates the two). Any reputable philosophy of science textbook will confirm what I have just said.

Let's look at two common proposals. First, something is said to be scientific if—and only if—it is *falsifiable* (this was Karl Popper's contribution). But, as J. P. Moreland observes, "The nature of falsifiability in nature is often difficult to clarify. . . . Seldom if ever are individual scientific propositions tested in isolation from other propositions or theories."[6] Given complicated theories and experiments with numerous variables, it is hard to discern what precisely has been falsified. There are other issues we could raise. So while falsifiability is relevant to scientific inquiry, it is not what provides the hard line of demarcation between what is science and what is not.

Another proposal is to define something as being science if—and only if—it deals with entities that are empirically testable or observable. However, it is fairly obvious that scientists deal with all sorts of theoretical entities like quarks and "strings" that no one has actually observed. It's great when predicted theoretical entities are empirically verified (like the Higgs boson particle), but this does not always happen. So while science *commonly* deals with empirically observable entities, this is not enough to separate science from nonscience. Now other pesky questions are raised: "Do the theories of science give a literally true model of the way the world is, or do they merely provide useful fictions, calculating devices, or convenient summaries of sensory experience that 'work' (e.g., help us control nature, predict phenomena, and so on)?"[7] There is a general consensus on the outlines of science (that science is generally empirical in nature, seeks publicly accessible results, employs rational inquiry, etc.), but as you can see, the parameters are not very neat and tidy.

Science Is Not the Only Game in Town When It Comes to Knowledge

An exalted view of science maintains that facts count as "real knowledge" *only* when they are discovered scientifically; what is not grounded in science is relegated to the realm of personal opinion (this view is often called scientism).[8] One of the main reasons to reject science as being the only game in town when it comes to knowledge is that there are other legitimate kinds of knowledge (see chapter 5, "Can We Know Anything at All?"). Moreover, scientism is actually self-refuting. As Moreland observes, "For one thing, the statement 'only what can be known by science or quantified and empirically tested is rational and true' is self-refuting. This statement itself is not a statement *of* science. It is a philosophical statement *about* science. How could the statement itself be quantified and empirically tested? And if it cannot, then by the statement's own standards, it cannot itself be true or rationally held."[9] This last observation raises the importance of recognizing the role philosophy plays in science.

Philosophy and Science Are Inseparable

Science rests on cool, hard fact; everything else is circumspect. *False.* Pure science is a myth; it always carries the residue of philosophical assumptions. As DeWeese and Moreland observe: "Science cannot be practiced in thin air.

It requires a number of philosophical theses that must be assumed if science is going to get off the runway. Each assumption has been challenged, and the task of stating and defending them falls to philosophy. The conclusions of science cannot be more certain than the presuppositions it rests on and uses to reach those conclusions."[10] Note some of the unscientifically derived assumptions of science:

1. The existence of a theory-independent, external world
2. The orderly nature of the external world
3. The knowability of the external world
4. The existence of truth
5. The laws of logic and mathematics
6. The reliability of our cognitive and sensory faculties to serve as truth gatherers and as sources of justified beliefs in our intellectual environment
7. The adequacy of language to describe the world
8. The existence of values used in science (e.g., "test theories fairly and report test results honestly")
9. The uniformity of nature and induction[11]

But why limit science to just this set of assumptions? Why not allow others to be included (perhaps from theology)? These are philosophical questions that need to be debated. One particular branch of science cannot proclaim its assumptions of what is and is not science without first providing a philosophical explanation of why certain criteria were selected and others excluded.

One obvious application of this point is contemporary science's use of methodological naturalism—the view that no nonnatural or supernatural entity or event can be invoked in a truly scientific explanation. We can't enter this discussion here, but this is an important question for you to do some thinking about. I think Paul Copan is right in his assessment that "the philosophical assumptions and biases made by certain scientists unfairly cordon off scientific inquiry to purely naturalistic explanations. However, if a God exists who created and designed the world, then these scientists are excluding a massively helpful source of explanation."[12]

Some Things Science Can't Tell Us

Science can and does enlighten us to many important and wonderful things about our world. Yet, we also need to be aware that science has its limits; there are some things that science just can't tell us. We have discussed the inability of science to "validate either scientific method itself or the presuppositions of that method."[13] But there are two other important issues that science cannot address. First, "science cannot give any ultimate naturalistic or mechanical explanation for the existence of the universe with which it deals."[14] Any explanations will appeal first to principles not generated by scientific reasoning.[15] Take the big bang theory, for example. In this event, all energy and matter came into existence some 13.7 billion years ago. If science can only deal with observable entities, then it does not have the right tools to address the cause of the big bang, because there was literally nothing (no gravity, no matter, no vacuum of bubbling particles, no energy, no space, etc.) in existence before that point.

Second, science cannot speak to ultimate purpose (i.e., teleology). Science of yesteryear attempted to incorporate teleology into scientific explanation by employing philosophical or theological observations, but no more. Science now concentrates on explaining the natural and mechanistic phenomena of the world. There is an important difference between mechanistic and teleological explanations. For example, science can tell us down to the last detail how an internal combustion engine works (mechanism), but it cannot tell us what it is for (teleology) without making some philosophical or theological assumptions. So in principle, strict scientific explanation cannot answer the "for what?" question in nature. Interestingly enough, this is the answer that we all long to discover.

Integrating Theology and Science

By now we have seen that science has resisted a hard-and-fast definition and admits some significant limitations. But if scientists incorporate theology into their science, many wonder if that will lead to the answer "God did it." The short answer to that is it doesn't have to. Addressing this concern requires first answering how science and theology relate. Though this would take a book of its own, we can oversimplify and mention two views: (1) the two realms/complementarity view and (2) the theistic science/direct interaction view.[16] View (1) maintains that "science and theology focus on two distinct, nonoverlapping areas of investigation—viz. the natural and the supernatural. Science and theology involve two different, complementary approaches to and descriptions of the same reality from different perspectives." Basically, keep them separate because they are addressing different questions. However, this approach diminishes Christianity as a robust knowledge tradition. This undesirable implication leads us to view (2), which "allows for the possibility that science and theology may directly interact with each other in epistemically positive or negative ways." Thus view (2) seems more at home in a robust Christian worldview because it allows us to incorporate all we know about the world (including theological knowledge) into our scientific theorizing. To wrap up this section, there are questions theology does not answer (e.g., the nature of chemical bonding) and there are questions science cannot answer (e.g., the cause of the big bang), but science and theology do overlap and can provide mutual support for the other.

We have only scratched the surface of this fascinating and challenging subject. There are many additional comments that could be made concerning the relationship between Christian theology and science.[17] So for now, we will conclude with Del Ratzsch's reminder that "Christianity puts science in proper perspective as being valuable but not the ultimate value; as being competent but not all-competent; as being a proper part of human life but not the whole; as being something humans do but not our highest calling; as providing solutions to some problems but not to the most fundamental human problem, alienation from our Creator."[18]

THE BIG IDEAS

- When push comes to shove, science and empirical data trump everything in our culture. This is how it is but not how it should be.

- God's two books—nature and the Bible—will be found to be in complete harmony when all is said and done. We need to remember that the latest theory in science is only a generation away from being redefined or replaced by a better theory.

- "Science cannot be practiced in thin air. It requires a number of philosophical theses that must be assumed if science is going to get off the runway. Each assumption has been challenged, and the task of stating and defending them falls to philosophy. The conclusions of science cannot be more certain than the presuppositions it rests on and uses to reach those conclusions." —DeWeese and Moreland

- When it comes to integrating science and theology, Christians should prefer an approach that allows us to incorporate all we know about the world (including theological knowledge) into our scientific theorizing.

- While science can tell us much about our world, it does have limits (what science itself is, its ultimate origins, and its ultimate purpose).

For Further Discovery

Bloom, John A. *The Natural Sciences: A Student's Guide*. Reclaiming the Christian Intellectual Tradition. Wheaton, IL: Crossway, 2015.

Collins, C. John. *Science and Faith: Friends or Foes?* Wheaton, IL: Crossway, 2003.

Copan, Paul. "Unless You Can Scientifically Verify or Falsify Your Belief, It's Meaningless." In *How Do You Know You're Not Wrong? Responding to Objections That Leave Christians Speechless*. Grand Rapids: Baker, 2005.

———. "You Can't Prove That Scientifically." In *How Do You Know You're Not Wrong? Responding to Objections That Leave Christians Speechless*. Grand Rapids: Baker, 2005.

DeWeese, Garrett J., and J. P. Moreland. "How Should Christians Think About Science?" In *Philosophy Made Slightly Less Difficult: A Beginner's Guide to Life's Big Questions*. Downers Grove, IL: InterVarsity Press, 2009.

Hannam, James. *The Genesis of Science: How the Christian Middle Ages Launched the Scientific Revolution*. Washington, DC: Regnery, 2011.

Lennox, John C. *God's Undertaker: Has Science Buried God?* Updated ed. Oxford: Lion, 2011.

Plantinga, Alvin. *Where the Conflict Really Lies: Science, Religion, and Naturalism*. Oxford: Oxford University Press, 2011.

Ratzsch, Del. *Science and Its Limits: The Natural Sciences in Christian Perspective*. Downers Grove, IL: InterVarsity Press, 2009.

Designed or Not Designed?

That Is the Question

It seems to me that, as it is usually presented, the current orthodoxy about the cosmic order is the product of governing assumptions that are unsupported, and that it flies in the face of common sense. . . . It is prima facie highly implausible that life as we know it is the result of a sequence of physical accidents together with the mechanism of natural selection.

—THOMAS NAGEL[1]

A fair result can be obtained only by fully stating and balancing the facts and arguments on both sides of each question.

—CHARLES DARWIN[2]

There exist natural systems that cannot be adequately explained in terms of undirected natural causes and that exhibit features which in any other circumstance we would attribute to intelligence.

—WILLIAM DEMBSKI[3]

"BIOLOGY IS THE STUDY OF COMPLICATED THINGS THAT GIVE THE appearance of having been designed for a purpose."[4] This is the intriguing conclusion arrived at by evolutionary biologist Richard Dawkins in his book *The Blind Watchmaker*. He has put his finger on the fundamental issues when it comes to exploring the origin of life: Does nature only appear to be designed or has it really been designed? Is the physical world we see today simply the result of a blind, random process with no end in mind (this is the proposal of modern neo-Darwinian evolution [NDE])?[5] Or has nature been intricately designed for a reason (this is the proposal of intelligent design

[ID])? It's hard to come up with more profound and important questions than these.

Do I believe in evolution? Well, it depends on how you define your terms. Because there is so much confusion on this issue, it is essential that we define our terms carefully. If by evolution, one means *change over time*, I have no problem with that. If somebody means *small changes occurring in nature over time within species*, I have no problem with that either. But I do have a problem with the view that argues that *at some point in the past, life arose from what was lifeless, commencing a blind, random, and gradual process of natural selection acting on genetic mutations that explains* all *the diversity and complexity we observe*. This controversial view is the one that fits under the umbrella of neo-Darwinian evolution. While Charles Darwin's theory, originally put forth in *On the Origin of Species*, has been modified over the past hundred and fifty years by adding population genetics, his main thesis of natural selection as the creative mechanism in nature remains essentially unchanged.

Now I am not a biologist, nor do I play one on TV. But I have spent a significant amount of time reading, studying, and thinking about these issues (and as you will see, the *philosophical assumptions* playing themselves out is where all the action is). My goal is not for you to come away from reading this chapter as an expert. My aim is to introduce you to the main ideas so that you will be able to engage them critically. At the outset, you should know that I find the case for NDE ultimately unpersuasive and inadequate to explain the available data. While there are biblical reasons for rejecting the core of NDE, we have no need to appeal to them here. The amount of scientific and philosophical evidence stacked up against NDE is sufficient.

Problems with Neo-Darwinian Evolution

So what's wrong with NDE? There are several issues that critics find problematic for this theory. First, there is the issue of how it all began. Somewhere in the finite past, there had to be a kickoff. Life had to arise from nonliving material. You have to get from chemistry to biology somehow. In other words, there has to be something for NDE to act upon. Phillip Johnson, author of *Darwin on Trial*, notes: "The basic difficulty in explaining how life could have begun is that all living organisms are extremely complex, and Darwinian selection cannot perform the designing even in theory until living organisms already exist and are capable of reproducing their kind. . . . The challenge of chemical evolution is to find a way to get some chemical combination to the point where reproduction and selection could get started."[6] So there needs to be an adequate naturalistic explanation of how chemical, nonliving matter evolved into biological, living matter.[7] And as of now, there has not been one. In fact the more we discover about the early earth's atmosphere, DNA, and RNA, the more challenging this appears. (I refer you to the excellent discussion of this topic by Stephen Meyer in *Signature in the Cell: DNA and the Evidence for Intelligent Design*.)

Let's allow for the sake of argument that this happened—life arising from something inanimate. The problems with this theory do not disappear. Accounting for transitions between species—from simple to complex—has proved difficult because this process, if true, is impossible to observe. The transition time is too slow. Therefore, in order to explain the development of radically different species over millions of years, scientists are forced to extrapolate a theory from the changes they observe occurring *within* species (e.g., Darwin observed while on the Galapagos Islands that the size of finch beaks varied over time due to wet/dry seasons and the availability of food). This extrapolation seems unwarranted based on the available evidence.[8] The information required to generate entirely new animal body plans is staggering (see the excellent discussion by Stephen Meyer in *Darwin's Doubt: The Explosive Origin of Animal Life and the Case for Intelligent Design*). The typical line of reasoning goes like this: "We are here, aren't we—then evolution happened." But NDE does not actually explain *how* it happened (sure, there are some just-so stories out there, but something less ad hoc is needed). And increasing numbers of scientists and philosophers are growing skeptical concerning the actual evidence for NDE (e.g., see the powerful critique by atheist Thomas Nagel in *Mind and Cosmos: Why the Materialist Neo-Darwinian Conception of Nature Is Almost Certainly False*).

Molecular biologist Jonathan Wells published a controversial book titled *Icons of Evolution* (an icon is a prominent symbol for a person or movement) that calls into question some long-standing "evidence" for evolution. Wells examines and compares "icons of evolution with published scientific evidence," discovering that "much of what we teach about evolution is wrong."[9] If you have had high school biology, then you are probably familiar with some of these icons: the Miller-Urey experiment, Darwin's tree of life, homology in vertebrate limbs, peppered moths, *Archaeopteryx*, Darwin's finches, Haeckel's embryos, and four-winged fruit flies. (If these are unfamiliar to you, you can look them up in the index of your biology text or Google them.) These prominent symbols achieve psychological influence for NDE far beyond what is warranted. Wells's point isn't that students should be taught religious dogma in the classroom; rather, he desires that the truth concerning these icons be taught so students can critically evaluate the merits of NDE.

NDE also has an "information problem."[10] There is a staggering amount of information contained in DNA, proteins, and cells. NDE suggests that species gradually—and randomly—progress from simple to complex, so where does the *new* information come from? Proponents of NDE have an exceedingly difficult time answering this question, so they don't answer it at all. They don't answer the question of *where* genetic information came from. Rather, they simply recognize it is there and then attempt to explain how it works.

The final shortcoming of NDE that I want to highlight is NDE's inability to explain immaterial human consciousness and the exclusively human capacities of high-level moral, abstract, and emotional reasoning, complex long-term goal-oriented planning, and genuine free will. It is illogical: an organism begins as a biological machine and randomly transitions to a species that experiences free will. Using NDE's own naturalistic rationale, if matter is governed by the laws of nature—and humans are purely physical beings—then there is no free will, only cause and effect (i.e., molecules in motion). But obviously humans *are* free to make choices according to their ability to reason and desire, and these are not wholly subject to chemical processes in the brain.

The fact of the matter is that NDE has been unable to adequately account for the origin of consciousness. Prominent neo-Darwinist philosopher Michael Ruse summarizes the situation: "Why should a bunch of atoms have thinking ability? Why should I, even as I write now, be able to reflect on what I am doing, and why should you, even as you read now, be able to ponder my points, agreeing or disagreeing, with pleasure or with pain, deciding to refute me or deciding that I am just not worth the effort? No one, certainly not the Darwinian as such, seems to have any answer to this. . . . The point is there is no scientific answer."[11] In short, how do you get something immaterial like a soul or mind from the purely material mechanism of NDE? The fact that there are no compelling explanations from the NDE camp is a significant shortcoming of the theory.[12] It does not explain what needs to be explained.

In light of these and other inadequacies of NDE theory, another scientifically grounded alternative is being proposed. The intelligent design movement has ignited national controversy, but this national attention has also led to much confusion. The fact of the matter is that a growing number within the scientific community "are skeptical of claims for the ability of random mutation and natural selection to account for the complexity of life . . . [and believe] careful examination of the evidence for Darwinian theory should be encouraged."[13] For reasons based on empirical evidence and research—not prior religious commitments—many of these scientists are in favor of exploring the scientific theory of ID because it seems to have more explanatory power and scope than NDE.

Intelligent Design

Confusion abounds concerning what ID is and isn't, so we must be careful to clearly define it. The media for the most part errs by calling ID a form of creationism (we will discuss the difference below). And opponents of ID label it creationism for rhetorical reasons: to classify ID in the category of beliefs and theories that are not backed by scientific evidence. Instead of engaging with the scientific evidence marshaled by ID scientists and philosophers,[14] NDE often resorts to name calling and institutional bullying. To get at the truth, the following are some definitions straight from leading ID proponents.[15]

William Dembski argues that the basic claim of ID is that "*there exist natural systems that cannot be adequately explained in terms of undirected natural causes and that exhibit features which in any other circumstance we would attribute to intelligence.*"[16] For example, imagine you are driving through the mountains and suddenly come across a rock face that demands your attention—it is different from the others. Whereas wind and erosion can account for the random appearances of most of the mountains you have seen that day, it cannot account for the four shapes embedded in this rock face. Why not? Because *there is a recognizable pattern of intelligence* that went in to the formation of this mountain. This becomes obvious by the fact that there are four specific patterns matching the faces of four former presidents of the United States—Mt. Rushmore. The natural inference here is not to the blind and unguided natural processes of wind and erosion but rather to design.

Specified Complexity

Consider another example from the science of archaeology.[17] When archaeologists excavate sites and sift through dirt, how do they distinguish between authentic artifacts and rocks? Answer: they look for highly improbable patterns or marks of design; this is what Dembski calls *specified complexity*:

> Life is both complex and specified. The basic intuition here is straightforward. A single letter of the alphabet is specified without being complex (i.e., it conforms to an independently given pattern but is simple). A long sequence of random letters is complex without being specified (i.e., it requires a complicated instruction-set to characterize but conforms to no independently given pattern). A Shakespearean sonnet is both complex and specified.[18]

Irreducible Complexity

Now what happens when scientists look for design in biology at the molecular level? After careful research, Michael Behe observed that some systems (e.g., bacterial flagella) cannot be accounted for by blind natural selection.[19] In fact, he concluded from his research that the most probable inference for the origin of irreducibly complex systems is design. A system is irreducibly complex if "it consists of several interrelated parts for which removing even one part completely destroys the system's function."[20] If this concept is still a little fuzzy, think of a mousetrap. In order for a mousetrap to work it must have all its parts (wood, spring, cheese, latch, etc.) working together. It is obvious that a block of cheese can't catch any mice, but adding a spring makes it possible. Then adding a block of wood makes it a probability. The point is that the individual components serve no function *by themselves*. It is only when they function together *as a whole* that you get a beneficial function.

Charles Darwin in 1859 admitted, "*If it could be demonstrated that any complex organ existed which could not possibly have been formed by numerous, successive, slight modifications, my theory would absolutely break down.*"[21] Obviously Darwin didn't think it did, but that's quite a statement! Can NDE, which understands nature as a closed system of random causes, account for the emergence of complexity? After one hundred and fifty years, NDE still comes up short. So by Darwin's own standard, his theory is breaking down. It should also be noted that as we learn more and more about the complexity of the cell and DNA, the problem is only going to get worse for NDE.

ID Has Religious Implications

It is imperative to recognize that ID is not making a claim based on religious presuppositions. On the contrary, scientists and philosophers have observed the relevant data and inferred ID is the best explanation for the origination of life. Gaps exist in the understanding of molecular biology that the theory of NDE has no way of bridging. There is a limit to the creative power of evolution.[22] NDE is stuck with the problem of accounting for where information comes from and how it is transferred. ID has a reasonable explanation for this as well. Contrary to what you might encounter online or in the classroom, ID is an argument from evidence, not ignorance. This is not a "design of the gaps" argument—we don't know how it works; therefore, it was designed. Why? Because DNA contains information. And our uniform and repeated experience confirms that information is always the product of a rational mind.[23]

The systems and organisms in nature *appear* designed because they *are* designed. Now to be sure, ID research has religious *implications* (just as NDE does) but it is not religious *in nature*. It does not claim to say *who* this designer is or what this being is like—that is a question for theology and philosophy of religion to debate. ID is not creationism in sheep's clothing. Unlike ID, creationism affirms the truthfulness of the special creation recorded in Genesis 1–2[24] and the biblical God.

A word of clarification is needed here. I believe that the God of the Bible is the designer referred to in ID and that He created all there is. But believing in ID does not require this conclusion, even though it is consistent with it. For example, a Muslim or Jewish follower could affirm ID along with the Christian. But this is a good thing because once a designer is inferred, people can then discuss *who* that designer is and *what he is like*. I am confident that a compelling case can be made that the God of the Bible—and what He has revealed—makes the most sense of the world in which we live.[25] The important point to understand, and help others understand, is that ID is not making religious claims and calling them science. Rather ID makes scientific observations with conclusions that have religious and theological implications.

I would be remiss if I didn't answer one strategy that NDE employs to undercut the force of ID's arguments. Since many of those within the ID movement are Christians, NDE accuses ID scientists of being religiously biased and incapable of doing "pure science." This charge does not hold water. Oxford evolutionist Richard Dawkins made the statement that "Darwin made it possible to be an intellectually fulfilled atheist."[26] As we can see, the knife cuts both ways. ID proponents are no more or less biased than those of NDE. But what should be abundantly clear by now is that how one answers certain *philosophical* questions will drive how the empirical evidence gets interpreted.

In the end, charges of hidden agendas will not advance the discussion. We need to stop name-calling and seek the truth—no matter how uncomfortable that may make us. We must be willing to question a theory that has been around a while. In this case, it is becoming increasingly evident to those who have eyes to see that the reason why nature *appears* to be designed is that it really *has* been designed.

POSTSCRIPT: How to Engage on Questions of Origins

Once Christians recognize that the real battle exists between theism and naturalism, we can put the current debate about origins into perspective. I have two suggestions that may help us better navigate these issues.

First, Christians need to present a united front opposing naturalism in the public square while also standing up for academic freedom, so that questions of origins can be rigorously discussed without fear of censorship, denial of tenure, or the loss of research money.

Second, and closely related, Christians must be charitable toward other Christians who disagree about which particular interpretation of Genesis is the most accurate (for example, the young/old earth debate). This is especially true when we discuss this topic on the Internet, on TV or radio, or in print. All the watching world sees are angry Christians not loving one another and bickering over which view of the flat-earth theory is correct. But in the same breath, we can and should develop careful exegetical and theological views on creation. All Christians who take the Bible seriously should be able to agree *that* God purposefully created, even if they disagree concerning the *how* and the *when*.

I suggest we carry out this cultural conversation according to the following priorities:

1. In the public square, make a positive scientific and philosophical case for theism and argue against naturalism.

2. At the public level and in our churches and youth groups, have conversations about the significant scientific evidence that undermines the plausibility of neo-Darwinian evolution and points toward intelligent design.

3. Only after spending significant energy on the first two priorities, turn to the in-house discussion concerning the various interpretive options of Genesis 1–2 and the age of the earth question (intelligent design is a big-tent approach that is compatible with various understandings of biblical creationism). Moreover, as students entering the university, you need to know that there is more than one plausible and biblically faithful interpretation of Genesis available for you to consider. In other words, you don't have to have it all figured out before you're eighteen!

In our age of science, these issues aren't going away anytime soon. As Christians we must prepare to speak intelligently to the questions of faith and science raised by our culture.

THE BIG IDEAS

- Four reasons to doubt the adequacy of NDE are (1) its failure to explain how life can arise from something lifeless, (2) its inability to account for where new information comes from, (3) the dubious status of many popular icons of evolution, and (4) its inability to account for the origin of human consciousness.

- The fundamental claim of ID is that "there exist natural systems that cannot be adequately explained in terms of undirected natural causes and that exhibit features which in any other circumstance we would attribute to intelligence." —WILLIAM DEMBSKI

- ID is not creationism in sheep's clothing, and it is not a religiously motivated theory (though like NDE, it has religious implications).

- When it comes to questions of origins, the real battle is between theism and naturalism. Once you settle that question, the other questions become easier to navigate.

For Further Discovery

Axe, Douglas. *Undeniable: How Biology Confirms Our Intuition That Life Is Designed.* New York: HarperOne, 2016.

Collins, C. John. *Did Adam and Eve Really Exist? Who They Were and Why You Should Care.* Wheaton, IL: Crossway, 2011.

Dembski, William A. *The Design Revolution: Answering the Toughest Questions About Intelligent Design.* Downers Grove, IL: InterVarsity Press, 2004.

Dembski, William A. and Sean McDowell. *Understanding Intelligent Design: Everything You Need to Know in Plain Language.* Eugene, OR: Harvest House, 2008.

Lennox, John C. *Seven Days That Divide the World: The Beginning According to Genesis and Science.* Grand Rapids: Zondervan, 2011.

Meyer, Stephen C. *Darwin's Doubt: The Explosive Origin of Animal Life and the Case for Intelligent Design.* New York: HarperOne, 2013.

———. *Signature in the Cell: DNA and the Evidence for Intelligent Design.* Grand Rapids: Zondervan, 2009.

Moreland, J. P., et al., eds. *Theistic Evolution: A Scientific, Philosophical, and Theological Critique.* Wheaton, IL: Crossway, 2017.

Richards, Jay, ed. *God and Evolution.* Seattle, WA: Discovery Institute Press, 2010.

Ross, Hugh. *Improbable Planet: How Earth Became Humanity's Home.* Grand Rapids: Baker, 2016.

———. *Navigating Genesis: A Scientist's Journey Through Genesis 1–11.* Covina, CA: RTB Press, 2014.

Whorton, Mark, and Hill Roberts. *Holman Quicksource Guide to Understanding Creation*. Nashville: B&H Publishing, 2008.

———————————

Evolution News and Views at www.evolutionnews.org.

Reasons to Believe at www.reasons.org.

Dealing with Doubt

Doubt is not the opposite of faith, nor is it the same as unbelief.
Doubt is a state of mind in suspension between faith and unbelief
so that it is neither of them wholly and it is each only partly.

—OS GUINNESS[1]

Unless you teach your moods "where they get off," you can never
be either a sound Christian or even a sound atheist, but just a
creature dithering to and fro, with its beliefs really dependent on
the weather and the state of its digestion.

—C. S. LEWIS[2]

I do believe, but help me overcome my unbelief!

—MARK 9:24 NLT

CONFESSION TIME. *I HAVE DOUBTS.* I HAVE PRAYED "THE PRAYER OF SAL-
vation" on more than one occasion—just to "make sure it took." I have
doubted at times that there is a heaven, that Jesus really has forgiven my
sins, that prayer does anything, and that God really loves me (I could go on).
Now what makes this confession more egregious is that I am a "professional
Christian" with graduate degrees in biblical studies, theology, and philosophy. I enjoy reading books on apologetics, and I believe Christianity to be
true. If anyone should have doubts, it shouldn't be someone like me, right?
Ha! You have probably had some of these same doubts but perhaps have
never voiced them to anyone else out of fear of what people might think. It
can be very painful to be left alone with your doubts.

Christians who publicly express their doubts are often looked upon as
if they uttered a four-letter word. Doubt is often viewed as the unforgivable
sin. But this is one of the many myths flying around out there about doubt.
Another—one of the biggest—is that spiritual people don't doubt; they just

need to conjure up more faith.[3] But this is just false. The Bible contains many examples of Christians who doubted. Do you remember Abraham—*the* man of faith? Do you recall his doubts getting the better of him when God said that he and Sarah would have a child in their old age? Abraham laughed— even in spite of how far God had led them and the promises He had made to them (Gen. 17:17). Or take John the Baptist who while in prison doubted that Jesus was really who He claimed to be (Matt. 11:2–3). Another common myth asserts that doubt is always bad; it's not. People can grow in their faith and mature as they deal with doubt. So if you find yourself doubting, there is nothing to be ashamed about; you just need to find out how to deal with it.

Flavors of Doubt

Not all doubts are created equal; they come in various shapes, flavors, and sizes. Think of doubt like a check engine light when it comes on in the dashboard of your car. You now know something is wrong; you just don't know what will solve the problem—an oil change or a new transmission. Your soul is your dashboard and doubt is the check engine light that needs to be diagnosed and addressed.

In this chapter I want to primarily focus on one kind of doubt, one that is common, frustrating, and painful.[4] The first kind that usually comes to mind is intellectual doubt. People *do* struggle with factual or content-related doubts about Christianity (these kinds of doubts can usually be remedied by further study, getting specific about what your doubts are, and reading helpful books), but many more struggle with emotional doubt—and this is where I want to focus our discussion. Because if you are anything like me, you received precious little training on how to deal with emotional doubts.

The doubts that I confessed at the beginning of the chapter are emotional doubts. Now I don't have everything figured out, but intellectually I am solidly convinced of the truthfulness of the core aspects of Christianity. My problem is that I let my emotions get the best of me. Listen to what Os Guinness has to say about the power of emotional doubt:

> The problem is not that reason attacks faith but that the emotions overwhelm reason as well as faith, and it is impossible for reason to dissuade them. . . . [This kind of] doubt comes just at the point where the believer's

emotions (vivid imagination, changing moods, erratic feelings, intense reactions) rise up and overpower the understanding of faith. Out-voted, out-gunned, faith is pressed back and hemmed in by the unruly mob of raging emotions that only a while earlier were quiet, orderly citizens of the personality. Reason is cut down, obedience is thrown out, and for a while the rule of emotions is as sovereign as it is violent. The coup d'état is complete.[5]

Who among us hasn't experienced a time when what we believe to be true was swamped by emotions, the nagging what-ifs of life? Many times, what we interpret as intellectual doubt is, in reality, unruly emotions.

Dealing with Emotional Doubt

In Philippians 4:6–9 Paul imparts some excellent advice concerning how Christians can overcome everyday expressions of anxiety and emotional doubt:

> Do not be anxious about anything, but in every situation, by prayer and petition, with thanksgiving, present your requests to God. And the peace of God, which transcends all understanding, will guard your hearts and your minds in Christ Jesus. Finally, brothers and sisters, whatever is true, whatever is noble, whatever is right, whatever is pure, whatever is lovely, whatever is admirable—if anything is excellent or praiseworthy—think about such things. Whatever you have learned or received or heard from me, or seen in me—put it into practice. And the God of peace will be with you.

Gary Habermas derives a four-step process of dealing with emotional doubt from this passage.

1. *Pray.* When we experience anxiety and doubt, we should first cast our anxieties and fears on God in prayer because He cares for us and will help us. And the peace He offers will guard our hearts and minds in Christ Jesus.

2. *Express thanksgiving and praise.* After praying, we should then intentionally praise God for the blessings in our life and express thanksgiving to Him for hearing our prayers.

3. *Change your thinking.* The most essential step in this process is to change our thinking from anxious thoughts to what is true. We need to remind ourselves of what is true in this situation regardless of how we feel.

4. *Practice.* In verse 9 Paul tells us to put this method into practice—in other words, do it. The natural inference is that whenever we encounter anxiety or emotional duress, we should repeat this process. We should practice this when life is going well and especially when we are being inundated by unruly emotions.[6]

In addition to this biblical method of dealing with emotional doubt, we also need to make sure that we are exercising regularly, sleeping enough, eating well, and not isolating ourselves from life-giving friendships as these contribute to our overall emotional and mental health. The remedy to your emotional doubt may just be getting a good night's sleep or grabbing some good food with some friends!

Changing Your Thinking

Let's unpack the third step a bit more since it is so crucial to dealing with emotional doubt. Our thought life is central to living a vibrant Christian life. In Romans 12:2, Paul says that the way we resist the pattern of this world is by renewing our *minds.* Now he could have said a lot of different things instead of mind—heart, emotions, worship—but he didn't. The reason is that what we think about and what we believe are critical to how we live. Dallas Willard, a Christian philosopher who has done a lot of work in the area of spiritual formation, offers penetrating insight into the interplay of thoughts and emotions:

> Our thoughts are one of the most basic sources of our life. They determine the orientation of everything we do and evoke the feelings that frame our world and motivate our actions. Interestingly, you can't evoke thoughts by feeling a certain way, but you can evoke and to some degree control feelings by directing your thoughts. Our power over our thoughts is of great and indispensable assistance in directing and controlling our feelings, which themselves are *not* directly under the guidance of our will. We cannot just choose our feelings.[7]

We don't have direct control over how we feel. But we can *indirectly* affect our emotions by thinking in certain ways. If we want to get at the root of the emotional doubt, then we have to change our thinking and stop allowing ourselves to believe lies. We must tell ourselves the truth—God's truth—until we accept it.[8] Again, this is not a one-time remedy; it's a habit we need to build into our life.

In light of this, I hope that you will no longer feel ashamed when you experience doubt, nor idly sit by and allow emotional doubt to paralyze you with fear. I will let the poignant words of Oswald Chambers conclude our discussion: "Unless we train our emotions they will lead us around by the nose, and we will be captives to every passing impulse or reaction. But once faith is trained to control the emotions and knows how to lean resolutely against weakness of character, another entry way of doubt is sealed shut forever. . . . Much of our distress as Christians comes not because of sin, but because we are ignorant of the laws of our own nature."[9]

THE BIG IDEAS

- "Doubt is not the opposite of faith, nor is it the same as unbelief. Doubt is a state of mind in suspension between faith and unbelief so that it is neither of them wholly and it is each only partly." —OS GUINNESS

- That "spiritual Christians" can't doubt is one of the biggest myths floating around out there (e.g., Abraham and John the Baptist).

- Of all the varieties of doubt we encounter, emotional doubt is the most painful and powerful form.

- Paul gives a four-step method of overcoming emotional doubt and anxiety: (1) pray, (2) express thanksgiving and praise, (3) change your thinking, and (4) practice.

- While we can't directly control our emotions, we can *indirectly* affect them by our thinking.

For Further Discovery

Backus, William, and Marie Chapian. *Telling Yourself the Truth*. Grand Rapids: Baker, 2014.

Craig, William Lane. "Doubt." In *Hard Questions, Real Answers*. Wheaton, IL: Crossway, 2003.

Guinness, Os. *God in the Dark: The Assurance of Faith Beyond a Shadow of Doubt*. Wheaton, IL: Crossway, 1996.

Habermas, Gary. *Dealing with Doubt*. Chicago: Moody Publishers, 1990. This book is available to download for free on his website, along with other helpful audio resources on doubt and apologetics, at GaryHabermas.com.

McGee, Robert S. *The Search for Significance*. Student ed. Nashville: Thomas Nelson, 2003.

McGrath, Alister. *Doubting: Growing Through the Uncertainties of Faith*. Downers Grove, IL: InterVarsity Press, 2007.

Moreland, J. P., and Klaus Issler. "Defeating Two Hardships of Life: Anxiety and Depression." In *The Lost Virtue of Happiness: Discovering the Disciplines of the Good Life*. Colorado Springs: NavPress, 2006.

———. "Embracing the Hiddenness of God." In *The Lost Virtue of Happiness: Discovering the Disciplines of the Good Life*. Colorado Springs: NavPress, 2006.

———. "Forming a Thoughtful Mind Stayed on God." In *The Lost Virtue of Happiness: Discovering the Disciplines of the Good Life*. Colorado Springs: NavPress, 2006.

Willard, Dallas. "Transforming the Mind, 1: Spiritual Formation and Our Thought Life." In *Renovation of the Heart: Putting on the Character of Christ*. Carol Stream, IL: Tyndale House, 2014.

———. "Transforming the Mind, 2: Spiritual Formation and Our Feelings." In *Renovation of the Heart: Putting on the Character of Christ*. Carol Stream, IL: Tyndale House, 2014.

Good News to Share

The good news is that Jesus Christ has provided a way of salvation. Jesus Christ, because of who He is and what He has done, has provided us with a wonderful gift, a way of salvation. Sinners need a Savior, and Jesus Christ is that Savior.

—DOUG CECIL[1]

When they believed Philip as he proclaimed the good news of the kingdom of God and the name of Jesus Christ, they were baptized, both men and women.

—ACTS 8:12[2]

Now, brothers and sisters, I want to remind you of the gospel I preached to you, which you received and on which you have taken your stand. By this gospel you are saved, if you hold firmly to the word I preached to you. Otherwise, you have believed in vain. For what I received I passed on to you as of first importance: that Christ died for our sins according to the Scriptures, that he was buried, that he was raised on the third day according to the Scriptures.

—1 CORINTHIANS 15:1–4

IT WAS THE SUMMER BEFORE MY JUNIOR YEAR OF HIGH SCHOOL IN KNOX-ville, Tennessee. I had spent the summer mowing lawns, working at Kroger, chasing girls (although I never managed to catch any), and trying to be cool—like most high schoolers. On the other hand, a guy named Mike spent a week of his summer at a "sharing your faith" conference in Chicago. During that time, he developed a "five most wanted" list of people at school who needed Christ. Yours truly made the list. So later that fall, as God's providence would have it, we ended up grabbing a bite to eat after a football game, and Mike shared the gospel with me. Over a plate of hot wings he used a "knowing God personally" tract to lead me to Christ. I placed my trust in Jesus that night. Though I had been baptized as an infant and confirmed at the end of elementary school in the Episcopal church, this night was the first time I recall ever *hearing* the gospel.

I am eternally grateful that Mike was faithful to share the gospel with me. It took courage. I could have laughed at him or said that I didn't need Jesus. But God was working in my heart and it was the right time. Mike was prepared to share the good news of Jesus Christ with someone who needed to hear it that day. Are you?

God Is Already Working

Before we talk about what the good news is and how to share it, we first need to recognize a very important truth: God is already working in people's hearts (John 16:8–11). As we speak, the Holy Spirit is convicting people of their sin and their need for a savior. So when you or I come along to share the gospel with someone, we can trust that God has already been working.[3] This truth was driven home to me in a powerful way when I was a sophomore in college and went on a summer project in Clearwater Beach, Florida. On Saturday we would go out on the beach for a few hours and share our faith. I remember sharing my faith with a guy on vacation from Switzerland. After I had finished, I asked him if he wanted to pray to receive Christ—he did. I was shocked! God had prepared the soil of his heart.

Why We Don't Share the Gospel

Almost every reason we don't share the gospel with others boils down to fear. We are afraid that we will look foolish or will offend someone. After all, we want to be liked. We don't want to be like one of those religious freaks on TV, do we? Worse still, what if we don't know how to answer a question they have? Deep down, though, we all know these are sorry excuses to not share the gospel. The first thing we should do is to confess our fears to God and pray for His boldness to share the good news. Next, we can practice so that we know what we want to say and have some good questions to ask when opportunities arise. This is another area where training is necessary. Finally, we can do some homework and learn how to respond to the most common objections to Christianity and explore why we believe what we believe. I'm convinced that many students (and adults for that matter) don't share their faith because they are not convinced that Christianity is actually true (this is why reasons for faith are so important). Even if we don't know what to say, we can learn the art of asking good questions. We'll cover that in a minute, but first the good news.

Good News?

Jesus *is* the good news. Listen to the angel that announced His birth: "I bring you good news that will cause great joy for all the people. Today in the town of David a Savior has been born to you; he is the Messiah, the Lord" (Luke 2:10–11). All of humanity lay in darkness, rebellion, and sin, in need of a savior, when Christ stepped out of eternity and into a manger so that He might become the crucified and resurrected Savior of the world (John 3:16). That is why we celebrate Christmas (His incarnation) and Easter (His passion and resurrection). That is the heart of the good news, and when hearing it there are only two responses: receive it or reject it. You and I have been called to proclaim this good news: "We are therefore Christ's ambassadors, as though God were making his appeal through us. We implore you on Christ's behalf: Be reconciled to God" (2 Cor. 5:20).

There are three essential parts of the good news: (1) all have sinned, (2) Christ died for my sins and arose from the dead to prove it, and (3) salvation is by faith alone. If these aren't in there somewhere, then according to Paul (1 Cor. 15:1–4), it isn't the gospel. Let's look briefly at each aspect.

1. *All have sinned.* The Bible unequivocally affirms that humans have fallen into sin and rebellion: "We all, like sheep, have gone astray, each of us has turned to our own way" (Isa. 53:6), and "all have sinned and fall short of the glory of God" (Rom. 3:23). Sin is "anything contrary to the character and nature of God"[4] and earns everyone death (Rom. 6:23). We all do things we should not, and we don't do the things we should. How good does someone have to be to earn heaven? As good as God. Sin and our impending judgment are the bad news.

2. *Christ died for my sins and arose from the dead to prove it.* While much occurs at the cross of Christ,[5] the core of the gospel is that Jesus

Christ took our sins upon Himself and died in our place to satisfy God's justice and wrath. Peter says, "Christ also suffered once for sins, the righteous for the unrighteous, to bring you to God. He was put to death in the body but made alive in the Spirit" (1 Peter 3:18). And Paul declares, "God demonstrates his own love for us in this: While we were still sinners, Christ died for us" (Rom. 5:8); also, "God made him who had no sin to be sin for us, so that in him we might become the righteousness of God" (2 Cor. 5:21; see also Col. 2:14). Not only did Christ die for my sins, but He rose from the dead to prove it: "He was delivered over to death for our sins and was raised to life for our justification" (Rom. 4:25). The death and resurrection of Christ are the heart of the good news we are to proclaim.[6]

3. *Salvation is by faith alone.* The Bible is clear that salvation cannot be earned (Titus 3:5). Our good deeds are like filthy rags in the presence of a holy God (Isa. 64:6). Paul emphatically states that "it is by grace you have been saved, through faith—and this not from yourselves, it is the gift of God—not by works, so that no one can boast" (Eph. 2:8–9). Trusting in Christ is necessary for the message of the gospel to become effective. Faith that saves involves "transferring your trust from whatever you are currently trusting in to make yourself right with God . . . to what Christ has already accomplished on the Cross on your behalf."[7] Jesus said, "To all who did receive him, to those who believed in his name, he gave the right to become children of God" (John 1:12). The good news must be received.[8]

Sharing Your Testimony

In chapter 23, "Getting to Know You," you will find a plan to discover how God has shaped your life story. Your testimony for sharing your faith is a little different. An evangelistic testimony should briefly and succinctly include your life before Christ, what factors led to your accepting Christ, a restatement of the gospel, and the difference Christ has made in your life since then. Aim for three to five minutes. Then memorize it so that you can work it into a conversation when an opportunity arises. The goal in any gospel presentation is clarity of what the good news is, followed by an offer to respond.

Trusting Christ Is Only the Beginning

But as Darrell Bock has said, "The gospel is about far more than heaven."[9] We don't just get our eternal ticket punched for fire insurance and then put it away for safekeeping. The good news that Christians share with unbelievers provides them the opportunity to "enter his eternal kind of life now"[10] through Jesus Christ. But this is only the beginning—the more we explore what God has said, done, and promised, the greater the good news gets! The kingdom story we find ourselves in begins with creation, encompasses all of reality, and culminates with a Christian being finally transformed into the image of Christ and the restoration of all things in the new heaven and the new earth. There are four elements of the true story of reality that we need to help people find themselves in: creation, fall, redemption, and restoration. Now more than ever, people don't know the whole story so our offer of redemption makes little sense to them. We need to back up and help them see why God created, why the world is such a mess, what God has done about it in Jesus, and how all of us can be redeemed and made a part of the restoration of all things.

Be Creative!

When sharing the good news, be creative. Think outside of the box. I remember as a freshman on spring break with Cru in Panama City, one guy just started digging a hole at the beach. People would ask him what he was doing and he would tell them, "Digging a hole—want to help?" So they picked up the extra shovel to help and he would share Christ with them.

During college, I swam regularly at our apartment pool. It had a hot tub, so one day I began a conversation with a guy about Jesus. Since he had just gotten in the hot tub it would have been rude for him to leave, so we had a good discussion! Bottom line, if you have the core of the good news memorized with some clear illustrations, then the sky is the limit for how you can share it.[11]

The Art of Asking Good Questions

One of the best skills you can acquire to effectively and confidently share your faith, as well as deal with those who challenge your faith, is to learn to ask good questions. As Christians we sometimes feel like we need to do all the talking. Not true. A strategically placed question can be far more powerful than a thirty-minute lecture (see Jesus's use of questions in Matt. 17:25; 21:28–32; Luke 20:1–4, 22–26). This kind of approach is modeled well by Randy Newman in *Questioning Evangelism* and *Corner Conversations*.[12] Both books are excellent. Greg Koukl, author of *Tactics*, has developed a question-based approach called the "Columbo tactic"[13] in which a person can go on the offensive in a disarming way. Columbo was a bumbling TV detective who everyone thought was harmless, yet he had the annoying habit of discovering the truth by asking a series of innocuous questions. Asking good questions will be much better received than preaching at someone. The following are two basic questions with an optional follow-up question:

1. *What do you mean by that?* This is an information-gathering question that clarifies what the other person is saying. For example, someone says, "There is no God." You could respond, "What do you mean by 'God'?" This question is important because it engages the other person and challenges them to think more deeply about what they are saying (maybe they don't know what they mean by "God" because no one has ever asked them).

2. *How did you come to that conclusion?* The first question helps you know *what* they think; this question explores *why* they think this way. What are their reasons for believing this? Of course this assumes that they have thought through why they believe something; this provides them the opportunity to give an account of why they believe it. Suppose that a person says, "God is everything and everywhere." Rather than saying, "No he isn't; God is omnipresent yet distinct from creation," you could ask, "How did you come to believe that?" This will be much more effective!

3. *Have you ever considered . . . ?* If you are comfortable with the conversation and would like to press a point further, ask this third question. After listening to what a person believes and why, you may discover a weak point to expose. Do this with a question: "It seems that you are saying that you and I are 'God,' but also that the waste flowing through a sewer pipe is 'God' too, is that correct?" By asking questions you have exposed an absurd argument. Perhaps they will abandon it and be more open to what you have to say about the historical Jesus.

Memorize these questions and start working them into your conversations. Employing this approach will put you in the driver's seat for most of the conversations you will have. (This works especially well on professors who try to bully Christians in class. Don't make any claims; keep the burden of proof on them by asking questions.)[14] You don't have to have all the answers; you just need to learn how to ask good questions.

Some Plant, Some Water, but God Causes the Growth

We all have a part to play in the process of people coming to know Christ. For example, you may encounter someone in college whose grandmother has been praying for him for the past fifteen years, and his parents have shared the gospel with him several times. Yet, God may give you the privilege of leading this person to Christ. Or your role may be to plant a seed that someone else down the road will water. God's Word reminds us that we all play a part, but it is God alone who causes the growth (1 Cor. 3:6–7). A productive spiritual conversation means helping people move closer to trusting Jesus. It may become obvious that our role in a conversation is to help remove some bad reasons for rejecting belief in God. We need to remind ourselves that our goal in sharing Christ is being faithful to do it: "Success in evangelism is simply communicating Christ in the power of the Holy Spirit and leaving the results to God."[15]

THE BIG IDEAS

- We must all be prepared to share the good news of Jesus Christ, and with God's help we can overcome our fear of sharing our faith with others.

- There are three essential parts of the good news:
  (1) all have sinned;
  (2) Christ died for my sins and arose from the dead to prove it; and
  (3) salvation is by faith alone.

- The gospel is about far more than heaven; it is about eternal life *now* as well. We need to help people find themselves in the true story of reality: creation, fall, redemption, and restoration.

- Learn the art of asking good questions. This will help take the pressure off of you as you get into conversations about the good news.

- "Success in evangelism is simply communicating Christ in the power of the Holy Spirit and leaving the results to God." —WILLIAM LANE CRAIG

For Further Discovery

Bock, Darrell L. *Recovering the Real Lost Gospel: Reclaiming the Gospel as Good News*. Nashville: B&H Publishing, 2010.

Cahill, Mark. *One Thing You Can't Do in Heaven*. Bartlesville, OK: Genesis Publishing, 2004.

Cecil, Douglas M. *The 7 Principles of an Evangelistic Life*. Chicago: Moody Publishers, 2003.

Coleman, Robert E. *The Master Plan of Evangelism*. 2nd ed., abridged. Grand Rapids: Revell, 2010.

Hull, Bill. *The Complete Book of Discipleship: On Being and Making Followers of Christ*. Carol Stream, IL: Tyndale House, 2014.

Koukl, Gregory. *Tactics: A Game Plan for Discussing Your Christian Convictions*. Grand Rapids: Zondervan, 2009.

Moreland, J. P., and Tim Muehlhoff. *The God Conversation: Using Stories and Illustrations to Explain Your Faith*. Downers Grove, IL: InterVarsity Press, 2009.

Newman, Randy. *Corner Conversations: Engaging Dialogues About God and Life*. Grand Rapids: Kregel, 2006.

———. *Questioning Evangelism: Engaging People's Hearts the Way Jesus Did*. 2nd ed. Grand Rapids: Kregel, 2017.

To the Ends
of the Earth

When he saw the crowds, he had compassion on them, because they were harassed and helpless, like sheep without a shepherd. Then he said to his disciples, "The harvest is plentiful but the workers are few. Ask the Lord of the harvest, therefore, to send out workers into his harvest field."

—MATTHEW 9:36–38

How, then, can they call on the one they have not believed in? And how can they believe in the one of whom they have not heard? And how can they hear without someone preaching to them?

—ROMANS 10:14

The gospel is bearing fruit and growing throughout the whole world—just as it has been doing among you since the day you heard it and truly understood God's grace.

—COLOSSIANS 1:6

"FOR GOD SO LOVED THE WORLD." IF YOU HAVE GROWN UP ANYWHERE near the church, then you are familiar with this passage from John 3:16. Unfortunately, this extraordinary verse has become all too ordinary to us. Grass is green, the sky is blue, and God loves the world—*what else is new?*

It shouldn't be this way, because this is truly a remarkable verse. The God and Creator of everything passionately loves, and actively desires to have a relationship with, every single person on the earth (1 Tim. 2:3–5). And He pursues us in spite of our helpless, rebellious, and sinful state (Rom. 5:8)! As

Christians we should love the world because God loves the world. Moreover, we are called to represent Christ to our world: "We are therefore Christ's ambassadors, as though God were making his appeal through us" (2 Cor. 5:20). Billions desperately need to be reconciled to God through the life-giving message of Jesus Christ.

Aren't We All Missionaries?

Every Christian, by virtue of being a follower of Christ, has the same general calling: to follow Christ in every area of life. But contained within this general calling we discover a specific sense of calling, the expressions of which vary from person to person according to gifting, desires, and life experiences. Just as some Christians are called to be pastors, or others to be business owners or scientists, some are called to be cross-cultural missionaries. We need missionaries who will go to the places that the impact of the gospel has barely touched.

If you are a Christian, then you are a minister of the gospel (1 Peter 2:9). Ministry is not just for the paid professionals. One of the joys of life is discovering God's purpose for us in His kingdom—whether that means serving faithfully in your local community or ministering to unreached people groups. Who knows, God may be tugging at your heart even as you read these words to consider going on a short-term mission trip. He may be calling and preparing you to go proclaim His message to an unreached people group one day. The world is full of places that need Jesus. Pray for an open heart to consider wherever God may lead.

The World Needs Jesus

Some have answered the call to go to the ends of the earth, but many more are needed. According to the Joshua Project,[1] there are 7.38 billion people in the world, which translates into 16,508 people groups. Of these, 6,686 people groups have been unreached by the gospel. This amounts to about 3.11 billion people. Many of them are concentrated in the "10/40 Window"—an area of the world that contains the largest population of non-Christians in the world (this area extends from ten to forty degrees north of the equator, and stretches from North Africa across to China). The need is clear. Jesus put it like this: "The harvest is plentiful but the workers are few. Ask the Lord of the harvest, therefore, to send out workers into his harvest field" (Matt. 9:37–38).

God Is at Work in the World

God is moving in powerful ways all over the world. Whole books have been written recounting stories of devotion, redemption, and personal sacrifice for the name of Christ.[2] It encourages my faith to learn of the work God is doing. Here is an amazing story I came across from the Jesus Film Project:

> Most of the people living in the village of Moogu are farmers, and many who reside in the northern region of Ghana follow pagan gods. Only 3 percent practice Islam, and the remaining 2 percent follow Jesus. The "JESUS" film team decided this was a good place to show the film and perform an outreach in the spring of 2003.
>
> The population in the town of Moogu exceeds 3,000. Four hundred and fifty of those decided to attend the screening of the "JESUS" film last March. At the completion of the movie, the team invited audience members to pray a prayer and give their lives to the Lord—but no one moved. Discouraged, the team thanked those who came to see the film, and began to pack up the equipment. While they were doing so, a man named Mbugri approached the team and asked for prayer. The team prayed for him and he gave his life to Jesus. The people were amazed. They couldn't figure out how Mbugri understood the movie and prayer—because he was deaf.
>
> Mbugri explained that, in the middle of watching the movie, he began to hear for the first time! He listened intently to the gospel message, and believed it was the healing hand of Christ that allowed him to hear. Because of the miracle, his entire family of eight placed their faith in Jesus, as did many others at the film showing.[3]

Wonderful stories like this could be multiplied. God is using ordinary Christians to be a part of extraordinary works as the good news is proclaimed around the globe! Faithfulness, availability, and obedience are all He requires.

How You Can Get Involved

As a college student, how can you get involved in God's kingdom program around the world? Here are three suggestions:

1. *Pray.* First, pray for God to give you a heart for the world. Next, buy a copy of Jason Mandryk's *Operation World* and begin praying for a country a day during your devotions (prayer guides are available online as well as at www.operationworld.org/country-lists). Finally, pray that God would show you if He is calling you to go and proclaim the good news of Jesus Christ to the world.

2. *Support.* You can give to the work of missionaries around the globe. There are always needs. But beyond the financial needs, people need to be made aware of the opportunities and needs around the world. Brainstorm how you can help get the word out (explore the resources at the end of this chapter). Finally, encourage people you know who are thinking of going into the mission field. Consider writing these missionaries via social media, email, or letter (or even go old school and send care packages); the missionaries I have talked with tell me this is a great encouragement to them!

3. *Go.* You have a precious commodity as a collegian—freedom. At this stage of life, many of you have no house payment, spouse, or children to consider yet. You will likely never be as free as you are right now. You also have spring breaks and summers off. So, prayerfully consider talking to a group of your friends and then go on a short-term mission trip together; it will forever change your life and the lives of those you encounter. Also, consider taking a road trip to Urbana (InterVarsity's annual student mission conference; www.urbana.org). Along with thousands of other college students, you will discover what God is up to around the world and how you can get involved further.

As followers of Christ, what we cannot afford to do is *nothing*—the need is too great and the news too wonderful.

Not Without a Price

I wish I could report that the world always embraces the gospel with joy and celebration. But the sad reality is that people are blinded to the truth and hostile to the things of God. Countless brothers and sisters in Christ are being persecuted for the name of Christ every day. For example, former Muslims have been disowned, beaten, raped, tortured, and killed because they converted to Christianity. Jesus Christ told His disciples, "'A servant is not greater than his master.' If they persecuted me, they will persecute you also" (John 15:20). We need to pray for our brothers and sisters as they make the ultimate sacrifice to take the gospel to people groups who have never heard it. For how to pray more specifically for the persecuted church, visit the Voice of the Martyr's website at www.persecution.com.

THE BIG IDEAS

- "For God so loved the world that he gave his one and only Son, that whoever believes in him shall not perish but have eternal life" (John 3:16).
- The need is great, the news is wonderful, and God is calling you to get involved: (1) pray, (2) support, and (3) go.
- Pray for the persecuted church.

For Further Discovery

Corduan, Winfried. *Neighboring Faiths: A Christian Introduction to World Religions*. Downers Grove, IL: InterVarsity Press, 2012.

DC Talk, and The Voice of the Martyrs. *Jesus Freaks: Martyrs, Stories of Those Who Stood for Jesus: The Ultimate Jesus Freaks*. Minneapolis: Bethany House, 2014.

Mandryk, Jason. *Operation World: The Definitive Prayer Guide to Every Nation*. Downers Grove, IL: InterVarsity Press, 2010.

Moreau, A. Scott, Gary Corwin, and Gary B. McGee. *Introducing World Missions: A Biblical, Historical, and Practical Survey*. Encountering Missions. Grand Rapids: Baker, 2015.

Café 1040 at www.cafe1040.com.

Camino Global at www.caminoglobal.org.

International Mission Board at www.imb.org.

Jesus Film Project at www.jesusfilm.org.
New Tribes Mission at www.ntm.org.
Operation Mobilization at omusa.org.
Operation World at www.operationworld.org.
Pioneers at www.pioneers.org.
Send International at www.send.org.

Getting to Know You

I praise you because I am fearfully and wonderfully made;
your works are wonderful,
I know that full well.
My frame was not hidden from you
when I was made in the secret place,
when I was woven together in the depths of the earth.
Your eyes saw my unformed body;
all the days ordained for me were written in your book
before one of them came to be.

—PSALM 139:14–16

We shall not cease from exploration
And the end of all of our exploring
Will be to arrive where we started
And know the place for the first time.

—T. S. ELIOT[1]

The unexamined life is not worth living.

—SOCRATES

MIDDLE SCHOOL IS ABOUT SURVIVAL. IS THERE ANY MORE AWKWARD period of life? High school is a transition from survival to fitting in. Social status is divvied out according to various activities, clubs, girlfriends/boyfriends, sports. But college is a unique mix of survival, transition, fitting in, and personal definition. You will begin at the bottom of the social food chain yet again. But there is a world of difference between college and high school. College has a unique ability to squash you into a certain mold—this shape is mostly determined by the people you spend the majority of your time with in the context of your newfound freedom from your parents. As the book of

Proverbs reminds us, "Whoever walks with the wise becomes wise, but the companion of fools will suffer harm" (13:20 ESV). In fact, one of the ways to ensure that you build a strong Christian faith that lasts far beyond the college years is surrounding yourself with wise relationships (e.g., parents, peers, mentors, and significant others).

One of the most important aspects of maturing as a human being and a follower of Christ is becoming increasingly more aware of your identity. Knowledge of who you are and especially who you are in Christ will provide stability as you walk through tumultuous emotional and social situations in college (e.g., whether to give in to peer pressure or potentially face ridicule for Christ's sake) and as you engage in authentic relationships with others. This doesn't happen overnight; it's a process. In this chapter we are going to explore what makes you . . . you. Who are you? Are you a social chameleon taking on the characteristics and expectations of whatever group you happen to be around? Are you quiet and reserved, or loud and outgoing? (Ever asked yourself why?) Are you energized by being in a large group or by being by yourself? How does the way Christ sees you affect your daily life? How have your various life experiences contributed to the person you are becoming— for good or ill? These are just some of the important questions we will be exploring. Much of what will be learned as a result of this chapter depends on your engaging the process of honest self-discovery. Find out who you are and then be that person on purpose. It will free you from a lot of pressure to perform, and it will allow you to focus more on how God wants to use you for His glory.

Natural Identity

There are certain aspects of our lives that we all have in common simply because we're human, and regardless of whether we are a Christian or not.[2] For lack of a better title, let's call this category *natural identity*. There are five key aspects that make up your natural identity: *image of God, roles, gender, temperament,* and *heritage.*

- *Image of God.* Everyone on the planet is made in the image of God and thus is invested with intrinsic dignity. Your dignity is not grounded in what you are able to do or not do or what color your skin happens to be; you are valuable because God created you (Gen. 1:26; 9:6). Period.

- *Roles.* Another part of our natural identity is the particular roles we happen to play during various seasons of life. This is part of the larger discussion around vocation/calling. For example, right now you are a student and a son or daughter. These are God-given roles you play—they can and do change in life. This is why it is not good to confuse your roles with your understanding of your core identity. Roles *express* who you are in a season of life; they do not *constitute* who you are.

- *Gender.* Our gender is integral to who we are. We view life as a male or as a female.[3] Though equal in value and dignity, male and female are different by God's design (Gen. 1:27; Matt. 19:4). Admittedly we need to move past stereotypes like all real men climb mountains and have beards while real women can't be assertive or strong leaders. And it is unwise to allow the prevailing winds of culture to define what it means to be male or female; we need to look to the Scriptures for our definition. We must resist the temptation to understand "equal" as "sameness."

- *Temperament.* Temperament is another aspect of our natural identity. We all tend to respond in different ways to different situations. Some people are energized by being alone (introverts), while others love being in groups (extroverts). Personality tests (e.g., Myers-Briggs or DISC) organize people according to patterns of behavior or tendencies. These general categories are neither good nor bad, but they often give us helpful insight into why certain situations frustrate us or make us feel comfortable.

- *Heritage.* This is the final aspect of our natural identity. Everyone has a heritage. We were all born to parents in a particular part of the world. Most of you reading this book have been born in America, and that fact significantly shapes your outlook on life. And within American culture there are subcultures that have shaped us as well. For the most part, heritage is something that happens to us; we don't choose it. However, we can choose how we will respond to our heritage and what kind of legacy we intend to leave.

Supernatural Identity

In addition to our natural identity, we also have a supernatural identity (those aspects of our lives that we possess by virtue of being in Christ). Our supernatural identity is comprised of our kingdom values, identity in Christ (both individual and corporate), and spiritual gifts.

When we became Christians, God "rescued us from the dominion of darkness and brought us into the kingdom of the Son he loves" (Col. 1:13; see also Matt. 6:33). Our perspective and orientation have changed at a fundamental level. We now seek to value what God values and to live for Him, not just ourselves. And living in light of this new kingdom reality will deeply affect who we are.

It is safe to say that when we trusted Christ, a lot of really important things happened. There are things true of us now that weren't before. God now sees us in a certain way—in Christ. Here are just a few of our spiritual blessings in Christ: we become redeemed and forgiven people (Eph. 1:7), God's workmanship (Eph. 2:10), children of God (John 1:12; Rom. 8:15–17), new creations (2 Cor. 5:17), friends of Christ (John 15:15), and fellow heirs with Christ (Rom. 8:17). This list is astounding. For more of what is true of you now that you are in Christ, read Romans 5:1–11 and Ephesians 1–2.

Not only does being in Christ have individual benefits, it has corporate implications as well. We have been baptized into the body of Christ (1 Cor. 12:13) and are individually members of one another (Rom. 12:5). With this new corporate identity comes certain privileges and obligations (see Eph. 4 and Col. 3), and these new realities are key to understanding who we are. For practical implications like how to avoid the performance trap, I highly recommend reading the student edition of *The Search for Significance* by Robert McGee.

When you trusted Christ, you were indwelt and sealed by the Holy Spirit (Eph. 1:13–14). One of the implications of this is that God's Spirit has supernaturally gifted you for serving and edifying the body of Christ. God has specifically designed the function you are to play within the body of Christ. Everyone has been given at least one spiritual gift (1 Peter 4:10). One of the best ways to discover your spiritual gift is to start serving in different areas in your local church and then allow other Christians to observe you and give you feedback.[4]

Shaped by Your Life Experiences

Through my involvement both as a member and eventually as the equipping pastor at Fellowship Bible Church, and my time on staff with Spiritual Formation at Dallas Theological Seminary, I was exposed to a process called *life story*. This process really helped me become more aware of who I am as a person and also my fit within the body of Christ. I am far more comfortable in my own skin than I used to be. While I can't walk you through this whole process in just one chapter, I can outline some important questions for you to ask as you begin this important process of self-discovery.

We often underestimate the effect our upbringing has had on shaping our lives. A core part of your life story can be gleaned from the four *h*'s—heritage, heroes, high points, and hard times. As you reflect on the questions below, take out a sheet of paper and jot down the thoughts that immediately come to mind. Don't evaluate, filter out, or organize any of your answers yet—just write. Brainstorm through this list and then later you can come back through and highlight the especially formative experiences (i.e., the ones that significantly shaped you). Also look for themes during different stages of life (e.g., moved a lot, insecurity, isolation, tangibly cared for by others, successful, popular). Then gather these themes together and weave them into your life story. Perhaps the most important and scary part of the life-story process is sharing it with others in your life—inviting them to get to know the real you, warts and all. But the best part is being unconditionally loved and accepted.[5]

1. *Heritage* involves the fundamental and seemingly ordinary elements of your life. The contents of this category rarely appear striking or extraordinary. Your heritage may contain elements you would write off as mundane, commonplace, or uneventful, but you may discover experiences and relationships of great significance. Some questions to ask as you think through this category are

   • How have my parents or primary caregivers influenced me?

   • What was the general atmosphere in my home as I grew up?

   • How have my ethnicity and culture played an important role in my life?

- What have my peer relationships (with those my own age) been like over the years?
- Have I moved around a lot? What effect do I think this has had on me?

2. *Heroes* are people who make a distinctly positive impression on your life through words or actions. They can be nearly anyone: a parent, relative, neighbor, teacher, friend, or coach. Heroes also can be people you have never met, such as political leaders or historical figures. Somehow, heroes touch you in life-changing ways. Heroes can come into your life at any time. A hero may be a person from your heritage (such as your mom, dad, or friend), a person you associate with at a high point in your life (such as a teacher, coach, camp counselor, or political figure), or a person who helped you in a hard time (such as a relative or even an author). Some questions to ask as you think through this category are

- Who has influenced me for good? How did they specifically do so?
- After whom would I like to model my life? Why?
- Who has shaped my character or direction in life? How? Why?

3. *High points* are those periods or events that have a distinctly positive meaning in your life. High points are often the best and most fulfilling seasons or experiences of your life. These times might include winning a district championship, making the honor roll, receiving an award, going on a vacation, visiting a long-distance friend, having a year of peace in the home, enjoying two years at a great job, or getting married. Some questions to ask as you think through this category are

- What accomplishments have brought me fulfillment or special recognition? How? Why?
- What events or people have brought me great joy?
- At what points in my life did I feel particularly good about life? Why?
- When have I made my greatest contributions to life or others? How?

4. *Hard times* are those seasons of life or relationships that have been particularly difficult or painful. Hard times might include divorce, the loss of a friend or relative, struggle with an addiction, times of abuse, a breakup with a boyfriend or girlfriend, an injury or sickness, a period of

loneliness, or a time of great pressure and anxiety. Some questions to ask as you think through this category are

- What incidents in my life are hard to talk about with others? Why?
- Who or what has been a source of pain in my life? When? Why?
- Toward whom do I harbor anger or bitterness?
- Whom do I struggle to forgive? Why?
- What has brought me great disappointment? Why?
- To what addictions or abuses have I been exposed either in my own life or in the lives of others?

5. *General questions*
- What have been the most influential experiences in my life?
- What life dreams have I had in the past?
- When I think of my parents, what memories come to mind?
- What are significant questions with which I have wrestled in my lifetime?

This process may seem tedious at first, but in our fast-paced society it is rare for people to think about the experiences that have molded them into who they are. Remember that God wastes nothing. Don't be afraid to enter into this transformative process. It can get messy, but some of the most significant growth we experience happens in the messiest places. So press on and answer these questions honestly; they may reveal some breakthrough areas of discovery for you. They also might reveal some potential blind spots that need to be dealt with in the process of becoming the man or woman God desires you to be.

Some Things I've Learned About Myself Along the Way

As I went through a process like the one above, I discovered a major theme about my life: the progression of moving from pure dependence on myself to dependence on God and others. Due to various life experiences, I tend to do things on my own. I learned early that people disappoint you, so I stopped opening myself up to the disappointment. But God has used circumstances later in my life to reshape this unhealthy approach to relationships. I am now learning to depend on God and others in a healthier way.

Another theme I discovered was my fear of disappointing those whom I am close to or look up to. I feel the weight (to an unhealthy degree) of not wanting to let anyone down. Being aware of this struggle helps me in the process of relating to others. Overall, knowing my life story—my strengths and struggles—allows me to be more intentional about areas in my life that I am asking the Spirit of God to transform.

THE BIG IDEAS

- Our *natural identity* includes the image of God, roles, gender, temperament, and heritage.

- Our *supernatural identity* includes kingdom values, identity in Christ (both individual and corporate), and spiritual gifts.

- A core part of your life story can be gleaned from the four *h*'s: heritage, heroes, high points, and hard times.

For Further Discovery

Allender, Dan B. *To Be Told: Know Your Story, Shape Your Future.* Colorado Springs: WaterBrook, 2009.

Anderson, Neil. *Who I Am in Christ.* Grand Rapids: Baker, 2001.

Center for Christian Leadership at Dallas Theological Seminary. *Community: Discovering Who We Are Together.* Transforming Life Series. Colorado Springs: NavPress, 2004.

———. *Identity: Investigating Who I Am.* Transforming Life Series. Colorado Springs: NavPress, 2004.

Cloud, Henry. *Changes That Heal: The Four Shifts That Make Everything Better . . . And That Everyone Can Do.* Grand Rapids: Zondervan, 2009.

Fey, Marc, Don Ankenbrandt, and Frank Johnson. *210 Project: Discover Your Place in God's Story.* Birmingham, AL: Alliance Publishing Group, 2011.

McGee, Robert S. *The Search for Significance.* Nashville: Thomas Nelson, 2003.

Rees, Erik. *S.H.A.P.E.: Finding and Fulfilling Your Unique Purpose for Life*. Grand Rapids: Zondervan, 2008.

Seidel, Gail. "Life Story and Spiritual Formation." In *Foundations of Spiritual Formation: A Community Approach to Becoming Like Christ*. Edited by Paul Pettit. Grand Rapids: Kregel, 2008.

Zacharias, Ravi. *The Grand Weaver: How God Shapes Us Through the Events of Our Lives*. Grand Rapids: Zondervan, 2010.

Zacharias, Ravi, and R. S. B. Sawyer. *Walking from East to West: God in the Shadows*. Grand Rapids: Zondervan, 2010.

---

210 Project at 210Project.com. "Discover your place in God's story."

Here's to Your Health

Anxiety weighs down the heart.
—PROVERBS 12:25

A cheerful heart is good medicine,
but a crushed spirit dries up the bones.
—PROVERBS 17:22

An ounce of prevention is worth a pound
of cure.
—HENRY DE BRACTON[1]

GOD DESIGNED US TO FUNCTION AS WHOLE PEOPLE. UNFORTUNATELY humans generally prefer disintegration! You and I are pretty complicated creatures. When something goes wrong in our life, there is no "easy button" to push that can fix everything; the root of the issue could be physical, spiritual, social, emotional, or mental. To complicate matters further, each of these aspects of human nature is interrelated. Throw in the fact that sin has corrupted every aspect of our being and the relationships we enter into, and we've got a real mess on our hands. For example, if we are worried in our soul or heart, it negatively affects our brain chemistry. When we don't eat well or sleep enough, our emotions can get all out of whack and we can feel depressed. If you've had a fight with your roommate, your mom, or the person you are dating, this can affect your intellectual ability to finish a paper. The goal of this chapter is twofold. First, I hope to convince you to take your overall health in college seriously. And second, I want to help you diagnose whether or not you are firing on all cylinders and then determine what part of you could use a tune-up.

Physical

Everybody desires to be physically healthy, so why aren't we? There are several reasons, but probably the biggest one—if we are honest—is lack of self-discipline. (That's what it boils down to for me.) We simply become lazy or complacent. As Christians, we have additional incentive to take care of our bodies because we only get one, and it has been bought with a price (1 Cor. 6:20). We are called to be good stewards of what God has entrusted to us. Moreover, it would be tragic to spend the first part of life preparing to attempt great things for God only to be sidelined by poor health decisions. As we begin to assess our physical health, we can address three categories: *exercise, sleep,* and *nutrition.* Here are a few diagnostic questions:

1. Besides walking to class, list the physical exercises you engage in during an average week (kind of activity), how often per week (frequency), and the time you spend (duration). Use a Fitbit or download a health app to help with this.

2. On average, how many hours of sleep do you get each night? What is your usual bedtime? What is your usual wake-up time?

3. I assume many of your meals are from the cafeteria. Buffet style can be dangerous, so what process do you normally go through to select the food you eat, and how much? Or is it food at first sight?

Here are some suggestions to improve your overall physical health:

1. Watch your portion size when it comes to food. (This is convicting for me!) Try not to eat too late at night, and limit the fast food!

2. Exercise. Swimming is my favorite form of exercise. It's a great workout (cardio and muscle training) in about thirty minutes (I usually throw in some push-ups and sit-ups). Not only is there a great physical benefit, but it also reduces stress and anxiety as well as clears the mind.

3. Join an intramural sports team with some friends.

4. If you are a morning person, set your devotional time right before breakfast; this will help you get up at a consistent time.

5. Take a twenty-minute power nap when you get the chance to reenergize. Sleep is good!

Spiritual

We are spiritual beings, so it is important to cultivate our spiritual life. Since there is already a chapter dealing with this (chapter 9), I won't revisit that material here. Instead, I want to focus on the social expression of your spiritual life—your engagement with a local church and campus ministries. One of the reasons I enjoyed college so much was my involvement with Cru; it made all the difference. Not only did I meet great friends, but it also gave me a place to participate, serve, and lead in ministry with others. This opportunity was a catalyst for my spiritual growth.

While it is more difficult to find and plug into a church when away at college, you really need to make an effort to do this. Being connected to the body of Christ is not optional for the Christian. A campus ministry will connect you with your peers on campus; the church will connect you with a more diverse group of God's people. By the way, a good way to find a church is to ask around and also look online. Be sure to check the doctrinal statement to make sure that it is a biblically based church. Odds are, if you are involved with a campus ministry, then the staff could recommend a good church. Both are helpful and needed in college. Here are some questions to help assess your spiritual health:

1. How often do you read the Bible (not so God will love you more, but so you will grow spiritually)? How often do you pray?

2. Where do you attend church? How often? Would you be missed by anyone if you stopped attending, or have you remained anonymous? Where are you serving others?

3. What campus ministries are you currently involved in?

Now for some suggestions for improving your spiritual health:

1. Set a goal for the week of having a consistent time in God's Word and in prayer.

2. Join a small group at church and/or volunteer to serve the body of Christ in some capacity.

3. Seek out a campus ministry to join. Three excellent ones are Cru (www.cru.org), InterVarsity Christian Fellowship (www.intervarsity.org), and The Navigators (www.navigators.org).

Social

Going off to college affects both you and your family in significant ways. Whether you are a commuter student or living on campus, the dynamics will be different than they were in high school, and this has to be navigated together. Many of you will become more of a familiar visitor. Some things will change relationally, yet others will stay the same. Like some of you, my parents divorced when I was young. Navigating relationships in a family affected by divorce adds another layer of difficulty to your family picture. Or, maybe your home was a volatile environment you couldn't wait to exit. Whatever your situation, part of the process of growing up is learning how to relate to your parents as an adult, while still honoring them (Eph. 6:2). This is not always easy.

All of us have a tendency toward isolation, believing the lie that we don't need anyone but ourselves. Therefore, developing and maintaining healthy friendships will take some effort and intentionality on our part. But it is definitely worth it. The highlight of my college experience was the friends that I made. We had fun together and we served Christ together. I honestly don't know that I would have survived and flourished in college had it not been for my close friends.

Some questions to ask when checking your social health:

1. When was the last *significant* conversation you had with a friend? What was it about?
2. If you received bad news today, who would be the first person you would talk to?
3. Would you describe yourself as a loner? Would others describe you that way?
4. Do you shy away from vulnerability in relationships? Why?
5. How often do you speak with your family? Is it all surface conversation, or is there some depth?
6. As a Christian, are your one or two closest friends also serious about following Jesus?

Some suggestions for improving social relationships:

1. Be intentional about spending time with close friends. Your inner circle needs to be serious about following Jesus (2 Tim. 2:22).

2. Take deep friendships that have become comfortable to the next level. For example, the longer we know someone, the easier it is not to *really* share what's going on inside.

3. Call home—connect regularly with family . . . or at least make the effort.

4. When you go home for Christmas and the summer, don't revert to being the kid your parents have to take care of. Be responsible and act more like an adult around them (make your own bed, put your dishes away, ask how you can help, etc.).

Emotional and Mental

How we feel (emotional) and what we think about (mental) have a *huge* impact on our overall health. In fact, if something is off emotionally, we can often feel it physically. If I am starting to gain weight, I can go to the gym to remedy this. But if I am being constantly bombarded by negative thoughts and irrational fears, then what can I do? We covered some of these issues in the chapter on dealing with doubt (chapter 20), so in this section, I want to address the difficult issues of anxiety and depression.

Can a genuine Christian struggle with anxiety and depression? The answer is yes. If a Christian struggles in these areas, does that mean they are not very spiritual? Unfortunately many think so, but this is false. The answer to some forms of depression and anxiety can be spiritual (e.g., demonic attack[2] or spiritual apathy). But many times it is due to either a repeated habit of negative thinking which deeply affects the emotions or a chemical imbalance in the brain. It is here where Christian therapists and prescription drugs can be of great help to a struggling believer.[3]

In my senior year of college, the year leading up to my marriage, I experienced a period of dark depression. I remember that it had become so bad that I could no longer push a broom at my construction job. There were issues in my past that I needed to address, and my Christian therapist determined that I needed some mild prescription drugs to help me deal with it. Antidepressants don't fix the problem; their role is to help put us in a place where our emotional highs and lows are more normal. I am not embarrassed by sharing this. It is no more a sign of spiritual weakness to take an aspirin for a headache than it is to take a prescribed antidepressant to help regulate your brain chemistry. By God's grace, through meeting with a counselor for several months and taking medication for a season, I was able to overcome this period of depression. If you struggle with these kinds of issues, you are not alone.[4] Here are some questions to ask:

1. What do you think about most often?
2. Would you say that you have healthy patterns of thinking or does your negative thinking tend to spiral out of control?
3. What do you do when you experience negative thoughts? How do you handle them?
4. Do you have the same unhealthy, defeating thoughts over and over again?
5. Do you live at the mercy of your emotions?
6. How do you respond emotionally in tense situations or conflict?

Some suggestions for improving your mental and emotional health:

1. Pray for God's help, dwell on God's Word, and tell yourself the truth.
2. Recognize some of the unhealthy patterns in your emotional life and seek help from a mentor, a qualified professional, or a deep friend.
3. Exercise regularly, get enough sleep, and eat right.
4. Spend time with friends, and laugh often and loud.

Have Fun!

College is a wonderful opportunity to enjoy life with friends and have some fun. There are many stories I could tell to back up this claim, but one that stands out is a spring break trip to Colorado. Tim and I loaded up a borrowed Nissan Pathfinder with a case of Mountain Dew and drove from Murfreesboro, Tennessee, to Denver, Colorado, to go skiing—on a shoestring budget. In not one of our finer moments, we wired the portable CD player directly off the car battery. Somewhere in Kansas, I was driving along and heard Tim yell. I saw him trying to put out the car mat that had caught fire due to the heat of the wire connected to the CD player! This was only the beginning of an unforgettable trip, which involved being snowed in at the house of his old friend instead of skiing most of the week, my painful first attempt at snowboarding, paying for expensive repairs to our friend's Nissan so we could get home, and visiting a very scary truck stop in Oklahoma at three in the morning. But I will never forget it; even now, it makes me smile.

So here you are in college with friends, a little money, someone's car, and time. Take a road trip somewhere. You have to be within striking distance either of something interesting or worthy of ridicule. Add some experiences to your life. Hop in the car and go—make some memories that you can then embellish as you get older for dramatic effect. (Just so you know, the details in my story are all true!) You will be amazed at what this will do for your overall health—minus the burgers and fries—and perspective on life.[5]

THE BIG IDEAS

- God designed us to function as *whole* people (physical, spiritual, social, emotional, and mental).

- The physical, spiritual, social, emotional, and mental parts of us all affect each other. In order to live a healthy life, you have to give yourself a regular checkup and then be intentional about pursuing health in that area.

For Further Discovery

Backus, William, and Marie Chapian. *Telling Yourself the Truth*. Grand Rapids: Baker, 2014.

Biebel, David B., and Harold G. Koenig. *Simple Health: Easy and Inexpensive Things You Can Do to Improve Your Health*. Lake Mary, FL: Siloam, 2005.

Hart, Archibald D. *The Anxiety Cure: You Can Find Emotional Tranquility and Wholeness*. Nashville: Thomas Nelson, 2001.

Ingram, Chip. *The Invisible War: What Every Believer Needs to Know About Satan, Demons, and Spiritual Warfare*. Grand Rapids: Baker, 2015.

Moreland, J. P., and Klaus Issler. "Cultivating Spiritual Friendships." In *The Lost Virtue of Happiness: Discovering the Disciplines of the Good Life*. Colorado Springs: NavPress, 2006.

———. "Defeating Two Hardships in Life: Anxiety and Depression." In *The Lost Virtue of Happiness: Discovering the Disciplines of the Good Life*. Colorado Springs: NavPress, 2006.

Sticks and Stones

Words kill, words give life;
   they're either poison or fruit—you choose.
                              —PROVERBS 18:21 MSG

Do not let any unwholesome talk come out of your mouths, but only what is helpful for building others up according to their needs, that it may benefit those who listen.
                              —EPHESIANS 4:29

Those who consider themselves religious and yet do not keep a tight rein on their tongues deceive themselves, and their religion is worthless.
                              —JAMES 1:26

"STICKS AND STONES MAY BREAK MY BONES, BUT WORDS WILL NEVER hurt me." Yeah, right! This has to be one of the biggest lies we learn as kids. I don't know about you, but I can think of plenty of times I would have rather been hit with a stick, bludgeoned with a stone, or even punched in the face than endure a deftly chosen insult or malicious word. Bruises fade with time, but the internal wounds of the heart often stay raw and fresh. Proverbs bluntly states, "Death and life are in the power of the tongue" (18:21 NASB). Two facts put us in a highly combustible environment: words are powerful, and we must communicate with one another. So we have to be careful. The goal of all Christians should be to speak the truth in love and build up others; therefore, we need to recognize the power of our words to bring either life or death (Eph. 4:15, 29). In college you will say a lot of words; what effects will they have?

The Bible is crystal clear that God cares about how we communicate with one another. The following are some questions to consider as we begin this conversation:

1. Do you have a verbal filter or do you immediately say the first thing that comes to mind?
2. Do you enjoy arguing, especially the winning part?
3. Do you have a black belt in verbal manipulation?
4. Are you ever wrong?
5. When was the last time you actually asked for forgiveness for a harsh word or inappropriate comment?
6. Are you holding a grudge against someone that you know you should forgive?
7. When was the last time you spoke life into someone?

Taming the Tongue, Renovating the Heart

It has been said that the tongue is the only weapon that gets sharper with use. The more we insult, the more skillful we become at it! James knew this all too well. In one of the most intensely practical and convicting books in the Bible, James describes our battle with our tongues. If you read James 3:1–12 you will find yourself squirming in your chair, because you will be unable to escape the truth about how you often use your words. Here is a sample:

> Likewise, the tongue is a small part of the body, but it makes great boasts. Consider what a great forest is set on fire by a small spark. The tongue also is a fire, a world of evil among the parts of the body. It corrupts the whole body, sets the whole course of one's life on fire, and is itself set on fire by hell.
>
> All kinds of animals, birds, reptiles and sea creatures are being tamed and have been tamed by mankind, but no human being can tame the tongue. It is a restless evil, full of deadly poison.
>
> With the tongue we praise our Lord and Father, and with it we curse human beings, who have been made in God's likeness. Out of the same mouth come praise and cursing. My brothers and sisters, this should not be. (James 3:5–10)

If you haven't been convicted enough yet, flip back a few pages and read Ephesians 4:15–5:4.

So we all know we have a problem taming our tongues, but what is the root? Jesus gives us the answer in Matthew 12:34: "For the mouth speaks what the heart is full of." If you constantly spit venom at people, then the problem is your heart,[1] not your mouth. As Dallas Willard observes, "The greatest need you and I have—the greatest need of collective humanity—is *renovation of our heart*. That spiritual place within us from which outlook, choices, and actions come has been formed by a world away from God. Now it must be transformed."[2]

The Basics of Communication— Talking and Listening

Talking is not always about the words you say. Most of the time the problem is not *what* has been said but *how* it has been said (Prov. 25:11). Studies show that our body language and tone of voice communicate far more than the words we actually say. Is your body speaking louder than your words? By the way, yelling *never* helps; you are much more likely to be heard if you keep your voice steady and calm. Being calm takes self-control and is a work of the Spirit (Gal. 5:22–23). So keep one eye on what you say and the other eye on how you say it.

Listening is an acquired skill. Few things are more frustrating than baring your soul to someone who is not listening. The first rule of good listening is looking into the eyes of the person who is talking with you. Next, don't formulate what you are going to say next while the person is still talking; listen. (I really have trouble with this one!) Finally, be aware of your body language. You may be unaware of the way you look when you listen to other people (e.g., a deer in the headlights look). People may misinterpret your posture as boredom or disinterest. Try to become a good listener with your whole body. It sounds cheesy I know, but give it a shot.

How to Fight Clean

Now I need to confess that I am not a conflict guru. I blow it just like everyone else . . . just ask my wife. But by God's grace, I am trying to be more intentional about resolving conflict biblically.[3] Since you are now an extremely intellectual college student, here's an equation for you to memorize: Y + R = C. Translation: you + roommates = conflict. It is not a matter of *if* but *when* you will have conflict. Now, you can swallow it, sweep it under the rug, run away, blow up at people, or resolve it. The last option should really be your only option!

Unresolved conflict is cancer to relationships, yet we are hesitant to confront conflict because we want people to like us. So how do we handle this? First of all, some things aren't worth fighting over. Listen to Proverbs 19:11: "A person's wisdom yields patience; it is to one's glory to overlook an offense." If your roommate accidentally leaves dirty dishes out or clothes on the floor, cut them some slack. Maybe they are going through a difficult time, so don't jump on them for petty stuff—be the bigger person. Now if this is a daily habit, it needs to be addressed. You are not—and should not pretend to be—their mommy and daddy. So if conflict needs to be addressed, Ken Sande offers this biblical way to go about it:

1. *Glorify God*: How can I please and honor the Lord in this situation?

2. *Get the log out of your own eye*: How can I show Jesus's work in me by taking responsibility for my contribution to this conflict?

3. *Gently restore*: How can I lovingly serve others by helping them take responsibility for their contribution to this conflict?

4. *Go and be reconciled*: How can I demonstrate the forgiveness of God and encourage a reasonable solution to this conflict?[4]

It is amazing how these four little questions will change your attitude and the face of your relationships!

I want to close this chapter by including The Peacemaker's Pledge.[5] Take some time to read over it. If we live what this passage says—rather than like petty, unforgiving toddlers—God will be glorified, and the watching world will be astonished.

The Peacemaker's Pledge

As people reconciled to God by the death and resurrection of Jesus Christ, we believe that we are called to respond to conflict in a way that is remarkably different from the way the world deals with conflict. . . . Therefore, in response to God's love and in reliance on His grace, we commit ourselves to responding to conflict according to the following principles.

Glorify God

Instead of focusing on our own desires or dwelling on what others may do, we will rejoice in the Lord and bring him praise. . . .

Get the Log Out of Your Own Eye

Instead of blaming others for a conflict or resisting correction, we will trust in God's mercy and take responsibility for our own contribution to conflicts. . . .

Gently Restore

Instead of pretending that conflict doesn't exist or talking about others behind their backs, we will overlook minor offenses or we will talk personally and graciously with those whose offenses seem too serious to overlook. . . .

Go and Be Reconciled

Instead of accepting premature compromise or allowing relationships to wither, we will actively pursue genuine peace and reconciliation—forgiving others as God . . . has forgiven us. . . .

By God's grace, we will apply these principles as a matter of stewardship, realizing that conflict is an opportunity, not an accident. We will remember that success in God's eyes is not a matter of specific results, but of faithful, dependent obedience.

THE BIG IDEAS

- Our words bring either life or death.
- A Christian is called to communicate in love and for another's benefit.
- The root issue of our problem with the tongue is our heart.
- Practice the skill of talking and listening.
- Have the wisdom and grace to overlook petty issues.
- Approach conflict with a biblical checklist: *glorify God, get the log out of your own eye, gently restore, go and be reconciled.*
- God will be glorified . . . the world will be astonished!

For Further Discovery

Cloud, Henry, and John Townsend. *Boundaries: When to Say Yes, How to Say No.* Grand Rapids: Zondervan, 2008.

Nelson, Tommy. *The Book of Romance: What Solomon Says About Love, Sex, and Intimacy.* Nashville: Thomas Nelson, 2007.

Sande, Ken. *The Peacemaker: A Biblical Guide to Resolving Personal Conflict.* Revised and updated ed. Grand Rapids: Baker, 2004.

Sande, Ken, and Kevin Johnson. *The Peacemaker: Handling Conflict Without Fighting Back or Running Away.* Student edition. Grand Rapids: Baker, 2008.

Tripp, Paul David. *War of Words: Getting to the Heart of Your Communication Struggles.* Phillipsburg, NJ: P&R Publishing, 2000.

Willard, Dallas. *Renovation of the Heart: Putting on the Character of Christ.* Carol Stream, IL: Tyndale House, 2014.

Peacemaker Ministries at www.peacemaker.net.

Relational Wisdom 360 at www.rw360.org.

26

Has the Church Lost Her Mind?

> *Your intellectual life is important . . . for the simple*
> *reason that your very character, the kind of person you*
> *are and are becoming, is at stake. Careful oversight of*
> *our intellectual lives is imperative if we are to think*
> *well, and thinking well is an indispensable ingredient*
> *in living well.*
>
> —W. JAY WOOD[1]

> *Our churches are filled with people who are spiritually*
> *born again, but who still think like non-Christians.*
>
> —WILLIAM LANE CRAIG[2]

> *Thinking is a dying discipline in a society that throbs*
> *with activity.*
>
> —RAVI ZACHARIAS[3]

THE CHURCH HAS LOST HER MIND.[4] I DON'T MEAN THAT CHRISTIANS ARE crazy, just that most Christians no longer value thinking well about Christianity and our world. Os Guinness sums up the unfortunate state of many within the American church: "buns of steel—brains of silly putty!"[5] The last century witnessed Christians retreating from the public square (though this retreat began to slow down in the 1970s). While Christians have made some modest inroads in terms of influence, and there are growing examples of Christians faithfully living out their vocation in all walks of life, the fact remains that evangelical Christians are not the ones setting the agenda at the highest levels of culture (such as Hollywood, mass media, and education). These are still the lingering effects of early generations largely abdicating their roles in "secular" institutions and starting their own "Christian" institutions. (By the way, I am not against Christian institutions; I am simply noting how many Christians have withdrawn from engaging society.) Well-meaning believers marginalized Christianity when they withdrew from the world of ideas. Christianity's absence from the public square in the early 1900s created a vacuum that secularism quickly filled. Christian philosopher J. P. Moreland observes that "we now find ourselves largely marginalized in the culture and ingrown in the issues we address, the activities we perform, the books we read, and the categories in which we think and speak. Our marginalization and ingrown texture are the result of several decades of academic bullying from the outside and intellectual cowardice or indifference on the inside."[6] Thankfully, there are indicators that this is beginning to change, but we still have a lot of work to do, and you may have a major part to play in that.

God Wants Our Hearts and Minds

You might be wondering how this could happen. Good question! I will only be able to summarize a couple of reasons here, but if you want a more thorough explanation, take a look at Moreland's excellent book *Love Your God with All Your Mind*. The short answer is that Christians made a choice they never had to make. Many thought they had to choose between valuing the heart *or* the mind. Even though this was a false dichotomy, they chose the heart and emotions and surrendered the life of the mind to "secular" people. They reasoned, "We will keep our emotions and faith, and you can have science and knowledge." Much of what we see in the church today is a result of this kind of approach to Christianity.

Even so, this false dichotomy invites the question, "Do our minds matter to God?" Jesus affirmed that our minds do matter to God when He gave the greatest commandment: "Love the Lord your God with all your heart and with all your soul and with all your mind" (Matt. 22:37). Far from a fragmented view of worship, this passage reveals an integrated devotion to the Creator and Sovereign Lord. Our worship should not be only emotional (heart) or only intellectual (head) but *both*. By emphasizing one over the other, Christians end up with a lopsided faith and become deficient disciples.

Unfortunately some within the church have understood Jesus, and by extension, Christianity, as encouraging anti-intellectualism. But as Douglas Groothuis argues, this is certainly not the case: "Jesus never demeaned the proper and rigorous functioning of our God-given minds. His teachings appealed to the whole person: the imagination (parables), the will, and reasoning abilities."[7] Groothuis goes on further to describe the implications of Jesus's words and example for our task of loving God fully: "For all their honesty in reporting the foibles of the disciples, the Gospel writers never narrated a situation in which Jesus was intellectually stymied or bettered in an argument; neither did Jesus ever encourage an irrational or ill-informed faith on the part of His disciples. With Jesus as our example and Lord, the Holy Scriptures as our foundation (2 Tim. 3:15–17), and the Holy Spirit as our Teacher (John 16:12–15), we should gladly take up the biblical challenge to outthink the world for Christ and His kingdom (2 Cor. 10:3–5)."[8]

Since all truth is God's truth, Christians should be committed to seeking the truth wherever it is found; and a "commitment to truth implies, in turn, a resolve to cultivate the mind as a part of our discipleship under the lordship of Christ."[9] Jesus Christ perfectly modeled what living a life of integrated devotion looks like. We must not lose sight of the close connection between truth, worship, and the knowledge of God: "It is not simply advantageous to love the Lord with the mind; it is also good, sweet, holy, beautiful, and honoring to God. The last reward to be had from the exercise of a Christian mind is to know God better, and that reward requires no other justification."[10]

Part of living well means thinking well. Our beliefs are the rails upon which our lives run. What we think about and how we think are important for life. But they are even more important for becoming conformed to the image of Christ. Paul puts it like this: "Therefore, I urge you, brothers and sisters, in view of God's mercy, to offer your bodies as a living sacrifice, holy and pleasing to God—this is your true and proper worship. Do not conform to the pattern of this world, but be transformed by the renewing of your mind. Then you will be able to test and approve what God's will is—his good, pleasing and perfect will" (Rom. 12:1–2; see also Phil. 4:8). We are not to allow the world to squeeze our minds and patterns of thinking into its mold. Rather, God's Word is to shape the way we think and live. This can only be achieved if we are actively pursuing God's truth in our thought life.

Waking Up

Thankfully the church is beginning to wake up from this intellectual slumber. One clear example of this can be observed in the renaissance of Christians within philosophy departments. Many philosophy classrooms are becoming less hostile toward talk of God. This is due largely in part to the rigor and sophistication of Christian intellectuals like Alvin Plantinga who have taken their calling seriously as disciples of Jesus. (We are seeing this kind of resurgence as well in historical Jesus studies with scholars like N. T. Wright.)

Now I don't mean to imply that Christianity is the dominant worldview in university philosophy departments. But I do want to make you aware that the arguments Christians are putting forth for the existence of God, and the plausibility of theism, are well studied and intelligent. Christian philosophers are a noteworthy example of living out the call to Christian scholarship.

The university is not the only area in which Christians have stopped hitting the intellectual snooze button. In local churches all over the country, pastors are applying serious study to equip Christians for the work of ministry (Eph. 4:12). Our culture is in desperate need of answers to the big questions of life, and the church is where they should find them. There is certainly much to be encouraged by today.

What You Can Do

As a college student, you have an amazing opportunity to think Christianly for the glory of God. Of course you also have the choice to coast along in intellectual neutral. I hope you will choose the first option. I want to challenge you to examine your life: ask yourself if you are loving God with your mind. Then ask what that might look like for you because everyone is unique. You are not in college just to learn how to make a living. As a Christ-follower, you are called to live your life fully for God. College is a time when you begin to discover where and how you are supposed to invest your time, talents, and resources for God's kingdom.

The following are some ideas to get you started:

- Cultivate the habit of reading books that matter (this is a skill you can learn). After leaving college, many Americans read mostly for entertainment. It's fine to read some fiction (I do) but also read nonfiction. For better or for worse, those who wield the most influence in our culture are readers. Readers are leaders.

- As a Christian, learn *what* you believe and *why*. College is a time of exploration and adventure. That is why I have listed numerous resources at the end of each chapter for you to peruse. Take advantage of the time you have now to think and discover. Grab a cup of coffee and stretch your mind. But in the process don't become so open-minded in college that your brains fall out![11]

- Stay up on current events and politics. Try to catch the headlines on a regular basis. I like to use Feedly and Twitter mostly for online news sources. I also try to build lists that include conservative as well as liberal outlets and news sources to compare how the same events are being reported.

- Ask God to lead you in making choices about your vocation and to confirm how He has gifted you to serve others. Spend some time dreaming about how you might embrace that calling with devotion.

Take advantage of the time you have to cultivate your intellectual life. My own journey led me to pursue graduate school. My calling is to help a new generation of Christ-followers think Christianly in an increasingly secular world. My passion for God has not diminished as I have thought more deeply and carefully about my faith. Rather, it has blossomed, and I am more excited about engaging our world with the gospel than ever before. Why? Because Christianity is really true—it best explains and illuminates all of reality! Wherever you are and whatever God calls you to do in life, please don't buy into the false dichotomy that you must choose between having a heart for God or a mind for God. God desires that your heart and mind be united in an integrated devotion to Him—for His kingdom and glory.

THE BIG IDEAS

- The choice between loving God with either your heart or your mind is a false dichotomy. God desires *both*.
- Jesus is the ultimate example of living life with integrated devotion.

- Part of living well means thinking well.

- As a college student, you have an amazing opportunity to think Christianly for the glory of God. You can either seize it or squander it. The choice is yours.

For Further Discovery

Moreland, J. P. *Kingdom Triangle: Recover the Christian Mind, Renovate the Soul, Restore the Spirit's Power.* Grand Rapids: Zondervan, 2009.

———. *Love Your God with All Your Mind: The Role of Reason in the Life of the Soul.* Revised and Updated ed. Colorado Springs: NavPress, 2012.

Morrow, Jonathan. *Think Christianly: Looking at the Intersection of Faith and Culture.* Grand Rapids: Zondervan, 2011.

Pearcey, Nancy. *Total Truth: Liberating Christianity from Its Cultural Captivity.* Wheaton, IL: Crossway, 2008.

Stott, John. *Your Mind Matters: The Place of the Mind in the Christian Life.* Downers Grove, IL: InterVarsity Press, 2013.

Willard, Dallas. *Knowing Christ Today: Why We Can Trust Spiritual Knowledge.* Grand Rapids: Zondervan, 2009.

Zacharias, Ravi. *Recapture the Wonder.* Nashville: Thomas Nelson, 2005.

JoanthanMorrow.org. Learn how to better understand why you believe what you believe and how to think Christianly about all of life.

Overcoming
Syllabus Shock

Procrastination: Hard work often pays off after time, but laziness always pays off now.
—DEMOTIVATOR POSTER[1]

Sluggards do not plow in season;
    so at harvest time they look but find nothing.
—PROVERBS 20:4

Therefore be careful how you walk, not as unwise men but as wise, making the most of your time, because the days are evil.
—EPHESIANS 5:15-16 NASB

ALL IS QUIET NOW. IT'S TWO IN THE MORNING AND THE ONLY SOUND IS the fizz of a freshly poured glass of Mountain Dew. Most sane people are asleep right now; too bad I'm not! It's just me and my way overpriced anthology of modern British literature. My "groundbreaking" analysis of James Joyce is due first thing in the morning—ten pages down, just fifteen more to go!

If I would have known then what I know now—what I'm going to tell you in this chapter—I could have avoided this all-nighter by planning ahead.

While it is true that you will be learning many life lessons outside the classroom, you will be spending a *significant* amount of time listening to lectures, writing papers, reading books, and taking tests. You *will* encounter the college phenomenon affectionately referred to as "syllabus shock." Syllabus shock is the state of incredulity, despondency, and acute confusion students experience after taking their first glance at the sheer volume of work that will have to be completed in a given semester. Often this takes place the first week of school. However, in more severe cases it afflicts those who have waited until halfway through the semester to read the syllabus *for the first time!*

College is exciting; there is always something to do and someone to meet. But at some point (I would advise sooner rather than later) you need to develop a plan of attack for your classes. Like most things in life, having a plan is crucial to success. I can't offer you magic reading glasses that allow you to achieve one-hundred-percent reading comprehension. And I can't sell you a "quick-quotes quill" like you'd find in a Harry Potter novel. But I can offer you some wisdom I have picked up along the way from teachers, classmates, and my own experience. These suggestions aren't infallible, and you won't hurt my feelings if you decide not to use them all. (Although I do have three graduate degrees and must have done something right.)

Go to class. Do I even have to say this? Yes. Here's why. I saw a lot of my fellow students skip class and then try to catch up later. It never ended well. If you go to class and pay attention, you will almost always get a C or better. If you study in addition to going to class and do the assigned reading and papers—A, here you come!

Find and learn how to use the library. Most universities require a library orientation class. I know this can be dreadfully boring. However, if you will learn how to be efficient with your time in the library (as opposed to floundering around like a fish out of water until you get frustrated to the point of giving up and just going to sleep), things will go well with you. Make friends with the librarians; they can help you quickly find what you need.

Learn to read. I know you can discern words on a page, but can you *read*? How's your reading speed and comprehension? This may be the most important study tip I give you for two reasons. First, *every* class will require you to read textbooks; this process can either be painful or profitable. Second, ideas are contained in books and they are very important. It sounds cheesy, but readers are leaders. So what can you do?

- You need to be patient with yourself—not everyone is a genius, but everyone can improve with effort.

- As soon as you can, take a speed-reading class and/or read *Breakthrough Rapid Reading* by Peter Kump.
- Treat your book like a map: first read the table of contents, then the introduction and conclusion, then scan the headers of the chapter you are about to read. Read the last page of the current chapter *first* to see where the author is headed (unless you are reading a novel that you don't want to find out the end of), and then start reading the chapter.
- TIP: Use your finger or a pen to trace the words you are reading—and keep it moving. This will keep you from reading the same word and sentence two hundred times and will significantly speed up your reading. Now you may think you will look silly while reading with your finger. Maybe. The alternative? You can "look cool" reading in your dorm room long after everyone else is finished and out with friends because they took my advice.

Learn to write. You don't have to win a Pulitzer Prize, but if you want to survive college then learning to write well is essential. The normal structure for most papers is introduction, body paragraphs, and conclusion. The introduction will contain your thesis statement (i.e., what the paper will be about). Be as specific and precise as you can with your thesis. Argue for your main points in supporting paragraphs, including clear transitions between them. The conclusion is the restatement of your thesis (never include new information in your conclusion). There are two schools of thought when it comes time to start writing: outline first then write, or write first then outline later. I try to write an outline first. It helps me stay on task while writing. But others just start writing what comes to mind and then organize it later. Try both and see what works best for you. By the way, the more you read, the better your writing will be.

Study for exams. Get some sleep the night before and eat something substantial for breakfast—not a lot of sugar (if you do, you will start off with a bang but be mentally sluggish thirty minutes into it). I find eating Altoids or peppermints during exams helps, and studies have shown this improves test taking. Take a deep breath and do your best. Read all of the directions; this will keep you from wasting time on answering questions they aren't asking. If you are allowed a blank sheet of paper, after the test begins write down key information you are worried about forgetting, then take the test. Keep an eye on the clock so you have enough time to spend on each question.

Plan ahead. You *will* experience syllabus shock. If it isn't one class that overwhelms you, it will be the cumulative force of them all. But this is manageable if you are wise. Take a few hours at the beginning of each semester to look at all of your syllabi. Make a spreadsheet by week and by subject for the whole semester. List all of your reading (chapters and page numbers), paper due dates, and exam dates. Then you will have one master sheet that has everything you have to do on it (color code it if you want—whatever works for you). You can then check things off as they are completed. This will help keep you from feeling overwhelmed. Take one assignment at a time.

Work ahead. This has been the secret to my sanity. Life inevitably happens. Either something fun or something not fun will interrupt life. If you are a week ahead you can take the time for the unexpected without tanking your semester. This isn't always possible, but if you hit the books hard the first weekend of the semester, you will thank yourself later on. Over Christmas break and summer vacation find out what some of your textbooks are going to be for the spring and fall (respectively) and get a head start. It's like putting money in the bank for a rainy day. Trust me, it is far more comfortable riding ahead of the homework wave than being repeatedly swamped and battered by it.

Discover your learning style. Learning how you best process information will be important for you. Some of you may really enjoy lecture-style teaching. Others learn better by doing. I am both a visual and auditory learner. I like seeing things sketched out in front of me in charts and diagrams. But I also remember more when I listen to recorded lectures on my iPhone. Google "learning styles test" and take some of them. This will help you maximize your learning experience.

Take classes with friends and form study groups. College and graduate school would not have been nearly as enjoyable or productive if I hadn't scheduled classes with friends. You need to have people in your corner cheering you on. If nothing else, the fact that someone else is as miserable as you are is great comfort! Also, there is strength in numbers. Take your review sheets, divide up the questions, and then conquer them together. Process the answers out loud—this alone will help you learn.

Review often. You may find it helpful to type up your notes after each class. This will help you review concepts and key information. But it will also prepare you to study well for the exam. You will have to organize the material then anyway; it's much easier to do this as you go along. If your professors will allow it, record the lectures for later review. If you go walking or running, listen to key lectures on your smartphone for review. Rank your classes in level of difficulty and pay attention to the ones that need more work. For example, foreign languages require daily review.

Study in the library. One hour in the library is usually equivalent to three hours of distracted study elsewhere. This is a fact. Your dorm room or apartment is a distracting place. You can always find something else to do besides homework. Xbox Ones and friends lurk there waiting to get you off task. Go study and get it over with. You can either pay the price now or pay later; it's your choice!

Get off to a good start. There is no substitute for getting your college career off to a good start grade-wise. It is much easier to start with a high GPA and then maintain it than it is to blow off the first semester of school and spend the rest of college trying to climb out of the basement.

Manage your class schedule. Don't take too many hours your first semester. I'd start with fifteen or sixteen hours rather than eighteen. You can always take more hours next semester if you see you can handle it. There is a lot to adjust to without being overwhelmed by too many classes. Also, don't schedule 8 a.m. classes if you can help it; college happens at night and it will be way too tempting to sleep in.[2] Work on your class schedule for the next semester before the day you are supposed to register, and always register at your scheduled time. This will ensure that you get the classes you need and want. Meet with your academic advisor *each* semester (I'm serious . . . you don't want to show up the semester you think you are graduating only to find that you need sixteen more hours). Take mostly general requirements your first two semesters. You have to take these anyway. Over time, you will have a better idea of what electives you want to take and what you may want to major in. If you take too many electives early on, you will find that only a certain number of them will count toward your degree track once you declare a major. That gets expensive.

Redeem the time. Always have a book or notebook with you. If you are going to get a haircut or an oil change, take a book to read. You will be shocked at how much you can get done while waiting at places. This will also reduce the stress of waiting—just pull out a book or some flash cards. You are being efficient while everyone else is getting frustrated. Find creative ways to redeem the time.

Exercise. The body fuels the mind. There will be times when the best thing you can do is shut the books and go for a run or play some basketball. Exercise helps clear your head. Swimming is my favorite exercise—minimum time, maximum benefit, and I feel refreshed afterward.

Do not cheat. Do not cheat on tests or say you read pages you didn't read. Your integrity and a clear conscience are worth far more than an unearned grade. It will be tempting to cut corners; don't do it.

Be diligent. "Hard work beats talent when talent doesn't work hard." This is the slogan that is painted on the wall of the University of Oklahoma's football weight room. While you may not be taking on a three-hundred-pound all-American defensive tackle, the principle is clear. There are really gifted people who don't work hard and are thus not successful. If you apply yourself and work hard, then you will be successful in the classroom. Learning—in most cases—is an acquired skill.

More could be said. But this will help you get off on the right foot and inoculate you against further episodes of syllabus shock. Whatever approaches you take to your studies, just don't be passive. If your goal is to make the academic aspect of your college experience miserable, then do exactly the opposite of what I've suggested in this chapter. You have been entrusted with a wonderful opportunity to learn, and as a Christian you want to be a good steward. Don't squander the time; before you know it, you will be walking across that platform being handed a diploma. Make the most of it! Enjoy the world of ideas.

POSTSCRIPT: Learning the Art of Self-Leadership

Influential business leader Peter Drucker made the following observation: "In a few hundred years, when the history of our time will be written from a long-term perspective, it is likely that the most important event historians will see is not technology, not the Internet, not e-commerce. It is an unprecedented change in the human condition. For the first time—literally—substantial and rapidly growing numbers of people have choices. For the first time, they will have to manage themselves. And society is totally unprepared for it."[3] You and I are bombarded by a mind-numbing amount of choices every day. In the midst of all of that, we have to learn how to lead ourselves. To be decisive, intentional, principled, and purposeful. This will be especially true as you begin to transition out of college and launch into your adult years. If you don't choose what to focus on, someone else will choose it for you. Before you leave college, I highly recommend reading *Essentialism: The Disciplined Pursuit of Less* by Greg McKeown. As much as you will want to, you can't do everything. This book will help you begin to think through and zero in on the contribution God is calling you to make in this world.

THE BIG IDEAS

- Don't be passive when it comes to your studies; make a plan and work hard.
- Learn to read and write well.
- Read this chapter again and make a list of what you need to do to succeed in the classroom.

For Further Discovery

Drucker, Peter F., and Joseph A. Maciariello. *The Daily Drucker: 366 Days of Insight and Motivation for Getting the Right Things Done.* New York: HarperCollins, 2011.

Duhigg, Charles. *Smarter, Faster, Better: The Secrets of Being Productive in Life and Business.* New York: Random House, 2016.

Kump, Peter. *Breakthrough Rapid Reading.* Upper Saddle River, NJ: Prentice Hall, 1999.

McKeown, Greg. *Essentialism: The Disciplined Pursuit of Less.* New York: Crown, 2014.

Newport, Cal. *How to Become a Straight-A Student: The Unconventional Strategies Real College Students Use to Score High While Studying Less.* New York: Broadway, 2007.

Page, Mary, and Carrie Winstanley. *Writing Essays for Dummies.* Chichester: Wiley, 2009.

Paul, Kevin. *Study Smarter, Not Harder.* Bellingham, WA: Self-Counsel Press, 2014.

———

Evernote at evernote.com. "Evernote: The note-taking space for your life's work."

Show Me the Money

The rich rule over the poor,
and the borrower is slave to the lender.

—PROVERBS 22:7

No one can serve two masters. Either you will hate
the one and love the other, or you will be devoted to
the one and despise the other. You cannot serve both
God and money.

—MATTHEW 6:24

Remember this: Whoever sows sparingly will also
reap sparingly, and whoever sows generously will also
reap generously. Each of you should give what you
have decided in your heart to give, not reluctantly
or under compulsion, for God loves a cheerful giver.
And God is able to bless you abundantly, so that in
all things at all times, having all that you need, you
will abound in every good work.

—2 CORINTHIANS 9:6–8

MONEY DOESN'T GROW ON TREES! I WISH IT DID. I'VE OFTEN THOUGHT life would be much simpler if we didn't have to worry about money. Like it or not, money is a big part of life. God knows this. That is why so much is written in the Bible concerning money and the pursuit of it. There is a wise way and there is a foolish way to handle the money with which you have been entrusted. One way is pleasing to God and it leads to blessing. The other way is dishonoring to God and it leads to heartache. You might wonder why there is a chapter on money in a book to college students. Good question. While most college students are not rich, you have at least *some* money to manage.

Moreover, there is no time like the present to start making wise financial choices. You are already, or soon will be, making significant decisions about loans, cars, and jobs—not to mention the basics like food and shelter. Now some of you have already had to learn some hard financial lessons in life. But others of you may have never received any guidance on managing money, so the financial independence thing is new for you. This chapter is here not only to keep you from getting your adult life off to a really bad start by making poor financial decisions, but it also will help you think about how to honor the Lord with the money you do have.

More Is Never Enough

We live in an affluent society; money is everywhere. We have entire television shows dedicated to the posh houses of the rich and famous—their pools, cars, and toys. Our culture worships wealth. If we are honest, we all struggle with wanting more money and stuff. We think—like all the generations who have come before and will come after us—that more money will satisfy us. This lie is so attractive that we believe it in spite of the testimonies of the rich! John D. Rockefeller lamented, "I have made many millions, but they have brought me no happiness."[1]

Wisdom reminds us: "Cast but a glance at riches, and they are gone, for they will surely sprout wings and fly off to the sky like an eagle" (Prov. 23:5). In the New Testament Paul states bluntly, "Those who want to get rich fall into temptation and a trap and into many foolish and harmful desires that plunge people into ruin and destruction. For the love of money is a root of all kinds of evil. Some people, eager for money, have wandered from the faith and pierced themselves with many griefs" (1 Tim. 6:9–10). And yet, we still tend to think that wealth will satisfy and that money can buy happiness. The sooner we can disabuse ourselves of this lie, the better off we'll be.[2]

Owned by God

At the end of the day, there is really just one principle that we need to grasp when it comes to "stuff"—*God owns it all*. "The earth is the LORD's, and everything in it, the world, and all who live in it" (Ps. 24:1). Notice God's ownership extends over all of humanity as well. But those who have been redeemed by Christ are owned by God in a special way because we have been bought with a price (1 Cor. 7:22–23). Since God owns it all, then we are *stewards* of His stuff. Randy Alcorn summarizes, "A steward manages assets for the owner's benefit. The steward carries no sense of entitlement to the assets he manages. It's his job to find out what the owner wants done with his assets, then carry out his will."[3] Luke 19:11–27 (see also Matt. 25:14–30) reveals that Christ-followers have been entrusted with time (twenty-four hours in a day), talents, abilities, opportunities for influence, and money to steward for God and the benefit of His kingdom. He will return one day and call us to account—rewarding the faithful (1 Cor. 3:12–15). Those whom He finds "making a profit for him" will hear, "Well done, good and faithful servant. . . . Enter into the joy of your master" (Matt. 25:21 ESV).

The Discipline of Generosity

One of the Bible verses still unwittingly quoted by our culture is Jesus's pronouncement that "it is more blessed to give than to receive" (Acts 20:35). This principle is one of the reasons Christmas is so much fun! People remember the blessing of giving. I love watching a friend or loved one unwrap a gift that I have purchased for them—not because they deserve it, but because I want to bless them. A central theme in Scripture is that Christians have been blessed by God in order to be a blessing to others. It's OK if you don't have much. Begin now to cultivate the habit of sacrificially and joyfully giving to the Lord's work and trusting in His provision for your needs—there never is an easy time to start.

Christians are called first to give to their local church and then to various needs outside of their local church and other worthy ministry opportunities. How much should a Christian give? Paul answers that question by stating, "Each of you should give what you have decided in your heart to give, not reluctantly or under compulsion, for God loves a cheerful giver" (2 Cor. 9:7). In one of the most convicting passages in the entire Bible, a widow gave all she had to live on to the Lord (Mark 12:41–44). How we give reveals what we treasure. Recall Jesus's words, "Where your treasure is, there your heart will be also" (Matt. 6:21). None of us is where we ought to be in this category, but we can ask God to work in our hearts and to move us in the right direction by His grace.

Of Budgets and Bank Accounts

Now that we have looked at some general biblical principles, let's apply them to your situation in college. One of the first things you need to do when arriving on campus is make a budget. If not, you will soon be asking, "Where did all the money go?" (This question will usually be prompted by your growling stomach.) One of the best ways to do this is to create a simple spreadsheet (or use an app like Mint or Mvelopes). Determine how much money you have coming in and going out each month. Some possible sources of income in college are a job, financial aid, student loans, and money from mom and dad. Common expenditures to include in a budget are rent, food, car, gas/oil, repairs, clothes, health insurance, car insurance, giving, tuition/books, savings, and entertainment (these will look different depending on your situation). Most important is that your budget is accurate and detailed enough to be helpful.

Observe how you do with your budget for a couple of months and then adjust accordingly. Obviously, if more is going out than is coming in, something needs to change—especially if you are charging it on a credit card. One of the benefits of having a checking/savings account (most banks offer free accounts to students if you ask) is that you will be able to check your balance online and easily monitor what is being spent. If you are trying to be a good steward of what God has entrusted to you, then budgeting is a necessary first step. The basic priority should be this: Give. Save. Spend.

Credit Card Blues

"Want a free T-shirt? It's yours free when you sign up for this credit card!" *Run!* If you want a new T-shirt, buy one and then skip a meal. But don't sign up for a credit card just to get a T-shirt (or whatever else they are "giving" away). We live in an instant gratification society. We want it now and our way. *Why wait? Life is short after all!* Don't fall into this sort of thinking—this is exactly the kind of reasoning that keeps credit card companies in business. The majority of Americans are in debt up to their eyeballs,[4] and many have filed bankruptcy because they couldn't pay off their debts. Proverbs offers the sobering reminder that "the rich rule over the poor, and the borrower is slave to the lender" (22:7). Being in debt causes us to worry and be anxious, and because all our money is already spoken for, our ability to be flexible and generous is limited. By the way, if you find yourself in debt, as Dave Ramsey likes to say, stop digging! Then apply the debt snowball by paying off the lowest balance first and then the next and so on to get momentum. Break free!

In my opinion, for most students it is the better part of wisdom to avoid signing up for a credit card in college—the temptation usually proves too much for most students. If you do sign up for a credit card in college to begin establishing good credit, then be wise and disciplined about it. First, have only one card, and by one, I mean not seven. (Get one with no annual fee and one that gives you miles/points.) Next, use it like a debit card—pay the balance off each month and on time. Thirty-five-dollar late fees add up in a hurry. Credit card companies stay in business by earning 20 percent a month in interest and finance charges based on your account balance. Finally, avoid impulse purchases. No one sets out to run up ten thousand dollars in credit card debt. Most students do it one pizza at a time. Be careful.

But what if borrowing money is unavoidable? In a couple of cases it can be. Buying a house or borrowing money to pay for school are two such examples (though a house is more like an investment, and your college degree can also be an investment as long as your job in that field has a reasonable chance of paying well enough for you to get the loan paid off). If you must borrow, then do so as responsibly as possible; this means only borrowing money as a last resort and only for the amount you actually need. Also, begin paying off your debt as soon as you can (especially if it is accruing interest daily). If you are considering borrowing money for tuition, explore the possibility of working a part-time job to help pay some of your semester bill as you go. Apply for scholarships, grants, and financial aid, and consider companies that have employer reimbursement for college. Get creative! Pay now or pay later: it's up to you. Every little bit helps!

College is an opportunity to start healthy, God-honoring financial habits. God's Word sets forth a high standard when it comes to money, and none of us will perfectly attain it. But by His grace and through the Holy Spirit, we can seek to be good stewards of our Master's things.

THE BIG IDEAS

- The Bible has a lot to say about a person's use and pursuit of money.

- No amount of money satisfies, and the blind pursuit of it will lead to disastrous consequences for you and those around you.

- Since God owns it all, our role is to be good and faithful stewards of His possessions.

- Beware of incurring debt. In doing so you become the lender's slave. Be wise when deciding whether or not to sign up for and use a credit card. And be *very* careful how much you take out in student loans.

- If you are trying to be a good steward of what God has entrusted to you, then budgeting is a necessary first step.

For Further Discovery

Alcorn, Randy. *The Treasure Principle: Unlocking the Secret of Joyful Giving*. Sisters, OR: Multnomah, 2005.

Getz, Gene. *Rich in Every Way: Everything God Says About Money and Possessions*. New York: Rosen, 2010.

Selingo, Jeffrey J. *There Is Life After College: What Parents and Students Should Know About Navigating School to Prepare for the Jobs of Tomorrow*. New York: HarperCollins, 2016.

Stack, Carol, and Ruth Vedvik. *The Financial Aid Handbook: Getting the Education You Want for the Price You Can Afford*. Franklin Lakes, NJ: Career Press, 2011.

Stanley, Andy. "Crazy Like Us." North Point Community Church. November 2015, http://northpoint.org/messages/crazy-like-us/.

———. *The Principle of the Path: How to Get from Where You Are to Where You Want to Be*. Nashville: Thomas Nelson, 2010.

Tyson, Eric. *Personal Finance for Dummies*. 8th ed. Hoboken, NJ: Wiley, 2015.

Whitney, Donald S. "Stewardship." In *Spiritual Disciplines for the Christian Life*. Carol Stream, IL: Tyndale House, 2014.

———

Crown Financial Ministries at www.crown.org.

Dave Ramsey at www.daveramsey.com.

Mvelopes.com. "Take Charge of Your Personal Finances."

Becoming More Like Jesus

The concept of eternal life in the New Testament is not primarily one of living forever in heaven, but of having a new kind of life now. This new kind of life is so different that those without it can be called dead, truly. This is a life of human flourishing; a life lived the way we were made to function; a life of virtue, character, and well-being lived like and for the Lord Jesus.

—J. P. MORELAND AND KLAUS ISSLER[1]

Now the Lord is the Spirit, and where the Spirit of the Lord is, there is freedom. And we all, who with unveiled faces contemplate the Lord's glory, are being transformed into his image with ever-increasing glory, which comes from the Lord, who is the Spirit.

—2 CORINTHIANS 3:17–18

Beloved, now we are children of God, and it has not appeared as yet what we will be. We know that when He appears, we will be like Him, because we will see Him just as He is.

—1 JOHN 3:2 NASB

EARLIER IN THE BOOK WE DISCOVERED THAT THE GOSPEL IS ABOUT FAR more than heaven. Heaven will be wonderful one day—and we should always live in light of the next world—but if you are a Christian, then eternal life has *already* begun because the core of eternal life is knowing Jesus (John 17:3). Jesus came that we might have abundant life (John 10:10).

As a college student, you have the opportunity to embrace eternal life by growing in your relationship with Jesus Christ. But you can also become distracted, thus missing out on the good life God intends for you to have. But the good life doesn't just happen by accident; you will have to be intentional about your pursuit of it. In what follows, I will give you an overview of what the Bible says about the process of becoming like Christ, and then conclude by listing some practical ways to meet with God in your busy college schedule.

Being Spiritually Formed into the Image of Christ

It is common to hear the term "spiritual formation" discussed today. It is a synonym of "the spiritual life" and "sanctification" (I will use all of these terms as well as "the good life" to refer to the same process). A more technical definition of spiritual formation is "the holistic work of God whereby He transforms a believer increasingly into the image of His Son, Jesus Christ, by the power of the Holy Spirit." This may seem complicated, but the basic idea is a simple one: God is working to reproduce the life, habits, attitudes, character, and actions of Jesus Christ in the believer's life. The goal is "to be conformed to the image of his Son" (Rom. 8:29). To be sure, you and I have a long way to go, but we can be encouraged that God is completely committed to this process. Paul reminds us: "He who began a good work in you will carry it on to completion until the day of Christ Jesus" (Phil. 1:6).

I want to briefly say something about what spiritual formation *is not* about; it is not a list of moral dos and don'ts. One of the themes I have tried to communicate throughout this book is that Christianity is not about saying no to stuff; it's about saying yes to the good life God has designed for us. When we walk in the ways God has for us, we will flourish as human beings. By God's grace we can experience a taste of the quality of life we were intended to have before life was corrupted by sin. Included in the good life are duties, obligations, and commands of God to obey (i.e., contained in Scripture), but we are primarily concerned with becoming the *right kind* of person, a person of virtue. The Christian life is about who we are becoming. When we lose sight of this goal, we all too easily fall into the joyless pit of legalism, and that is no way to live.

The Believer's Resources

God has given us everything we need for the spiritual life. Peter writes of this promise: "His divine power has given us everything we need for a godly life through our knowledge of him who called us by his own glory and goodness" (2 Peter 1:3). The believer's resources in the process of spiritual formation are God's Word, God's Spirit, and God's people.

God's Word

The first essential resource is exposure to God's Word. By its truth our thinking is renewed and we are able to break free from the anti-Christian mold the world presses us into (Rom. 12:1–2). God's Word is the primary source of truth about Christ and what it means to follow Him; it equips us for every good work (2 Tim. 3:16–17). Moreover, it is a lamp to the feet and a light to the path (Ps. 119:105), alive and active (Heb. 4:12), sweeter than honey and more precious than gold (Ps. 19:10), perfect and trustworthy (Ps. 19:7), and true and righteous (Ps. 19:9). Exposure to God's Word provides us with stability (Eph. 4:12–15), gives insight and guidance (Ps. 119:9–10; Prov. 3:5–6), and leads us into spiritual maturity (1 Cor. 3:1–3; Heb. 5:14; 1 Peter 2:2–3).

God's Spirit

The third person of the Trinity, the Holy Spirit, is another essential resource for our spiritual formation. When Jesus spoke to His disciples during the Upper Room Discourse, He promised another helper, the Holy Spirit, would not only be *with* them but—after His death, resurrection, and ascension—would be *in* them (John 14:17). The Holy Spirit indwells every Christian and is at work in our lives. He is a person, not a force. In short, there is no spiritual formation if there is no activity of the Holy Spirit. As theologian Gordon Fee has aptly said, "The Spirit is . . . the empowering presence of God for living the life of God in the present."[2]

God's People

The final essential resource for spiritual formation is the body of Christ. The Christian life is not to be pursued in isolation. James Emery White says a "myth [about the spiritual life] is that a personal relationship with God through Christ is synonymous with a private relationship with God through Christ. The truth, however, is that becoming a truly spiritual person is a team sport."[3] The bottom line is that we need one another to be conformed to the image of Christ. It is significant that the image of Christ also has a communal expression (see Gal. 4:19—*you* is plural here). Even our knowledge of God is incomplete without one another. As Klaus Issler points out, "God is so grand and majestic, and each relationship is so person specific that there will be much to learn about God from the stories of other believers' experiences with God. The fullest knowledge of God attainable by human beings will only come about within a growing and God-knowing community of saints. Thus, to know God more fully cannot be accomplished without the larger community of believers."[4]

Spiritual Formation Is a Cooperative Process

It is important to recognize that both God and the believer are involved in this process. God initiates and enables, and then we respond in faith by cooperating with the work He desires to do in us. This spiritual cooperation is the picture we find in Scripture: "Therefore, my dear friends, as you have always obeyed—not only in my presence, but now much more in my absence—continue to work out your salvation with fear and trembling, for it is God who works in you to will and to act in order to fulfill his good purpose" (Phil. 2:12–13; see also 1 Thess. 2:13; 2 Peter 1:3–8).

Spiritual Formation Is Holistic

As we think about the transformative work that God is doing in us, we need to remember that spiritual formation is holistic—it affects all aspects of life (i.e., physical, spiritual, mental, emotional, intellectual, and social). This truth is seen in Luke 10:27: "'Love the Lord your God with all your heart and with all your soul and with all your strength and with all your mind'; and, 'Love your neighbor as yourself.'" Our lives are to be lived in authentic community with others and with an integrated devotion to Christ.

The Role of the Spiritual Disciplines

One of the ways Christians can be intentional about their spiritual formation is by practicing the spiritual disciplines. Paul has this to say about the importance of discipline in a believer's life: "Discipline yourself for the purpose of godliness; for bodily discipline is only of little profit, but godliness is profitable for all things, since it holds promise for the present life and also for the life to come" (1 Tim. 4:7–8 NASB). Christians throughout church history have employed various spiritual disciplines to help them grow in Christ. The best definition of the spiritual disciplines I have found comes from Dallas Willard: spiritual disciplines are the "indirect means that allow us to cooperate in reshaping the personality—the feelings, ideas, mental processes and images, and the deep readiness of soul and body—so that our whole being is poised to go with the movements of the regenerate heart that is in us by the impact of the Gospel Word under the direction and energizing of the Holy Spirit."[5] The disciplines are not the end goal but only the means to the end, which is becoming more like Christ. Practicing the disciplines creates a context and opportunity for the Spirit to work in our lives. While some shy away from the disciplines because of the fear of becoming legalistic (i.e., becoming more concerned about the discipline than truly becoming like Christ), this should not keep Christians from practicing them. We don't practice the disciplines to master them; rather, we practice them to experience God more fully. The disciplines facilitate the transformation of sinful habits into godly, healthy patterns in our life (see Rom. 6:12–13). When the disciplines are rightly practiced, freedom is the reward. The following is a list of some of the most common spiritual disciplines:[6]

1. *Solitude and silence.* This allows us to remove ourselves from the frantic activity and pressures of the day and retreat into the presence of God so that we can hear His voice.

2. *Prayer.* This allows us to commune with the living God, releasing our cares and burdens to Him. Also, we can learn to practice His presence throughout the day.

3. *Journaling.* This allows us to record the ways God is working in our lives over time (i.e., the fruit of our study, prayer, and meditation times).

4. *Study and meditation.* The goal here is to discover God's Word and then renew our mind with His truth, values, priorities, and attitudes. In contrast to Eastern meditation, which empties the mind, biblical meditation fills the mind with the things of God (see Josh. 1:8).

5. *Fasting.* This allows us to abstain from physical nourishment or certain activities for a period of time in order to cultivate dependence on God.

6. *Secrecy.* This allows us to look to God alone for recognition and approval, helping us be free from living our lives according to the opinions and expectations of others.

7. *Confession.* This allows us to be vulnerable and transparent with trusted friends as we confess our sins to them. The purpose of confession is to overcome the dominion and control that hidden sins have on us, as well as to receive grace and encouragement.

8. *Fellowship.* This allows us to be encouraged and built up by intentionally spending time with brothers and sisters in Christ.

9. *Simplicity, stewardship, and sacrifice.* These three go together and allow us to overcome the distractions of the stuff and possessions of this world. Also, living simply and sacrificially and showing good stewardship help us treat what we have as God's possessions and not our own.

10. *Worship and celebration.* This allows us to be fully occupied in both individual and corporate settings, that we might celebrate who God is and how wonderful He is. Also, instead of grumbling about present circumstances, we thank God for all He has done for us.

11. *Service.* This allows us to pay attention to others' needs instead of our own. We look to seek the good of others, expecting nothing in return.

12. *Witness.* This allows us to step out of our comfort zone and, as the Spirit leads, look for opportunities to invest in the lives of unbelievers for the purpose of introducing them to Jesus.

Though these are all biblical and beneficial, it is not as though we have to practice all of them all of the time. God leads us into different areas of maturity during different seasons of life. It may be that you need to grow in dependence on God instead of the things of this world for comfort. If so, fasting would be a way to grow in this area. Remember that the spiritual life is not a sprint; it is a marathon. Becoming more like Christ takes farsighted vision; it is a life of consistent obedience.

Another time-tested way of connecting with God is called "sacred reading," or in Latin, *lectio divina*. *Lectio divina* incorporates the disciplines of study, meditation, and prayer into one activity. Let's look at an example:[7]

Scripture

"Come to me, all you who are weary and burdened, and I will give you rest. Take my yoke upon you and learn from me, for I am gentle and humble in heart, and you will find rest for your souls. For my yoke is easy and my burden is light" (Matt. 11:28–30).

Reading

Slowly read the Scripture passage several times.

Meditation

Take some time to reflect on the words and phrases of the text. Which words, phrases, or images speak to you?

Prayer

Offer the internalized passage back to God in the form of a personalized prayer of adoration, confession, renewal, petition, intercession, affirmation, or thanksgiving.

Contemplation

What word or image captures the spirit of this passage for you?

Response

Take a few minutes to present yourself before God in silence and yieldedness. When your mind wanders, center yourself by returning to the spirit of the passage.

Practical Tips for Meeting with God

Here are some practical tips that may help you have a more fruitful time meeting with God.

1. It is probably best not to have your quiet time in your bed first thing in the morning; falling back asleep is too tempting! (Although I do remember dreaming through some good quiet times.)

2. Find a place to meet with God where you can avoid distractions. It would be good to turn off your smartphone, or if you use a Bible app like YouVersion, find a way to turn off all notifications and read offline for a focused amount of time. However, if you find yourself unable to muster the self-control to not constantly check social media and text messages, I'd encourage you to power it off and read a printed Bible version.

3. If your mind wanders to everything you have to do that day, keep a sheet of paper handy to write down whatever it is that comes to mind so you don't stress out about it. Then refocus on God and His Word.

4. Buy a recent translation of the Bible. For Bible study I prefer the accuracy of the New American Standard Bible; for ease of reading, I have enjoyed the New Living Translation. If you are going to buy a study Bible, I would recommend the *Life Application Study Bible* in the translation of your choice.[8]

5. Set a regular time for your time with God and try to be consistent— either morning or night.

6. Develop a plan. However, don't be too ambitious in the beginning. Set a reasonable goal for the first week, a goal that will not be overwhelming. When we mess up, we tend to get discouraged and convince ourselves that we are spiritual losers while everyone else seems to be a spiritual superhero. Then we give up. If you miss a day, pick up at the same place the next day (remember, it's not a sprint).

7. On a note card, write out a verse you want to meditate on and carry it with you in your pocket that day.

8. If you are musically gifted, then sing to the Lord; this will help soften your heart. (Even if you are not musically gifted, you can still make a joyful noise!)

9. Some find it easier to pray while walking . . . with your eyes open, of course. This could be a great opportunity to pray for your campus building by building.

10. Start a journal/prayer diary to record answers to prayer or ways God has shown up in your life recently.

A Sample Thirty-Minute Quiet Time

1. Take a deep breath and clear your mind of distractions. Be still and quiet your heart (Ps. 131:2). Then ask God to meet with you today.
2. Read a chapter from either the Old or New Testament.
3. Select a verse out of today's reading that you would like to meditate on, using the sacred reading example as a guide.
4. Spend some time in prayer using the ACTS method.

   Adoration. Praise God for who He is and what He has done.

   Confession. Confess your sins to God and receive His forgiveness.

   Thanksgiving. Thank God for what He is doing in your life and the lives of others.

   Supplication. Pray for others and their needs as well as your own.[9]

There is no one way to have a quiet time, but this at least gives you a place to begin. Be creative and flexible, but be intentional about it or it won't happen. We are all works in progress, but by God's grace and the Holy Spirit we are striving to become more like Jesus (Phil. 3:14).

THE BIG IDEAS

- The gospel is about more than just going to heaven (as important as this is); it's about knowing Jesus in the here and now.
- The basic idea of spiritual formation is that God is working to reproduce the life, habits, attitudes, character, and actions of Jesus Christ in the believer's life; the goal is for us "to be conformed to the image of his Son" (Rom. 8:29).
- The spiritual life is a cooperative activity. God initiates and enables, and then we respond in faith by cooperating with the work He desires to do in us.
- The spiritual disciplines—and especially sacred reading—can be helpful in becoming more like Jesus. When they are rightly practiced, freedom, not legalism, is the reward of the disciplines.
- We are all works in progress, but by God's grace and the Holy Spirit we are striving to become more like Jesus (Phil. 3:14).

For Further Discovery

Hawthorne, Gerald F. *The Presence and the Power: The Significance of the Holy Spirit in the Life and Ministry of Jesus.* Eugene, OR: Wipf and Stock, 2003.

Issler, Klaus. *Wasting Time with God: A Christian Spirituality of Friendship with God.* Downers Grove, IL: InterVarsity Press, 2001.

Johnson, Jan, and Dallas Willard. *Renovation of the Heart in Daily Practice: Experiments in Spiritual Transformation.* Colorado Springs: NavPress, 2006.

Keller, Timothy, and Kathy Keller. *The Songs of Jesus: A Year of Daily Devotions in the Psalms.* New York: Viking, 2015.

Moreland, J. P., and Klaus Issler. *The Lost Virtue of Happiness: Discovering the Disciplines of the Good Life.* Colorado Springs: NavPress, 2006.

Morrow, Jonathan. "Introducing Spiritual Formation." In *Foundations of Spiritual Formation: A Community Approach to Becoming Like Christ.* Edited by Paul Pettit. Grand Rapids: Kregel, 2008.

———. *Think Christianly: Looking at the Intersection of Faith and Culture.* Grand Rapids: Zondervan, 2011.

Ortberg, John. *The Me I Want to Be: Becoming God's Best Version of You.* Grand Rapids: Zondervan, 2009.

Whitney, Donald S. *Simplify Your Spiritual Life: Spiritual Disciplines for the Overwhelmed.* Carol Stream, IL: Tyndale House, 2014.

Yancey, Philip. *What's So Amazing About Grace?* Grand Rapids: Zondervan, 2003.

Discovering the Will
of God

The way of fools seems right to them,
but the wise listen to advice.
—PROVERBS 12:15

Take delight in the LORD,
and he will give you the desires of your heart.
—PSALM 37:4

He has shown you, O mortal, what is good.
And what does the LORD require of you?
To act justly and to love mercy
and to walk humbly with your God.
—MICAH 6:8

WHO AMONG US HAS NOT WONDERED WHAT GOD HAS IN STORE FOR OUR lives? Should I ask her out on a date? If she says yes, is she the one (though this may be a bit presumptuous)? What career should I pursue? Where should I live? Should I buy this car? Does God want me to go overseas and be a missionary?

These are only a handful of the questions we ask. Some seem pretty black and white while others are extremely complex and challenging. So how do we know God's will for our lives?[1] Is there some formula that we can memorize and then plug the appropriate data into? Unfortunately, there isn't. If someone had this magic formula, they would be richer than the owners of Google. (Has anyone else noticed that they're taking over the world?) Discovering God's will is more of an organic and dynamic process. It's kind of like learning to dance. God leads and then you take a step. God leads and then you take another step. But how do you know which step to take? Since there is no formula for discovering God's will for your life, I want to suggest some principles that will aid you in discerning what God would have you do as you travel through life. My list is not exhaustive, but Christians from all walks of life have found these in particular to be helpful. I won't be able to develop each principle fully here, but there will be more than enough to get you thinking in some different ways about discovering God's will (more details can be found in the books I suggest at the end of the chapter).

PRINCIPLE 1: Consult the Word of God

If you want to know God's will for your life, start with the Bible. Spend time learning what God desires you to do and then, empowered by the Holy Spirit and enabled by grace, seek to obey. Charles Swindoll, one of my heroes of the faith, observes, "The better you get to know the Word of God, the less confusing is the will of God. Those who struggle the least with the will of God are those who know the Word of God best."[2]

Paul encouraged Timothy to continue growing in his understanding of God's Word: "But as for you, continue in what you have learned and have become convinced of, because you know those from whom you learned it, and how from infancy you have known the Holy Scriptures, which are able to make you wise for salvation through faith in Christ Jesus. All Scripture is God-breathed and is useful for teaching, rebuking, correcting and training in righteousness, so that the servant of God may be thoroughly equipped for every good work" (2 Tim. 3:14–17; see also Ps. 119). After only a little time and effort, you will discover that God's general will for your life as a Christian is not mysterious. For example, these are all part of God's will for our lives:

- That we be saved (2 Peter 3:9)
- That we be filled with the Holy Spirit (Eph. 5:18)
- That we mature spiritually and become more like Jesus Christ (Rom. 8:29; Col. 2:6–8; 1 Thess. 4:3)
- That we flee from sexual immorality and impurity (2 Cor. 7:1; 1 Thess. 4:3–7)
- That we put others' needs before our own (Phil. 2:3–5)
- That we submit to proper authorities (Rom. 13:1; 1 Peter 2:18)

- That we honor our parents (Eph. 6:1)
- That we maintain a posture of prayer and gratitude (1 Thess. 5:16–18)
- That we are generous with our money (2 Cor. 9:7)
- That we think Christianly about all of life (Luke 10:27; Rom. 12:2)
- That we tell others how they can have a personal relationship with God and help others learn from Jesus how to live (Matt. 28:19–20; Acts 1:8)
- That we act justly, love mercy, and walk humbly with God (Mic. 6:8)

This little list is enough to keep us busy for quite a while.

One more thing: God's leading in your life will *never* contradict His Word. Simply having a strong emotion about something doesn't trump what God has clearly revealed in Scripture. It is not as though someone can say, "Well I prayed about it, and I think God is telling me to leave my spouse for another woman because, after all, God wants me to be happy." (Unfortunately, this is not a hypothetical example. Some people actually *use* this!) Now sometimes God's Word doesn't unilaterally condemn or endorse a certain activity (e.g., drinking alcohol).[3] If you find yourself facing a decision concerning matters of conscience and personal conviction, consult the principles found in Romans 12–14 and 1 Corinthians 8–10. Then pray about it and ask for God's wisdom.

Here's a key question you need to ask based on this principle: What has God already said in the Bible about the decision, circumstance, relationship, or opportunity you are considering? Are you consistently setting aside time to read, study, and apply God's Word so that you would know the answer to this question? The bottom line is this: obeying God in the areas that He has *already* spoken will prepare us to make wise decisions in the areas the Bible doesn't *specifically* address. The vast majority of God's will we don't have to wonder about or pray about—he has already revealed it to us.

PRINCIPLE 2: Cultivate a Heart for God

This principle is an extension of being transformed by God's Word and Spirit. Do you find yourself increasingly desiring the things God desires? As you watch Jesus in action in the Gospels, are you beginning to see a little more of Him in your life? Seek to cultivate the virtues you observe in the life of

Christ (practicing spiritual disciplines is one way to begin doing this). Pray with the psalmist: "Teach me your way, LORD, that I may rely on your faithfulness; give me an undivided heart, that I may fear your name" (Ps. 86:11). Here is the bottom line: when you delight yourself in the Lord, He will give you the desires of your heart (Ps. 37:4). This occurs because your heart has conformed to His heart, and as we mature in Christ, we can begin to follow our hearts with more confidence. God's will is to transform our hearts so that we can increasingly follow our desires as we mature because they are aimed at what is good, true, and beautiful.

PRINCIPLE 3: **Pray for God's Wisdom and Leading**

If you are unsure what God's will is for your life . . . ask Him! There are numerous examples of prayers for wisdom in the Bible. The following are two of them. James says, "If any of you lacks wisdom, you should ask God, who gives generously to all without finding fault, and it will be given to you" (1:5). One of the passages that has been especially meaningful to me is Psalm 143:8, 10: "Let the morning bring me word of your unfailing love, for I have put my trust in you. Show me the way I should go, for to you I entrust my life. . . . Teach me to do your will, for you are my God; may your good Spirit lead me on level ground." It is so easy for us to forget to ask God for wisdom in making decisions; prayer is absolutely essential to this process.

PRINCIPLE 4: **Seek Good Advice and Wise Counsel**

In America, we are infected with the lone-ranger mentality: "I can do it on my own. After all, who knows what I need to do with my life better than me?" Let me be honest with you: this is a foolish way to go through life. We have too many blind spots! Others can often see things we can't because we are simply too close to a situation to have a healthy perspective on it. The book of Proverbs is full of passages encouraging us to bring wise counsel into the process of seeking God's will. For example: "Listen to advice and accept discipline, and at the end you will be counted among the wise" (Prov. 19:20). Here's another: "The way of fools seems right to them, but the wise listen to advice" (Prov. 12:15).

Haddon Robinson suggests three kinds of counsel:[4]

1. *Biblical counsel.* Who is someone in your life saturated with the Word of God who can help you discover what the Bible says about your situation?

2. *Experienced counsel.* Who is someone who has been in this same situation?

3. *Best available counsel.* Who has special expertise in the area where you need advice? Suppose you are considering pursuing a job in the music industry. Before you act on this, it would be wise for you to set up a meeting with a leading representative in that field. Although it is tempting, don't go it alone—you will regret it. Take the risk of being told something you may not want to hear, but need to hear.

Here is the key question to ask at this stage: Who are the wise people in your life who you can go to when you face difficult, confusing, and time-sensitive decisions? List three names: _____, _____, _____. (If you can't list any, those would be some great relationships to start pursuing!) God has given us strategic relationships to help us wisely navigate life.

PRINCIPLE 5: Examine Your Motives

Earlier we said that the more we mature in Christ, the more we will be able to follow the desires of our heart. But we also need to critically examine our motives, because the blinding effects of sin often keep us from seeing how selfish we can be. The first thing we have to do is to admit that we have the uncanny (and very dangerous) capacity to justify anything to ourselves—we have PhDs in self-deception! The prophet Jeremiah put it this way: "The heart is more deceitful than all else and is desperately sick; who can understand it?" (17:9 NASB). Andy Stanley is spot-on when he observes, "We can never be free as long as we're in the habit of lying to ourselves about the reasons behind the choices we make and the paths we take. Telling yourself the truth will free you to move from where you are to where you want and need to be."[5]

It is good to ask yourself some tough questions: *Why am I really doing this? Am I being selfish here? Will others benefit if I do this?* Sometimes we can become so preoccupied with finding God's will that it becomes unhealthy. Either we are presented with several options and freeze up (paralysis by over-analysis) or we walk around thinking and talking about ourselves all the time! Listen to the counsel of Dallas Willard: "My extreme preoccupation with knowing God's will for me may only indicate, contrary to what is often thought, that I am overconcerned with myself, not a Christlike interest in the well-being of others or in the glory of God."[6]

Ask God to reveal to you the motives of your heart. One way of doing this would be to pray as David prayed in Psalm 139:23–24: "Search me, God, and know my heart; test me and know my anxious thoughts. See if there is any offensive way in me, and lead me in the way everlasting."

PRINCIPLE 6: Use Your Head

A mind is a terrible thing to waste. God gave us minds to think and reason with. Now, we are not infallible beings or anything, but we possess the ability to think critically about life situations. It is good to wait on God's direction and leading. However, this doesn't mean that weighing various options or scenarios is unspiritual—far from it. It is wise to envision how a decision would affect not only next week but also the next ten years. Take choosing a job, for example. Ask yourself: *What makes good sense in this situation? Does this position fit my training, education, goals, or passions?* You will be surprised how much this line of questioning will help!

PRINCIPLE 7: Believe That God Is at Work in the Circumstances of Life

God is always at work in the circumstances of life. Sometimes His providence is imperceptible to us, but other times He will reveal His thoughts and ways . . . if we are paying attention. Consider the apostle Paul. He observed an open door God had provided for ministering in Ephesus, and he chose to stay in Ephesus for a while—in spite of opposition (1 Cor. 16:7–9). However, an open door doesn't always mean we should walk through it. On another occasion, Paul recognized an open door in Troas, but he decided to move on because he didn't have peace of mind about the circumstances (2 Cor. 2:12–13). While circumstances can be a guide to the way the Lord is leading, our interpretation of them should be checked by the other principles we have discussed (the book *Experiencing God* has a helpful chapter on circumstances).[7]

PRINCIPLE 8: Be Sensitive to the Leading of the Holy Spirit

This one makes some people nervous. Who hasn't heard the words "God told me to . . ." and then cringed at what was said next? There have certainly been abuses to the "I just have a peace about it" approach . . . too many to count actually. But does the fact of the abuse of this statement make all cases of God's leading in this way illegitimate? Of course not. We must be reminded that we should be wise as we try to discern whether the Holy Spirit is prompting us or not.[8] Many people, myself included, have experienced the strong leading or prompting of the Holy Spirit in a situation. We must not ignore Him in our decision-making. Even though this is a subjective process, God could be trying to get your attention; are you listening and open to what He may say?[9]

Now this principle is best understood in light of the others we have discussed, and we should always test our "impressions" with God's Word and with wise counsel. The Spirit's leading is not a trump card to be used selfishly—remember to check your motives.

Before we wrap up our discussion, here is one more bit of advice—*pay attention to your moods.* If at all possible, don't make decisions late at night or after a deeply emotional experience. Of course, sometimes decisions have to be made on the spot with little or no time to reflect, but most often decisions afford a little time before they must be made. The bigger the decision, the less you will want to make it in the heat of the moment. Rather than deciding the course of your life at three in the morning, sleep on it—things may look a lot different in the morning!

The Best Question Ever

Would you like to avoid a lot of pain, frustration, and heartache? Then have the courage to ask this question and then be honest with yourself. Here's the question that has been developed by Andy Stanley: "*In light of your past experiences, current circumstances, and future hopes and dreams, what's the wise thing to do?*"[10] This question is based on Paul's letter to the Ephesians: "Be very careful, then, how you live—not as unwise but as wise, making the most of every opportunity, because the days are evil. Therefore do not be foolish, but understand what the Lord's will is" (Eph. 5:15–17). Understanding the will of the Lord is connected to wisdom.

Notice the power of this question—it cuts through a lot of your excuses. For example, if you go to the Bible and are relieved to find there is not a verse against whatever you are about to do, that's not wisdom and it doesn't necessarily mean God is for it. "Is there a verse against it?" and "Is it the wise thing for me to do?" are very different questions. Also, the question is not, "Is it wise for my friend or coworker?" . . . but is it wise for *you*.

So let's make it really practical and apply the best question ever to dating. In light of who you are at this point in your life and the last time you dated someone who was cute but not serious about their faith (i.e., your track record), and given that you really haven't changed a whole lot yet, and that you would someday like to be married to someone who loves Jesus, is it wise for you to date this person right now? Well, if you put it that way . . . That's the power of this question.

Have the courage to ask the best question ever and you will avoid a lot of really bad decisions in life.

Reflection on Discovering the Will of God in the Most Affluent Nation on Earth

As an American Christian, I have wrestled with how to know that I'm not following the path of least resistance and calling it God's will. In America it's easy—too easy—to buy into the lie that God's will is always that you be healthy and wealthy. (Our brothers and sisters around the world have a much different experience.) Now, there is nothing wrong with being healthy or wealthy, and these can be seen as God's blessing. But remember that with health and wealth come responsibility and stewardship.

On the other hand, sometimes we can feel guilty for being born in America—the land of opportunity. But we need to remember that God providentially arranged where we would be born (Acts 17:26–27). So if you find yourself in an affluent, comfortable, or influential situation, then consider how you can advance God's kingdom in ways that others without your privileges or status could not (e.g., we can create an awareness of how God is working globally and how Christians can get involved). Be a good steward of this influence. However, just because we encounter suffering, adversity, or persecution, don't immediately interpret these as reasons to change course. Sometimes we must courageously trim our sails and head directly into the wind. The Christians in 1 Peter and Hebrews 11 are a testimony to this reality and serve as our courageous examples.

So as you seek the will of God for your life, employ the principles in this chapter. And then make a decision! God is with you. Be open to whatever God has for you and always live life for His glory, not your own (1 Cor. 10:31). If you have this attitude, you can't go wrong.

THE BIG IDEAS

- Since there are no formulas for discovering the will of God, we ought to utilize biblical principles. The ones we explored in this chapter were (1) consult the Word of God, (2) cultivate a heart for God, (3) pray for God's wisdom and leading, (4) seek good advice and wise counsel, (5) examine your motives, (6) use your head, (7) believe that God is at work in the circumstances of life, and (8) be sensitive to the leading of the Holy Spirit.

- Have the courage to ask the best question ever: "*In light of your past experiences, current circumstances, and future hopes and dreams, what's the wise thing to do?*" —ANDY STANLEY

- Following the will of God in America comes with its own opportunities and challenges that we need to be aware of.

For Further Discovery

Blackaby, Henry T., Richard Blackaby, and Claude V. King. *Experiencing God: Knowing and Doing the Will of God.* Nashville: B&H Publishing, 2008.

DeYoung, Kevin. *Just Do Something: A Liberating Approach to Finding God's Will.* Chicago: Moody Publishers, 2014.

Heath, Chip, and Dan Heath. *Decisive: How to Make Better Choices in Life and Work.* New York: Crown, 2013.

Issler, Klaus. "Communication: Hearing the God Who Speaks." In *Wasting Time with God: A Christian Spirituality of Friendship with God*. Downers Grove, IL: InterVarsity Press, 2001.

Stanley, Andy. *The Best Question Ever*. Sisters, OR: Multnomah, 2009.

———. *The Principle of the Path: How to Get from Where You Are to Where You Want to Be*. Nashville: Thomas Nelson, 2011.

Swindoll, Charles R. *The Mystery of God's Will: What Does He Want for Me?* Nashville: Thomas Nelson, 2001.

Willard, Dallas. *Hearing God: Developing a Conversational Relationship with God*. Downers Grove, IL: InterVarsity Press, 2012.

When Someone
You Love Dies

The LORD *is close to the brokenhearted
and saves those who are crushed in spirit.*

—PSALM 34:18

*I am the resurrection and the life. The one who
believes in me will live, even though they die.*

—JOHN 11:25

*Then I saw "a new heaven and a new earth." . . . And
I heard a loud voice from the throne saying, "Look!
God's dwelling place is now among the people, and
he will dwell with them. They will be his people, and
God himself will be with them and be their God. 'He
will wipe every tear from their eyes. There will be no
more death' or mourning or crying or pain, for the old
order of things has passed away." He who was seated
on the throne said, "I am making everything new!"*

—REVELATION 21:1–5

The first day I'll never forget. I will always remember the summer before my senior year of high school. I was about to go to work at Kroger when the phone call came. I recall standing in my driveway in Knoxville, Tennessee, as my dad told me that my oldest brother had been killed in a car wreck (he had apparently committed suicide). Life had become too much for him, and he was alone. Evidently hopelessness and pain won that day. As I reflect back, I feel twinges of guilt for not being able to do something (though I don't know what I would have done, since he lived in Florida and I lived in

Tennessee). I also want to know why God allowed this to happen. But only God knows the answer to this question. Death has a way of stealing some of the innocence and glitter of life.

The second day I'll never forget. My wife and I were visiting a prospective graduate school in California. We were leaving the school heading out to lunch when my cell phone rang. My father had passed away. He had been battling illness after illness for years, but it was still a shock. It was as if I had been punched in the gut, and I found it hard to breathe. I had planned to fly out to see him in the next two weeks—though I know he would not have wanted me to remember him that way. He would have wanted me to remember him in the good times: throwing a baseball at his apartment in Knoxville, or the drives out in the country when I was a kid. Still, he died too young and never met his grandchildren. I have my questions for God on this one as well. I suppose we will always have our questions when it comes to the timing of loved ones' deaths.[1] Death reminds us that life is short and that we are not promised tomorrow.

How Do You Deal with Death?

Having walked through the loss of a brother and a father by the time I was twenty-six, I want to share some of the things I have learned through these experiences. Why take the time to write such a depressing chapter? Because odds are you will receive a phone call like this one day—maybe even during college. And when you lose someone you love, there are certain things that you will need to hear—I know I did. So here are some of my reflections on how to walk through dark days:

1. *Allow yourself to honestly grieve.* Even if you know your loved one was a Christian and you will see them again someday, that doesn't mean you shouldn't grieve. You don't need to put a "spiritual mask" on at the funeral. When you are grieving, it is OK to not feel that "all things work together for good" (Rom. 8:28 KJV). Part of the healing process is being able to cry and feel the pain of loss. Give yourself permission to grieve.

2. *God is big enough for your honest questions and feelings.* God knows your heart anyway, so you might as well share it with Him. Jesus understands what you are going through; talk to Him.

3. *Try not to spend too much time alone.* There will be times when you need to be by yourself. Maybe you just want to sit and remember for a while. But be careful that you don't shut out the people who love you and are trying to walk with you through this time. Just having others around will be a huge help. It was huge for me.

4. *Let people minister to you.* Pride is a funny thing. Even in a moment of desperate emotional need we may still find an excuse to not allow others to help us—because that would admit need. Well, the sooner that myth is obliterated, the better. Allow people to help you.

5. *Talk about it.* You need to talk about it. Swallowing it will get rid of it temporarily, but it will eventually need to come out. It is healthy to talk to someone. Find a friend, pastor, or counselor. Maybe keep a diary; this could be a way to express what you are feeling. But it is always best to talk to a person about this. Unlike a sheet of paper, they can love you back.

6. *You are still alive, and that's OK.* It is OK to live your life again. You are not disrespecting their memory by moving on; notice I did not say *forgetting.* Resist the temptation to feel guilty. There is still a lot to live for.

How Do You Minister to Family and Friends Who Mourn?

It is hard to know how to minister to someone who has lost a loved one—especially if you have never been through anything like it yourself. They usually don't teach courses on this, so here are some practical suggestions:

1. *Have a ministry of presence in their life.* Just *be there* for them. Don't say anything—especially cliché Christian sayings like, "They're in a better place." Listen far more than you speak. Job's friends rightly take a lot of criticism for the way they treated Job, but at least they started off well: "Then they sat on the ground with him for seven days and seven nights. No one said a word to him, because they saw how great his suffering was" (Job 2:13).

2. *Pray.* Never underestimate the power of prayer. Pray specifically for healing, peace, protection, and grace. In the darkest moments, only the reality of God's presence comforts.

3. *Don't ask, do!* If you wait for them to tell you what they need, you will be waiting a long time—they may never ask. Rather than ask if you can bring a meal, go buy a gift card for a restaurant, place it in a card, write them a note, and drop it at their place. That way when they are hungry, they can just go eat or have someone go get the food. Be creative.

4. *Don't avoid them.* They will already be feeling different anyway. They need human contact and touch. Go give them a hug and pray with them. Sit with them during a meal; invite them out with friends or to a movie. This will be healing to them.

5. *Continue to be available.* Grieving takes longer than a week. When they will need you most is in the days ahead when the shock has worn off and the casseroles, flowers, and cards have stopped coming and they have to face the reality of life again. But sadly, most people have gone on with life as usual at this point. Take the initiative to call and check in or stop by and say hello. These are probably the loneliest days. Also, pay attention to holidays or anniversaries of the day they lost a loved one. Send a text to just let them know you are thinking of them.

6. *Be patient.* Give them time. Also, you probably need to develop thicker skin. They may respond in uncharacteristic ways because they are hurting. Don't take it personally; the pain has to go somewhere.

After the Last Tear Falls

There will come a day when every broken heart has been mended, every illness healed. God will set the world right. Death will not have the final word—Jesus Christ made certain of that. One day, perfect love will drive out all of our fears (1 John 4:18). So even in the darkest hours, I trust in God. One day, God will no longer have to count the tears we cry, because they will all be wiped away (Ps. 56:8; Isa. 25:7–8).[2]

POSTSCRIPT: With My Brother to the End

The older I get the more death seems to interrupt life. Honestly I am growing weary of it and am tired of funerals. But God wastes nothing so I want to share with you two important lessons I learned by walking with my brother through his battle with cancer.

The first lesson I would share is to never give up on people. I had given up on my brother, but I shouldn't have. Let me explain. My relationship with my older brother was complicated and virtually nonexistent for over ten years (based on what we later discovered was a big misunderstanding). We had chosen very different paths. I had chosen to follow Jesus, which led me to finish college, get married, start a family, and pursue graduate school. Because of a lot of pain in his life and unresolved wounds, my brother had run down a path away from God and experienced many of the consequences that came with it. But that's not what served as the wake-up call. Cancer did. Through some providential relationships and circumstances, I learned that he was battling stage IV cancer. And compressing a very emotional and significant story of healing, not only did my brother and I reconcile, but also over months of talking again I was able to lead my brother to place his trust in Jesus Christ as his Savior. I never saw that coming . . . but God did. Lesson number one: no one is ever too far gone for God's grace. We can only see through the lens of our circumstances. If someone is coming to mind right now—don't give up on them!

The second lesson I learned is that the years I had spent studying the evidence for the resurrection prepared me for a path I would have never chosen to walk. The good news was that my brother's cancer was in remission for a season. He married a wonderful and loving woman and they had a sweet baby girl. But then the cancer came back with a vengeance and my brother fought so hard and I was so proud of him. As the cancer stole the life from my brother, we talked about what was true and said what we needed to say to each other, and I tried my best to support and love him well. I also watched as his wife loved him and sacrificially cared for him during an unspeakably hard and painful time. But one of the things my brother and I talked about and I reminded him of often was that because Jesus really was raised from the dead, we would be too someday. Because he was a follower of Jesus, this life was not the end for him. God's true story continues.

I had the privilege of being with my brother and holding his hand as he took his last breath. In those last few seconds I was reminding him that it was going to be OK, and he could go to be with Jesus, and I loved him. God's grace and peace along with the knowledge that the resurrection is really true are what sustained me during those difficult days. And they sustain me in the good days too. My brother died at the age of forty, which is way too young. Life is a gift—don't waste it or take it for granted. And remember this: because the resurrection of Jesus is true, it changes everything.

THE BIG IDEAS

- Unless the Lord returns before, death will interrupt your life.
- Allow yourself to grieve and be ministered to.
- Minister to others with grace and action.
- One day, there will be no more tears.

For Further Discovery

Carson, D. A. *How Long, O Lord? Reflections on Suffering and Evil*. 2nd ed. Grand Rapids: Baker, 2006.

Habermas, Gary R., and J. P. Moreland. *Beyond Death: Exploring the Evidence for Immortality*. Eugene, OR: Wipf and Stock, 2004.

Keller, Timothy. *Walking with God through Pain and Suffering*. New York: Dutton, 2013.

Lewis, C. S. *A Grief Observed*. New York: HarperCollins, 2009.

———. *The Problem of Pain*. New York: HarperCollins, 2009.

Sittser, Jerry L. *A Grace Disguised: How the Soul Grows Through Loss*. Grand Rapids: Zondervan, 2009.

Swindoll, Charles R. *Hope Again: When Life Hurts and Dreams Fade*. Dallas: Word, 1996.

Yancey, Philip. *Where Is God When It Hurts?* Grand Rapids: Zondervan, 2010.

Zacharias, Ravi. *Cries of the Heart: Bringing God Near When He Feels So Far*. Nashville: Thomas Nelson, 2002.

Gentlemen, Become Who You Were Born to Be

> *Be strong, therefore, and show yourself a man. Keep the charge of the LORD your God, to walk in His ways, to keep His statutes, His commandments, His ordinances, and His testimonies, . . . that you may succeed in all that you do and wherever you turn.*
>
> —1 KINGS 2:2–3 NASB

> *A good name is more desirable than great riches;*
> *to be esteemed is better than silver or gold.*
>
> —PROVERBS 22:1

> *If a man knows not what harbor he seeks, any wind is the right wind.*
>
> —SENECA

THERE ARE SOME MOMENTS IN YOUR LIFE YOU NEVER FORGET . . . THIS was one of them. Standing on a rocky beach as the sun was setting over the Pacific Ocean, I was surrounded by fifty young college-aged men. We had just concluded twenty-four weeks of exploring biblical manhood together that year. In order to graduate, each of the young men had completed a manhood action plan (MAP) and then shared specific action steps with dates attached to them with their small group so they would follow through. If you were in that group, here are some of the things you would have heard: important conversations they needed to have with their own fathers to give and receive forgiveness, what standards of integrity and purity they would have in their dating life, what they wanted to be like as husbands and fathers someday, and what they wanted written about them in their obituary when all was said and done.

As I delivered a charge for them to pursue biblical manhood and invited them to step up into this community of men, I couldn't help but think of a similar experience I had seven years earlier. But that night I was the one who had finished a year of investigating what biblical manhood looked like with a band of brothers and then been called up to join a group of older men in pursuing God's vision for manhood. I had committed to be a man of Christ, and someday—if it was part of God's calling for me—to be a godly husband and loving father.

These were two of the most significant experiences of my life, and by God's grace the effects from commitments made there continue to impact my family and friends—all because some other men had invited me to pursue God's ideal of biblical manhood. In this chapter, I want to invite you to do the same. God is calling you to more.

Are Men Necessary?

Are men necessary? Columnist Maureen Dowd wrote a book addressing this question titled *Are Men Necessary? When Sexes Collide.*[1] I came across an answer she gave in a CNN interview: "'So now that women don't need men to reproduce and refinance, the question is, will we keep you around? And the answer is,' she added puckishly, 'you know we need you in the way we need ice cream, you'll be more ornamental.'"[2] So, guys, are we really necessary? Who are we? What does manhood really look like?

When Men Are Absent

When men don't show up, take responsibility, and follow through, bad things happen. As the National Center for Fathering confirms, "More than 20 million children live in a home without the physical presence of a father. Millions more have dads who are physically present, but emotionally absent. If it were classified as a disease, fatherlessness would be an epidemic worthy of attention as a national emergency."[3] A heartbreaking 40 percent of babies born in the United States are delivered by unwed mothers.[4] And CNN has reported that "more than 72 percent of children in the African-American community are born out of wedlock."[5] Children raised in a home without a dad face dire consequences. Here are only a few:

- Nine times more likely to drop out of school
- Ten times more likely to abuse chemical substances
- Seventy percent of teen pregnancies happen in a fatherless home
- Eleven times more likely to exhibit violent behavior
- Twenty times more likely to be incarcerated
- Nine times more likely to be raped or sexually abused in a home without a biological father[6]

This is what happens when fathers are absent. What is going on?

Manhood Is in a State of Confusion

William Bennett, author of *The Book of Man*, makes the following observation: "For the first time in history, women are better educated, more ambitious and arguably more successful than men. Now, society has rightly celebrated the ascension of one sex. We said, 'You go girl,' and they went. We celebrate the ascension of women but what will we do about what appears to be the very real decline of the other sex?"[7] There is absolutely no question that feminism has accomplished many important achievements for women's rights over the past two centuries. These should be celebrated and promoted because they are consistent with God's design of women as co-image-bearers worthy of all the dignity, respect, and rights that men are (see Gen. 1–2). However, one of the unintended consequences of feminism is the promotion of the false idea that there really is no meaningful difference between men and women, between moms and dads. What is abundantly clear is that you won't find manhood celebrated in our culture today. When was the last time you saw a strong, smart, virtuous, and patient dad celebrated on TV shows or in Hollywood? More often than not, TV shows paint a picture of men as passive, aloof, oversexed, and in serious need of a strong woman to keep them in line (nothing wrong with a strong woman, but I am merely highlighting what this indicates concerning the state of manhood). It seems like each new sitcom keeps this caricature of manhood alive and well.

In looking at today's culture, one thing is crystal clear: manhood is in a state of confusion. A majority of men live lives of confusion, isolation, frustration, and quiet desperation.[8] Time only intensifies these emotions. Our society offers a lot of pressure but little by way of encouragement for this generation of men. On the contrary, men get a healthy dose of ridicule before being dismissed as unnecessary. This sentiment is tragic in and of itself, but even more tragic when this same confusion, isolation, frustration, and quiet desperation is occurring among Christian men. Men are floundering today because they find their identity in performance, possessions, and pleasure. There is a lack of vision that calls men beyond themselves to serve others.

This leads many men to self-medicate by escaping to video games, fantasy football, and porn. Obviously I am not saying there is anything inherently wrong with playing some video games or fantasy football, but if it were possible to add up the total number of hours spent on these activities each year by all the males in our culture, I think we would be shocked!

Our society offers no compelling definition of manhood to boys today and provides no encouragement to find one. The consequences have been devastating as men routinely escape into their careers, being largely passive in the home, with their wives and children unsure what role—if any—the men are supposed to play. This confusion extends into their role in society as well, which perpetuates the cycle.

Where are you, as a college man, to look for a definition? At the end of the chapter, we will unpack and explore the biblical definition of manhood I talked about at the beginning of this chapter, which you can apply to any situation in life. We will then highlight ten biblical ideals to pursue. But before we get to that, let's briefly take a look at how we got here.[9]

So How Did We Get Here?

In some ways, manhood has gone downhill since exiting the garden of Eden after the fall—but we won't go back that far! There is a lot to this answer, but I just want to highlight two particularly powerful sociological factors in America. The first was the *Industrial Revolution*. Before the twentieth century, sons would typically learn from their fathers because they would go out in the field with them to watch them work or be around them to observe how they lived. But when the Industrial Revolution occurred, some fathers went off to work in the city, or the new jobs required fathers to be gone more, leaving the young men with no role model, no picture of what it means to be a man. Simply put, dad was not around very much anymore. Mentoring is crucial to cultivating manhood, and societal factors have made that increasingly difficult to replicate.

A second factor that contributed to today's state of manhood confusion was the *sexual revolution*. The loss of restraint and the elevation of satisfying one's desires as the highest good haven't been good for anyone—especially men. The lie is that you can have sex without responsibility. Then the epidemic of pornography came along, offering to satisfy sexual desires without relationships. Women were seen as objects to be used, not loved and protected. Freedom became redefined apart from virtue and responsibility. Instead "freedom" became the ability to do what you want to do whenever you want to do it—and this mind-set has had disastrous consequences for men and for society as a whole.

A Bit of My Journey to Manhood

I want to share a bit of my story with you. I grew up in a broken home. My parents divorced when I was eight years old. My mom raised me until I was in seventh grade; then my dad was given custody of me. In many ways, I was left to figure out life on my own. Though there were good times, my relationship with my dad was unfortunately characterized by formality and superficial conversation: get good grades, stay out of big trouble, that sort of thing. But he never talked to me about being a man. He never told me how to date or filled me in on what sex was all about.

High school was pretty tough to navigate—a lot of insecurity and uncertainty. But then things began to change. My junior year I became a Christian and almost immediately a youth volunteer started to mentor me. He had me over to his house, his wife cooked me manicotti, and we would talk about what growing in Christ looks like. They both listened to me. I have long since told Neal how much I appreciate him and the time he gave me—the fact that he, as an older man, took the time to invest in me breathed life into my soul.

I was then off to college, and that is where I met mentor number two. Rich was the campus director of Campus Crusade for Christ at Middle Tennessee State University. For four years we met regularly and I watched his life; I learned a ton. Upon graduation I got married (the same day!). Now I faced my next hurdle: What was I supposed to do as a husband?

Enter my third mentor: Monty. Being able to talk to him about marriage and ministry was huge! I was part of a church plant, and the first thing our church did was go through a curriculum from Men's Fraternity. This process changed my life. Through it I received a biblical vision for manhood, marriage, and family. Not only that, but I gained friends whom I could trust and who would call me to a higher standard as a Christian man.

I have now been married fifteen years, and I have three children. I am still learning and growing, but I have to tell you that I love being a husband and a father because I have a vision for what this ought to look like. Not only that, but I have men in my life who encourage me to pursue that vision. I look forward to one day sharing it with my son.

A Biblical Definition of Manhood

As Christian men, our instruction manual is the Bible. The pages of Scripture reveal two prominent men: the first man, Adam, and the last Adam, Jesus Christ (Gen. 1–3; 1 Cor. 15:45–49). Adam lived life separated from God; Jesus Christ lived in union with God. As men, you and I will live in the shadow of one or the other. The following definition is derived from comparing and contrasting the lives of these two predominant men: *"a real man is one who . . . rejects passivity, accepts responsibility, leads courageously, [and] expects the greater reward . . . God's reward."*[10] Let's briefly discuss each of the four aspects (you can further explore this definition of manhood and more in the resources found at AuthenticManhood.com).[11]

- First, a real man *rejects passivity*. Genesis 2:16–17 reveals that Adam had been given a clear word from God that neither he nor his wife were to eat from the tree of the knowledge of good and evil. And yet, Adam exhibited passivity by standing idly by as his wife was tempted by the serpent to eat the fruit. Eve ate, and though he was right next to her, he did nothing (Gen. 3:6). In contrast, Jesus Christ rejected passivity and displayed initiative in coming to save humanity held captive by sin. Listen to how the second Adam is described: "Have this attitude in yourselves which was also in Christ Jesus, who, although He existed in the form of God, did not regard equality with God a thing to be grasped, but emptied Himself, *taking the form* of a bond-servant, *and* being made in the likeness of men. Being found in appearance as a man, He *humbled* Himself by *becoming obedient* to the point of death, even death on a cross" (Phil. 2:5–8 NASB, italics added). Jesus Christ did not stand idly by and do nothing.

- Second, a real man *accepts responsibility.* "Like Adam, Jesus Christ was also given three specific responsibilities from His Father. Our Lord was entrusted with a *will* to obey (His Father's), a *work* to do (redeem the lost), and a *'woman'* to love (the church)."[12] While Adam rejected his responsibilities, Jesus Christ joyfully accepted these responsibilities even in the midst of great difficulty (see John 4:34).

- Third, a real man *leads courageously.* Men were created to lead; notice I didn't say "dominate" or "abuse" (see 1 Cor. 11:3). In the garden "Adam relinquished his leadership . . . when he refused to step forward with God's Word and lead his wife."[13] In contrast, when presented with the opportunity to succumb to emotional, spiritual, and physical pressures in the Judean wilderness, Jesus Christ led with the truth of God in the face of adversity and temptation (Matt. 4:10).

- Finally, a real man *expects God's greater reward.* Why was Jesus able to persevere through hardship and ultimately the cross? The author of Hebrews writes, "Let us run with endurance the race that is set before us, fixing our eyes on Jesus, the author and perfecter of faith, *who for the joy set before Him* endured the cross, despising the shame, and has sat down at the right hand of the throne of God" (12:1–2 NASB, italics added). Jesus Christ looked forward to a joyful reward! That is what kept Him going. And if you and I struggle well and remain faithful, then we will be rewarded as well. At the end of life Paul said, "In the future there is laid up for me the crown of righteousness, which the Lord, the righteous Judge, will award to me on that day; and not only to me, but also to all who have loved His appearing" (2 Tim. 4:8 NASB).

Ten Biblical Ideals to Pursue

The following are ten biblical ideals you can pursue as a Christian man.[14] Pray that God would build these qualities into your life.

1. *Loyalty.* "For I delight in loyalty rather than sacrifice, and in the knowledge of God rather than burnt offerings" (Hos. 6:6 NASB).

2. *Servant-leadership.* "Whoever wants to become great among you must be your servant, and whoever wants to be first must be your slave" (Matt. 20:26–27).

3. *Kindness.* "What is desirable in a man is his kindness" (Prov. 19:22 NASB).

4. *Humility.* "Do nothing out of selfish ambition or vain conceit. Rather, in humility value others above yourselves" (Phil. 2:3).

5. *Purity.* "Let no one look down on your youthfulness, but rather in speech, conduct, love, faith and purity, show yourself an example of those who believe" (1 Tim. 4:12 NASB).

6. *Honesty.* "Therefore, laying aside falsehood, speak truth each one of you with his neighbor, for we are members of one another" (Eph. 4:25 NASB).

7. *Self-discipline.* "But have nothing to do with worldly fables. . . . On the other hand, discipline yourself for the purpose of godliness; for bodily discipline is only of little profit, but godliness is profitable for all things, since it holds promise for the present life and also for the life to come" (1 Tim. 4:7–8 NASB).

8. *Excellence.* "Do you not know that those who run in a race all run, but only one receives the prize? Run in such a way that you may win" (1 Cor. 9:24 NASB).

9. *Integrity.* "He who walks in integrity walks securely, but he who perverts his ways will be found out" (Prov. 10:9 NASB).

10. *Perseverance.* "Let us not lose heart in doing good, for in due time we will reap if we do not grow weary" (Gal. 6:9 NASB).

Become Who You Were Born to Be

J. R. R. Tolkien's *Lord of the Rings* is a masterpiece. There is a scene toward the end of Peter Jackson's *The Return of the King* film adaptation that powerfully captures what we have been talking about. Aragorn is leading an outmanned army to defeat the dark lord Sauron. But then Elrond shows up with a gift—

the sword called Anduril. Yet Aragorn still fears his past and is reluctant to embrace his destiny as king of Gondor. Then, at the moment of decision, Elrond whispers, "Put aside the ranger; become who you were born to be." Aragorn embraces his destiny and courageously leads his army to victory. As Winston Churchill famously put it: "There comes into the life of every man a task for which he alone is uniquely suited. What a shame if that moment finds him either unwilling or unprepared for that which would be his finest hour."[15]

You and I have a similar choice before us. Either we can remain ensnared by sin, our past, and passivity, or we can embrace God's call upon our lives as men and take initiative. Which will you choose? Our world desperately needs real men, not dominating, unforgiving, abusive, manipulative, and selfish boys. *Become the man you were born to be.*

THE BIG IDEAS

- Manhood is in a state of confusion. Two main sociological reasons for this are the lack of mentoring ushered in through the Industrial Revolution and the redefinition of freedom and responsibility during the sexual revolution.

- A real man rejects passivity, accepts responsibility, leads courageously, and expects God's greater reward.

For Further Discovery

Arterburn, Stephen, Kenny Luck, and Mike Yorkey. *Every Man, God's Man: Every Man's Guide to Courageous Faith and Daily Integrity.* Colorado Springs: WaterBrook Press, 2011.

Köstenberger, Andreas J., and Margaret Elizabeth Köstenberger. *God's Design for Man and Woman: A Biblical-Theological Survey.* Wheaton, IL: Crossway, 2014.

Nelson, Tommy. *The Book of Romance: What Solomon Says About Love, Sex, and Intimacy.* Nashville: Thomas Nelson, 2007.

Rainey, Dennis. *Stepping Up: A Call to Courageous Manhood.* Little Rock: FamilyLife, 2011.

Weber, Stu. *The Four Pillars of a Man's Heart: Bringing Strength into Balance*. New York: Crown, 2013.

———. *Locking Arms: Shoulder to Shoulder, Man to Man . . . God's Design for Masculine Friendships*. Sisters, OR: Multnomah, 1995.

———. *Tender Warrior: Every Man's Purpose, Every Woman's Dream, Every Child's Hope*. Sisters, OR: Multnomah, 2006.

Men's Fraternity at www.mensfraternity.com.

Ladies, Pursue Real Beauty

Above all else, guard your heart,
for everything you do flows from it.

—PROVERBS 4:23

Charm is deceptive, and beauty is fleeting;
but a woman who fears the LORD is to be praised.

—PROVERBS 31:30

Flee the evil desires of youth and pursue righteousness,
faith, love and peace, along with those who call on the
Lord out of a pure heart.

—2 TIMOTHY 2:22

I HAVE A CONFESSION: *I AM NOT A WOMAN.* BUT IF IT MAKES YOU FEEL any better, I am listening to various women artists on Spotify to get in the spirit of things as I write this chapter. Obviously, I cannot speak from personal and common experience like I can to the guys.

Think of me as an older brother in Christ. Having a little sister and being the father of two girls has sobered me to how hard it must be to be a Christian woman in today's society. That is why I wanted to take this opportunity to share a handful of insights from God's Word about what it means to be a woman of God. As to my further credentials, I watch the occasional chick flick—there, I said it (if any guys are reading this chapter, I also watch action films). But most importantly, I am married to a godly, beautiful woman. She is a wonderful mother to our three children, and I have learned a lot about biblical womanhood simply by observing her follow Christ.

Becoming a Woman of the Word

Becoming a woman of God means becoming a woman of the Word (this is part of what it means to fear the Lord—see Proverbs 31:30). It is vitally important that you saturate your heart and mind with God's truth. Meditate on the Word of God (Josh. 1:8). Renewing your mind is not optional if you want to grow as a woman in Christ (Rom. 12:1–2). As we will discuss in a moment, you are constantly being bombarded with images and expectations that are contrary to God's unique design for you as a woman. If you don't want to be squashed into the world's mold—and as a result miss out on God's best for you—then you must make time with God in His Word a daily priority during this season of life.

Listen to the advice of David: "How can a young person stay on the path of purity? By living according to your word. I seek you with all my heart; do not let me stray from your commands. I have hidden your word in my heart that I might not sin against you" (Ps. 119:9–11). From this passage, we learn that the way to live a pure life is by obeying what God's Word says and then hiding this truth in our heart. Also, David had placed himself under its authority. Remember that God's Word is alive and at work in you as you submit to its authority (Heb. 4:12; see also 1 Thess. 2:13). So if you want to be a woman of God, then meditating on God's Word regularly is nonnegotiable.

Rejecting a Barbie Worldview

Again, I'm not a woman—but I can only imagine the pressure of living in our airbrushed society with pencil-thin models on the cover of every magazine and selling every product under the sun. While I don't agree with a lot of what Meghan Trainor sings about, I do applaud her pushing back against our photoshopped culture by pulling her "Me Too" music video after editors airbrushed her. Daily, you face the pressure to be, well, *perfect*. But what does perfect mean? To look like a Barbie doll, a runway model, or a busty, seductive blond on the cover of *Cosmo*? To have perfect abs and a great tan? This is not true beauty (much of it is artificially enhanced with computer programs, lighting, and makeup anyway). I'd like to recommend a book that I came across called *Wanting to Be Her: Body Image Secrets Victoria Won't Tell You* by Michelle Graham.[1] This book honestly addresses the critical issue of body image far better, and with much more candor, than I ever could.

I'm not saying your body is unimportant. On the contrary, it is important to be healthy and take care of your body—primarily because it is the temple of the Holy Spirit and you only have one body with which to serve God. Also, it is not wrong to try to look your best—but your outward appearance should not *consume* your time, energy, and money. Remember, you are God's precious, adopted daughter (Rom. 8:15–17), and He intricately designed you from the earliest stages of life; you are fearfully and wonderfully made (Ps. 139:14–16). His everlasting love is not conditioned upon whether you own the latest jeans or fit into a size two or fifteen (see Jer. 31:3).

It is not as though the Bible demeans physical appearance (e.g., Gen. 29:17 tells us that Rachel "had a lovely figure and was beautiful"). It's just that God values other things *more* than outward appearance, namely the heart (1 Sam. 16:7). By way of illustration, when considering a man to date, look for a godly character and a good reputation (Prov. 22:1). If he's handsome, that's a bonus. Character is sexy (trust me on this). Being attracted to whomever you date and eventually marry is natural and good. Solomon's bride-to-be longed for him because of his character and appearance, but they also showed restraint until they were married (Song 2:3–7).[2]

Here is a great proverb: "Like a gold ring in a pig's snout is a beautiful woman who shows no discretion" (Prov. 11:22). Among other things, this passage teaches that virtuous character and a pure heart are much more important than whether someone is drop-dead gorgeous, or plain, or overweight. While it is hard at your youthful age to imagine that your body will one day deteriorate, the truth is it will. This is why it is so foolish for us to ground our sense of identity or base our relationships with the opposite sex on physical beauty. One day, outward beauty will fade; then what will be left? Life is too short to pursue an unrealistic and unhealthy agenda set by a culture that does not have your best interests in mind.

Pursuing Real Beauty

Real, biblical beauty goes beyond the physical and focuses on the heart. Let's briefly examine two passages that clearly show how God defines real beauty.

Proverbs 31:10–31 describes what a virtuous woman looks like. But the crowning jewel and summary verse of this passage is verse 30: "Charm is deceptive, and beauty is fleeting; but a woman who fears the LORD is to be praised." A virtuous and truly beautiful woman is one who fears the Lord. She is the one who follows the path of wisdom (see Prov. 1:7). The things the world looks to as attractive and valuable are a hollow substitute for the real thing. God's Word says charm is deceitful. One commentator observes that charm "deceives because it promises a lifetime of happiness that it can't deliver."[3] Charm is like an advertisement that lures someone into a store but then there is nothing of real value to purchase.

Notice that this verse also claims that beauty is fleeting. The word *fleeting* literally means "a puff of air."[4] It is gone before you know it (I know, not a comforting thought). Charm and beauty are only the shell; the fear of the Lord is what gives substance and weight to a woman's soul. Proverbs 31:30 defines beauty as cultivating the fear of the Lord.

First Peter 3:3–4 states, "Your beauty should not come from outward adornment, such as elaborate hairstyles and the wearing of gold jewelry or fine clothes. Rather, it should be that of your inner self, the unfading beauty of a gentle and quiet spirit, which is of great worth in God's sight."[5] There is a lot here, but I just want to call your attention to a couple of observations. First, what signifies the beauty of a woman is not her outward appearance; it is her inner self (i.e., her heart). Moreover, in contrast to physical beauty that fades over time, "a gentle and quiet spirit" remains beautiful. God highly values the inner beauty of the heart.[6]

These two passages lead to one convicting question: Which aspect of beauty receives more of your attention, your heart or your outward appearance? Is your answer in line with what God values the most? Here are three pieces of big-brotherly advice: First, keep on the lookout for guys who value your heart more than your body; this will keep you from a lot of heartache. Second, your heavenly Father loves you more than you can possibly imagine and you are His precious daughter—that is your primary identity. No matter how you mess up or the guilt and shame you feel, you can always run to Him. Finally, when it comes to dressing modestly, help out your brothers in Christ by not wearing clothes with words written across your rear end or chest. Guys struggle enough with keeping their wandering eyes under control; they don't need any more incentive from strategically placed advertising or slogans.

OK, the brotherly sermon is over now.

On Being a Biblical Woman in Today's World

Our society has come a long way when it comes to women's rights, and we should celebrate this progress. Unfortunately, however, the latest wave of feminism has gone far beyond demanding equal rights. Our culture is slowly eroding genuine gender distinctions. You were created female, and I was created male, and that didn't occur by accident. Though both male and female equally bear the image of God (Gen. 1:26–27; 5:2), are equal in value, and are coheirs with Christ, God designed us to function in specific ways that *complement* one another. So while we are *equal* in God's eyes, that does not mean we are or have to be the *same*. As a woman of God, there are aspects of being a follower of Christ that you have in common with men, but there are also specific aspects that are core to your calling as a woman.

As I conclude with some final observations about biblical womanhood and culture, you need to know that I am not saying that all women should be barefoot and pregnant, cooking in the kitchen. Neither am I saying that women must stay in abusive or oppressive relationships. I am not saying that women aren't as smart or talented as men, that they can't be good leaders, or that they can't be strong, independent, or athletic.

Just as I included a biblical definition of manhood for the guys, here is the best attempt I have seen at capturing a concise but accurate definition of biblical womanhood: a real woman "rejects worldly temptations for significance, believes in God's priorities, nurtures the next generation, and expects God's greater reward."[7]

Being a godly woman in today's world will require you to go against the grain. However, a biblical woman finds her significance in God's priorities, not the ever-changing murmurings of culture. For most women, this most probably includes marrying and embracing the high calling of being a virtuous wife and a nurturing mother, and investing considerable intellect, gifting, and talent in family first.[8] Contrarily, our society says that a career is the highest calling for a woman and is where her significance should lie.[9] As a father of three, I can tell you that I thank God that my wife desires (and is able) to be at home with our children during these formative years. It is not always easy, but she nurtures and loves them well. Sure, there are days when anything would be preferable to more diapers, dirty clothes, and nursery rhymes, but she loves being a mom—and is a great one at that! Could she be making important contributions to the workplace instead? Absolutely!

My wife is creative, resourceful, and hardworking. But what could be more important than being there every step of the way for our young children?

Now, you may be wondering why I chose to include this touchy discussion in a chapter to a bunch of unmarried college women. Your college years are largely when you will form your values and priorities, and I have sat through enough college classes and talked to enough students to know that this is the *last perspective on womanhood you will get in a secular classroom.* In fact, what I have said will be seen by many as a step backward for you as a woman. The world says that being a wife and mother is not as significant as being the CEO of a company. God disagrees.[10] The vast majority of you reading this book will eventually get married and have a family, and this is a high calling in and of itself. Interestingly, a Gallup poll indicates that "more than half of women, 56%, who have a child younger than 18 would ideally like to stay home and care for their house and family."[11] In the days and years ahead, it will be up to you to seek God's face, study His Word, and set your priorities accordingly as you walk the path of womanhood and discover your calling. Just be careful that you don't mistake the prevailing winds of cultural opinion for the voice of God. If you are obedient to God and faithful to His priorities and calling on your life, you will find that His approval and reward far outweigh anything else the world has to offer.

THE BIG IDEAS

- If you want to be a woman of God, then meditating on God's Word regularly is nonnegotiable.

- Real, biblical beauty goes beyond the physical and focuses on the heart.

- A real woman "rejects worldly temptations for significance, believes in God's priorities, nurtures the next generation, and expects God's greater reward." —ROBERT LEWIS

- It will be up to you to seek God's face, study His Word, and set your priorities accordingly. Just be careful that you do not mistake the prevailing winds of cultural opinion for the voice of God.

For Further Discovery

Baldwin, Tindell. *Popular: Boys, Booze, and Jesus: A Memoir*. Carol Stream, IL: Tyndale House, 2013.

Courtney, Vicki. *Cherish: Cultivating Relationships with Parents, Friends, Guys, and More*. Nashville: B&H Publishing, 2016.

Ethridge, Shannon, and Stephen Arterburn. *Every Young Woman's Battle: Guarding Your Mind, Heart, and Body in a Sex-Saturated World*. Colorado Springs: WaterBrook Press, 2009.

Feldhahn, Shaunti, and Robert Lewis. *The Life Ready Woman: Thriving in a Do-It-All World*. Nashville: B&H Publishing, 2011.

Graham, Michelle. *Wanting to Be Her: Body Image Secrets Victoria Won't Tell You*. Downers Grove, IL: InterVarsity Press, 2005.

Köstenberger, Andreas J., and Margaret Elizabeth Köstenberger. *God's Design for Man and Woman: A Biblical-Theological Survey*. Wheaton, IL: Crossway, 2014.

Moore, Beth. *So Long, Insecurity: You've Been a Bad Friend to Us*. Carol Stream, IL: Tyndale House, 2010.

TerKeurst, Lysa. *Unglued: Making Wise Choices in the Midst of Raw Emotions*. Grand Rapids: Zondervan, 2012.

Proverbs 31 Ministries with Lysa TerKeurst at www.proverbs31.org.

The Dating Game

Above all else, guard your heart,
for everything you do flows from it.
—PROVERBS 4:23

Love is patient, love is kind. It does not envy, it does not boast,
it is not proud. It does not dishonor others, it is not self-seeking,
it is not easily angered, it keeps no record of wrongs. Love does
not delight in evil but rejoices with the truth. It always protects,
always trusts, always hopes, always perseveres. Love never fails.
—1 CORINTHIANS 13:4–8

The issue is not how to fit our spiritual life into our dating life;
rather, it is how to fit our dating life into our spiritual life.
—HENRY CLOUD AND JOHN TOWNSEND[1]

I COULDN'T BELIEVE IT. I WAS STUNNED. THERE I WAS AT RED LOBSTER, looking across the booth at my date and then back down at the menu. I am in high school, for goodness' sake, and this girl just ordered the most expensive item on the menu—Alaskan snow crab! This delicacy weighed in at a costly $22.95. And given that I only had about $25 in my wallet, I quickly realized that water and a side salad were my only available dining options. "Not hungry?" she asked. "Yeah, my stomach is a little upset." Needless to say, that was our last date.

Ah, dating . . . It's fun, isn't it? While my story only set me back some cash and some time, a bad dating relationship can cause way more damage. It can lead to a lot of pain, frustration, and heartache. I was recently at a coffee shop, and a teenage girl walked in wearing a T-shirt that had the words "You break it . . . you buy it" just above a picture of a broken heart. That pretty well sums it up.

If you've grown up anywhere cold (or if you have seen *A Christmas Story*), then you know sticking your tongue to a frozen flagpole is not a great idea. You aren't going to get out of that without leaving a little bit of you on that pole. The same is true of a bad dating relationship. You may break up, but it will definitely cost you something. So how in the world do you date? Or as some have suggested, should you even date at all?[2]

What does the Bible say about dating? If by that you mean, does the Bible describe what a twenty-first-century dating relationship in America should look like, then no, the Bible does not have much to offer. But God has not left us in the dark about dating, love, sex, and marriage (see Song of Solomon). God's Word provides us with many principles that can be applied to dating relationships. For this topic, I thought it would be helpful to list some common questions and issues, and then share some biblical, time-tested principles for dating well.

When Are You Ready to Date?

How is your relationship with God? Do you spend regular time studying and meditating on God's Word (1 Peter 2:2–3) and in prayer (Col. 4:2)? Do you have a community of friends that encourages and challenges you to be more Christlike (Heb. 10:24–25)? If dating is for those seeking to be mature (notice I didn't say you had to be perfect to date), then I would suggest focusing on your spiritual health before trying to add the challenges that dating can bring to your life. If you are doing your best to follow Christ, then I would offer three things you need to do *before* you start dating.

First, you need to come up with a picture of *the kind of person* you are looking for; that way you will not settle for less. You don't need to know who "the one" is, but you need to think about what qualities that person needs to have. Stop looking for *the one* and start looking for *the right kind of one*. If you have no clue what you are looking for, then take some time to pray for guidance, search the Scriptures, talk with friends, and observe healthy dating relationships. Odds are if you begin seriously dating the first guy or gal that comes along—with no idea what you are looking for—you may get comfortable in a relationship that is not good for you . . . and end up kicking yourself two years later. Or worse yet, you may end up in a marriage that is less than God's best for you. It is unwise to waste your time seriously dating someone you couldn't see yourself marrying some day. It is not fair to either person in the relationship. Don't date potential, date actual.

The second way you'll know if you are ready to date is when you are more interested in and focused on *becoming* the right kind of person than *finding* the right person. I can say with 99 percent certainty that if you get married someday, someone will read the love chapter at your wedding (see 1 Cor. 13:4–7): "Love is patient, love is kind. It does not envy, it does not boast, it is not proud. It does not dishonor others, it is not self-seeking, it is not easily angered, it keeps no record of wrongs. Love does not delight in evil but rejoices with the truth. It always protects, always trusts, always hopes, always perseveres." But let me ask you a question: Are you becoming a more loving person now? Having that passage read at your wedding won't magically make you a more loving person. Another question worth thinking about is this: Is the kind of person you are looking for, looking for the kind of person you are becoming? If you remember nothing else, remember this: character is sexy.

The third way to know if you are ready to date is when you know what physical, moral, and emotional boundaries you will not compromise in order to get that other person to go out with you. And you must be willing to remain single rather than compromise your integrity and your relationship with God. Let me put this bluntly: ladies, if a guy is pressuring you physically or morally to cross boundaries you have set, then you need to drop him—it's better to be single. I promise. By the way, if he is pressuring you during the dating relationship, that tells you he doesn't respect and obey God. And if he doesn't respect God's authority and obey now in a dating relationship while he's pursuing you, what makes you think he will submit to God's authority in a marriage relationship someday? Ladies, if no one else is telling you this, I will: you are worth waiting for! Putting a ring on his finger doesn't magically make him spiritually mature or give him character. And guys, your integrity and relationship with God are far more precious than staying in a relationship with a girl who is stringing you along—no matter how good it feels to be cared for by somebody. You don't have to find the perfect person—but you do need to find one who is perfectible by growing in their love and obedience to Christ.

Is It Time for a Break?

Do you need to take a break from dating? There are many different scenarios: perhaps you have been in and out of numerous relationships, or have become too physically or emotionally involved and have been deeply wounded as a result. Maybe you tend to wrap your identity up in the person you are dating, or in whether you are dating. Or every time you get in a relationship, your walk with God goes in the toilet.

I have known people who needed to take time off from dating for a while so they could mature and regain perspective. In saying that *some* people shouldn't date, I'm not saying that *everyone* shouldn't date. The problem is not inherent in dating. Rather, the issue is the physical, emotional, social, and spiritual maturity of the person. Dating can be healthy and God-honoring if individuals proceed wisely.

Now, if God has given you a conviction on whether or not to date right now, stick with it. I am not trying to change your mind. But it is a good idea to examine this conviction every now and then, as well as to ask for the wise counsel of Christian friends *who will be honest with you* (not just tell you what you want to hear). Honestly, some of you need to take a break from dating for a season, but others of you are free to give it a chance. Here's a hint: if, as you have been reading this chapter, someone comes to mind who in your wiser moments you know is not good for you, pay attention to that. That wasn't just a random thought.

What About Dating Non-Christians?

This is one of the most frequently asked dating questions. God's Word says that believers are not to be unequally yoked with unbelievers (2 Cor. 6:14). While the immediate context of this passage is not addressing dating, the principle certainly can be applied here. Let me ask you a question. Would you marry a non-Christian? Then why would you date one? It is God's job to change people, not yours. Missionary dating is simply not wise. Yes, there have been a few (and I emphasize *few*) fantastic stories in which a person led someone to Christ and then they got married and lived happily ever after. And I am not trying to put God in a box. So, I am not going to tell you it is wrong to date an unbeliever (by wrong I mean the Bible specifically prohibits it), but I am going to say that it is unwise and unfair to both people.

How Do You Know If Your Dating Relationship Is Healthy?

A good dating relationship needs time in order to progress. Both people also need to be cultivating respect and tenderness toward one another. And finally, you need to show restraint—both physically and emotionally. Are you acting like a married couple but have only been dating for three weeks? Also, you both should be on the same page. After five or six dates, you need to talk. And guys ought to take the lead here. Express where you think the relationship is at and where you see it going. Talk about it together and preferably in person. Neither person in the relationship should have to guess about how serious it is. (Hey guys, this is a great opportunity to reject passivity and lead courageously!)

An important question to ask yourself: *Is this relationship producing life in me, or is it dragging me down emotionally, physically, and spiritually?* As a Christian, does this person challenge you to deepen your relationship with God, or have they become a distraction? Has this relationship sapped your zeal for the things of God only to replace it with worry, apathy, or jealousy? You be the judge. Better yet, have your friends help you judge. Sometimes these things are hard to see when you're in the midst of a relationship. Have the courage to ask (and actually listen to) a close friend to tell you what they see.

How Far Is Too Far?

This is a two-part question—emotionally and physically. Emotionally, you need to establish boundaries. It is not a good idea to share your whole life story and all your dirty laundry on the first date. This is kind of like emotionally dumping everything inside on the other person. Too much emotion too early can bond you too quickly for unhealthy reasons. You need to allow a relationship to progress at an emotionally appropriate pace. Falling in love feels great and it is sometimes hard to keep your emotions in check. But a good question to ask yourself is this: Am I looking to this other person in order to feel good about myself? If so, then you might be a little too emotionally dependent on them.

You also need to develop physical boundaries. I am going to talk to the guys for a second. As we discussed in the chapter on biblical manhood, the biblical pattern is for men to take the lead in obedience to God. And in this case your marching orders are clear: "Flee sexual immorality" (see 1 Cor. 6:18). You should not put a girl in the position of having to say "no further." I will save our discussion of God's design for sexual intimacy in marriage for chapter 35, "Sex, Sex, Sex," but God's will for all of His children is that we not be sexually immoral (1 Thess. 4:3). Premarital sex and related activities form a bond not meant for those outside of marriage. Passion looks like love, but it is a cheap imposter. Now, I know that some of you have fallen into unhealthy and sinful physical relationships. But take heart: the good news is that God can forgive you and help you change. No one is beyond God's grace (Eph. 2:8–9).

Back to our question of how far is too far. I would suggest that this is the wrong question. We should ask instead: What would a pure, God-honoring relationship look like? Guys: a good rule of thumb is not to start kissing a girl until you are ready to hold her heart (remember our calling to love and protect?). Kissing is trivialized in our culture, but it's a big deal—especially open-mouth kissing (see Song 4:11). This is sensuous stuff meant to lead somewhere. I have good friends whose first kiss was at their wedding—that was their conviction. I did not kiss my wife-to-be until I told her I loved her and was ready to make a commitment to her. You will need to see where your convictions are on this and establish boundaries (again guys, you take the lead here). I am not trying to be legalistic or guilt-trip anyone, but I honestly don't see how anything beyond holding hands, hugging, or mouth-to-mouth kissing is pleasing to God or appropriate for a couple in a dating relationship.[3] If you find yourself resistant to what I am saying and are trying to argue against me in your mind right now, it's worth asking yourself, "Why?"

God's Word reminds us not to make provision for the flesh in regard to its lusts (Rom. 13:14). Wisdom would challenge us to not play with fire. A desire for passion and intimacy with the person you love is good, normal, and God-given. But this passion is to occur in the context of holiness and within marriage. Giving in to passion is wonderful . . . when the time is right.

Handle with Care

I'll never forget walking up to the front door of a girl I was going to take on a date in high school. Her dad walked me to the car and reminded me that I was carrying precious cargo. He was right. As you date, remember that the person you are dating will be either your future spouse or someone else's. How would you want someone to be treating your future spouse right now? You would want them to be treated with courtesy and respect, not manipulated, abused, or exploited to fulfill someone's selfish desires. More than that, as Christians, the people you date are sons and daughters of the most high God (Gal. 4:6), and you ought to treat them as such. Christ died for them and loves them with an everlasting love. Handle with care.

For Those Who Are Frustrated and Tired of Waiting

As hard as it sounds, be patient. Continue to trust God, pray, and keep your eyes open. But even if a relationship does not happen in your timing, don't compromise just to be in one. Having hope that God will provide that perfect match is far better than being in a hopelessly miserable relationship (especially if it leads to a hopelessly miserable marriage).

In the meantime, spend time hanging out in large groups going to movies, football games, or service projects. These were some of my favorite memories from college.

And Now the Rest of the Story

Confession time. I didn't intentionally take a break from dating for much of high school and college. I was frustrated, but God knew what He was doing. Big surprise, huh? While in college, I went through a study on the Song of Solomon by Tommy Nelson. Finally I had a God-centered vision for attraction, dating, love, and sex (like what we have been talking about in this chapter and the next). It made all the difference. Not because girls were lining up at the door to date me, but because I knew what I was looking for and was willing to wait on it. In the meantime I was going to run hard after God and hopefully find a girl one day who could keep up.

In November 1999, God brought me the kind of girl I was waiting on. We both knew from very early on that we were made for each other. We dated for four months and then became engaged. Eight months later—and on the same day I graduated from college—Mandi and I were married. (Take my word for it, the shorter the engagement, the better.) Let me tell you, I did not settle! I am married to a wonderful, beautiful, funny, godly woman who challenges me to be more like Christ. She is my best friend. So as we wrap up this chapter, remember that it only takes getting one relationship right. Hang in there, run hard after Jesus, and don't compromise.

THE BIG IDEAS

- Some people *should* take a break from dating for a season, but others have the freedom to give dating a chance. Dating is not the issue; maturity is.

- It is important in dating to have a picture of the kind of person you are looking for; don't settle for less. Part of this silhouette should be that they are a follower of Christ. Also, you should know what you will not compromise just to be in a relationship.

- An important way you'll know if you are ready to date is when you are more interested in and focused on *becoming* the right kind of person than *finding* the right person.

- It is imperative that you establish emotional and physical boundaries in your dating relationship.

- Treat the person you are dating the same way that you would want someone to treat your future spouse. Remember that they are a son or daughter of the most high God. Handle with care.

- Instead of asking, "How far is too far?" ask, "What would a pure, God-honoring relationship look like?"

For Further Discovery

Cloud, Henry, and John Townsend. *Boundaries in Dating: How Healthy Choices Grow Healthy Relationships.* Grand Rapids: Zondervan, 2009.

Keller, Timothy, and Kathy Keller. *The Meaning of Marriage: Facing the Complexities of Commitment with the Wisdom of God.* New York: Dutton, 2011.

Nelson, Tommy. *The Book of Romance: What Solomon Says About Love, Sex, and Intimacy.* Nashville: Thomas Nelson, 2007.

———. *Song of Solomon.* DVD. Student ed. Available at https://www.rightnow.org/Content/Series/135.

Stanley, Andy. *The New Rules for Love, Sex, and Dating.* Grand Rapids: Zondervan, 2015.

Sex, Sex, Sex

When it comes to sex, one cannot leave out marriage. The no to sex outside marriage seems arbitrary and cruel apart from the Creator's yes to sex within marriage.

—LAUREN F. WINNER[1]

That is why a man leaves his father and mother and is united to his wife, and they become one flesh. Adam and his wife were both naked, and they felt no shame.

—GENESIS 2:24–25

If we think of sex as only a physical activity to be engaged in at our pleasure, and only for our pleasure, . . . [and] if we think our makeup is limited to satisfying appetites, we'll conclude that we can engage in sexual activity, enjoy it on a physical level, and totally disassociate these acts from the rest of what we are as human beings—but we'll be sadly mistaken.

—JOE S. MCILHANEY AND FREDA MCKISSIC BUSH[2]

NOW THAT I HAVE YOUR ATTENTION. SEX SELLS, AND IT SEEMS THAT everyone's buying. My wife and I recently saw a commercial in which they were using sexual innuendo to sell carpet spot remover! We live in a sex-crazed society. It is unavoidable. You may be checking out at the grocery store next to the latest busty blond or brunet on the cover of *Cosmopolitan* magazine announcing "five instant seduction tips." Or maybe you just rented the latest movie where a couple had *one* date together and then jumped in the sack. We now live in a culture where 69 percent of US adults believe "any kind of sexual expression between two consenting adults is acceptable."[3] Forty percent of practicing Christians believe this as well. Not good.

On campus, if you haven't been already, you will be bombarded with sexual temptation—whether it is at parties with drunk but attractive people, or whether you are watching a movie on the couch with your significant other. Feelings of sexual desire and attraction are completely natural, but the burning question you will need to answer in your own heart is, *why wait?*

Everybody in our culture is talking about sex, so why is the church's message on it either overly negative or silent? Is it embarrassing? Is God blushing up in heaven with one hand over an eye? Some might say, "People can't talk about sex in church—this is the house of the Lord!" *Right* . . . better to let the next generation learn about it on the side of a gas station bathroom stall, the Internet, or late-night HBO. Makes sense to me. (Is my sarcasm thick enough?)

Pastor Tommy Nelson observes, "So many people within the body of Christ seem to be wounded and maimed emotionally and psychologically by issues and problems related to sexual intimacy, and yet nobody in the church wants to discuss these issues."[4] The simple fact of the matter is that most parents don't talk about sex with their children because it is too embarrassing and awkward. If the kids are lucky they get a bird and a bee here and there, but what they don't get is a compelling vision for sexual intimacy worth waiting for.

Since I never really had "the sex talk" with my parents, I was fortunate enough to be taught about biblical sexuality in college through the *Song of Solomon* study by Tommy Nelson.[5] This study changed my life. It not only changed the way I thought about sex; it showed me the kind of man I needed to become and the kind of woman I wanted to spend the rest of my life with. After meeting the woman who would become my wife my senior year of college, we kept our relationship pure until our honeymoon night. I assure you, it was not easy. We were in love, and we wanted each other. But by God's grace we waited. It is hard to say *no* to a pleasurable experience in the here and now if you don't have something better to say *yes* to in the future. This chapter hopefully will give you a vision of a sexuality to say *yes* to!

That's in the Bible?

Isn't the Christian view of sex all about having kids? Don't get me wrong, kids are great—and certainly a major aspect of the union between husband and wife.[6] But the Bible has plenty to say about the sexual relationship between husband and wife that doesn't mention procreation as a goal.

(Doesn't that make sex sound fun? Imagine a wife coming home from running errands and saying to her husband, "You wanna procreate at eight-thirty?") People are often surprised by how explicitly the Bible talks of the beauty and passion of sexual intimacy. Check out what Proverbs 5:15–20 has to say. The New Living Translation really captures the heart of this passage (the man's sexuality is symbolized by a "spring" and the woman's is imagined as a "well"):

> Drink water from your own well—
> share your love only with your wife.
> Why spill the water of your springs in the streets,
> having sex with just anyone?
> You should reserve it for yourselves.
> Never share it with strangers.
>
> Let your wife be a fountain of blessing for you.
> Rejoice in the wife of your youth.
> She is a loving deer, a graceful doe.
> Let her breasts satisfy you always.
> May you always be captivated by her love.
> Why be captivated, my son, by an immoral woman,
> or fondle the breasts of a promiscuous woman?

This passage is about pure pleasure and enjoyment for the man and woman! Who knew that breasts and fondling were mentioned in the Bible? Notice too that this passage speaks of sexual bliss within the safety and parameters of the marriage relationship.

The book of the Song of Solomon is as racy as it comes—even with our toned-down translations of the Hebrew text.[7] As I understand it, Jewish children weren't allowed to read it until they came of age because it was said to ignite the passions. Having read it, that seems like sound advice! In order to help you understand the imagery of this book, the woman's sexuality is referred to as a garden. Look at this steamy description of Solomon and his wife's interaction from chapter 4, which is their honeymoon night. In chapters 1–3 we have seen this couple's desire grow along with their restraint, culminating in the wedding day at the end of chapter 3. Now they are ready to enjoy God's gift of sex:

You have captured my heart,
    my treasure, my bride.
You hold it hostage with one glance of your eyes,
    with a single jewel of your necklace.
Your love delights me,
    my treasure, my bride.
Your love is better than wine,
    your perfume more fragrant than spices.
Your lips are as sweet as nectar, my bride.
    Honey and milk are under your tongue.
Your clothes are scented
    like the cedars of Lebanon.

You are my private garden, my treasure, my bride,
    a secluded spring, a hidden fountain.
Your thighs shelter a paradise of pomegranates
    with rare spices—
henna with nard,
    nard and saffron,
    fragrant calamus and cinnamon,
with all the trees of frankincense, myrrh, and aloes,
    and every other lovely spice.
You are a garden fountain,
    a well of fresh water
    streaming down from Lebanon's mountains.

YOUNG WOMAN Awake, north wind!
    Rise up, south wind!
Blow on my garden
    and spread its fragrance all around.
Come into your garden, my love;
    taste its finest fruits.

YOUNG MAN I have entered my garden, my treasure, my bride!
    I gather myrrh with my spices
and eat honeycomb with my honey.
    I drink wine with my milk.

YOUNG WOMEN Oh, lover and beloved, eat and drink!
OF JERUSALEM Yes, drink deeply of your love!

(SONG 4:9–5:1 NLT)

And this is just one of the sex scenes in this book! The point of this passage is to show you that uninhibited, passionate sex is intended for married people, and also that God is not a prude; who do you think designed sex? Sex is exciting, creative, and wonderful, but there is a time and place for it. OK . . . rein in your imagination and go take a cold shower!

It would be fun to say more, but I think you get the big idea. I am not getting paid to say this, but if I were to make a required reading list for you on this topic, Tommy Nelson's *The Book of Romance: What Solomon Says About Love, Sex, and Intimacy* would be at the top of it. You owe it to yourself and your future spouse to read this book *as soon as you can*—not only will it give a positive vision for biblical sexuality, but it will also keep you from making a lot of painful mistakes.

Marriage was designed by God. God created sex for the context of marriage as an expression of oneness—because there is trust, holiness, love, and commitment in the marriage relationship. This is the ideal (though you see in the Bible many instances of less than ideal relationships and their consequences). I don't want you to hear me saying that marriage is *all* about sex and the pleasures that accompany it. Neither do I want you to get the idea that biblical sex leads to self-centeredness; on the contrary, oneness is an expression of selflessness. The relationship is the entrée; sexual intimacy is the dessert. But the dessert sure is lots of fun!

Of Love and Lighter Fluid

Now that we have seen the ideal for sexuality within marriage, why would anyone settle for less? If sex within marriage is like a hot, blazing fire with deep embers and lots of dry wood burning brightly in the safety of a fireplace, then premarital sex is like spraying lighter fluid on wet logs.[8] The flame will burn bright and hot for an instant, but then it is gone. The fire will not last—unless you keep spraying lighter fluid on the flame. (And then there is always the possibility of the can blowing up in your hand.) Of course, after a while people discover that they have to spray on more and more passion to reach the same intensity of the heat they had the first time that felt so good. The problem with premarital sex is that you think you have more than you really have. *It looks like the real thing—a roaring fire that will keep you warm for a long time.* But in the end, it will leave you burned and with a fire that will not last.[9] Not only does premarital sex give you a false sense of intimacy with this other person—because sacrificial love, holiness, and commitment are absent from it—but it will also undermine your future relationships. Remember, your past relationships become part of your future relationships. Be really careful here. That is why God tells you to run away from sexual immorality. It will consume you and undermine the flourishing God desires for you.

People sometimes think Christianity is all about rules—what we can and can't do. But God gives us boundaries because He loves us, wants to protect us, and desires us to flourish. God's will for us is our increasing holiness, not sexual immorality: "It is God's will that you should be sanctified: that you should avoid sexual immorality; that each of you should learn to control your own body in a way that is holy and honorable, not in passionate lust like the pagans, who do not know God" (1 Thess. 4:3–5). God wants us to experience life, not hollow substitutes. God prohibits certain activities for our benefit, not because He doesn't want us to have fun or enjoy ourselves. The temptation will be strong; no one is denying that. But some things are worth waiting for. Say yes to God's design, because He is your heavenly Father who loves you! Pray for God's grace and seek out a group of like-minded believers to encourage you along the way.

The Myth of "Try Before You Buy"

Our hookup culture has led to the crisis of cohabitation today. Astonishingly, "more than 60 percent of all marriages are preceded by some form of cohabitation."[10] This may seem harmless, but this is a personal and cultural disaster at multiple levels, which will deeply affect generations to come.

Practically, this makes relationships *more complicated*, not less. Here's the basic idea: since we can't seem to get along very well while dating and even having sex, let's move in together to see if we are compatible. Bad idea! And that's what sociologists will tell you, not just the Bible. Cohabitation is especially harmful to women. Glenn Stanton sums up the research:

> If a woman wants to significantly increase the likelihood of getting a husband who:
>
> 1. is less committed than she is to the marriage
> 2. is less committed to her and to marriage than noncohabitating husbands

3. displays unhealthy problem-solving skills

4. is less likely to be emotionally and practically supportive

5. is more generally relationally negative and

6. displays violent behavior towards her . . .

. . . then the science tells us that living with a future husband before marriage is one of the most efficient ways to get each of these. And all by just living with him first![11]

That's not a pretty picture. Save yourself a lot of heartache and pain. Listen to wisdom . . . don't move in together!

Another myth of our hookup culture is that sex is just physical, right? Friends with benefits? Nothing could be further from the truth. In *Hooked*, Dr. Joe McIlhaney (founder of the Medical Institute of Sexual Health) and Dr. Freda McKissic Bush explain the devastating effects of promiscuous sex:

An individual who is sexually involved, then breaks up and then is sexually involved again, and who repeats this cycle again and again is in danger of negative emotional consequences. People who behave in this manner are acting against, almost fighting against, the way they are made to function. When connectedness and bonding form and then are quickly broken and replaced with another sexual relationship, it often causes damage to the brain's natural connecting or bonding mechanism.[12]

McIlhaney and Bush use the vivid illustration of tape losing its stickiness after it is repeatedly applied and removed to compare what is going on in our brains. So what does the science say? If you want a fulfilling and sexually satisfying relationship in marriage then don't give in to premarital sex. You are stealing from your future when you do.

Restoring the Years the Locusts Have Eaten

What if you are reading this and realize you've blown it? You have already had sex, maybe with more than one person. Maybe you're addicted to pornography and no one knows. Maybe you feel weighed down with guilt and regret. The first thing you need to understand is how God views you. Romans 8:1 says, "Therefore, there is now no condemnation for those who are in Christ Jesus." If you are in Christ, then you are a new creation and you have been washed clean from your sins (2 Cor. 5:17; see also Ps. 103). Own your sin and then accept God's forgiveness in Christ.

Unfortunately, this truth does not eliminate or undo the pain and consequences of bad decisions. But you can begin anew right now. You can resolve to stay sexually pure from this day forward. His grace can reach you wherever you are at, no matter how much of a lost cause you think you are. Don't believe me? Test Him and see. He will change you from the inside out, if you will allow Him to. There is a wonderful passage in Joel 2:24–26 describing God's redemption of loss. Years of Israel's wheat crop had been destroyed by swarms of locusts, but God promised that He would restore the years the locusts had eaten. That promise symbolically stands today. God can take those places of pain, regret, and shame and plant joy, true intimacy, and purity if you will cry out to Him and follow His ways.

THE BIG IDEAS

- Sex is everywhere, and Christians need to be discussing it.
- God is not a prude; He created sex for a man and woman to enjoy in marriage. Married sex is worth waiting for! (See Prov. 5:15–20; Song 4:9–5:1.)
- Premarital sex is like spraying lighter fluid on wet logs—the flames look big and bright but will quickly fade. It's a hollow imitation of the real thing.
- Reject the cohabitation and "sex is only physical" myths—our hookup culture is lying to you!
- If you will let Him, God can restore the years the locusts have eaten in your life and give you a fresh start.

For Further Discovery

AbuJamra, Lina. *Thrive: The Single Life as God Intended*. Chicago: Moody Publishers, 2013.

Burk, Denny. *What Is the Meaning of Sex?* Wheaton, IL: Crossway, 2013.

Gresh, Dannah. *What Are You Waiting For? The One Thing No One Ever Tells You About Sex*. Colorado Springs: Waterbrook Press, 2011.

Harris, Joshua. *Sex Is Not the Problem (Lust Is): Sexual Purity in a Lust-Saturated World*. Sisters, OR: Multnomah, 2005.

Köstenberger, Andreas J., and David W. Jones. *God, Marriage, and Family: Rebuilding the Biblical Foundation*. 2nd ed. Wheaton, IL: Crossway, 2010.

McLlhaney, Joe S., and Freda McKissic Bush. *Hooked: New Science on How Casual Sex Is Affecting Our Children*. Chicago: Moody Publishers, 2008.

Nelson, Tommy. *The Book of Romance: What Solomon Says About Love, Sex, and Intimacy*. Nashville: Thomas Nelson, 2007.

Stanley, Andy. *The New Rules for Love, Sex and Dating*. Grand Rapids: Zondervan, 2015.

Stanton, Glenn T. *The Ring Makes All the Difference: The Hidden Consequences of Cohabitation and the Strong Benefits of Marriage*. Chicago: Moody Publishers, 2011.

Family Life at www.familylife.com.

Tommy Nelson's Song of Solomon resources at www.dbcmedia.org/sermons/love-song-a-study-in-the-song-of-solomon/.

A Call to Purity

How can a young person stay on the path of purity?
By living according to your word.

—PSALM 119:9

Blessed are the pure in heart, for they shall see God.
—MATTHEW 5:8 NASB

But keep away from youthful passions, and pursue
righteousness, faithfulness, love, and peace, in company
with others who call on the Lord from a pure heart.
—2 TIMOTHY 2:22 NET

SOME IMAGES STICK WITH YOU. I REMEMBER WAKING AS A KID, WAY OUT in the country in Deer Lodge, Tennessee, to a foot of snow on the ground. It was one of the most beautiful sights I have ever seen. I put on my boots and walked outside. I was met by the brilliant reflection of morning sun off of freshly fallen snow. There were no footsteps, no blemishes, just a sparkling blanket of purity. If we are in Christ, then God has washed us so that we are whiter than snow (Ps. 51:7). Because of the work of Christ on our behalf, this is the way that God sees us: white like freshly fallen snow. But that doesn't mean that we have arrived spiritually. God is calling us to pursue purity. Paul put it this way: "Since we have these promises, dear friends, let us purify ourselves from everything that contaminates body and spirit, perfecting holiness out of reverence for God" (2 Cor. 7:1). In this chapter, I want to share some of my reflections on the topic of purity. Some of these I heard during college; others, I needed to be reminded of. Odds are that you will need to hear some or all of these at some point in your college career. But just so you don't miss the big idea of the chapter, here it is: you must plan for purity; you won't just drift into it.

It's not about saying no; it's about saying yes to something much better. Sin in general leads us to desire other things more than God. This is the heart of idolatry—making good things our *ultimate* things. But we will never say no to the immediate pleasures of sin (and they are pleasurable . . . for a moment) unless we have something better to say yes to. The psalmist invites us to "taste and see that the LORD is good" (Ps. 34:8). We are invited to delight in the Lord (Ps. 37:4). God is our ultimate satisfaction—everything else is, quite literally, second best. Our plans are never as good as God's. This is especially true when it comes to sexual issues (see chapter 35, "Sex, Sex, Sex"). Cultivating a vision for sexuality in marriage, and the good life as lived in line with God's design, will help you say no to the daily lures of lust and sexual temptation. You can only say no so many times—that is, unless you have something far more beautiful to say yes to.

Don't go it alone. American Christianity has bought a big fat lie: "I can make it on my own, thanks." This is the battle cry of lone-ranger Christianity. But the New Testament teaches nothing of the sort. Paul called young Timothy to "keep away from youthful passions, and pursue righteousness, faithfulness, love, and peace, *in company with others who call on the Lord from a pure heart*" (2 Tim. 2:22 NET, italics added). Pursuing purity is a team sport. I was blessed to have great roommates and friends in college who were unified in pursuing purity; it made all the difference. What happens when we don't stand together? Proverbs answers, "Whoever isolates himself seeks his own desire; he breaks out against all sound judgment" (18:1 ESV). Unfortunately, I learned this lesson the hard way in college, one weekend when my roommates were all out of town. I should have either asked for accountability or made plans to be with a group. Instead, I just stayed home and allowed a subtle temptation to intensify. So after a while, I gave in—because after all, who would know? I went and rented something that I never should have watched. Of course, I was ashamed afterward. But there was no one there to help me stand against the strong wind of temptation; I had isolated myself. Trust me, you can't do it alone. We need each other.

We have an enemy. In our scientific age, it's easy to forget that we have an adversary who seeks to kill and destroy us (John 10:10). He has personalized schemes with which to attack us (2 Cor. 2:11). Peter admonishes us to "be of sober spirit, be on the alert. Your adversary, the devil, prowls around like a roaring lion, seeking someone to devour. But resist him, firm in your faith, knowing that the same experiences of suffering are being accomplished by your brethren who are in the world" (1 Peter 5:8–9 NASB). Satan is a roaring lion—if you want this image driven home to you in a powerful way, watch *The Ghost and the Darkness* on Netflix sometime.[1] If we don't recognize Satan as an obstacle to our purity and holiness, then we are toast. As in those Discovery Channel shows depicting what happens to an animal when it strays from the herd, we will be devoured before we know what hit us. Constant vigilance is required.

Call it what it is . . . sin. In our struggle for purity we face a potential pitfall concerning our sin. We can actually come to a point with a sin that we have struggled with for so long that we begin to view it as not as bad as it is. Or worse, we tell ourselves it is OK. We now live in a cultural moment when teens and young adults consider not recycling more immoral than viewing pornography.[2] James describes how easily temptation can turn into sin: "Each person is tempted when they are dragged away by their own evil desire and enticed. Then, after desire has conceived, it gives birth to sin; and sin, when it is full-grown, gives birth to death" (1:14–15). If you have seen or read *The Lion, the Witch and the Wardrobe,* then you know that we all have our "Turkish delight"—that temptation that repeatedly leads us astray. It is better to fall a hundred times and confess it a hundred times than to stay on the ground and call that which is sinful *good* (Prov. 24:16). We must be honest with the bitterness of our sin before we can embrace the sweetness of God's forgiveness and grace.

God forgives. Sometimes we just need to rest in the forgiveness of God. We can find ourselves battered by the guilt and shame that accompany sin. But sometimes we keep on beating ourselves up for particular sins (I am not talking about conviction of sin here). We convince ourselves that somehow we must atone for this particularly nasty sin. Yet this makes a mockery of the cross of Christ. In that moment, we need to hear the author of Hebrews say, "Now where there is forgiveness . . . there is no longer any offering for sin" (10:18 NET). As the hymn says, Jesus paid it all (Heb. 10:10). In times where you need to experience the God who forgives, rest in Him by meditating on Psalm 103.

Do whatever it takes. Desperate times call for desperate measures (this is especially applicable to us guys when it comes to lust and Internet pornography). Job said, "I made a covenant with my eyes not to look with lust at a young woman" (Job 31:1 NLT).[3] We must resolve to do whatever it takes to keep us from lust. If that means giving up the convenience of high-speed Internet, keeping your smartphone out of your bedroom, or not watching certain shows or movies, so be it. The cost of sin in this area is too high. If it goes unchecked it will cripple you and your ministry for life.[4] It will flat take you out. We must stop storing up for ourselves illicit images that will be used against us at a later date by our enemy! We had satellite when I was a kid, and of course my brothers and I found the pornography channels. I can still remember the images I saw when I was seven. Another way of putting it is, "Don't feed the tiger today that you will have to fight tomorrow." One of the students I mentored in college recognized his temptation while online, so he removed the ability to connect to the Internet from his room and only checked email and wrote papers in the computer lab. Is this kind of behavior extreme? Not if it keeps you from corrupting your mind.

One more thing: Internet filters and monitoring software are no longer optional for Christian men. As a college man seeking to follow Christ, if you own a laptop and smartphone and do not have some sort of Internet accountability, you are being foolish.[5] I am not trying to pick on anyone; I'm just shooting straight with you. I know guys who still resist doing this, saying they don't struggle in this area. Praise God—however, you are asking for trouble if you aren't proactive. Satan won't come after you when you are at your strongest; he will wait to pounce when you are weary, vulnerable, and least expecting it. My advice is to do whatever it takes. A final note to girls about pornography: there is a growing trend for younger girls to experiment with and become ensnared in porn. A study from Barna Group with Josh McDowell Ministry has found that "33% of women, ages 13–24, seek out porn at least once a month compared to 12% of women over age 25."[6] Know that you don't need to struggle alone or be embarrassed because you are a girl and you think you shouldn't struggle with this. That's a lie. God can set you free.

There is always a way out. God promises us a way of escape; our job is to have the courage to take it. Paul says, "No temptation has overtaken you except what is common to mankind. And God is faithful; he will not let you be tempted beyond what you can bear. But when you are tempted, he will also provide a way out so that you can endure it" (1 Cor. 10:13). Stay alert! The sad thing is that when we do see the way out and ignore it, it's because we would rather sin . . . *ouch*. We need God to transform our desperately sick hearts (Jer. 17:9).

The pure in heart experience God in a special way. If we are in Christ, then nothing can sever that relationship (Rom. 8:31–39). But if we find ourselves in a pattern of disobedience and habitual sin, we won't experience God *to the degree that we could* if our hearts were pure before Him.[7] God is personal, and we are in a relationship. Sin diminishes our ability to relate to God. Listen to the words of Jesus from the Sermon on the Mount: "Blessed are the pure in heart, for they will see God" (Matt. 5:8). I don't know about you, but I want to see and experience all the intimacy with God that I can. Because God is holy, and because shame and guilt prompt us to run from God, we must pursue purity.

Pursue the sweet sleep of integrity. Proverbs tells us, "He who walks in integrity walks securely, but he who perverts his ways will be found out" (10:9 NASB). As a graduate student, I did most of my work on the computer late at night when everyone was asleep. This could have been a recipe for disaster. But as a married man and father, I thank God for helping me to stay pure when it comes to where I go online. I am not so arrogant to think myself incapable of stumbling, but I will do everything I can to see that it doesn't happen. This side of heaven, we will all have a divided heart at some level (Ps. 86:11). Still, what a blessing to be able to rest your head on your pillow at the end of the day because you are living life with integrity—especially in the area of sexual purity. You don't have to be tormented by thoughts of whether or not someone will find you out. You don't have to cover things up and then lie about it.

A lot has been said—more could be. But I wanted to leave you with a reminder of the three resources God has provided for you in your pursuit of purity in life: God's Word (Ps. 119:9, 11), God's Spirit (2 Peter 1:3–4), and God's people (Gal. 6:2; 2 Tim. 2:22; James 5:16). We explored these in more detail in chapter 29, "Becoming More Like Jesus."

THE BIG IDEAS

- God is calling us to purity, and this pursuit will require courageous intentionality on our part. We must plan for purity; we won't just drift into it.
- The resources that God has given us for our pursuit of purity are God's Word (Ps. 119:9, 11), God's Spirit (2 Peter 1:3–4), and God's people (Gal. 6:2; 2 Tim. 2:22; James 5:16).

For Further Discovery

Harris, Joshua. *Sex Is Not the Problem (Lust Is): Sexual Purity in a Lust-Saturated World*. Sisters, OR: Multnomah, 2005.

McDowell, Sean. "What's the Big Deal About Porn?" Vimeo video, 47:35. May 7, 2015. http://seanmcdowell.org/videos/whats-the-big-deal-about-porn.

Wilkinson, Bruce. *Personal Holiness in Times of Temptation*. Eugene, OR: Harvest House, 1998.

Willard, Dallas, and Jan Johnson. *Renovation of the Heart in Daily Practice: Experiments in Spiritual Transformation*. Colorado Springs: NavPress, 2006.

Covenant Eyes at www.covenanteyes.com. Internet filtering and accountability software.

Set Free Summit at www.setfreesummit.org.

Your Brain on Porn at www.covenanteyes.com/brain-ebook/. Free e-book; learn the five ways porn warps your brain and biblical ways to renew it.

Christianity, Homosexuality, and the Bible

When people we love come to us and tell us about a part of their life that is out of line with Scripture, we have some choices: We can kick them out of our life. We can ignore it. We can change our beliefs so there's no tension between us. Or we can keep loving them and hold our beliefs firm. For me, the last option has always worked the best.

—CALEB KALTENBACH[1]

For two thousand years, orthodox Christianity has believed that marriage is between a man and a woman and that such sexual difference is necessary. . . . It would take a rather earth-shattering series of arguments to overturn such well-established tradition.

—PRESTON SPRINKLE[2]

Long before there was a debate about same-sex anything, far too many heterosexuals bought into a liberal ideology about sexuality that makes a mess of marriage: cohabitation, no-fault divorce, extramarital sex, nonmarital childbearing, pornography, and the hook-up culture all contributed to the breakdown of the marriage culture.

—RYAN ANDERSON[3]

HOMOSEXUALITY IS NOT JUST AN ISSUE TO BE DISCUSSED OR ARGUED; IT involves real people on all sides who are made in the image of God. It's complex and emotions can run high. There are very real hurts, fears, regrets, desires, misunderstandings, and relationships that have been broken. You may have friends who identify as gay or lesbian. Maybe you've struggled with how to make sense of all of this as a Christian. You know what your parents think or what your youth pastor thinks, but what do you think? What does the Bible say? After all, you don't want to be seen as a hateful bigot or homophobe, right?

If homosexuality hadn't already become part of the national consciousness, then it certainly did in June of 2015 when the US Supreme Court legalized same-sex marriage. LGBT issues and questions are not only part of the cultural conversation; they are now part of public policy. So in this chapter I want to do my best to give you a distinctly Christian view of homosexuality that takes God's Word seriously. Obviously this is a massive topic, but it's important to give an overview of some of the most important questions, issues, and principles for you to think through as a student because there is so much confusion on this topic. Also, I encourage you to read the resources I suggest at the end of this chapter, as they will help answer further questions you might have.

A Distinctly Christian Starting Point for This Conversation

Before we begin wading into these important questions, I want to start with three distinctly Christian affirmations. These need to be the baseline for any conversation.

First, *all are broken.* Let me speak as clearly as I can: we are all broken; we just express our brokenness in different ways. The Bible is very clear that all of us fall short of God's perfect standard of holiness. None of us has it all together. So there is definitely no room for a self-righteous, I'm-better-than-you attitude.

Second, *all are welcome.* The gospel is good news for everyone. Period. You don't have to clean yourself up before you come to Jesus. You don't have to get yourself together. No matter what anyone has done or struggled with, they are welcome. That's the amazing, scandalous grace that Jesus offers.

Last, *all are called to repentance.* Once someone becomes a follower of Jesus by placing their trust in Him alone and receiving His forgiveness, we are all called to change and grow. And we all need to change and grow, right?

There are sins we need to stop doing (sins we really enjoy, by the way). This is a universal call to discipleship to our Lord Jesus Christ over a lifetime and involves what Eugene Peterson calls "a long obedience in the same direction."[4]

Asking and Answering the Right Questions

Over the past thirty years, the church has not always responded well to those who struggle with or outright embrace homosexuality. In fact, I would say that some responses have been downright sinful and shameful. It's OK for us to apologize to our LGBT friends for how they have been treated in a very un-Christlike manner by some Christians (doing so doesn't mean we are apologizing for the Bible or what it teaches, by the way).

There are several reasons why Christians have not always responded well, but one of the big reasons is because many times Christians were answering one question when another question was being asked. To help us all have better conversations about this moving forward, I want to suggest three different questions we need to be prepared to engage:

1. What does the Bible teach about homosexual practice? (This is a factual and interpretive question.)
2. How should the church help people who are struggling with homosexual sin? (This is a relational and spiritual question.)
3. Is same-sex marriage good for society? (This is a question of public policy and the common good.)

So if my friend is struggling with temptation and sin (question 2), they probably don't need a lecture on what Leviticus teaches about homosexuality (question 1). Likewise many Christians have tried answering public-policy questions (question 3) with Bible answers (question 1). All three questions are legitimate and important, but they are different questions that require different approaches.

What does the Bible teach about homosexual practice?

The Bible includes homosexual behavior among a long list of sinful behaviors outside of God's design for human sexuality. Homosexual behavior is specifically addressed as sinful in Genesis 19:4–9; Leviticus 18:22, 20:13; Romans 1:26–27; 1 Corinthians 6:9–10; and 1 Timothy 1:9–10. There is not a single passage in the entire Bible that speaks positively of homosexuality.

While some people may throw the Bible out as morally outdated,[5] many are still reluctant to get rid of Jesus altogether when it comes to this issue. Instead, people try to get Jesus to be on their side of the argument by saying that in the end he would side with love and not judging people.[6] Some even say that Jesus never addressed homosexuality in his teaching. What's the truth? A helpful way to get at an answer is to ask if Jesus, as the most loving person who ever lived, would approve of homosexual behavior.

While it's technically true Jesus never used the word *homosexual* in his recorded teachings, it would be incorrect to conclude from this that he did not say anything concerning it. We know this from at least two occasions.

First, notice how Jesus reaffirms God's original design for sexuality grounded in creation when questioned by the Pharisees:

> Some Pharisees came to Jesus, testing Him and asking, "Is it lawful for a man to divorce his wife for any reason at all?" And He answered and said, "Have you not read that He who created them from the beginning made them male and female, and said, 'For this reason a man shall leave his father and mother and be joined to his wife, and the two shall become one flesh'? So they are no longer two, but one flesh. What therefore God has joined together, let no man separate." (Matt. 19:3–6 NASB; see also Gen. 1:27; 2:24)

Jesus affirmed that God's intention was the complementary sexes of male and female committing to a permanent one-flesh union. This was the pre-fall standard that Jesus, the most loving man who ever lived, appealed to.

Second, in Mark 7:21–23, Jesus said, "For it is from within, out of a person's heart, that evil thoughts come—*sexual immorality*, theft, murder, adultery, greed, malice, deceit, lewdness, envy, slander, arrogance and folly. All these evils come from inside and defile a person" (italics added). The Greek word for "sexual immorality" used here is *porneia*, which denotes things like unlawful sexual intercourse, prostitution, unchasteness, and fornication. Jesus did not need to specifically condemn homosexual behavior because the first-century Jewish context and worldview already assumed it was *one* of many ways to commit sexual sin.[7] There is no indication whatsoever in Scripture that Jesus either rejected or revised the prohibition of homosexual behavior found in the Torah. The bottom line is that Jesus still has some credibility in this conversation, so if you are given the opportunity to share your views on homosexual behavior, I would start with Jesus and explain His views in context. You can simply say that your view is the same one held by Jesus. Have you ever considered what He taught?

Now that we have covered Jesus's view, let's briefly look at what the rest of the Bible teaches. While we don't have room here to explore all the passages in detail, I do want to quickly summarize the revisionists' interpretation and the traditional response so you can get the basic contours of the debate. (Again, I encourage you to research these passages further by reading the resources I recommend at the end of the chapter.)

- *Genesis 19:4–9*. This passage is the least clear of all the passages that address homosexual behavior because there are several sins being committed. Contrary to the revisionists' interpretation that Sodom and Gomorrah were judged by God for inhospitality or attempted homosexual rape, this passage in context reveals that Sodom and Gomorrah were exceedingly wicked and judged for many sins *including* homosexual behavior (see 2 Peter 2:6; Jude 7).

- *Leviticus 18:22, 20:13*. Contrary to the revisionists' interpretation that this only refers to priestly practices or only condemns temple prostitution, the context clearly indicates otherwise. Surrounding this prohibition, "do not have sexual relations with a man as one does with a woman; that is detestable," is the condemnation of adultery, bestiality, incest, and child sacrifice. Clearly these are universally condemned and not just restricted to those who have priestly duties. And to the charge that Christians just pick and choose which Old Testament laws we still apply, there are some commandments that are contained in the law that transcend the law because they are rooted in creation norms (Gen. 1–2) and reaffirmed in the New Testament.

- *Romans 1:26–27*. Contrary to the revisionists' interpretation that this only refers to temple prostitution, pederasty (in that culture, older men would have sex with younger boys), or people who violate the sexual orientation that comes naturally to them, the context of Romans 1–3 makes it clear that Paul is universally condemning homosexual behavior. Here's why. Romans 1 is a creation narrative with literary features that parallel Genesis 1, in which Paul highlights the rational step of inferring obvious conclusions from observing and reflecting on nature. Then Paul argues in Romans 2–3 that all people with or without the law, Jew or Greek, are under sin and accountable to God. Furthermore, "natural desires" are not what Paul is discussing here. "Against nature" (*para physis*) in this context refers to the created order. Paul is appealing to the natural "function" (*chresis*) of males and females. The words he uses for male (*arsen*) and female (*thelys*) highlight their specific genders. Paul is arguing on the basis of how males and females are biologically and anatomically designed by God to operate in a sexually complementary way. Men were designed to function sexually not with men but with women. Paul's word choice could not have been clearer. Homosexual behavior is a clear violation of God's creational order, the complementary design of men and women, and the command to be fruitful and multiply (Gen. 1:26–27; 2:18–24).

- *1 Corinthians 6:9–10 (also 1 Timothy 1:9–10).* Contrary to the revisionists' interpretation that this only refers to temple prostitution or abusive homosexual practices, here Paul is contrasting the unrighteous with those who have been made righteous because of the work of Christ. Homosexual behavior is *but one* of the ways that unrighteousness is manifested. Revisionists argue that the word translated "homosexuals" here means "male prostitutes." This isn't the case because Paul actually coined this word to clearly make his point. He uses the Greek translation of the Hebrew Scriptures (the Septuagint) to reference the prohibition of homosexual behavior in Leviticus 18:22. He takes the two words "male" (*arsen*) and "bed" (*koite*) from Leviticus 18:22 and combines them to form this new word (*arsenokoites*) to describe sex between men in 1 Corinthians 6:9.[8] Paul's countercultural statement in this passage condemns both roles (passive and active) of homosexual behavior common in Corinth.

In summary, then, if we are trying to answer the factual question of what the Bible teaches about homosexual behavior, the answer is clear. It falls outside of God's design for human sexuality and is therefore sinful. Christopher Yaun, who tells of his struggle with homosexuality in *Out of a Far Country: A Gay Son's Journey to God*, shares why experience alone cannot be the only lens through which we read these passages: "Experiences do inform our interpretation of Scripture. As a racial minority, biblical texts on sojourners and aliens mean more to me than to someone who is not a racial minority. However, experiences can also hinder the interpretation of Scripture. Although it is impossible to completely distance the interpretive process from one's experiences, it is important to recognize our biases and do our best to minimize them. A high view of Scripture involves measuring our experience against the Bible, not the other way around."[9] Not only do we need to be careful how we let our experience shape our understanding of the Bible, we also need to be careful how we use the Bible. As Caleb Kaltenbach, who grew up with three gay parents, reminds us, "God's Word should never be a catalyst for us to mistreat those who are different from us."[10]

How should the church help people who are struggling with homosexual sin?

How should you as an individual and us as a church community help people who are struggling with sexual sin in general and homosexual sin in particular? The Bible teaches that holiness, not heterosexuality, is the goal of the spiritual life. Let me explain what I mean. All of us are broken; we just express our brokenness in different ways. As we repent and are empowered by the Holy Spirit, we pursue holiness. The goal is being conformed to the image of Jesus Christ (see Rom. 8:29). Unfortunately, when these goals get talked about in the context of homosexual sin, some well-meaning Christians have indicated that the goal is for this person to live a heterosexual lifestyle. This may or may not happen. But we need to be clear that whatever our struggle, holiness is the goal.

Christians may find that they still struggle with same-sex attraction but are convinced that this is contrary to God's design and will as revealed in the Bible. Therefore, under the lordship of Jesus, they say no to acting on their desires. But saying no to sinful desires is not a specifically homosexual issue; it is a fallen-human issue. Recognizing this dynamic will help us have appropriate compassion with each other as we struggle toward holiness and

Christlikeness together. As a Christian who struggles with same-sex attraction, Wesley Hill shares:

> Slowly, ever so slowly, I am learning . . . that my struggle to live faithfully before God in Christ with my homosexual orientation is pleasing to him. And I am waiting for the day when I will receive the divine accolade, when my labor of trust and hope and self-denial will be crowned with his praise. "Well done, good and faithful servant," the Lord Christ will say. "Enter into the joy of your master."[11]

We must create space in our churches for people to struggle well. And we need to be a source of encouragement and community to our brothers and sisters as they seek to submit to the lordship of Jesus. As Peter Hubbard rightly says, "The remedy is not complicated. In Jesus we are loved, so we can be honest about our own sin. And we can love other sinners. We can listen, asking good questions even when we don't understand or agree. And we can speak. God will give us helpful words, for we live in and for His kingdom, not our own."[12]

Is same-sex marriage good for society?

Why can't we stay out of politics and just preach the gospel? There's a lot that could be said here but I will simply summarize that according to the Bible we are called to love our neighbors well (Mark 12:31) and seek the welfare of the city in which we've been planted (Jer. 29:7). We are called to be faithful whether we are in the majority or the minority.

Think of it this way. Imagine our society is all in a giant inflatable raft out at sea and half of the people decide to take knives and start punching holes in the raft, and it starts taking on water. The choices of some affect the reality of many. That is the way public policy works.

While the Supreme Court has ruled on this, that doesn't mean we should give up making the case for traditional, natural marriage. Why? In 1973 *Roe v. Wade* was decided and abortion legalized, but the pro-life movement didn't end. Since that ruling, it has worked to do good for others, protect the unborn, help mothers with unwanted pregnancies by starting crisis-pregnancy centers, and make the case for life anew in each generation. For the good of the next generation, we need to do the same for marriage. As Ryan Anderson puts it so well:

> Whatever the law or culture may say, we must commit now to witness to the truth about marriage: that men and women are equal and equally necessary in the lives of children; that men and women, though different, are complementary; that it takes a man and a woman to bring a child into the world. It is not bigotry but compassion and common sense to insist on laws and public policies that maximize the likelihood that children will grow up with a mom and a dad.[13]

Here are four reasons why people should support and promote the public good of natural marriage (for a full treatment I would start with *Same-Sex Marriage: A Thoughtful Approach to God's Design for Marriage* by Sean McDowell and John Stonestreet):

1. Marriage is not the creation of the state; therefore, the state cannot redefine marriage. The basic social purpose of marriage, which existed prior to the state, is that it attaches mothers and fathers to their children and to each other. The natural institution of marriage is foundational for civilization to flourish.

2. Same-sex marriage will ultimately harm children because it denies them—by definition—the opportunity to be raised by either their biological mother or father. Decades of published research in psychology, social science, and medicine demonstrate that children do best when raised by their biological mother and father in a long-term marriage (this is the ideal).[14] The tragedy of this social experiment is that no one is thinking of the child's rights or desires in any of this discussion.

3. Same-sex marriage will restrict religious freedom. We are seeing more and more of this with bakers, photographers, and adoption agencies being fined if they do not comply and approve. Public policy is demanding people violate their conscience in the name of tolerance. We all lose when this happens. Religious liberty is a public good for people of all faiths or no faith at all.[15]

4. Same-sex marriage will remove any logical reason to deny other forms of marriage. Once you separate biology and the potential for natural

childbearing from marriage, on what rational basis can you prohibit other relationships that people desire and want to have approved by the state as marriage? We are already seeing challenges based on this logic for polygamy, polyamory (group marriage), and incestuous relationships. While it may not *yet* be culturally palatable, it will be one day and there will be no rational basis to exclude these "new family" structures and relationships.

When talking in the public square with people who do not believe in the Bible, quoting Bible verses is not the best way forward. In fact, it just makes the argument easier for opponents to dismiss as "religious" (read bigoted and homophobic) rather than "rational." It's important to learn how to make a strong case for natural marriage in a secular culture.

Three Cultural Myths About Homosexuality

There is a lot of misinformation out there and it's important to know the truth. And while knowing this information shouldn't cause us to respond to anyone any differently, these myths are repeated so often that people think they are true when they are not.

The first myth is that *10 percent of the population is gay*. This is based on a completely debunked study reported in a 1948 book by Alfred Kinsey called *Sexual Behavior in the Human Male*. A more accurate number is the 2011 UCLA study by the Williams Institute on sexual orientation and gender identity that incorporated and analyzed data from previous prevalence studies. It found that *1.7 percent* of the adult population identified as either gay or lesbian.[16] Again the point of this is not to belittle or diminish the importance of the issue or the reality of the struggle. But it is important to have a more accurate understanding of the scope of the situation.

Another often repeated myth is that *homosexuals are born that way*, as if this is proven science. Related to this is the idea that God made me this way. Is this true? While the Bible does not teach that people are born gay, it does teach that all people are born sinful. We no longer inhabit a sin-free garden. The reality is that we live in a fallen world in which sin affects all of us on physical, genetic, psychological, relational, and emotional levels (see Rom. 3:23; 5:12–21). There are plenty of sinful desires we should not act on or consider "natural" that can be overcome as we grow more like Christ. This is the hope and power of the gospel: we can struggle well. As Mark Mittelberg reminds us, "We must correct the idea that because a desire seems natural it must be from God and is therefore okay. As fallen humans we all have many desires that seem natural to us but that are not from God."[17]

But hasn't science shown that people are born gay? Actually, no. Alan Shlemon summarizes the state of the scientific evidence:

> The American Psychological Association (APA), for example, once held the position in 1998 that, there is "evidence to suggest that biology, including genetic or inborn hormonal factors, play a significant role in a person's sexuality." However, a decade of scientific research debunked this idea and caused the APA to revise their view in 2009. Their new position reads: "Although much research has examined the possible genetic, hormonal, developmental, social, and cultural influences on sexual orientation, *no findings have emerged that permit scientists to conclude that sexual orientation is determined by any particular factor or factors.*"[18]

You can be sure that if the evidence did exist, the APA would have cited it. Openly gay Harvard geneticist Simon LeVay, who is widely cited as discovering the gay gene, offers this clarification: "It's important to stress what I didn't find. I did not prove that homosexuality is genetic, or find a genetic cause for being gay. I didn't show that gay men are born that way, the most common mistake people make in interpreting my work. Nor did I locate a gay center in the brain."[19] Dean Hamer, another openly gay geneticist, when asked if homosexuality was rooted solely in biology, responded, "Absolutely not. From twin studies, we already know that half or more of the variability in sexual orientation is not inherited."[20] These are just a few of the many scientific studies that could be cited.

The point to be made here is that even if someone was more genetically predisposed toward certain desires or behaviors, that does nothing to alter what God has already revealed about his design for sexuality. Because of the fall, it is entirely possible that we may discover the effects of sin to be deeply bound up in our genetic information. To recognize this fact does not legitimize the behavior. On the other hand, it is also critical to understand that people don't choose to be gay either. The best evidence at this time indicates that conscious gender identity and homosexual desires *develop* over time from early childhood throughout adolescence. So while it is accurate to say that behavior is always chosen, one's desires are not.

A final myth we need to engage is that *it's not possible for people to change their homosexual orientation.* Many people are saying that it's harmful to even try. Now because I don't want to be misunderstood, I want to acknowledge that there have been instances of harmful attempts at change through counseling, special camps, abuse, and other dubious activities that should not be practiced. However, that doesn't tell the full story.

With this in mind, we are better positioned to engage the claim that gay people can't change. The first thing to point out is that the Bible demonstrates that change had happened in Corinth. One of the most hope-filled passages in the entire Bible is 1 Corinthians 6:9–11:

> Or do you not know that wrongdoers will not inherit the kingdom of God? Do not be deceived: neither the sexually immoral nor idolaters nor adulterers nor men who have sex with men nor thieves nor the greedy nor drunkards nor slanderers nor swindlers will inherit the kingdom of God. *And that is what some of you were. But you were washed, you were sanctified, you were justified in the name of the Lord Jesus Christ and by the Spirit of our God.* (italics added)

Moreover there are plenty of people who have struggled with and overcome same-sex attraction.[21] And as long as at least one has changed, then change is at least possible for those who struggle with same-sex attraction. Again, Shlemon's comments are helpful here:

> Does everyone who tries to change succeed? No. In fact, most people fail. Is it an easy process for those who achieve a measure of change? Absolutely not. Does change always entail complete transformation? Rarely. Do some people return to homosexuality? Of course. But is it possible for some to experience substantial and enduring change? Yes. That's good news, given that there are many people with unwanted SSA [same-sex attraction]. They have hope.[22]

What Does Love Require of You?

As we wrap up this chapter I would like to suggest some next steps for you to consider. First, no more gay jokes. Don't laugh at them, and gently but firmly don't tolerate them being said in your presence. Do you think Jesus would laugh? Second, realize that acceptance is not the same thing as approval. We can accept, love, and maintain relationships with our LGBT friends without approving of everything they say or do. Third, learn to listen and have genuine empathy for people struggling with sin and who have been wounded by others in the process. People are watching our responses as Christians, so let's love well.

But let's also think well. You need to know that it will not be possible for you to stay on the sidelines of this and not come to a conclusion and hold a conviction. If you don't come to a conviction intentionally you'll drift into one along with the culture around you. Study the Bible, read the suggested resources, know why you believe what you believe on this, and then be ready to talk about it. If you are asked what you believe about homosexuality or same-sex marriage, Greg Koukl has some very helpful advice: "You know, this is actually a very personal question you are asking. I don't mind answering, but before I do, I want to know if it's safe to offer my views. So let me ask you a question: Do you consider yourself a tolerant person or an intolerant person on issues like this? Is it safe to give my opinion, or are you going to judge me for my point of view? Do you respect diverse points of view, or do you condemn others for convictions that differ from yours?"[23]

For the good of everyone involved, we must move past the slogans and name-calling. The Bible will seem culturally out of step with our society. But as Christians we must prepare ourselves to courageously stand our ground on the truth of Scripture while at the same time compassionately moving toward those who struggle with same-sex attraction with the radical love Christ offers to us all.

THE BIG IDEAS

- A distinctly Christian starting point to this conversation is that all are broken, all are welcome, and all are called to repentance. The gospel is good news for us all.

CHRISTIANITY, HOMOSEXUALITY, AND THE BIBLE | 301

- The three main questions we need to be ready to engage are (1) What does the Bible teach about homosexual practice? (This is a factual and interpretive question.) (2) How should the church help people who are struggling with homosexual sin? (This is a relational and spiritual question.) (3) Is same-sex marriage good for society? (This is a question of public policy and the common good.)

- There is not a single passage in the entire Bible that speaks positively of homosexuality.

- Science has not shown that there is a gay gene. The best evidence at this time indicates that conscious gender identity and homosexual desires *develop* over time from early childhood throughout adolescence. So while it is accurate to say that behavior is always chosen, one's desires are not.

- The Bible teaches that holiness, not heterosexuality, is the goal of the spiritual life.

For Further Discovery

Allberry, Sam. *Is God Anti-Gay?* London: Good Book Company, 2013.

Anderson, Ryan T. *Truth Overruled: The Future of Marriage and Religious Freedom.* Washington, DC: Regnery, 2015.

Butterfield, Rosaria Champagne. *The Secret Thoughts of an Unlikely Convert: An English Professor's Journey into Christian Faith.* Pittsburgh: Crown and Covenant Publications, 2014.

Dallas, Joe. *Speaking of Homosexuality: Discussing the Issues with Kindness and Clarity.* Grand Rapids: Baker, 2016.

DeYoung, Kevin. *What Does the Bible Really Teach About Homosexuality?* Wheaton, IL: Crossway, 2015.

Hill, Wesley. *Washed and Waiting: Reflections on Christian Faithfulness and Homosexuality.* Grand Rapids: Zondervan, 2016.

Kaltenbach, Caleb. *Messy Grace: How a Pastor with Gay Parents Learned to Love Others without Sacrificing Conviction.* Colorado Springs: WaterBrook Press, 2015.

McDowell, Sean, ed. *A New Kind of Apologist.* Eugene, OR: Harvest House, 2016.

McDowell, Sean, and John Stonestreet. *Same-Sex Marriage: A Thoughtful Approach to God's Design for Marriage.* Grand Rapids: Baker, 2014.

Shlemon, Alan. *The Ambassador's Guide to Understanding Homosexuality.* Signal Hill, CA: Stand to Reason, 2013.

Sprinkle, Preston M. *People to Be Loved: Why Homosexuality Is Not Just an Issue.* Grand Rapids: Zondervan, 2015.

Yuan, Christopher, and Angela Yuan. *Out of a Far Country: A Gay Son's Journey to God, A Broken Mother's Search for Hope.* Colorado Springs: Waterbrook Press, 2011.

Unplugged and Offline

In silence we close off our souls from "sounds," whether those sounds be noise, music, or words. Total silence is rare, and what we today call "quiet" usually only amounts to a little less noise. Many people have never experienced silence and do not even know that they do not know what it is.

—DALLAS WILLARD[1]

If anything, my information-overloaded brain needs daydream breaks now more than ever. Yours probably does too, so take time on occasion to do nothing—in the presence of God and to the glory of God.

—DONALD S. WHITNEY[2]

Be still, and know that I am God.
—PSALM 46:10

IN 2015, FACEBOOK HAD OVER ONE BILLION USERS ONLINE AT THE SAME time. Yep, that's one in seven people on earth online at the same time on one digital platform. This is just one indication of the digital and social media revolution we are all living through. Everyone is online. As a college student and digital native you are more plugged in and online than any generation in history: Instagram, YouTube, Facebook, Twitter, smartphones, Netflix, Spotify, messaging, wireless everything, and laptops. You didn't ask for this. What this means is that you probably can't remember a world without touch screens and Wi-Fi, and this provides you with some unique opportunities and challenges.

But is this a good thing? That depends. Now before you tune me out, let me explain. I am not saying that these are all evil or that you should throw all your high-tech gadgets in the trash, opting instead for a telegraph machine and a quill. But there is a growing societal concern that this media excessiveness is not good for people. In a TED talk based on her provocative book *Alone Together*, MIT psychologist Sherry Turkle is blunt:

> We expect more from technology and less from each other. . . . Technology appeals to us most where we are most vulnerable. . . . We're lonely, but we're afraid of intimacy. And so from social networks to sociable robots, we're designing technologies that will give us the illusion of companionship without the demands of friendship. We turn to technology to help us feel connected in ways we can comfortably control. But we are not so comfortable. We are not so in control.[3]

My main goal in this chapter is to challenge you to be an active participant and not a passive observer in your online experiences. I want you to examine the *amount of time* you spend plugged in and then consider the benefits and drawbacks of time spent online and on social media and how that is affecting your identity (i.e., how are you trying to manage the impressions others have of you through your posts?). How is communicating only on your terms affecting those around you? Consider what it would look like to steward your digital influence for God's glory and your neighbors' good. Honestly assess what kind of digital footprint you are leaving. BTW, your kids will be able to see *all* your posts one day. That's sobering!

Connected . . . but Not Really

Walking across a college campus these days is interesting. Almost everyone I pass is either listening to or looking at a smartphone, and wherever their destination, I am positive another screen won't be far away. This is a generation far more connected than any other. What was once global has become local due to advances in technology. Ironically, however, people have never felt more isolated.[4] We are a touchscreen away but still disconnected. In our day and age being online is difficult to avoid, but that does not mean that we have to be online and sharing everything *all the time.*

One of the drawbacks of digital communication is that it depersonalizes human interaction. There is no body language or voice inflection in an email or message; it is merely text that shows up and must be encoded with your emotions—typically whatever emotions you happen to be feeling at the time. Moreover, email allows us to hide behind our computer and say things we would never say to people if they were standing in front of us. I call this digital courage. Communication via digital media is a paradox: it brings people close and keeps them at a distance at the same time.

CHALLENGE: *The next time you get on Instagram or Snapchat (or whatever platform is next) with someone you go to school with, sign out and go grab a meal or coffee together and talk face-to-face. Put your phones down on the table. It will do your soul good.*

Your Own Little World

We all need to escape from reality from time to time and decompress—I get that. However, it is quickly growing apparent that technology is allowing us to disengage from the world around us and retreat to digital worlds of our own creation. And this is not good—especially as followers of Jesus Christ. We are to spend our time engaging our world, not avoiding it. If we are not careful, then we will begin to lose touch with what is going on around us and become self-absorbed.

CHALLENGE: *Find a way to serve at a local food bank or after-school program in your community on a regular basis.*

Be Careful Online

Online predators are real and they prey on the naive. This ranges from stealing your credit card information to stealing your identity. The stark truth is that you can't really know who was sitting at the other end of the email or text you received. Unfortunately this is a messed-up world and people have to be careful online—especially children and women. The Internet is a tool; in the wrong hands, it becomes a weapon. Do not put personal contact information on your public online accounts. This is too easy to track. Make your Instagram private so that you know who is following you. Create screen names that hide your real identity and important information. Be extremely cautious about agreeing to meet people in person from the Internet. If for some reason you decide to, meet in a very public place and with a group of friends. If the online "friend" is unwilling to agree to these conditions, don't go! Lastly, don't participate in cyberbullying of any kind; instead, become a voice for the voiceless who are being bullied. The emotional distress cyberbullying causes is extremely harmful. It breaks my heart to hear of students who commit suicide because they were bullied. If you are aware of something going on, go to the proper authorities (teacher, counselor, dean, parent, or the police). We must stop this.

CHALLENGE: *Make sure your social media accounts do not have too much of your personal information on them, making you a vulnerable target. Remember, some things are just not wise or appropriate to share. Serve and protect others online.*

Quiet Please

One of the great things about the game of golf is when the marshal walks up on the tee box and holds up the "quiet please" sign. If you are like me, you are in need of this guy to come track you down and hold that sign in your face! It's hard to be still and quiet. I love music—I think life should have a sound track. But there are times when we just need to shut up and be quiet. This is especially important in order to be attentive to God's leading.

CHALLENGE: *Turn off your smartphone and do a social media fast for a day or even a week. Find a quiet place somewhere off the beaten path to just sit in God's presence and reflect.*

Wasted Time

There are only twenty-four hours in a day. My buddy Austin and I have been trying to figure out how we can add a few more hours to the day. No luck yet. Time waits for no one—it just ticks on. Not to sound morbid, but we will never experience the moments again that have just passed, and we will run out of moments someday. Do we really want to spend hours of our day on mundane chatter and purposeless updates and notifications? Paul has a good word for us: "Be very careful, then, how you live—not as unwise but as wise, making the most of every opportunity, because the days are evil" (Eph. 5:15–16).

CHALLENGE: *During a time you normally get online, redeem those moments by doing something either to cultivate your spiritual life or to further God's kingdom in some way. Find another human being to serve and encourage in person.*

The Discipline of Self-Reflection

Odds are you are overcommitted and overstimulated. You have somewhere to be and something that requires your mental energy. Endless to-do lists are the mortal enemies of self-reflection and personal evaluation. Part of maturing as a person requires us to take stock of our lives from time to time. Where are you going in life? Take time to evaluate your plans, emotional health, relationships, hopes, dreams. Ask yourself, what areas do I need to grow in?

CHALLENGE: *Take out a notebook or journal and clear your schedule for a morning or afternoon. Then evaluate where you are at in life. Write out your thoughts so that you can review them on occasion. Ask God to give you wisdom about what you should say no and yes to as opportunities arise.*

THE BIG IDEAS

- We are more connected than any other generation. The global has become local due to advances in technology. Ironically however, people have never felt more isolated. Pursue real relationships.

- Spending time alone in silent reflection in the presence of God is a wonderful discipline to start while in college.

- Be careful about basing your identity on how many likes your post got or how people talk about you on social media. This is an exhausting and dangerous way to live. You are valuable because God created you and loves you.

- Be careful and wise about what you post online. Remember that your digital footprint is always there and your future employer and future kids will be able to read everything you post. Think twice before posting once.

For Further Discovery

Koch, Kathy. *Screens and Teens: Connecting with Our Kids in a Wireless World.* Chicago: Moody Publishers, 2015.

Moreland, J. P., and Klaus Issler. *The Lost Virtue of Happiness: Discovering the Disciplines of the Good Life.* Colorado Springs: NavPress, 2006.

Postman, Neil. *Technopoly: The Surrender of Culture to Technology*. New York: Knopf Doubleday, 2011.

Turkle, Sherry. *Alone Together: Why We Expect More from Technology and Less from Each Other*. New York: Basic Books, 2011.

Whitney, Donald S. *Simplify Your Spiritual Life: Spiritual Disciplines for the Overwhelmed*. Carol Stream, IL: Tyndale House, 2014.

Winter, Richard. *Still Bored in a Culture of Entertainment: Rediscovering Passion and Wonder*. Downers Grove, IL: InterVarsity Press, 2002.

Zacharias, Ravi. *Recapture the Wonder*. Nashville: Thomas Nelson, 2005.

39

Compassionately
Engage Your World

Learn to do good;
Seek justice,
Reprove the ruthless,
Defend the orphan,
Plead for the widow.
—ISAIAH 1:17 NASB

"Do you become a king because you are competing in cedar?
Did not your father eat and drink
And do justice and righteousness?
Then it was well with him.
He pled the cause of the afflicted and needy;
Then it was well.
Is not that what it means to know Me?"
Declares the LORD.
"But your eyes and your heart
Are intent only upon your own dishonest gain,
And on shedding innocent blood
And on practicing oppression and extortion."
—JEREMIAH 22:15–17 NASB

Paul does not expect life in this world to be heaven on earth,
but he does expect believers to be good citizens, to give
generously to the poor, to live in society in a way that features
their Christian faith. . . . Paul does not endorse a private
Christianity, where one's individual salvation does not affect
public living. New life in Christ embraces and touches every
dimension of the life of believers.

—THOMAS SCHREINER[1]

WE LIVE IN A GLOBAL SOCIETY. NEWS AND IMAGES ARE INSTANTANEOUSLY bounced off satellites and relayed to and from the remotest parts of the globe. In the twenty-first century, people are more aware than ever before of the injustices and atrocities that are occurring around the world. As Christians, what are you and I doing in light of this new information? What can be done? What should we do? How do we engage? What does biblical compassion look like? I will confess up front that I don't have all the answers, and I am trying to figure out what this looks like for me as a follower of Christ. But I think God's Word reveals some principles for us to put into practice, regardless of the society we happen to live in.

Salt, Light, and Good Works

One of the purposes for which Christ saved us was for us to be a "people . . . zealous for good deeds" (Titus 2:14 NASB; see also 1 Peter 2:12).[2] As we seek to be conformed to the image of Christ, we need to be mindful that one of Jesus's primary roles on earth was to glorify the Father. One way we "image the Son" is by bringing glory to the Father. In the Sermon on the Mount Jesus said, "Let your light shine before others, that they may see your good deeds and glorify your Father in heaven" (Matt. 5:16). Just prior to this verse Jesus reminds us that we are to be a preserving agent (salt) and a voice of truth (light). Christ-followers are to be publicly engaged, because transformation occurs as individuals within communities live out the good news of the kingdom.[3] Christ was a public figure who impacted the world with the words of life that He spoke, the quality of life that He lived, and the acts of service and compassion that He performed.

Christianity is not just private, requiring our attention for only two hours on a Sunday morning; it is public and should affect the totality of life (i.e., a thoroughgoing Christian worldview). Unfortunately, many Christians have withdrawn from ethical, social, political, educational, and cultural issues and institutions. As Christians, we need to enter into dialogue in the public square and become part of the solutions, not just heralds of the problems. Throughout the history of Christianity, followers of Jesus have understood their responsibility to share the fruit of a Christian way of life (e.g., build hospitals, orphanages, rescue centers).[4] We need to follow their lead. We need to get past viewing our relationship with God as only this private experience.

Rather, as Francis Schaeffer put it, "True spirituality—the Christian life— flows on into the total culture."[5] Meaning, we need to view our activity from Monday morning to Saturday night as just as important as two hours on Sunday morning.

Social Justice and Action

Justice both reflects the heart of God and connects us to the heart of God.[6] There are numerous passages in the Old Testament that speak to this idea (Isa. 10:1–4; 58:3–12; Jer. 5:26–29; 22:13–19; Amos 2:6–7; 4:1–3; 5:10–15), but perhaps the most powerful instance occurs in Jeremiah 22:16. In this passage, God is pleading the cause of the afflicted and needy and asks: "Is that not what it means to know me?" The implication is as convicting as it is obvious: those who know God plead the cause of the poor and the afflicted.

Ronald Sider defines social action as "that set of activities whose primary goal is improving the physical, socioeconomic, and political well-being of people through relief, development, and structural change."[7] While the proclamation of the good news is the priority of the church (see Matt. 28:19–20), good works and social action should not be neglected. Unfortunately, in the well-founded zeal to proclaim Christ, some Christians have neglected appropriate and biblically informed social action. A document titled "For the Health of the Nation: An Evangelical Call to Civic Responsibility" accurately describes an appropriate interplay between good news and good works:

> From the Bible, experience, and social analysis, we learn that social problems arise and can be substantially corrected by both personal decisions and structural changes. On the one hand, personal sinful choices contribute significantly to destructive social problems (Prov. 6:9–11), and personal conversion through faith in Christ can transform broken persons into wholesome, productive citizens. On the other hand, unjust systems also help create social problems (Amos 5:10–15; Isa. 10:1–2) and wise structural change (for example legislation to strengthen marriage or increase economic opportunity for all) can improve society. Thus Christian civic engagement must seek to transform both individuals and institutions. While individuals transformed by the gospel change surrounding society, social institutions also shape individuals. While good

laws encourage good behavior, bad laws and systems foster destructive action. Lasting social change requires both personal conversion and institutional renewal and reform.[8]

Our society and the world need both individual and institutional transformation. The need for justice and relief is almost overwhelming. Today it is estimated that there are over thirty-five million slaves worldwide.[9] AIDS is ravaging entire countries in Africa. Genocide is a sickening reality. The poor suffer starvation, and children die daily due to the lack of clean drinking water. We still have racial injustice. The sex trade is booming with girls being kidnapped and sold into a life of slavery. Well over one million abortions are still legally performed each year in this country alone (only a tiny fraction of which are due to rape, incest, or imminent threat to the mother's health).[10]

When faced with these issues, what can we do? First, we can pray for God's mercy to be poured out and justice to be done. Next, we need to raise awareness within the church; we need to get the word out. Christians ought to be leading the charge in addressing these needs (a great example of this is William Wilberforce's campaign to abolish slavery in England, which was accomplished on July 26, 1833, just a few days before his death—see the 2006 film *Amazing Grace*).[11] Finally, we can go and be part of the solution. Are you still figuring out what God is calling you to do with your life? Why not spend a summer feeding the poor or digging wells that provide clean drinking water?[12]

Political Engagement

Institutional change primarily occurs through politics. As Christians living in a democratic society like America we have both the blessing and responsibility of civic engagement (see Rom. 13:1–7; 1 Peter 2:13–17). Not only are we to participate in the democratic process, but the New Testament also calls us to pray for our leaders (1 Tim. 2:1–2). So if we are seeking change, then we must engage the political process. (If you are eighteen, then you should register to vote.)

You will be happy to learn that God is neither a democrat nor a republican. Both political parties have strengths and weaknesses. While individual Christians align themselves politically depending on the issues of the day, we need to be careful not to naively believe that our particular political party is perfect. I think it is much more profitable for Christians to vote according to worldview considerations rather than according to political platforms. For example, a candidate or piece of legislation protecting the sanctity of human life ought to be supported by the Christian community. By the same token, in the name of human dignity derived from creation in God's image, we ought to oppose any legislation that knowingly exploits the poor or underprivileged or leads to systemic injustice.

Here are two quick words of wisdom about Christians and political engagement. First, we must be careful to be humble and civil in our treatment of those with whom we disagree—even over emotionally intense issues. Nothing is gained by attacking people, though we lose our integrity when this happens. Second, change comes slowly and with compromise. We need to have realistic expectations of what can be accomplished. We don't compromise on what the Bible says is right or wrong, but the nature of politics is such that concessions have to be made—it's the nature of the game. So, "compromise leading to incremental good is still good."[13] While biblically speaking we want to hit a grand slam, politically and socially it would be beneficial if we hit a single! To use a hot-button issue as an example: when laws were being challenged and legislation written regarding abortion, if Christian voters and conservative politicians would have conceded to allow abortion in the limited cases of rape, incest, and imminent threat to the mother's life, then perhaps we would have saved millions of innocent lives.[14] Not all, but some.

Before closing out our discussion, I want to briefly address two possible objections to what we have talked about.

Isn't There a "Wall of Separation" Between Church and State?

In our increasingly secular culture, the issue of the "separation of church and state" has come front and center. But this slogan is nowhere in the constitution. Don't take my word for it. J. Budziszewski, professor of government at the University of Texas, speaks to this myth. He points out that "even when you include the amendments, the Constitution says only three things about religion," only two of which relate to our discussion here:

- ARTICLE VI: "no religious test shall ever be required as a Qualification to any Office or public Trust under the United States."

- AMENDMENT I: "Congress shall make no law respecting the establishment of religion, or prohibiting the free exercise thereof."

Meaning: (1) The government is not allowed to make people take a religious test in order to qualify for holding federal office. (2) Congress is not allowed to set up an official national church. (3) Congress is not allowed to stop people from practicing their religions. . . . These three rules are meant to protect your liberty to follow God, not to abolish it. That famous slogan about a "wall of separation" just isn't there . . . Christians are free to act according to their convictions in politics, just as atheists are free to act according to theirs.[15]

We Can't Legislate Morality, Can We?

Another common myth is that people shouldn't legislate their morality—especially Christians. But this is false as well. For as Michael Bauman explains, "All laws, whether prescriptive or prohibitive, legislate morality. All laws, regardless of their content or their intent, arise from a system of values, from a belief that some things are right and others wrong, that some things are good and others bad, that some things are better and others worse. In the formulation and enforcement of law, *the question is never whether or not morality will be legislated but which one.*"[16] The law is undergirded by moral and value judgments. This is inescapable. Now, this does not mean that as Christians we should seek legislation outlawing sins like lust or gossip, but rather we should seek the passage of laws supporting human dignity, sanctity of life, and justice, while outlawing the atrocities of incest (consensual or not), child pornography, and rape. As Jeremiah reminds us, we should seek the welfare of the city in which God has planted us (see Jer. 29:7). This is fully appropriate under a Christian worldview.

After all is said and done, we can't do everything—but we can do something. If we work together in humility and compassion we will be able to do good and meet *some* of the needs that are out there. We will not usher in the perfect kingdom of God; Scripture seems to indicate that before Christ returns, things will get worse, not better (2 Tim. 3:1–7). Just like in sharing the gospel, our responsibility is not to be ultimately successful but to be faithful and leave the results to God. We can be a voice for the voiceless and contribute in some way to see that justice is done. When we read the latest news feed, it reminds us that the world is not as it should be nor will it be so until Christ returns and reigns. *Come soon, Lord Jesus* (Rev. 22:20)!

THE BIG IDEAS

- Christians are called to be both salt and light in the world, as well as to do good works.

- When we plead the case of the needy or afflicted, we reflect God's heart.

- Christians are committed to both individual conversion through Jesus Christ and institutional/structural change in order to provide justice and relief for the oppressed.

- Engage in politics with humility, civility, and patience from a Christian worldview—rather than from the view of a particular political party. Compromise in the right direction is a good thing.

- The so-called wall of separation between church and state and the claim that people should not legislate morality are slogans that are false and should be rejected.

- Success is measured not by the ultimate outcome but by our faithfulness to what God has called us to.

For Further Discovery

Batstone, David. *Not for Sale: The Return of the Global Slave Trade and How We Can Fight It*. New York: HarperCollins, 2010.

Bauman, Michael. "Legislating Morality." In *To Everyone an Answer: A Case for the Christian Worldview*. Edited by Francis J. Beckwith, William Lane Craig, and J. P. Moreland. Downers Grove, IL: InterVarsity Press, 2009.

Beckwith, Francis. *Politics for Christians: Statecraft as Soulcraft.* Christian Worldview Integration Series. Downers Grove, IL: InterVarsity Press, 2010.

Corbett, Steve, and Brian Fikkert. *When Helping Hurts: How to Alleviate Poverty Without Hurting the Poor . . . and Yourself.* Chicago: Moody Publishers, 2014.

Guinness, Os. *A Free People's Suicide: Sustainable Freedom and the American Future.* Downers Grove, IL: InterVarsity Press, 2012.

Haugen, Gary A. *Good News About Injustice: A Witness of Courage in a Hurting World.* Downers Grove, IL: InterVarsity Press, 2009.

Keller, Timothy. *Generous Justice: How God's Grace Makes Us Just.* New York: Dutton, 2010.

Kinnaman, David, and Gabe Lyons. *Good Faith: Being a Christian When Society Thinks You're Irrelevant and Extreme.* Grand Rapids: Baker, 2016.

Moore, Russell. *Onward: Engaging the Culture Without Losing the Gospel.* Nashville: B&H Publishing, 2015.

Living Water International at https://water.cc.

International Justice Mission at www.ijm.org.

Watching Movies with Eyes Wide Open

Therefore I urge you, brethren, by the mercies of God, to present your bodies a living and holy sacrifice, acceptable to God, which is your spiritual service of worship. And do not be conformed to this world, but be transformed by the renewing of your mind, so that you may prove what the will of God is, that which is good and acceptable and perfect.

—ROMANS 12:1–2 NASB

Finally, brothers and sisters, whatever is true, whatever is noble, whatever is right, whatever is pure, whatever is lovely, whatever is admirable—if anything is excellent or praiseworthy—think about such things.

—PHILIPPIANS 4:8

As viewers, we must be sensitive to our own weaknesses and negative propensities. . . . We must be careful to draw personal lines that we will not cross, based upon what particular things affect us negatively when we are exposed to them in movies.

—BRIAN GODAWA[1]

AS A DAD I GET THE OPPORTUNITY TO BE A KID AGAIN AS I WATCH MY children grow up. I vividly remember when my son discovered the wonderful world of Play-Doh. Oh, Play-Doh . . . can't you just see those bright colors and smell that unique scent right now? My son particularly enjoyed squeezing big handfuls until the Play-Doh is pressed through his hands and onto the floor. Great fun!

Well, our emotions and thoughts are like that Play-Doh. Bizarre thought,

I know, but keep reading. Our emotions are easily moldable, able to take one shape and then another a second later. They are prone to being squeezed by all the stuff we come into contact with on a daily basis. What most people don't realize is that movies and TV have the ability to mold and condition our emotions over time. Producers and directors think, plan, direct, and edit based on their desire for our emotions to take a certain shape. Depending on the intent of the director, this can be a good or bad thing. News flash: when you watch movies and TV, you are not merely being entertained.

Like waves washing perpetually over a rock on the beach, media can dull the edges of our minds. While our minds *require* sharpening, movies and TV often subtly condition our emotional responses so that over time, we find our beliefs being changed. If visually embodied ideas can do this to current beliefs we hold (i.e., our worldview), what of those things we have never really thought of before? Simple—it sets its own opinion in our minds by default. Our plausibility structures—those things we find reasonable—are being affected on a daily basis unless we are actively resisting.

OK, here's what I mean: Imagine setting up your equalizer on your sound system or iTunes with all of the different frequencies and levels. Any music will now be heard according to those settings. Take, for example, the movie *The Cider House Rules* (1999). If you watch that movie without a solid opinion concerning the morality of abortion (and maybe even if you do), then it is most likely that you will be cheering for the girl to have an abortion by the end of the movie because that was the director's intent. (Now I am not being insensitive to the tragic circumstances surrounding this particular situation and don't want to enter the abortion debate here, but I do want to make the point that this movie was made specifically to shape your views on abortion by evoking a visceral response; more specifically you're making the transfer of emotion from a complex circumstance to the act of abortion itself.) If we are being shaped like this, then what do we do?

Renewing Your Mind

It is as though Paul anticipated our discussion when he wrote his letter to the Romans and challenged them to "not conform to the pattern of this world, but be transformed by the renewing of your mind" (Rom. 12:2; see also Eph. 4:17–24). The world is constantly trying to press us into its mold. And if we are passively sitting there, soaking it all in, then we are already being shaped. Here is a helpful and convicting barometer: pay attention to what you laugh at. People laugh at what they agree with at a fundamental level. Are you laughing at something that later on you know you shouldn't have?

But God has given us truth (John 17:17), and we are to allow the waters of His Word to wash over our minds, cleansing and shaping us according to His design and priorities. We're called to view and feel about the world the way God does, not some Hollywood director. Let me be clear that I am not advocating that we put our heads in the sand and withdraw from culture—it is good to be challenged by other worldviews at times in order to see if what we believe is really true. But it is imperative that we maintain a steady diet of biblical truth and form good thinking habits. Otherwise, we will find ourselves too easily influenced by the puppet masters of our day.

Watching with Wisdom and Discernment

We live in an age of unparalleled freedom of expression. Everybody's got an opinion, and they're not afraid to use it! Whether these opinions and ideas are expressed in movies, novels, prime-time news, blogs, artwork, magazines, or the Internet, the fact is they are out there for public consumption. If you find your media dinner plate full of ideas each day, you probably shouldn't "clean your plate," as your mom would say. A bit of discernment is necessary to see what on our plates is palatable and what we should allow the disposal to consume.

In thinking about how to go about this, I came across an excellent book by award-winning screenwriter Brian Godawa titled *Hollywood Worldviews: Watching Films with Wisdom and Discernment*. He makes some observations which I think are helpful in thinking about our consumption of media. We don't want to fall into either of two extremes. First, we don't want to completely desert or cut ourselves off from culture (he calls this "cultural anorexia"). Nor do we want to completely immerse ourselves in culture (he calls this "cultural gluttony").[2] Which one do you tend to lean toward? The following are some questions Godawa lists to help us answer that:

Cultural Anorexic

1. Do you generalize all movies as "worldly" or consider any depiction of sin as wrong without concern for context?

2. Are you unable to appreciate anything good in a movie because of some bad you see in it?

3. Do you consider art and entertainment to be wastes of time and therefore spend all of your leisure time on "spiritual" activities?

4. How many times have you been incapable of interacting with those around you because you were out of touch with their cultural experience?

Cultural Glutton

1. Do you watch every movie that interests you without considering beforehand whether its subject matter is appropriate?

2. Do you think movies and television are only entertainment without any real messages?

3. How many hours a week do you spend on entertainment? Now compare that with how many hours a week you read the Bible or other spiritual growth material.

4. How many times have you enjoyed a movie that you later came to realize was offensive to your beliefs or worldview?[3]

It is important that we give ourselves a periodic checkup to ensure that we are maintaining a balanced diet of media.

When it comes to entertainment, gender and your emotional history also raise some issues. There are many movies and shows that men just should not watch . . . *period*. I am not being dogmatic here; I just know I'm right! Men are more visually oriented and therefore should avoid lusty movies filled with gratuitous sexual innuendo—no matter how funny the movie may seem. This isn't a matter of conviction, but wisdom (see Job 31:1; 2 Tim. 2:22). Men's minds are like sponges when it comes to lustful, sexual images, and the "DVR of the mind" is always recording. So don't put stuff in there you don't want thrown back at you during your weakest moments.

Now if you are opposed to what I am saying on this point, ask yourself why. Could it be that you really enjoy these forbidden little treats and are reluctant to give them up? If so, you have just learned something important about yourself.

Women aren't immune from viewing inappropriate films either. Fantasy is an issue many women struggle with—it is not so much the sexual aspect (at least of the same *kind* that men deal with) as it is emotional fantasy.[4] As a woman, are your views of body image, self-worth, relationships with the opposite sex, and romance being determined by Hollywood? (BTW, men are not immune from struggling with body image as well . . . We can't all look like Chris Hemsworth from *Thor*.)[5] If so, you will become frustrated, disappointed, disillusioned, and ultimately you will suffer heartbreak. My point is that we must form our beliefs about these issues based on what God has said.

Emotions are powerful. Any movie worth its salt will stir the emotions—hopes, fears, dreams, laughter, empathy, and pain. A well-made movie will take you *there*. But there are some movies I can't watch due to my personal history and certain fears I have. It is not healthy for *me* to go there. There is also a place where it is not beneficial for you to go. Let's say you struggle with fear of bad things happening to you. Is it wise to open yourself up to powerful images that will reinforce those emotions? Remember that as Christians we have an enemy who seeks to take advantage of us any way he can (2 Cor. 2:11; see also 1 Peter 5:8). Do we really want to give him ammunition?

One final point: a person may believe they can watch something, claiming that the sex or violence or language just doesn't affect or bother them. The rationale is, it doesn't affect me, so it's OK to watch it. This person is in spiritual danger, because it means their conscience has been deadened and calloused by overexposure—they can't feel the conviction they *ought* to feel. Now this does not mean that it's universally wrong to watch movies if they contain sex, bad language, or violence, only that we should *always* be bothered, saddened, and appropriately moved by it.[6]

One more thing: Is it just me or is every other movie coming out these days a horror film? Each one seems to be more gruesome, disturbing, and maniacal than the one before (*The Walking Dead* is just one example of gratuitous violence gone mainstream). In case you were wondering, I don't think these kinds of movies and shows are good for the soul. Reality is scary enough. That's my two cents on that!

That's a Wrap!

So how much media should we eat off our plates each day? As Christians we should not be *cultural anorexics*, abstaining from all media, or *cultural gluttons*, uncritically devouring all the media set before us. Wise Christians need to find a middle road governed by a biblical worldview and our individual convictions (see Rom. 14). Always be aware of the worldviews that are being advocated. Here is a quick tip. If you follow the journey of the hero in the movie you are watching and see what ideas are attached to their moment of clarity, that is the worldview the director wants you to adopt. And if you follow the antagonist or villain and pay attention to the ideas they embody, that is the worldview the director wants you to reject (notice this is not done by rational argument but with imagination and emotion).

We can also look for the redemptive themes within films and use them to connect with the brokenness of those around us. A movie or TV show may be just the key to unlock a spiritual conversation we've wanted to have with someone. My hope and prayer is that you will no longer be a passive movie watcher being shaped and manipulated by the latest director's fancy, but instead that you will watch movies with your eyes wide open.[7]

THE BIG IDEAS

- Media does more than entertain; it shapes our emotions and thoughts. If you are not actively renewing your mind, then you are already being shaped into the world's mold (see Rom. 12:1–2). There is a very good chance your worldview has already been shaped without you realizing it on some of life's biggest questions.

- As Christians we should not be *cultural anorexics* or *cultural gluttons*. Wise Christians need to find a middle road governed by a biblical worldview and our individual convictions before the Lord (see Rom. 14). Always be aware of the worldviews that are being advocated.

- Pay attention to what emotions you are feeling as you watch. When you feel a strong emotion, see what idea is attached to it and that will tell you what the producer is trying to get you to feel and think—how they want to change your mind without a rational argument.

For Further Discovery

Godawa, Brian. *Hollywood Worldviews: Watching Films with Wisdom and Discernment*. Downers Grove, IL: InterVarsity Press, 2012.

Common Sense Media at https://www.commonsensemedia.org. Find out what's in the movie (sex, violence, innuendo) before you see it.

Plugged In at http://www.pluggedin.com. Another great site to review the content of music, video games, and movies.

VidAngel at https://www.vidangel.com. This is a great way to rent a movie and filter out the objectionable content.

A Christian View
of Alcohol

He causes the grass to grow for the cattle,
And vegetation for the labor of man,
So that he may bring forth food from the earth,
And wine which makes man's heart glad,
So that he may make his face glisten with oil,
And food which sustains man's heart.
—PSALM 104:14–15 NASB

Wine is a mocker and beer a brawler;
whoever is led astray by them is not wise.
—PROVERBS 20:1

It is better not to eat meat or drink wine or to do
anything else that will cause your brother or sister to fall.
—ROMANS 14:21

I CAN SAY ONE THING WITH CERTAINTY ABOUT WHEREVER YOU GO TO college: drinking will happen (much to the dismay of parents reading this book, and yes, it will happen at Christian schools too). This is one of those "not if, but when" issues. Here are the facts on college student drinking in America: "Full-time college students tend to drink more than others in their age group. In 2014, 60 percent of full-time college students reported any alcohol use, 38 percent reported engaging in binge drinking, and 12 percent reported heavy drinking during the past 30 days."[1] In light of the prevalence of drinking in college, how should you view drinking as a Christian student? What does the Bible have to say? To address these questions we'll first examine four popular myths about alcohol and then contrast these by examining four biblical truths. Then I will share a little from my experience.

Four Myths About Alcohol

Myth #1

Drinking makes you cool and desirable, allows you to be your "uninhibited self," and ensures you'll have more fun. As I reflect on this myth, I have to chuckle because it makes me think about a commercial I saw once. This ad shows a party on some mountain peak in Colorado with scantily clad women dancing. The camera zooms in on a few young men drinking the advertised beer with broad smiles painted on their faces as they realize that they have instantly become the most desirable males of the species! The right beer makes all the difference, right? Wrong. In reality, people generally don't care what kind of beverage you drink—or if they *do* use what you are or are not drinking as some sort of test, run the other way!

Doesn't drinking alcohol let out the real you? No. Alcohol creates someone who is not you at all. If you need to lighten up a bit, there are better routes to go. And it is simply false that you have to be drinking in order to have a good time. I went through college without drinking and had a blast! Most times the kind of "fun" you would have while under the influence of alcohol you will regret later—if you even remember it. The extras in those commercials were paid for their hour in the studio to sell you a lie, and then they went home to their normal life. If you buy the lie, I promise you'll be disappointed.

Myth #2

The wine spoken of in the Bible was really grape juice. The short answer is no. The words *wine* and *strong drink* show up hundreds of times in the Bible, but let's just take two examples that demonstrate wine is the sort of beverage that can get you drunk.

In Genesis we find that Noah got into an undesirable situation because of too much wine (Gen. 9:21–24). Noah's act of becoming drunk brought shame upon himself and dishonored God.

In the gospel of John we learn that Jesus performed His first recorded miracle at a wedding feast in Cana by turning water into wine (John 2:3–10). A New Testament scholar comments on the significance of this passage, saying that the headwaiter's response "makes perfect sense. . . . The reason why a man brings out the poorer wine later is because the good wine has numbed the senses a bit. Grape juice would hardly mask anything."[2] In addition to this, the verb John used in this passage, "drunk freely," almost always means "*to cause to become intoxicated*."[3] Taken together, these observations strongly suggest that the wine mentioned here is the kind of beverage that can lead to intoxication.

Myth #3

The Bible only speaks about wine and strong drink in a negative way. It is often said that the Bible *uniformly condemns* the drinking of wine. This is simply not the case. To be sure, there are many instances where God's Word warns against getting drunk or shows the foolish consequences of being seduced by too much wine. However, it may surprise you to learn that the Bible also speaks of wine in a positive light (see Deut. 14:22–26; Ps. 104:14–15). In fact, "wine becomes an important image of joy, celebration and festivity, often expressive of the abundant blessing of God."[4] Because of this, God's withholding wine from Israel is often a sign of judgment for their disobedience (e.g., Jer. 48:33). God is not against our pleasure, but He does want us to order our affections appropriately—with Him at the center as our *greatest* source of pleasure.

Myth #4

Mature Christians should not drink alcohol—period. It is completely appropriate for Christians to have a conviction against drinking alcohol. There are many legitimate reasons for people to think that drinking any alcohol is wrong for them (e.g., abuse and a history of alcoholism in the family). But this is a matter of conscience and personal conviction, not biblical teaching. As we have already seen, the Bible—while condemning drunkenness—does not condemn wine in and of itself. R. V. Pierard comments, "Christian liberty permits one to abstain or partake in moderation, but total abstainers are not justified in holding up their practice as the more biblical, virtuous, or spiritual of the two."[5]

As Christians, we are often stereotyped as being against everything—especially if it can be associated with having fun! Non-Christians often stumble over the fact that our Christian subculture views drinking as wrong. Now I am not suggesting that we need to lure people to the church with keg parties, but I am saying that Christians should do their best to put only the stumbling blocks in front of unbelievers that the gospel of Christ requires— the gospel is offensive enough.

Four Biblical Truths About Alcohol

Biblical Truth #1

If you are under the age of twenty-one in America, then it is illegal for you to drink alcohol—end of story. As a Christian, this is a matter of obedience, not conviction. Romans 13:1–7 informs us that we are to obey the law of the land, and American law states that you must be twenty-one to purchase and consume alcohol. If you were growing up in Italy where there is no legal drinking age, obedience would not be an issue. However, once you are of legal age, you still need to apply these next three biblical truths.

Biblical Truth #2

The Bible is crystal clear that you are not to get drunk. The apostle Paul states this unambiguously in Ephesians 5:18: "And do not get drunk with wine, for that is dissipation [i.e., wasteful indulgence], but be filled with the Spirit" (NASB). The New Living Translation renders this verse: "Don't be drunk with wine, because that will ruin your life. Instead, be filled with the Holy Spirit." When we are drunk, we are no longer in control, and this almost always leads us down an undesirable path. God's reason for not wanting us to get drunk isn't because He is a cosmic killjoy. Rather, He gives this command because He loves us and desires the best for us, even if we don't see things His way at first.

Biblical Truth #3

Christians of legal age, while having liberty to drink in moderation, should not drink if it is going to cause a brother or sister in Christ to stumble. Freedom exists so that we can choose to do the good and virtuous thing, not so that we can choose to do whatever we want. The Bible is clear that we are not to use our liberty to cause brothers and sisters to stumble. We are to look out for the interests of others (Phil. 2:4–11). This principle is illustrated by Paul in 1 Corinthians 8:7–13 (see also Rom. 14:21). It was common in ancient times for people to sacrifice animals to idols at a temple. After the animals had been sacrificed, the temple priests would sell the meat to make money—at a reasonable price. Mature Christians knew that it made no difference whether the meat had been sacrificed to idols, and being good stewards they purchased and ate the inexpensive meat. The problem arose when recent converts (who perhaps had been sacrificing animals at these very temples) witnessed Christians buying and eating the defiled meat. These converts had just separated themselves from this idolatrous lifestyle only to be confused by other Christians' seeming acceptance of it. This confusion caused them to stumble in their faith. Paul's response? It wasn't, "I have liberty to eat meat and they need to get over it." Rather, he said, "If my eating meat causes them to stumble, I'll never eat it again—my liberty isn't worth that!"

Because of this biblical principle, I chose not to drink in college even though I was of legal age. I found that too many people had negative associations with alcohol, and I did not want to send the wrong message. Some of the people I knew had recently left a partying lifestyle after committing their lives to Christ. Why use my liberty to trip them up? Seeing me with a beer in my hand might have been the very justification they were looking for to give in to the temptation to drink. I am not advocating that the correct course is abstaining from alcohol, but I am advocating that we must put the well-being of our brothers and sisters in the Lord above our liberty.[6]

Biblical Truth #4

Let your conscience be your guide; is it a sin for you? If you are of legal age, can you participate in drinking with a pure conscience? Scripture instructs us to ask ourselves this question (concerning activities the Bible does not specifically prohibit or endorse). In Romans 14:13–23, Paul again explicitly affirms biblical truth #3 in verse 21, but he also adds that we are not to violate our conscience or personal convictions before the Lord. The human conscience is complex and sometimes difficult to interpret. A person of legal age may be unable to sort out whether the hesitation to drink alcohol is from guilt—associated with past social or family experiences perhaps—or from a legitimate conviction of the Holy Spirit. Time, prayer, and a close community of Christian friends can help you process your feelings regarding alcohol.

The Dark Side of the Bottle

The reality is that for many of us alcohol is a gray area complicated by life experiences—neither fun nor happy. We must face the harsh emotional realities that accompany alcohol *when it is abused*. If you haven't experienced this firsthand, odds are someone close to you has, and you owe it to them to be sensitive regarding this.

My view of alcohol has not been shaped by positive experiences. I grew up in a home where alcohol was abused. My late father struggled most of his life with his addiction to alcohol.[7] His alcoholism led him to relate to people in abusive and unhealthy ways, which in turn caused a lot of pain. I witnessed how one beer to take the edge off of a hard day rapidly turned into a six-pack or more. I had a front-row seat to what alcohol brings when mixed with anger, stress, and frustration.

From late middle school into early high school, I experimented with alcohol to dull the pain of loneliness and escape the lack of purpose I felt in life. It didn't work. Every night spent forgetting was followed by a morning of remembering. The occasions when I did drink, I drank to get drunk. I didn't drink socially or to fit in. But after I came to Christ my junior year of high school, I abandoned this hollow attempt to dull the pain and fill the emptiness. It wasn't helping anyway. And besides, I had found something much better to devote my life to—becoming a disciple of Jesus Christ.

I also had plenty of opportunities to see the effects of alcohol abuse as a member of a national fraternity at a large state university. I watched friends lose control due to alcohol on many a Friday or Saturday night, sometimes losing their way for years at a time. I witnessed young women mistakenly think guys cared for them at parties only to wake up to regret, shame, and bitterness the next day. I don't say this to portray myself as holier-than-thou. I deeply loved (and still do) my fraternity brothers, and it broke my heart to watch some of the decisions they made. What I saw friends do week in and week out was destructive—even if it wasn't immediately apparent to them. Sometimes there were only temporary consequences, like a hangover or wasted money. But deep regrets also accompanied their poor choices. And they will live with those for the rest of their lives.

I do not speak of alcohol as one who has never tried it or seen its effects up close and personal. There is no denying the dark side of the bottle. Liberty comes with responsibility, and the consequences of abuse are painfully real.

Sticky Situations

Now you may find yourself—either due to your own foolishness or just as a victim of circumstance—in a situation that is not good and involves alcohol. If you end up in a bad situation, please don't make it worse by driving home drunk or riding with someone who has been drinking. I know money is tight in college, but call an Uber or a sober friend to come get you. This is not a matter of being considered uncool or weak. This is being wise. And this decision could save you a lot of future heartache . . . or it could even save your life. Over 1,700 college students die each year related to drunk driving.[8] Driving drunk is nothing to mess around with (and while we are on the topic, neither is texting and driving).[9]

You will find yourself in a situation where you are pressured to get drunk—even if you do not pledge a fraternity or sorority—and you must resolve beforehand what you will do. If you don't and are faced with a pressure situation, you are likely to cave in. It is tough to say no in the heat of the moment. When I pledged a fraternity, I was very clear about the fact that I didn't drink and was not about to start. I tried very hard not to be prideful or a jerk about it, but I would not yield when opportunities arose. And the others respected me for it.

To the women who are reading this book, you must know that many guys will attempt to use alcohol to lower your inhibitions so that they can get physical with you. Be on guard. And remember, a real man will pursue you with holiness and respect your convictions, not push you to compromise them.

Grace and a Fresh Start

I am aware that I am not writing to an audience who has never experimented with alcohol or been drunk before. So what if you've already blown it? I have good news for you. Drunkenness is not an unforgivable sin. This is not to dismiss sin as unserious. *All* sin grieves the heart of our Father. The wonderful truth of the gospel is that if you honestly confess your sin in faith, because of Christ's sacrifice at the cross on your behalf, God will forgive you. You can be washed clean and have a fresh start. Also, you have the opportunity for a new start when going to college. You can choose new friends. College is an opportunity to show yourself wise or foolish (see Prov. 23:29–35 and 1 Cor. 15:33).

Grace is a beautiful thing, but remember that even though God is graceful and promises to forgive you if you repent, He has also given you significant freedom with which to make meaningful decisions. And this means that the consequences of sin will follow you into your future. So be careful what you invite to come along.[10]

POSTSCRIPT: Should Christians Smoke Pot?

You may have noticed that recreational marijuana is now legal in several states. But just because it's legal in some places, does that mean God thinks it's a good idea for you? Odds are you have friends or know of people who have smoked marijuana. Maybe you've even tried it yourself.

According to new data from the Substance Abuse and Mental Health Services Administration, 77 percent of teens and adolescents believe it "isn't risky to smoke marijuana occasionally."[11] This is pretty amazing, as most people would say that smoking cigarettes is harmful because of all the public reinforcement that occurs in commercials and media—there are even trailers at the movies showing how scary cigarettes are! However, many young people don't have the same negative reaction to smoking marijuana because it is not being publicly discouraged (hopefully this will change in the future). While a lot could be said, I want to give you two reasons why Christians should not smoke marijuana recreationally.

First, while there is no verse that specifically mentions and prohibits smoking marijuana, the Bible clearly teaches that Christians should not be controlled by any substance (see Eph. 5:18). In the same way that drinking for the purpose of getting drunk (i.e., intoxicated) would be sinful for Christians, smoking marijuana for the purpose of becoming intoxicated would also be sinful. We are called to be sober minded and clearheaded so that we can honor God in our thoughts and actions (see 1 Peter 1:13). As Joe Carter summarizes:

> For marijuana, however, a much lower dosage is needed to induce a state of intoxication. Studies show that intoxication occurs at the ingestion of less than 7 mg of THC (the psychoactive ingredient in marijuana). That is approximately the equivalent to four puffs of a marijuana cigarette.
>
> If the purpose of consuming the marijuana was for nourishment and

taste, we would need to eat only an amount that would not cause the intoxicating effect—about 200 mg of marijuana leaves. In theory, then, it could be possible to ingest marijuana with no sinful intentions. But of course, in almost all cases, the recreational use of marijuana is done with the *intention* of achieving some level of intoxication. And if the intent of the recreational use of marijuana is to achieve some level of intoxication, then it is clearly a sinful motive and action.[12]

Second, it's not good for you—especially if you are under twenty-five. More research needs to be done, but studies already indicate that it affects brain development and other functions.[13] Why risk it? As my friend and president of the Colson Center for Christian Worldview John Stonestreet put it after investigating the negative effects of marijuana use on the body, "So if you don't care about eating, learning, remembering things, forming healthy relationships or having a happy life, by all means, light up! And, I should add, in light of all of these concerns, it's reckless for policymakers and the voting public to jump on the weed bandwagon simply in the name of more 'freedom' and tax dollars."[14]

The bottom line is that smoking marijuana is not wise—there is a pathway attached to this decision and the destination is not human flourishing. Choose a better path.

THE BIG IDEAS

* Four popular myths about alcohol:
  1. Drinking makes you cool and desirable, allows you to be your "uninhibited self," and ensures you'll have more fun.
  2. The wine spoken of in the Bible was really grape juice.
  3. The Bible only speaks about wine and strong drink in a negative way.
  4. Mature Christians should not drink alcohol—period.
* Four biblical truths about alcohol:
  1. If you are under the age of twenty-one in America, then it is illegal for you to drink alcohol—end of story (Rom. 13:1–7).

2. The Bible is crystal clear that you are not to get drunk (Eph. 5:18).
3. Christians of legal age, while having liberty to drink in moderation, should not drink if it is going to cause a brother or sister in Christ to stumble (1 Cor. 8:7–13).
4. Let your conscience be your guide; is it a sin for you (Rom. 14:13–23)?

- Always be sobered by the dark reality of alcohol when it is abused. Even if you find yourself in a sticky situation, be wise. Remember that God's grace is always available to the repentant, but that doesn't mean the consequences of your actions will simply disappear.

- Even though smoking marijuana recreationally may be legal, Christians should not smoke it because we should not be controlled by any substance, it's not good for our brains, and it does not lead to human flourishing.

For Further Discovery

Gentry, Kenneth L. *God Gave Wine: What the Bible Says About Alcohol*. Fountain Inn, SC: Victorious Hope, 2015.
Pierard, R. V. "Drinking of Alcohol." In *Evangelical Dictionary of Theology*. Edited by Walter A. Elwell. Grand Rapids: Baker, 2001.

Ethics in a
Brave New World

Most people would not want to live in a society in which morality was unimportant, in which conceptions of right and wrong carried little weight. In fact, it is unlikely that any sort of civilized society could continue unless it had concern for key moral values, such as fairness, justice, truthfulness, and compassion. Ethics are important because they give direction to people and societies who have some sense that they cannot flourish without being moral.

—SCOTT RAE[1]

Any time we can do something, we are suddenly forced to ask whether we ought to do it.

—PAUL CHAMBERLAIN[2]

All it takes for evil to prevail is for good men to do nothing.

—EDMUND BURKE[3]

WHAT DO *THE HUNGER GAMES, DIVERGENT,* AND *THE MAZE RUNNER* ALL have in common? They wrestle with significant questions about what it means to be human and what it means to be good. Is science humanity's only hope? If God does not exist, then does the one with the most power make the rules? Does the majority determine good? Which lives have value? Do the ends justify the means?

The fictional scenarios raised in these works should prompt us to think about the all too real-life scenarios people face in our country each day. For example, a young man is faced with what to do with a brain-dead parent who is only being kept alive by life support. Or a married couple has been unable to get pregnant and is exploring what reproductive technologies are available. Due to advances in genetics, it won't be too long before it will be widely available for parents to create designer children (increased intelligence, blond hair, blue eyes, athletic, etc.).[4] The question is, should they be allowed to? What about war? When is it justified? Have the rules changed with terrorism on the scene (i.e., strictly speaking there is no recognized nation to be at war with, only individuals)? These are not easy situations, to be sure. So how should Christians approach these and other issues in a way that honors the Lord? How do people figure out what their morally acceptable options are in any given situation?

Finding Our Moral Compass

We live in a culture that is at best unsure where the moral boundaries are in certain cases and at worst suggests that there are no lines out there at all. In chapter 26 we talked about the church losing her mind. One of the places this absence of careful thinking among Christians shows up is in the area of ethical reasoning.[5] In a culture that has lost its moral compass, the church has a wonderful opportunity to offer clear ethical thinking (with compassion and love) so that our culture will hear at least one voice speaking up for life, goodness, and dignity. The remaining part of this chapter will be spent introducing you to the important ethical debate concerning human personhood.

Before we move to that, I want to call your attention to the seriousness of these issues for your generation, because it is your generation that will inherit the consequences of today's ethical decisions. And honestly, much of it doesn't look good. But you don't have to stand idly by watching and waiting for the worst. You can choose to invest some time in learning how to think Christianly about ethics in this brave new world and then be salt and light among your peers. Even a small light makes a difference in a culture of increasing moral darkness. If you won't think carefully and biblically about these issues, then who will?[6]

What Does It Mean to Be a Person?

Here we are at the beginning of the twenty-first century and there is growing confusion over what it means to be a person. You would think we'd have this down pat by now. What it means to be human is already settled in virtue of genetic information (DNA); there is "no doubt scientifically that individual human life begins at conception and does not end until natural death."[7] For the sake of illustration, let's apply this discussion to the personhood of the unborn. So an unborn baby is a human, but is that unborn baby a person? This is a critical question because only *persons* deserve our respect and care. Philosophically speaking there are two views: the *functional view* and the *essentialist view*.

An increasing number of people like Princeton ethicist Peter Singer are arguing for a *functional view* of personhood today (this includes many within the pro-choice camp). This view seeks to distinguish a human person from a human being. An unborn child will of course be a human being, but he or she is not yet a person. Personhood is determined by satisfying certain criteria such as brain activity, consciousness, the ability to reason and think, the capacity to communicate, self-awareness, and self-motivated activity. In other words, if an entity functions in a certain way, then it is a person. One of the strongest criticisms of this view is that it understands personhood as something one can have in degrees (kind of like a barometer), and thus dignity and value are degreed properties as well. With this view, an unborn child does not satisfy the criteria for personhood and therefore does not have a right to life (this view also has disastrous consequences for the elderly or terminally ill).[8]

Also according to the functional view, a human embryo satisfies none of the criteria, and so it can be used for stem-cell research. But what is the difference between an embryo, a fetus, a thirty-year-old man in a coma on a ventilator, and someone who is asleep? All of them are human and none of them are functioning according to the criteria above. So is personhood withheld in all these cases? If it is argued that the man in a coma has the latent capacity to function in those ways when he wakes up, the same could be said of the embryo or fetus, for they possess the latent capacities to function in those ways at birth. For at least these reasons, this view of personhood seems arbitrary and artificial.

On the other hand, the *essentialist view* maintains that "a person functions as a person *because* she *is* a person and *not because* she *functions* as a person. That is, personhood is not something that arises when certain functions are in place, but rather something that grounds these functions whether or not they are ever actualized in the life of a human being."[9] Personhood is something you either have or you don't—there aren't degrees of persons. As philosopher Frank Beckwith puts it, "Intrinsic value is not a matter of degree; one either has it or does not. Intrinsic value, therefore, cannot be conditioned on the level of human capability, for if one had more capability, one would have more value."[10] Human life is valuable at every stage no matter how small or big, how young or old. In the essentialist view, "the unborn are not potential persons, but human persons with great potential."[11]

Use the SLED Test to Defend Life

Here's the bottom line in this discussion: philosophically, there is no relevant difference between an *unborn*, *newborn*, or *adult* human person. Using the SLED acrostic, we can clearly see the four differences between the unborn, newborn, and adult:[12]

- *Size.* We protect the basic rights of small people just the same as bigger people. Seven-foot-seven basketball player Yao Ming is not more valuable than someone who is four feet tall.
- *Level of development.* An elderly human is human; an adult human is human; a child human is human; a newborn human is human; an unborn human is human. We protect human rights independent of their stage of development.
- *Environment.* Our human rights are unaffected by our changes of location. *Where* one is is irrelevant to *who* one is (that is, inside the womb versus outside the womb). This exposes the horrendous logic people use for the barbaric practice of partial-birth abortion.
- *Dependency.* Toddlers, the elderly in nursing homes, people with pacemakers or artificial organs, people in need of blood transfusions to stay alive—*they are all dependent on something or someone else for life.* Human beings are intrinsically valuable—regardless of their level of dependency. Viability does not determine value.

There is no *morally significant* difference between unborn, newborn, and adult human persons.

You will also notice that the essentialist view is completely consistent with a biblical view of human persons. Biblically speaking, every human being is valuable, has dignity, and was created with the capacity for relationship with God for His glory (Gen. 1:26–27; 2:7; 9:6; Exod. 20:13; Ps. 139; Isa. 43:7; Acts 17:28).

This discussion has obvious implications for the physician-assisted suicide debate. Once a patient is unable to function in certain ways or enjoy a certain quality of life, does that individual cease to be a person who is worthy of care? In addition, does this individual's status as a nonperson mean that a doctor is morally permitted to end biological life? According to the functional view it seems hard to avoid this conclusion. However, an essentialist will regard all human life as inherently valuable and worthy of care regardless of the stage of development or deterioration.

In chapter 39 we talked about having compassion on those who are oppressed and in need of protection. With the essentialist view of a person this includes the unborn, the severely handicapped, and the invalid. These did not acquire their personhood once they were able to perform certain functions, nor do they forfeit their personhood when they are unable to perform these functions. They are persons because they are human. Where you land on this critical issue will greatly affect the challenging ethical decisions you'll face in our brave new world.

THE BIG IDEAS

- Society faces incredibly difficult ethical questions in our brave new world. Yet our culture has lost its moral compass. This provides the church with a wonderful opportunity to be agents of salt and light.

- Perhaps the most important issue to be settled is what it means to be a person. There are two views of human personhood: (1) a *functional view*, which maintains that personhood is determined by satisfying certain criteria such as brain activity, consciousness, the ability to reason and think, the capacity to communicate, self-awareness, and self-motivated activity. In other words, if an entity functions in a certain way, then it is a person. And (2) an *essentialist view*, which maintains that "a person functions as a person *because* she *is* a person and *not because* she *functions* as a person. That is, personhood, is not something that arises when certain functions are in place, but rather something that grounds these functions whether or not they are ever actualized in the life of a human being." —FRANCIS J. BECKWITH

• "Intrinsic value is not a matter of degree; one either has it or does not. Intrinsic value, therefore, cannot be conditioned on the level of human capability, for if one had more capability, one would have more value." —FRANCIS J. BECKWITH

For Further Discovery

Beckwith, Francis J. *Defending Life: A Moral and Legal Case Against Abortion Choice.* Cambridge: Cambridge University Press, 2007.

———, ed. *Do the Right Thing: Readings in Applied Ethics and Social Philosophy.* 2nd ed. Belmont, CA: Wadsworth, 2002.

Chamberlain, Paul. *Talking About Good and Bad Without Getting Ugly: A Guide to Moral Persuasion.* Downers Grove, IL: InterVarsity Press, 2009.

———. *Whose Life Is It Anyway? Assessing Physician-Assisted Suicide.* Norcross, GA: RZIM, 2002.

Ensor, John, and Scott Klusendorf. *Stand for Life: A Student's Guide for Making the Case and Saving Lives.* Peabody, MA: Hendrickson, 2012.

Klusendorf, Scott. *The Case for Life: Equipping Christians to Engage the Culture.* Wheaton, IL: Crossway, 2009.

Mitchell, C. Ben, et al. *Biotechnology and the Human Good.* Washington, DC: Georgetown University Press, 2007.

Moreland, J. P., and Scott B. Rae. *Body and Soul: Human Nature and the Crisis in Ethics.* Downers Grove, IL: InterVarsity Press, 2009.

Rae, Scott B. *Moral Choices: An Introduction to Ethics.* 3rd ed. Grand Rapids: Zondervan, 2009.

Center for Bioethics and Human Dignity at www.cbhd.org.

Life Training Institute at www.prolifetraining.com.

43

Beyond the Horizon

Calling is the truth that God calls us to himself so decisively that everything we are, everything we do, and everything we have is invested with a special devotion, dynamism, and direction lived out as a response to his summons and service.

—OS GUINNESS[1]

At the core of our being, there is also a particular heart call that defines the unique purpose for our existence. It is like a golden thread that runs through the fabric of our lives. It is the story line of our life that provides a sense of continuity and coherence in an otherwise fragmented and confusing world.

—GREG OGDEN[2]

I must keep alive in myself the desire for my true country, which I shall not find till after death; I must never let it get snowed under or turned aside; I must make it the main object of life to press on to that other country and to help others to do the same.

—C. S. LEWIS[3]

THE HORIZON IS THAT PLACE WHERE THE EARTH AND THE SKY SEEM TO meet. It is the place where you can see no farther. The funny thing is that even though we can move closer to yesterday's horizon, we can still never see beyond it. Life, and particularly our calling in life, is a lot like gazing at the horizon. We can see clearly up to a point what God is calling us to do, or what the next chapter of life may bring—but no further. So how do we discover what is to come next, who we are to be, and what we are to do?

On Following Your Dreams
and Discovering Your Calling

There are different schools of thought on this, but I will share with you the advice I received—and it has proven to be sound thus far. If you dream, there is always the possibility of disappointment. But what is the alternative? If you aim at nothing in life, then you will hit it one-hundred-percent of the time. I resonate with what William Carey once said, "Attempt great things for God and expect great things from God."[4] Who else will dream for you if you will not?

Here is the bad news: most dreams never come true . . . at least not in the way we initially conceive them. It seems that God uses our dreams to move us along to other dreams that would not have been possible had we not dreamed in the first place. (That's a lot of dreaming!)

After I graduated from college, one of my dreams was to attend seminary and be trained as a pastor. So my wife and I packed up and headed to Dallas. But it wasn't too long after we arrived that God put another dream in my heart. This dream expanded on the pastor dream and sharpened it. Next thing you know, we were heading off to Los Angeles to complete two degrees instead of one! What started off as one dream ended up leading to another better dream. And this new dream fit who I was so perfectly, and God knew that . . . because He knows me!

One of my roommates and best friends in college had a dream to write and perform music. Some people didn't think he had what it took to make it in the music business. Today, Dave Barnes is living his dream and impacting people with skillfully woven lyrics and melodies—for the glory of God.[5] Now did everything happen according to his original dream? No, but that dream enabled him to find the path he is on today.

What we dream about helps illumine what our calling in life is. In his book *Courage and Calling*, Gordon Smith talks about three expressions of a person's calling.[6] First, there is the *general call* to follow Jesus as a Christian. Then there is the *specific call* that encompasses an individual's mission to the world. And finally, there is the *immediate call* that includes the duties and tasks for which we are presently responsible. The middle one is the unique call on a believer's life, or what has been called by some the "heart call." Your heart call—whatever that is—will keep you awake at night and get you out of bed in the morning. One of the keys to building a lasting faith is having a compelling vision for life. So as you dream about doing great things for the kingdom of God, ask yourself the following important diagnostic questions. These will help you recognize and sharpen your heart call.

1. What are my gifts and abilities?

2. Have my experiences in life prepared me for a specific type of position or service?

3. What kinds of things do I enjoy doing? What is life-giving to me?

4. What is my heart's desire?

5. What ideas, issues, and subjects do I find myself thinking about the most?

6. What is my unique personality?

7. What are the kinds of activities that I frequently find myself having the opportunity to be involved with?

8. What are the areas that others have encouraged and affirmed me in?

9. Where do I most connect with the needs of the world?

10. If money were no object, what would I like to do?[7]

While we often arrive at increasing clarity of our heart calling as we go through life, this calling is—in a sense—ultimately mysterious, resting just beyond the horizon. Os Guinness describes this tension: "In many cases a clear sense of calling comes only through a time of searching, including trial and error. And what may be clear to us in our twenties may be far more mysterious in our fifties because God's complete designs for us are never fully understood, let alone fulfilled, in this life."[8]

Movies are powerful. Perhaps the movie that has had the most profound impact on my life is *Dead Poets Society*. Actually, this movie was a key ingredient the Lord used to soften the soil of my heart toward the gospel. This happened primarily because it invited me to ask a question I had never really pondered before. There is a wonderful scene in which Mr. Keating (Robin Williams) is teaching his students about what really matters in life. But it was the last question he asked that resonated deep within my soul, and I hope will resonate within yours as well:

We don't read and write poetry because it's cute. We read and write poetry because we are members of the human race. And the human race is filled with passion. And medicine, law, business, engineering—these are noble pursuits and necessary to sustain life. But poetry, beauty, romance, love— these are what we stay alive for. To quote from Whitman,

> Oh me! Oh life! of the questions of these recurring,
> Of the endless trains of the faithless, of cities filled with the foolish . . .
> . . . .
> . . . —What good amid these, O me, O life?
>
> *Answer.*
> That you are here—that life exists and identity,
> That the powerful play goes on and you may contribute a verse.

That the powerful play goes on and you may contribute a verse. What will your verse be?[9]

Of Sunsets and Sunrises

Sunsets and sunrises, both are beautiful in their own way. One day, sooner than you think, you will be hearing your name called as you walk across the stage at graduation. In that moment, the sun will be setting on your college experience, but about to rise on the next chapter of life. I want to ask you a serious question: *How do you want to remember your college years?* What story do you want to tell? With guilt and regret? Lamenting opportunities squandered? Living with painful reminders of walking in the company of fools? Or with fondness, wearing a satisfied smile knowing that you made the most of this God-given opportunity? So what story do *you* want to tell? It's up to you.

Some will tell you that the college years are the best years of your life. But this is not true. I like Morrie's approach (from *Tuesdays with Morrie*).[10] When faced with the years at the end of his life, he said in effect, "I had my chance to be twenty already, now is my chance to be old." Each year can be your best year if lived to the fullest—lived to the glory of God (1 Cor. 10:31). Fight the temptation to become a passive observer in life who thinks that college was "really living." Yes, college is crucial in setting the trajectory of your life's journey, but it's only a chapter in your life. And who wants only one good chapter in life?

Live your life in such a way that at the end you can be like Frodo, at the end of *The Return of the King*, who was ready to travel to the far country, leaving the stories of a life well lived as a legacy. Paul fought the good fight and finished the course (2 Tim. 4:7). Along with the author of Hebrews and countless other Christians we say, "Let us run with perseverance the race marked out for us, fixing our eyes on Jesus, the pioneer and perfecter of faith" (Heb. 12:1–2). That is my prayer. And I hope it is yours too.

Speaking as one who is a few miles ahead of you on the road of life, I hope you will take these words to heart. Who knows, maybe our paths will cross somewhere on life's journey. Or perhaps we will find a tall shade tree in the new heaven and new earth under which to talk about a journey well traveled by God's grace.

THE BIG IDEAS

- God seems to use our initial dreams to move us along to other dreams that would not have been possible had we not dreamed in the first place.

- There are three expressions of a person's calling. First, there is the *general call* to follow Jesus as a Christian. Then there is the *specific call* that is each individual's mission to the world. And finally, there is the *immediate call* that includes the duties and tasks for which we are presently responsible.

- Each year can be the best year if faithfully lived to the fullest—lived to the glory of God (1 Cor. 10:31).

- Run the particular race set before you with perseverance and by fixing your eyes on Christ.

For Further Discovery

Albom, Mitch. *Tuesdays with Morrie: An Old Man, a Young Man, and Life's Greatest Lesson.* New York: Crown, 2007.

Alcorn, Randy C. *Heaven*. Wheaton, IL: Tyndale House, 2009.

Fey, Marc, Don Ankenbrandt, and Frank Johnson. *210 Project: Discover Your Place in God's Story*. Birmingham, AL: Alliance Publishing Group, 2011.

Garber, Steven. *Visions of Vocation: Common Grace for the Common Good*. Downers Grove, IL: InterVarsity Press, 2014.

Guinness, Os. *The Call: Finding and Fulfilling the Central Purpose of Your Life*. Nashville: Thomas Nelson, 2003.

Keller, Timothy, and Katherine Leary Alsdorf. *Every Good Endeavor: Connecting Your Work to God's Work*. New York: Dutton, 2012.

Lewis, C. S. *The Weight of Glory*. New York: HarperCollins, 2009.

Morrow, Jonathan. *Think Christianly: Looking at the Intersection of Faith and Culture*. Grand Rapids: Zondervan, 2011.

Smith, Gordon T. *Courage and Calling: Embracing Your God-Given Potential*. Downers Grove, IL: InterVarsity Press, 2011.

Whelchel, Hugh. *How Then Should We Work? Rediscovering the Biblical Doctrine of Work*. Nashville: WestBow Press, 2012.

Zacharias, Ravi. *The Grand Weaver: How God Shapes Us Through the Events of Our Lives*. Grand Rapids: Zondervan, 2010.

---

210 Project at 210Project.com. "Discover your place in God's story."

Strengths Finder Assessment at www.strengthsfinder.com.

Strong Interest Inventory at www.cpp.com/products/strong/index.aspx.

What I've Learned Thus Far

WE HAVE REACHED THE END OF OUR TIME TOGETHER, SO I THOUGHT I might include some reflections on my journey thus far.

- Don't wait to enjoy life someday; start enjoying it now. We are not promised tomorrow. Life is not all about pleasure, but you will find that being fully present each day will lead to far more joy and contentment.

- Never underestimate the power of listening to good music or watching a good film with friends or family. God uses art to help us reflect in ways we ordinarily would not.

- Don't be afraid of silence. It will do your soul good to quiet the world around you.

- Have the courage and faith to follow wherever God leads you. He is big enough to go before you and promises to walk with you.

- Pursue deep relationships with brothers and sisters in Christ. We need each other far more than we realize. *Start today.*

- Resolve conflict quickly and learn to say these words: "I am sorry for _____; will you forgive me?" I have seen the enemy tear apart life-giving relationships because of pride and bitterness. Root these out quickly or they will consume you.

- It is amazing to experience the love of a woman who knows me—warts and all—and still loves me. She is my best friend and I am so glad we are on this journey together. God has used her to shape who I am in so many ways and heal significant wounds in my life. Find a spouse who loves God and has character.

- It is difficult to put into words the joy I feel in being with my children. Adventures. Wrestling and tickling. Reading and imagining together.

Hearing the words "love you" from these little human beings has changed me forever. I love being their daddy and am SO proud of them.

- God is faithful. Time and time again He has shown up in ways that I did not expect or deserve—many times through the sacrificial generosity and encouragement of others. Never underestimate the power of an encouraging word or an act of service done in love.

- Your integrity and good name are worth far more than the fleeting pleasures of sin. I promise you will never regret battling for a pure heart. When sin knocks you down, quickly ask God for forgiveness and get up and then keep walking in the truth.

- I need God and His grace and love more now than ever before. You never outgrow the gospel.

- At a fundamental level, we all must answer the question: Is this life all there is, or is it a mere prelude of a life yet to come? C. S. Lewis called this living in light of High Country. The answer we give—not with our mouths, but with our hearts—will largely determine how this life is lived. Live for something greater than yourself. Live for the God who created you, called you into a new way of life as His child, and has prepared good works for you to do for His glory (see Eph. 2:10).

> *If you read history you will find that the Christians who did most for the present world were just those who thought most of the next. . . . [They] all left their mark on Earth precisely because their minds were occupied with Heaven. It is since Christians have largely ceased to think of the other world that they have become so ineffective in this. Aim at Heaven and you will get earth "thrown in": aim at earth and you will get neither.*
>
> —C. S. LEWIS[1]

Acknowledgments

Remember your leaders who taught you the word of God. Think of all the good that has come from their lives, and follow the example of their faith.

—HEBREWS 13:7 NLT

THE BOOK YOU HOLD IN YOUR HANDS WOULD NOT BE POSSIBLE WITHOUT the grace of God. God rescued me from a place of confusion, pain, and loss, and He changed my life. Everything good and true that flows out of my life is a testimony to my Savior.

I am more convinced than ever that life is a team sport; community is not optional for the Christ-follower. The content of this book has been shaped by so many lives, and there are numerous people to acknowledge in this limited space.

I am so appreciative to Paul Copan, William Lane Craig, and J. P. Moreland for initially endorsing and encouraging this book project. I am grateful to Jim Weaver and Kregel for taking a chance on me as a young author. Jim, along with the rest of the team at Kregel, has been a joy to work with—thanks to Sarah, Amy, Miranda, Sara, and Joel. This book is better because of them.

Ever since taking my first steps on this journey with Christ as a junior in high school, there have been mentors showing me the way. (Who knows what great stuff I would have missed and what potholes I would have hit were it not for them?) I will mention three key men. Neal Ligon (along with his wife, Gayle) loved me during high school at a time when I really needed to be loved. In college, my life was marked by Rich Humphrey. He taught me how to study and read the Bible (e.g., 2 Timothy), gave me a passion for sand volleyball, and modeled the spiritual life for me in college; my life is forever marked by his intentionality and faithfulness. After graduating college and as a rookie in marriage and ministry, Monty Waldron helped me fill in the blank pages of my handbook to life. I don't have the words for all that I have learned from him and would not be the man I am today if it were not for his influence and investment. To the many others I have not named who have marked my life, thank you.

I am grateful to all of the wonderful and interesting people I traveled the college years with—the journey was a blast! It would take pages to include you all by name, but my roommates, friends from Campus Crusade (including summer projects in Clearwater), and fraternity brothers made it a great experience.

I want to thank people from my two years with the Howard G. Hendricks Center for Christian Leadership at Dallas Theological Seminary. Paul Pettit and Andy Seidel modeled the importance of authentic community to the spiritual formation process. It was wonderful serving with my good friends Jonathan Phipps and Tom Pussel as spiritual formation fellows. Last but not least, our time with our SF group was a sweet time of community and growth. During this season at DTS, two professors especially impacted me: Scott Horrell and Darrell Bock. Thank you both for your investment.

Our ministry support team for the past four years and counting has made my education and this book possible—Mandi and I are continually humbled by your generosity. Moreover, our families have been so supportive of us on our life journey—thank you all for your prayers and encouragement; we love you.

Our time at Talbot School of Theology and Biola University was joy filled and life changing. I want to thank our grace group (and our Grace EV Free family) for so warmly embracing us. I am grateful to student ministries at Biola University for providing me the opportunity to invest in students (a shout-out to all my former coworkers and the men of the Journey!).

The training I received at Talbot through the master's program in philosophy of religion and ethics was top-notch and my view of the world has forever been changed (and hopefully as you read this book yours has been as well). I want to express my gratitude to specific professors for their investment. J. P. Moreland has been a great encouragement to me from the beginning. He challenged me to view everything we do in light of God's kingdom program and to strive to believe what Jesus did about all of reality. William Lane Craig is an exemplar of careful and rigorous Christian scholarship and encouraged me to have a vision for life. Garry DeWeese taught me more about integration than anyone I've ever met; he is an incredible blend of theologian, philosopher, and pastor. Scott Rae showed me where what we believe intersects with the world around us; we all face difficult questions each day, and we are to engage those in a distinctively Christian and redemptive way. Dave Horner brought home in a powerful way the connection between ethics, worship, virtue, and the good life—in short, *eudaimonia*. Kent Edwards vividly modeled how to illustrate and image the truths of God's Word so that people can understand, remember, and apply them.

Two fellow philosophers and loyal friends read all of these chapters, made significant suggestions for improvement, and greatly encouraged me in the writing process: Matt Getz and Mike Good. Thank you both!

I saved the best for last: the love of my life and soul companion, Mandi. You have stood by me, believed in me, and encouraged me to follow God's calling. It hasn't always been easy or predictable, yet you have trusted God and loved me well. You are a precious daughter of God and a joy to me and to our children. Thank you for all that you are and all that you challenge me to be.

A Devotional Reading Plan for Your First Semester

Open my eyes, that I may behold
Wonderful things from Your law.
—PSALM 119:18 NASB

For this reason we also constantly thank God that when you
received the word of God which you heard from us, you accepted
it not as the word of men, but for what it really is, the word of
God, which also performs its work in you who believe.
—1 THESSALONIANS 2:13 NASB

YOUR TIME WITH GOD IN HIS WORD IS ESSENTIAL TO YOUR SPIRITUAL health and development in college. Why not start off your semester with a commitment to meet with God daily? I promise you won't regret it. In order to help you out, I have arranged a devotional reading plan for your first semester. There are fifteen weeks of readings. The goal will be to read six chapters per week (one per day, with one day off to catch up or read something else). While all Scripture is important and helpful, I selected these chapters according to what I thought would be encouraging to you at this stage of life. You won't have any trouble finding something to chew on— these are wonderful chapters! You will also notice that I have skipped around some; this is because I wanted to introduce you to the major themes of God's Word. As you become more familiar with the Bible, you will be able to better understand the context of each chapter and the flow of the books.

I am not a morning person (more power to you if you are), so I read the Bible mostly at night. The important thing is to pick a consistent time and set it aside to spend time in God's Word. The point of a spiritual discipline is not to be legalistic but to put yourself in a context where you can meet with

God. So if you miss a day, don't beat yourself up. Just start where you left off and pray for the discipline to set aside fifteen minutes a day to read through the passage and pray.

You could begin your time by praying that God would speak to your heart through His Word. Perhaps there is some sin in your life you need to confess (see 1 John 1:9). When it comes to reading the Bible, I am an underliner and highlighter—if you see something that speaks to you or that you want to remember, mark it! As you read each day, maybe take out a notebook or a journal to jot down some of your thoughts, discoveries, and prayers. Here are some questions you might ask of these chapters to get you started.[1]

- Is there an example for me to follow?
- Is there a sin to avoid?
- Is there a promise to claim?
- Is there a prayer to repeat?
- Is there a verse to memorize?
- Is there a command to obey?
- Is there a condition to meet?
- Is there an error to mark?
- Is there a challenge to face?

Important prayers in the Bible to memorize, meditate on, and pray back to God:

- Psalm 25:4–7
- Psalm 86:11
- Psalm 139:23–24
- Psalm 143:8–10
- Matthew 6:9–13

After you finish this Bible reading plan, pick out another one:

- ESV Online Reading Plans at http://www.esv.org/resources/reading -plans/
- Bible Gateway at https://www.biblegateway.com/reading-plans/
- YouVersion at https://www.bible.com/reading-plans

WEEK 1

- ☐ Psalm 1
- ☐ Psalm 19
- ☐ Psalm 119:1–88
- ☐ Psalm 119:89–176
- ☐ John 1
- ☐ Colossians 1

WEEK 2

- ☐ Hebrews 1
- ☐ 2 Peter 1
- ☐ 2 Timothy 1
- ☐ 2 Timothy 2
- ☐ 2 Timothy 3
- ☐ Proverbs 4

WEEK 3

- ☐ Isaiah 45:14–25
- ☐ Isaiah 55
- ☐ Psalm 139
- ☐ Genesis 1
- ☐ Genesis 2
- ☐ Genesis 3

WEEK 4

- ☐ Isaiah 53
- ☐ Psalm 103
- ☐ Isaiah 9:1–7
- ☐ John 11
- ☐ Luke 18
- ☐ Luke 19

WEEK 5

- ☐ Luke 23
- ☐ Luke 24
- ☐ Mark 14
- ☐ Mark 15
- ☐ Matthew 28
- ☐ 1 Corinthians 15

WEEK 6

- ☐ John 14
- ☐ John 15
- ☐ John 16
- ☐ John 17
- ☐ Acts 1
- ☐ Acts 2

WEEK 7

- ☐ Acts 3
- ☐ Acts 4
- ☐ Romans 1
- ☐ Romans 2
- ☐ Romans 3
- ☐ Romans 5

WEEK 8

- ☐ Romans 6
- ☐ Romans 7
- ☐ Romans 8
- ☐ Romans 12
- ☐ Romans 14
- ☐ Matthew 5

WEEK 9

- ☐ Matthew 6
- ☐ Matthew 7
- ☐ 1 Peter 1
- ☐ 1 Peter 2
- ☐ 1 Peter 3
- ☐ 1 Peter 4

WEEK 10

- ☐ 1 Peter 5
- ☐ Titus 3
- ☐ 1 Corinthians 1
- ☐ 1 Corinthians 2
- ☐ 1 Corinthians 3
- ☐ 2 Corinthians 3

WEEK 11

- ☐ 2 Corinthians 4
- ☐ 2 Corinthians 5
- ☐ 2 Corinthians 9
- ☐ Galatians 5
- ☐ Colossians 3
- ☐ Ephesians 1

WEEK 12

- ☐ Ephesians 2
- ☐ Ephesians 3
- ☐ Ephesians 4
- ☐ Ephesians 5
- ☐ Ephesians 6
- ☐ James 1

WEEK 13

- ☐ James 2
- ☐ James 3
- ☐ James 4
- ☐ 1 John 1
- ☐ 1 John 2
- ☐ 1 John 3

WEEK 14

- ☐ 1 John 4
- ☐ 1 John 5
- ☐ Job 1–2
- ☐ Job 38–40
- ☐ Job 41–42
- ☐ 1 Thessalonians 4

WEEK 15

- ☐ 1 Thessalonians 5
- ☐ 2 Peter 3
- ☐ Revelation 20
- ☐ Revelation 21
- ☐ Revelation 22
- ☐ 2 Timothy 4

Christian Versus Secular Colleges

Pros and Cons

> *Teach me your way, LORD,*
> *that I may rely on your faithfulness;*
> *give me an undivided heart,*
> *that I may fear your name.*
>> —PSALM 86:11

CHOOSING A COLLEGE IS STRESSFUL. IS IT BETTER TO ATTEND A CHRIS-tian or secular college? Now for many of you, this is a moot point since the decision has already been made. But some of you may still be scouring the Internet or sifting through piles of brochures trying to make a decision. If so, what should you consider? First, there is no universal answer on this one. It's not a moral issue and it is not more spiritual to go to one or the other. Also, this decision is person specific and based upon a combination of factors: your life experiences, gifts, abilities, aspirations, level of maturity, resources, and calling. I attended a large state school of twenty thousand plus students but have also worked in discipleship ministry with students at a prominent Christian university, so I have been fortunate enough to spend a good chunk of time in each setting. Here are *some* of the pros and cons as I see them—take it for what it's worth as you come to a wise decision. But before I share these I want to ask you to consider something that more and more students are doing to prepare for the college years.

Should I Take a Gap Year After High School?

I have taught, trained, and worked with high school and college students for over twelve years now, and I am increasingly convinced that most students are not ready for college when they graduate high school. That's not a slam on you. But it is reality and the sociological research underscores this. Some major sociological studies show that over 50 percent of students will disengage from their Christian faith during the college years (an increasing number doing so for intellectual reasons or doubts).[1] To put the point as clearly as I can, there are significant spiritual, intellectual, moral, and relational challenges waiting for you. It doesn't have to be that way nor should it be. As I have shared throughout this book, it is critical that you own your faith. So I have two possible action steps for you to prayerfully consider.

First, if you are still in high school or just recently graduated, come spend two weeks during the summer with me and other leading teachers at Impact 360 Immersion (impact360.org/immersion). Immersion is a two-week transformational worldview and apologetics experience for high school students where you will learn what you believe, why you believe it, and how to live it out in the real world. Be sure to check this out because every year students share how Immersion was a game changer for them as they headed into the college years with a more confident faith.

The second opportunity I want to encourage you to consider is coming and spending nine months with us at our Impact 360 Gap Year. I am one of the lead faculty. You will get top-notch training in biblical worldview, spiritual formation, and servant leadership as well as sharpen your understanding of your personal strengths and calling. On top of that you will develop lifelong friendships and travel internationally for a month, learning how to serve cross-culturally and broadening your understanding of God's heart for the world. If you are a high school graduate between eighteen and twenty, then this could be a great next step for you to go deeper in your faith and better understand what you want to get out of the rest of your college years, as you journey on your way to who God is calling you to become. Check out our website at impact360.org/gap-year.

Should I Attend a Secular College?

Pros

1. This isn't a scrimmage; it's game time! It most likely will not be popular to be a Christian. As a result it will cost you something to follow Christ

and be much harder to "play Christian." This will build your faith if you let it and are prepared.

2. You have the opportunity to be salt and light on your campus—it is a mission field at your doorstep.

3. You have the opportunity to interact with professors and ideas that you would usually not be exposed to at a Christian school. Experiencing diversity is a good thing.

4. Where you go after college—the workplace or graduate school—will probably respect a degree from a prestigious secular school more than one from a Christian liberal arts college. Unfortunately, academic pedigree matters. Honestly and realistically evaluate what your educational and professional goals are during this unique season of life.

Cons

1. This isn't a scrimmage; it's game time. You run the risk of being inundated and overcome with ideas hostile to your Christian worldview. You may be unequipped to deal with this, and it could lead to a faith crisis or simply spiritually "checking out" until after graduation. (One of the main reasons I wrote this book was to help you in this area.)

2. While temptations can be found anywhere, temptations are especially intense and explicit at a secular school.

3. If you don't find a solid group of Christian students or a campus ministry to plug into, then you will become increasingly isolated. And it is *much* more difficult to stay faithful to Christ and grow spiritually if you are on a relational island.

4. You will not have the benefit of taking classes that are friendly toward biblical Christianity and help you see how your Christian worldview informs your particular major and area of study.

Should I Attend a Christian College?

Pros

1. You will generally be surrounded by people who have similar Christian values and beliefs. Much growth and encouragement can occur in this kind of environment. Being of the same mind with the university is a blessing.

2. You most likely won't be forced to compartmentalize your faith from the rest of life. If the Christian school you are attending is worth their salt, they will help you in the process of integration and worldview formation.

3. You will be taught from a Christian worldview by professors who are Christians. This is an amazing opportunity to be mentored that few people get.

4. You will be prepared for certain types of ministry in ways that you wouldn't be trained at a secular school. And it could be that you go on to pursue a graduate degree at a secular school after you have laid a good foundation at a Christian college.

Cons

1. You will be surrounded by people who have similar values and beliefs. This *could* lead to a naive view of the world and perhaps even arrogance toward others—an us-against-them mentality. You can lose touch with unbelievers.

2. It is popular (or at least expected) to be a Christian. You likely won't encounter resistance or hardship on account of your faith. Struggle and adversity are some of the best catalysts for spiritual growth. You might have to battle apathy and complacency more than you would at a secular school if everyone is going through the motions "because we are all good Christians here."

3. You may not be exposed with sufficient rigor to the ideas you will encounter upon graduation in the workplace or broader culture.

4. Depending on your career path, people may not regard your degree as highly as someone who attended a secular school. While this shouldn't determine your decision, you do need to be aware of it.

So which one to choose? I can't tell you that. I would advise employing some of the principles in chapter 30, "Discovering the Will of God." Ask yourself what you would like to get out of your college experience. Is there a particular subject you want to major in or a part of the country you want to experience? Would you feel more comfortable at a larger or smaller school? And what kind of person would you like to be on the other side of your college experience? Then, take out a sheet of paper and make a list of pros and cons as you see them. Then ask someone who knows you well to talk through the list with you and pray together for wisdom.

It may be that God desires to use you to influence people for His kingdom at a secular school. Or a particular career path may point you toward a secular university. On the other hand, God may want to grow you in the kind of ways that best occur at a Christian school. Or maybe you need to take some more time during a gap year to better know yourself and deepen your faith before making that longer-term decision. Perhaps you are a new believer and need the nurturing of a Christian environment as opposed to a hostile secular environment. Even in spite of all these factors, don't allow this decision to paralyze you. God is bigger than the particular college you decide to attend. Whatever you do and wherever you find yourself, remember that God will be with you. Live your college years for the glory of God. May God guide your steps. Enjoy the journey!

For Further Discovery

Basie, John D. *Your College Launch Story: Six Things Every Parent Must Do.* Pine Mountain, GA: Impact 360 Institute, 2016.

Hewitt, Hugh. *In, but Not Of: A Guide to Christian Ambition and the Desire to Influence the World.* Nashville: Thomas Nelson, 2012.

Keller, Timothy, and Katherine Leary Alsdorf. *Every Good Endeavor: Connecting Your Work to God's Work.* New York: Dutton, 2012.

Morrow, Jonathan. *Think Christianly: Looking at the Intersection of Faith and Culture.* Grand Rapids: Zondervan, 2011.

JonathanMorrow.org. Visit my website for more resources to help you own your faith along the way.

Impact360.org. Learn more about the on-campus and online worldview and leadership experiences Impact 360 Institute offers for high school and college students.

APPENDIX
C

Resources for Philosophy

> *Good philosophy must exist, if for no other reason, because bad philosophy needs to be answered. . . . The learned life then is, for some, a duty.*
>
> —C. S. LEWIS[1]

SOME PEOPLE THINK THAT CHRISTIANS AND PHILOSOPHY DON'T MIX. Many misinterpret Colossians 2:8 to mean that *all* philosophy is bad. This is incorrect. Only that which is ultimately based on the ideas of *humans alone*, rather than Christ, is what is being critiqued. In the last fifty years, God went from being dead in the academy to being very much alive and well. Today theists, many of them Christians, are doing exemplary work in analytic philosophy. This continues the rich heritage of medieval Christian philosophers such as Augustine and Aquinas. So if you find yourself in a philosophy class where a theistic point of view isn't being given a fair shake, or if you are just interested in the big hairy questions of life, these resources are for you. Enjoy! These are not all the same level of difficulty: **(B)** = beginner, **(I)** = intermediate, and **(A)** = advanced.

Books

Alston, William P. *A Realist Conception of Truth*. Ithaca, NY: Cornell University Press, 1996. **(A)**

Beckwith, Francis J. *Defending Life: A Moral and Legal Case Against Abortion Choice*. Cambridge: Cambridge University Press, 2007. **(I)**

———, ed. *Do the Right Thing: Readings in Applied Ethics and Social Philosophy*. 2nd ed. Belmont, CA: Wadsworth, 2002. **(I)**

Copan, Paul. *Loving Wisdom: Christian Philosophy of Religion*. St. Louis: Chalice Press, 2012. **(B)**

Copan, Paul, and Paul K. Moser. *The Rationality of Theism*. London: Routledge, 2003. **(I)**

Craig, William Lane. *Philosophy of Religion: A Reader and Guide*. Edinburgh: Edinburgh University Press, 2002. **(A)**

Craig, William Lane, and J. P. Moreland, eds. *Naturalism: A Critical Analysis*. London: Routledge, 2002. **(A)**

DeWeese, Garrett J., and J. P. Moreland. *Philosophy Made Slightly Less Difficult: A Beginner's Guide to Life's Big Questions*. Downers Grove, IL: InterVarsity Press, 2009. **(B)**

Ganssle, Gregory E. *Thinking About God: First Steps in Philosophy*. Downers Grove, IL: InterVarsity Press, 2010. **(B)**

Kreeft, Peter, and Trent Dougherty. *Socrates' Children: Ancient–Modern*. 4 vols. South Bend, IN: St. Augustine's Press, 2016. **(B)**

———. *Socratic Logic: A Logic Text Using Socratic Method, Platonic Questions and Aristotelian Principles*. 3rd ed. South Bend, IN: St. Augustine's Press, 2010. **(I)**

Menuge, Angus J. L. *Agents Under Fire: Materialism and the Rationality of Science*. Oxford: Rowman & Littlefield, 2004. **(I)**

Moreland, J. P., and Scott B. Rae. *Body and Soul: Human Nature and the Crisis in Ethics*. Downers Grove, IL: InterVarsity Press, 2009. **(I)**

Moreland, J. P., and William Lane Craig. *Philosophical Foundations for a Christian Worldview*. Downers Grove, IL: InterVarsity Press, 2009. **(I)**

Morris, Thomas V. *Philosophy for Dummies*. Hoboken, NJ: Wiley, 2011. **(B)**

Plantinga, Alvin. *The Analytic Theist: An Alvin Plantinga Reader*. Edited by James F. Sennett. Grand Rapids: Eerdmans, 1998. **(I)**

———. *God, Freedom, and Evil*. Grand Rapids: Eerdmans, 1977. **(I)**

———. *Warranted Christian Belief*. Oxford: Oxford University Press, 2000. **(I)**

Quinn, Philip L., and Kevin Meeker. *The Philosophical Challenge of Religious Diversity*. New York: Oxford University Press, 2000. **(I)**

Important Journals

"*Philosophia Christi* is a peer-reviewed journal published twice a year by the Evangelical Philosophical Society (EPS) with the support of Biola University as a vehicle for the scholarly discussion of philosophy and philosophical issues in the fields of apologetics, ethics, theology, and religion." Quote taken directly from their website at www.epsociety.org/philchristi/.

"*Faith and Philosophy* is published quarterly by the Society of Christian Philosophers. The journal encourages discussions among philosophers representing a wide variety of theological perspectives and philosophical orientations that fall largely within the philosophy of religion. It seeks critical and reflective self-understanding of Christian faith carried out in dialogue with those who do not, as well as with those who do, share its Christian commitment." Quote taken directly from their website at www.faithand philosophy.com.

APPENDIX
D

Discussion Questions

CHAPTER 1: **Preparing for Campus Life**

1. What about college most excites you?

2. What about college scares you to death?

3. Have you noticed ways that God has already been at work in the details and situations of college life? Share about these.

4. Knowing yourself and your tendencies, which of the three pieces of wisdom do you think you will need to hear most often?

5. How significant were your parents or grandparents in shaping what you believe today? Do you own your faith or is it something that you were raised with but aren't sure what you really believe?

CHAPTER 2: **Think Christianly**

1. What is a worldview? How should people go about testing one?

2. What does the statement "all truth is God's truth" mean?

3. Are you living a fragmented life? If so, in what specific areas of your life do you see this happening? What could you do to change this?

4. What do you think it would look like on your campus, and in our world today, if more Christians lived like Christianity was true for more than just two hours on Sunday morning?

CHAPTER 3: **Getting Theological**

1. When you hear the word *theology*, what is the first image that comes to mind?

2. What does it mean to say that God has two books?

3. How much of a role do you think tradition ought to play in formulating our theology?

4. What is the goal of theology? How are you doing in your growth as a theologian?

5. If someone were to ask you what Christians believe, generally speaking, could you tell them?

6. Of the doctrines we looked at, which one did you find most encouraging? Why?

7. What do you think Augustine meant when he said, "In essentials, unity; in nonessentials, liberty; and in all things, charity"? Why is it important for Christians to be unified on the essentials before a watching world?

CHAPTER 4: Blinded by Faith?

1. Before reading this chapter, how would you have defined faith?

2. Why is the notion of blind faith incompatible with Christianity?

3. Why is sincerity not enough for faith?

4. Explain the three aspects of faith and why they are important.

5. Can you think of a recent time in your life when you have had to walk by faith and not by sight? What happened?

CHAPTER 5: Can We Know Anything at All?

1. Why do you think knowledge is important in life?

2. Explain the difference between empirical and nonempirical knowledge. Why is empiricism an incomplete picture of knowledge?

3. What is the difference between methodism and particularism? Why is this distinction important?

4. Have you ever been challenged by a skeptic and then felt the burden to demonstrate with one-hundred-percent certainty that you were correct? How did that conversation go? How has this chapter better equipped you to dialogue with skeptics?

5. What does a healthy skepticism look like? What does humility concerning the things we know, especially as Christians, look like?

6. Of the sources of knowledge we mentioned, which do you think is the most reliable? Why?

7. Would you consider yourself an intellectually virtuous person? Why or why not? How might you cultivate the intellectual virtues?

CHAPTER 6: Truth Matters

1. What do the people you interact with at college think of truth?

2. How is truth talked about differently in a math or science lecture versus an English literature class?

3. Why is it important to understand that truth is discovered, not created?

4. Why should Christians care about truth?

5. What does Jesus mean when He refers to Himself as the truth in John 14:6?

CHAPTER 7: A Moral Disaster

1. Have you encountered relativistic slogans before? How did you respond?

2. Why is disagreement overrated?

3. Explain the *reformer's dilemma* and *moral progress* arguments to the group.

4. If moral relativism faces such strong counter examples, then why do you think people still want to hold to moral relativism? What seems to be the root issue?

CHAPTER 8: True Tolerance

1. Can you think of any examples of the new definition of tolerance that you have seen on TV, in something you have read, or at the movies?

2. Have you ever found yourself in a situation in which you were viewed as intolerant for standing up for what you believe? What happened?

3. Have you ever seen a Christian stand up for the truth but do it in a way that was not loving or respectful? How did the other person respond?

4. From memory, explain the difference between what tolerance actually means versus the new definition of tolerance that shows up in classrooms and in the culture at large.

5. Look up Luke 12:11–12; Acts 4; and 1 Peter 3:15–16. Discuss what you observe in these passages.

CHAPTER 9: **How to Read the Bible**

1. Are you intimidated by the Bible? Why?

2. What about this chapter challenged or encouraged you the most?

3. Why is observation so important to Bible study?

4. Who determines the meaning of a passage: the author or the reader?

5. On a scale from one to ten, how would you rate your skill as an interpreter of the Bible?

6. Have you ever studied a book of the Bible in-depth? Why not?

7. What are the four themes of the Bible?

CHAPTER 10: **Can I Trust the Bible?**

1. Before reading this chapter, how did you think the Bible came to be?

2. Even though we don't possess the original documents, how are we able to have confidence in the copies that we now possess?

3. What is the significance of the Dead Sea Scrolls being discovered at Qumran in 1947?

4. Of all the evidence for the reliability of the New Testament, what do you think is the strongest?

5. Why is it important to distinguish between a community's *recognizing* the authority of the books that became the Bible and *investing* them with authority?

6. What did Jesus say about the Old and New Testaments? See Matthew 5:17–18, Luke 24:25–32, and John 10:34–36.

CHAPTER 11: **Knowing Versus Showing Your Faith**

1. Has there ever been a time you have been challenged with an objection to Christianity that you did not know how to refute, but still just knew it had to be wrong? If so, when did this happen and what was the objection?

2. What doubts or questions are you currently wrestling with as a Christian?

3. How is your spiritual life? Would you say that you are experiencing fellowship with God or is sin keeping you from a vibrant relationship with God?

CHAPTER 12: No Apologies Needed

1. Have you ever found yourself in a situation in which you were embarrassed to be a Christian? Why do you think that was?

2. Take a minute to reflect on when you became a Christian. What were the most significant factors that led you to trust Christ?

3. Have you ever been in a situation in which you were called upon to give an answer for the hope within you? What happened?

4. What steps could you take right now to deepen your knowledge of what you believe and why?

CHAPTER 13: The Existence of God

1. If you do not believe in God, what do you think is your biggest obstacle? Of the arguments listed, which one do you find the most plausible? Why?

2. If you are a Christian, did any of these arguments (or others I didn't mention) help you come to trust Christ?

3. If during a conversation on campus someone asked you why you believe God exists, could you give them an answer? Which of the arguments we discussed, excluding Jesus, would you share first? Why?

4. Why is Jesus such a powerful argument?

CHAPTER 14: Do All Roads Lead to God?

1. Why do you think this question is so difficult and powerful?

2. How would you respond to the charge that you are arrogant or immoral for believing that Jesus is the only way to God?

3. Did God have to save anyone at all? Why or why not?

4. Explain the main difference between unsophisticated religious pluralism and sophisticated religious pluralism.

5. If people aren't judged for not hearing the name of Jesus, then how are they judged?

6. What are the four main passages that teach that salvation is found in no one else but Christ?

CHAPTER 15: **The Problem of Evil and Suffering**

1. Do you think that evil is the most powerful objection to belief in God? Why or why not?

2. Explain how atheism and pantheism deal with the problem of evil.

3. What is evil?

4. What logically possible, morally sufficient reason for God's allowing evil does Alvin Plantinga offer? Do you think this is a plausible explanation? Why or why not?

5. How is evil dealt with at the cross of Christ?

6. Which biblical story (Joseph, Job, or Lazarus) encouraged you the most? Why?

7. Give at least one reason why God has not yet finally dealt with evil.

CHAPTER 16: **Thirty-One Flavors of Jesus**

1. What flavor of Jesus do you often hear from your fellow students or in your classes?

2. What did you think of the passages from the so-called missing gospels?

3. What point was Jesus trying to make when He healed the paralytic in Mark 2:1–12?

4. Why is it important to let Jesus speak for Himself when we ask who He is?

5. It is often said that Jesus never claimed to be God. How could you use Mark 14:60–64 to show that He did?

6. Have you taken Jesus at His word by accepting His forgiveness and starting an eternal relationship with God? If not, what do you think is keeping you from doing so? If so, what can you do to ensure that relationship thrives during the college years?

CHAPTER 17: **Did Jesus Rise from the Dead?**

1. How does Paul's statement in 1 Corinthians 15:12–19 make you feel? Nervous or encouraged?

2. What is the "minimal facts approach"?

3. Why is it important to see the New Testament as a work of ancient literature first?

4. Without looking back at the chapter, see if you can list off the five historical facts regarding the resurrection of Jesus that are mentioned in this chapter.

5. Of the evidence mentioned in this chapter for the resurrection, which do you think is the strongest?

6. Why is it important that people understand that Christianity doesn't separate faith from history?

CHAPTER 18: Science Rules!

1. Why do you think people are so enamored with science?

2. Do recent scientific discoveries make you worry about the reliability of the Bible?

3. What is scientism? What is wrong with this view?

4. In what ways does science rely on philosophy?

5. What are some things that science cannot tell us?

CHAPTER 19: Designed or Not Designed?

1. What was your first exposure to neo-Darwinian evolution? When was it?

2. From what we have covered in this chapter, what do you think is the greatest weakness of NDE?

3. Had you ever heard of intelligent design before reading this chapter? If so, where did you learn of it?

4. How is ID usually portrayed in the media, positively or negatively?

5. What is the difference between ID and creationism? Can you affirm both?

6. What is the basic claim of ID?

7. In your opinion, what is the strongest argument for ID?

8. Why do you think opponents of ID resort to name-calling rather than engage the arguments?

CHAPTER 20: Dealing with Doubt

1. Have you ever doubted that you were saved? What did you do? What did others tell you to do? How did this make you feel?

2. What is the most common form of doubt?

3. What is the difference between doubt and unbelief?

4. Why is our thought life so important to our emotional life?

5. How are you doing when it comes to meditating on what God says is true?

CHAPTER 21: Good News to Share

1. When did you trust Christ? How did this happen?

2. What is your biggest fear in sharing the gospel?

3. Have you ever led anyone to Christ? What happened?

4. Explain the three central aspects of the gospel message.

5. Why is a person's decision to trust Christ only the beginning of the gospel?

6. What is the "Columbo tactic"? What are the three key questions to ask?

CHAPTER 22: To the Ends of the Earth

1. Has the truth of John 3:16 become commonplace to you? Try paraphrasing it in your own words.

2. Do you know any missionaries personally? Describe what work they do and where. How does their commitment and sacrifice challenge you?

3. Have you considered going on a short-term mission trip in college? What is stopping you?

4. Have you ever thought about being a missionary? What could you envision yourself doing?

5. What are some ways you can become more involved in what God is doing around the world?

CHAPTER 23: Getting to Know You

1. On a scale from one to ten, how well would you say you know yourself?

2. On a scale from one to ten, how comfortable would you say you are in your own skin?

3. Do you struggle with peer pressure, or do you find yourself able to stand firm on who you are and what you believe? (Be honest.)

4. Of the four *h*'s, which one has most significantly shaped you?

5. Why are we so afraid of others really getting to know us?

6. What aspects of your identity in Christ mean the most to you at this stage of life?

7. Do you know what your spiritual gifts are? How did you find this out?

CHAPTER 24: Here's to Your Health

1. Why is it important to view health holistically?

2. What did you need to be reminded of as you read this chapter?

3. Which of the areas we discussed do you think you are the healthiest in? The least healthy?

4. Spend some time answering the questions included in the chapter this week.

CHAPTER 25: Sticks and Stones

1. How did conflict take place in your home growing up? Was it healthy?

2. What is your normal response when conflict arises?

3. Which aspect of talking well do you think you most struggle to do?

4. Which aspect of listening well do you think you most struggle with?

5. Why is it so hard to say the words, "Will you forgive me?"

CHAPTER 26: Has the Church Lost Her Mind?

1. Did the church you grow up in value the life of the mind?

2. Do you tend to emphasize emotions or your thought life more? Why do you think that is?

3. Reflect on Romans 12:1–2. Are you passively allowing the world to squash your thought life into its mold?

4. What is one practical way you can start loving God with your mind?

5. Besides the required reading for your classes, what was the last book you read cover to cover? When did you read it? What motivated you to read it?

CHAPTER 27: Overcoming Syllabus Shock

1. What were your study habits in high school? How do they need to change to meet the demands of college?

2. Do you need to change your reading style to keep up with college assignments? Under "learn to read" in the chapter, what will be most helpful for you?

3. Why is it better to study in the library than in your dorm room?

4. After reading this chapter, what are some action steps you need to take?

5. How will you safeguard yourself from the temptation to cheat?

6. Do you already know what you want to major in? If so, who or what influenced that decision? If not, what steps can you take to help you make that decison?

CHAPTER 28: Show Me the Money

1. What are your current sources of income in college?

2. Are you responsible for your finances or do your parents handle this for you? Do you think you should begin to take a more active role in your finances? Why or why not?

3. Do you have any credit cards? If so, how many, and what are your spending habits?

4. Do you have a budget or do you just spend until the money is gone each month? What can you do to change this?

5. What impact will recognizing that God owns it all have on your approach to finances?

6. Do you give money to your local church? If not, why not?

7. Are you a generous person? Why or why not?

CHAPTER 29: Becoming More Like Jesus

1. How is the gospel about more than going to heaven?

2. What is God's goal in spiritual formation?

3. What are our three essential resources for spiritual formation? Which one do you currently use the most?

4. Why is it important to view the spiritual life as a cooperative activity?

5. What is the goal of a spiritual discipline? Have you ever practiced any of the disciplines in the list? Which ones? What was your experience like?

6. What does your time with God look like right now? What is your biggest struggle when it comes to meeting with God?

CHAPTER 30: Discovering the Will of God

1. Do you think that God has a specific will for your life? Why or why not?

2. How are you doing when it comes to learning what God's will is for your life from His Word?

3. What happens when we become too consumed by looking for God's will?

4. Which of the principles we discussed are the easiest to put into practice? Which ones do you find the most challenging?

5. What examples from Scripture can you think of where someone is not healthy or rich but is faithful to God?

6. Have you recently reached a difficult decision in a life situation, but you know this is the right thing to do? What happened?

CHAPTER 31: When Someone You Love Dies

1. Has someone close to you died? How do you think people did in ministering to you?

2. What does it mean to have a "ministry of presence" for someone?

3. Of all that was said in this chapter, what do you think was the most important thing to walk away with?

4. What are the ways in which you can minister to someone who has experienced the loss of a loved one?

CHAPTER 32: Gentlemen, Become Who You Were Born to Be

1. Where did you get your view of manhood?

2. Is there an area of your life in which you are being passive?

3. Is there an area of your life in which you need to accept responsibility?

4. Is there an area of your life in which you need to lead courageously?

5. Pick one of the ten biblical ideals and try to build that habit into your life.

6. Read one of the books suggested at the end of this chapter.

CHAPTER 33: Ladies, Pursue Real Beauty

1. Where did you get your view of what a woman ought to be?

2. Have you encountered a resistance to a biblical view of womanhood in your classes? What did this look like?

3. Why is it important to see that equality does not mean sameness?

4. Are you becoming a woman of the Word? If not, how can you make this more of a priority?

5. How do you define beauty? How does this differ from culture's definition? The Bible's definition?

6. Is there an area of your life in which you need to reject the priorities of the world and accept the priorities of God?

7. In addition to spending time in God's Word, make it a short-term goal to read one or more of the books suggested at the end of this chapter.

CHAPTER 34: The Dating Game

1. Are you in a spot where you need to take a break from dating for a while? Or are you at a place where you can give dating a chance?

2. When is someone ready to date?

3. What does a healthy dating relationship look like?

4. Why is it important to establish emotional and physical boundaries?

CHAPTER 35: Sex, Sex, Sex

1. Where did you first hear about sex? From whom? What was that conversation like?

2. Why doesn't the church talk about sex?

3. Were you a little surprised by the explicit passion contained in the Bible passages we looked at?

4. How is premarital sex like lighter fluid?

5. If you know Christian singles who are sexually active, how do they justify their behavior? What does the Bible have to say about it?

6. Do you think married sex is worth waiting for? If so, how can you be intentional about following through on this decision?

CHAPTER 36: A Call to Purity

1. Which of these nine reminders did you really need to hear? Why?

2. How are you pursuing purity in your life right now?

3. What are some ways you could be more intentional and proactive in pursuing purity?

4. Who in your life right now encourages you to pursue purity? What does this relationship look like?

5. Do you have any sort of monitoring or filtering service on your Internet? Why or why not?

CHAPTER 37: Christianity, Homosexuality, and the Bible

1. Which of the three distinctly Christian starting points do you resonate with?

2. Explain the Bible's position on homosexual behavior.

3. What does the current scientific evidence show about the question of whether people are born gay?

4. What does loving someone who struggles with same-sex attraction look like in the local church context?

5. Why and how should Christians care about making the case for natural marriage in the public square?

6. Which of the next steps suggested at the end of the chapter do you need to take?

7. What was the most important insight you learned in this chapter?

CHAPTER 38: Unplugged and Offline

1. How much time do you spend each day listening to Pandora, Spotify, or iTunes?

2. How much time do you spend each day online (email, surfing the Web, Instagram, Facebook, Snapchat, YouTube, etc.)?

3. How much of your day today was spent in silence or solitude? How about this past week?

4. When was the last time you got away from the busyness of life to reflect on how life is going? What is going well right now? What needs to change?

5. When was the last time you got alone and just sat silently in the presence of God?

CHAPTER 39: Compassionately Engage Your World

1. What does it mean to be salt and light in our culture?

2. What is social action and how is it different from sharing the good news of Jesus?

3. In your opinion, what is the most pressing social issue facing America today? The world?

4. The relationship of Christianity and politics is always a little complex. Of all that was said in this section, what stuck out to you the most?

5. How should you respond to the objection that you can't legislate morality?

6. What can you do to compassionately engage your world as a college student?

CHAPTER 40: Watching Movies with Eyes Wide Open

1. What is your favorite movie? Why?

2. Is there a disturbing or inappropriate image from a movie that you saw that you cannot forget? Is it burned into your mind's eye? How old were you?

3. As a group, answer some of the questions from earlier in this chapter to see if more of you tend toward Brian Godawa's category of cultural gluttony or of cultural anorexia.

4. How do you discover the idea the director or producer wants you to agree on after watching a movie?

CHAPTER 41: A Christian View of Alcohol

1. List all the beer commercials you can remember. After you do this, ask yourself how much your thinking or beliefs about alcohol have been shaped by the media. Next time you watch a TV show—especially a sporting event—count how many beer commercials come on.

2. Growing up, what was your experience with alcohol? Was it in the home? How was it viewed by your parents, church, or community?

3. Do you have a history of alcoholism in your family?

4. Which of the myths about alcohol most surprised you?

5. From memory, recall the four things the Bible says regarding the use of alcohol.

6. What is the reason we should not be *controlled* by another substance (see Eph. 5:18)?

7. Do you think it is morally OK for Christians to smoke pot? Why or why not?

CHAPTER 42: Ethics in a Brave New World

1. What do you think is the most important ethical issue facing our culture today?

2. Have you talked about any of these issues in class? How were they addressed?

3. As Christians, how does being salt and light relate to the ethical issues our society faces?

4. Which view of a person—a functional view or an essentialist view—do you think is correct? Why?

5. Does a human embryo possess the same moral status as a twenty-five-year-old woman? Why or why not?

6. If you were faced with some of the questions mentioned in the opening paragraph, would you have anything more than gut feeling to go on?

CHAPTER 43: **Beyond the Horizon**

1. What do you want to be when you grow up?

2. Spend time answering some of the diagnostic questions mentioned earlier in the chapter and share with the group. If they know you well, ask if they see the same things to be true of you.

3. Talk about the three aspects of calling. Brainstorm together about what sorts of responsibilities and activities would fall under each one.

4. When you walk across that stage at graduation, what do you want to be able to say of your college years?

5. If Mr. Keating is correct that everyone has a verse to contribute to this grand story we find ourselves in, what do you think yours will be? (While you may not have a specific answer, try to give a general one.)

Notes

CHAPTER 1: Preparing for Campus Life

1. J. R. R. Tolkien, *The Fellowship of the Ring*, The Lord of the Rings (New York: Ballantine, 1965), 102.
2. Albert Einstein, *The Einstein Reader* (New York: Citadel, 2006), 31.
3. Mark Twain, quoted in Gary Thomas, *Education: A Very Short Introduction* (New York: Oxford University Press, 2013), 2.
4. The resources at the end of this chapter are here to help you explore what college is and why it is the way it is (the history and influence of different ideas). The websites will be especially helpful as you explore many of the questions that will arise in the days ahead.

CHAPTER 2: Think Christianly

1. Arthur F. Holmes, *All Truth Is God's Truth* (Grand Rapids: Eerdmans, 1977), 14.
2. C. S. Lewis, *The Weight of Glory* (New York: Macmillan, 1965), 140.
3. There is a wonderful discussion of secularism and how Christians should engage ideas in the public square in Brendan Sweetman, *Why Politics Needs Religion: The Place of Religious Arguments in the Public Square* (Downers Grove, IL: InterVarsity Press, 2006).
4. Philip Graham Ryken, *Christian Worldview: A Student's Guide*. Reclaiming the Christian Intellectual Tradition (Wheaton, IL: Crossway, 2013), 18.
5. Sean McDowell and Jonathan Morrow, *Is God Just a Human Invention? And Seventeen Other Questions Raised by the New Atheists* (Grand Rapids: Kregel, 2011).
6. See Alvin Plantinga, *Where the Conflict Really Lies: Science, Religion, and Naturalism* (New York: Oxford University Press, 2011), and Angus J. L. Menuge, *Agents Under Fire: Materialism and the Rationality of Science* (Oxford: Rowman & Littlefield, 2004). Plantinga also addresses this issue in "An Evolutionary Argument Against Naturalism—Alvin Plantinga at USC," YouTube video, 1:18:24, from a public lecture hosted at University of Southern California, posted by "The Veritas Forum," February 23, 2013, https://www.youtube.com/watch?v=PwE_D9GUC0s.
7. Shane Hipps, *Flickering Pixels: How Technology Shapes Your Faith* (Grand Rapids: Zondervan, 2009), 11–12.
8. I will write more on this in chapter 39. But take Christianity and Islam for example. They are fundamentally different on this point. Islam, with its understanding of the Qur'an and Sharia law, is or becomes the state government. By contrast, Christians aren't supposed to take over the government by force or by military might, but we are supposed to allow God's truth and the power of His kingdom to influence all areas of life until Christ returns. Now the Bible says that we will not bring in a utopia, but it calls us to engage, not retreat from, culture.

9. Nancy Pearcey's book *Total Truth: Liberating Christianity from Its Cultural Captivity* (Wheaton, IL: Crossway, 2004) has challenged me to think more about what this looks like in our culture today. It's a great read!

10. For a helpful critique of naturalism, see Phillip E. Johnson, *Reason in the Balance: The Case Against Naturalism in Science, Law, and Education* (Downers Grove, IL: InterVarsity Press, 1995). For a more academic critique, see William Lane Craig and J. P. Moreland, eds., *Naturalism: A Critical Analysis* (London: Routledge, 2000).

11. Francis Beckwith, William Lane Craig, and J. P. Moreland, *To Everyone an Answer: A Case for the Christian Worldview* (Downers Grove, IL: InterVarsity Press, 2004), 373.

12. For more, see R. Scott Smith, *Truth and the New Kind of Christian: The Emerging Effects of Postmodernism in the Church* (Wheaton, IL: Crossway, 2005).

13. Beckwith, Craig, and Moreland, *To Everyone an Answer*, 373.

14. Christian theism is not the only game in town anymore. Islam is growing in its influence as a theistic option in America. See Alan Shlemon, *The Ambassador's Guide to Islam* (Signal Hill, CA: Stand to Reason, 2010), and Winfried Corduan, *Pocket Guide to World Religions* (Downers Grove, IL: InterVarsity Press, 2006).

15. John Stonestreet, "Who's Restoring What? Participating in God's Plan Without Overstepping Our Bounds," *BreakPoint*, April 6, 2016, http://www.breakpoint.org /bpcommentaries/entry/13/29116.

16. I don't want to be misunderstood at this point. I am advocating a critical (not skeptical) posture toward the things we are taught because it all flows from a particular worldview. We must simply examine the ideas and see if these things are so. I am not trying to vilify professors or universities. On the contrary, there is much to be learned from them.

CHAPTER 3: Getting Theological

1. J. I. Packer, quoted in Max Anders, *New Christian's Handbook: Everything New Believers Need to Know* (Nashville: Thomas Nelson, 1999), 89.

2. Rick Cornish, *5 Minute Theologian: Maximum Truth in Minimum Time* (Colorado Springs: NavPress, 2005), 29.

3. David S. Dockery, *Christian Scripture: An Evangelical Perspective on Inspiration, Authority, and Interpretation* (Nashville: B&H Publishing, 1995), 64. This is a clear, thorough, yet accessible discussion of these topics. For two robust arguments for the rationality of inerrancy and biblical authority, see J. P. Moreland, "The Rationality of Belief in Inerrancy," *Trinity Journal* 7, no. 1 (1986): 75–86, and Douglas Blount, "The Authority of Scripture," in *Reason for the Hope Within*, ed. Michael J. Murray (Grand Rapids: Eerdmans, 1999).

4. When I list these passages, I am intending to get you pointed in the right direction for further study of each doctrine. Always read them in context.

5. Wayne A. Grudem, *Systematic Theology: An Introduction to Biblical Doctrine* (Grand Rapids: Zondervan, 2000), 226.

6. The following categories are found in Anders, *New Christian's Handbook*, 3–7.

7. An interesting thought to ponder is that God calls us to be holy even as God is holy (1 Peter 1:16).

8. Examples of the "logically impossible" would be God making Himself not exist, to

create a married bachelor, or create a square circle. An example of God acting contrary to His nature would be lying.

9. Bruce A. Ware, "Male and Female Complementarity and the Image of God," in *Biblical Foundations for Manhood and Womanhood*, ed. Wayne Grudem (Wheaton, IL: Crossway, 2002), 79.

10. See John W. Cooper, *Body, Soul, and Life Everlasting: Biblical Anthropology and the Monism-Dualism Debate*, updated ed. (Grand Rapids: Eerdmans, 2000), and J. P. Moreland, *The Soul: How We Know It's Real and Why It Matters* (Chicago: Moody Publishers, 2014).

11. Cornelius Plantinga, *Not the Way It's Supposed to Be: A Breviary of Sin* (Grand Rapids: Eerdmans, 1995).

12. The lyrics to the praise song "In Christ Alone" powerfully capture many of these themes. Words and Music by Keith Getty and Stuart Townend. Copyright © 2001 Kingsway Thankyou Music.

13. See Robert L. Saucy, *The Church in God's Program* (Chicago: Moody Publishers, 1972).

14. David K. Clark, *To Know and Love God: Method for Theology*, Foundations of Evangelical Theology, ed. John S. Feinberg (Wheaton, IL: Crossway, 2003), 424.

15. These categories and the following discussion are based upon the fine work of Alan Kent Scholes, *What Christianity Is All About: How You Can Know and Enjoy God* (Colorado Springs: NavPress, 1999), 11–26.

16. Ibid., 21.

17. Ibid., 21–22.

18. Ibid., 22.

19. In the survey of doctrine I presented in this chapter, I included both convictional and persuasive issues.

20. This saying has traditionally been attributed to Augustine, but there is some doubt as to whether he actually said it. Regardless of its origin, it rings true as to the perspective that Christians ought to strive for.

CHAPTER 4: Blinded by Faith?

1. David K. Clark, *Dialogical Apologetics: A Person-Centered Approach to Christian Defense* (Grand Rapids: Baker, 1993), 20.

2. Mark Twain, quoted in Louis P. Pojman and Michael Rea, *Philosophy of Religion: An Anthology*, 7th ed. (Boston: Cengage, 2014), 555.

3. Dan Brown, *The Da Vinci Code* (New York: Doubleday, 2003), 341–42.

4. Lisa Miller, "Belief Watch: Arguing Against the Atheists," *Newsweek*, October 6, 2008, 16.

5. Craig J. Hazen, "Defending the Defense of the Faith," in *To Everyone an Answer: A Case for the Christian Worldview*, eds. Francis J. Beckwith, William Lane Craig, and J. P. Moreland (Downers Grove, IL: InterVarsity Press, 2004), 43–44.

6. Clark, *Dialogical Apologetics*, 20.

7. This began in 1517.

8. These are the corresponding Latin terms. Philosophically speaking, these three components are independently necessary and jointly sufficient conditions of saving faith. For a clear summary of what biblical faith looks like, see Peter Kreeft and Ronald K. Tacelli, *Handbook of Christian Apologetics: Hundreds of Answers to Crucial*

Questions (Downers Grove, IL: InterVarsity Press, 1994), 30–31. Also see Thomas A. Howe and Richard G. Howe, "Knowing Christianity Is True: The Relationship Between Faith and Reason," in *To Everyone an Answer*, 23–36.

9. R. C. Sproul, *Faith Alone: The Evangelical Doctrine of Justification* (Grand Rapids: Baker, 1995), 30.

10. Ibid., 31.

11. Ibid., 33.

12. Because the word *faith* in our culture has become so ambiguous, I think it is better to speak of *trust* when we are talking in the public square.

13. Sproul, *Faith Alone*, 40.

14. Robert L. Saucy, "Theology of Human Nature," in *Christian Perspectives on Being Human: A Multidisciplinary Approach to Integration*, eds. J. P. Moreland and David M. Ciocchi (Grand Rapids: Baker, 1993), 42.

15. Clark, *Dialogical Apologetics*, 25.

16. For an excellent discussion of faith, see ibid., 17–19.

17. C. S. Lewis is instructive on this point. "That is why Faith is such a necessary virtue: unless you teach your moods 'where to get off,' you can never be either a sound Christian or even a sound atheist, but just a creature dithering to and fro, with its beliefs really dependent on the weather and the state of its digestion. Consequently one must train the habit of Faith." From Lewis, *Mere Christianity* (New York: Simon & Schuster, 1996), 125.

CHAPTER 5: **Can We Know Anything at All?**

1. Mark Twain, quoted in Vernon McLellan, *Complete Book of Practical Proverbs and Wacky Wit* (Carol Stream, IL: Tyndale House, 1996), 131.

2. Robert Anthony, quoted in Sayre Van Young and Marin Van Young, *Tweet This Book: 1,400 Greatest Quotes of All Time in 140 Characters or Less* (Berkeley: Ulysses, 2011), 73.

3. Since this is a brief overview, I have chosen to ignore the more technical details of the so-called "Gettier-style" objections. Taking these into account, knowledge = justified true belief + "something else." For more on this, see Richard Feldman, *Epistemology*, Foundations of Philosophy Series (Upper Saddle River, NJ: Prentice Hall, 2003).

4. These categories come from ibid., 4.

5. I will adopt the view that our senses should be viewed as innocent until proven guilty.

6. For more on this, see Paul Copan, *How Do You Know You're Not Wrong? Responding to Objections That Leave Christians Speechless* (Grand Rapids: Baker, 2005).

7. In epistemology this is known as the "problem of the criterion."

8. Garrett J. DeWeese and J. P. Moreland, *Philosophy Made Slightly Less Difficult: A Beginner's Guide to Life's Big Questions* (Downers Grove, IL: InterVarsity Press, 2005), 77.

9. To see IBE applied to the question of Jesus's resurrection, see the outstanding article by William Lane Craig, "Did Jesus Rise from the Dead?" in *Jesus Under Fire: Modern Scholarship Reinvents the Historical Jesus*, eds. Michael J. Wilkins and J. P. Moreland (Grand Rapids: Zondervan, 1995).

10. James Beilby and David K. Clark, *Why Bother with Truth?*, The RZIM Critical Questions Booklet Series (Norcross, GA: RZIM, 2000), 48.

11. Ibid., 47.
12. I want to thank Garry DeWeese for the insights he shared with us during epistemology class at Talbot School of Theology—especially the distinction between knowledge, understanding, and wisdom.
13. See Nancy Pearcey, *Total Truth: Liberating Christianity from Its Cultural Captivity* (Wheaton, IL: Crossway, 2008).

CHAPTER 6: Truth Matters

1. Aristotle, quoted in Chad V. Meister, *Building Belief: Constructing Faith from the Ground Up* (Grand Rapids: Baker, 2006), 21.
2. C. S. Lewis and Patricia Klein, *A Year with C. S. Lewis: Daily Readings from His Classic Works*, 1st ed. (San Francisco: HarperSanFrancisco, 2003), 26.
3. Norman Geisler and Joseph Holden, *Living Loud: Defending Your Faith* (Nashville: B&H Publishing, 2002), 29, 31.
4. It is beyond our scope to describe how postmodernism is changing the way people view the truth, but suffice it to say, truth is understood as being created by the way people in different communities use their language. Reality then is linguistically constructed.
5. Of course the Bible wasn't written with the correspondence theory of truth in mind, but of the philosophical theories available to us today, this common sense view of truth is at home in the Bible.
6. A quick comment would be helpful here. Since all truth is God's truth, we can discover truths that are not included in the pages of Scripture. It is not as though we need the book of Romans to tell us 2 + 2 = 4, that grass is green, or that sodium and chlorine make salt. However, statements in the Bible revealed about God, salvation, sin, Jesus Christ, morality, history, and so on are true (i.e., they describe reality). They reveal information we could not have discovered apart from God's specific revelation to us. God gave us His Word because there is a limit to the amount of truth humans can discover by studying the natural world. For example, the splendor and complexity of nature reveals the truth that there must have been a designer. Scripture then reveals the truth about the identity of that designer—the triune God who desires a relationship with His creation.
7. C. S. Lewis, "Man or Rabbit?" in *God in the Dock: Essays on Theology and Ethics*, ed. Walter Hooper (Grand Rapids: Eerdmans, 1970), 108–9.
8. This is not *just* an intellectual experience; see chapter 5, "Can We Know Anything at All?"

CHAPTER 7: A Moral Disaster

1. Allan David Bloom, *The Closing of the American Mind: How Higher Education Has Failed Democracy and Impoverished the Souls of Today's Students* (New York: Simon & Schuster, 1987), 25.
2. John Ladd, quoted in Louis P. Pojman, *Ethics: Discovering Right and Wrong*, 3rd ed. (Belmont, CA: Wadsworth, 1999), 26.
3. Christian Smith et al., *Lost in Transition: The Dark Side of Emerging Adulthood* (New York: Oxford University Press, 2011), 24. See also Barna Group's recent research, "The End of Absolutes: America's New Moral Code," May 25, 2016, https://www.barna.com /research/the-end-of-absolutes-americas-new-moral-code/. Within moral relativism,

there are nuanced positions that are worth exploring, but that is not our current task. What we will talk about in this chapter could be applied loosely to any relativistic argument. For a more precise discussion, see Russ Shafer-Landau, *Whatever Happened to Good and Evil?* (Oxford: Oxford University Press, 2004).

4. Pojman, *Ethics*, 32.

5. Francis J. Beckwith, "Why I Am Not a Moral Relativist," in *Why I Am a Christian: Leading Thinkers Explain Why They Believe*, eds. Norman L. Geisler and Paul K. Hoffman (Grand Rapids: Baker, 2001), 19.

6. The best explanation for objective moral values understands them as grounded in the nature, character, and commands of God. See the resources at the end of the chapter, especially Paul Copan, "The Moral Argument," in *The Rationality of Theism*, eds. Paul Copan and Paul K. Moser (London: Routledge, 2003).

7. In my understating of this topic, I am indebted to so many people. But I want to highlight my appreciation here for the insight of one of my ethics professors, Dave Horner. His class solidified a lot of these concepts for me, and I am employing a couple of his arguments here (e.g., the reformer's dilemma).

8. Francis Beckwith and Gregory Koukl, *Relativism: Feet Firmly Planted in Mid-Air* (Grand Rapids: Baker, 1998), 67.

9. Dallas Willard, *Renovation of the Heart: Putting On the Character of Christ* (Colorado Springs: NavPress, 2002), 105.

10. Michael Novak, *No One Sees God: The Dark Night of Atheists and Believers* (New York: Doubleday, 2008), 283–84.

11. Greg Koukl, "Partial-Birth Abortion Is Not About Abortion," Stand to Reason, March 30, 2013, https://www.str.org/articles/partial-birth-abortion-is-not-about-abortion#.WC3VUHgwdXt.

12. John Stonestreet, "Vote Against Assisted Suicide in Colorado," *USA Today*, October 18, 2016, http://www.usatoday.com/story/opinion/2016/10/18/suicide-colorado-prop-106-euthanasia-column/91964372/.

CHAPTER 8: True Tolerance

1. Chad V. Meister, *Building Belief: Constructing Faith from the Ground Up* (Grand Rapids: Baker, 2006), 34.

2. This is the definition from Norman Geisler and Joseph Holden, *Living Loud: Defending Your Faith* (Nashville: B&H Publishing, 2002), 31.

3. Encarta Reference Library (Microsoft, 2005), CD-ROM, italics added.

4. Paul Copan, *True for You, but Not for Me: Overcoming Objections to Christian Faith* (Minneapolis: Bethany House, 2009), 35.

5. Dallas Willard, quoted in Brad Stetson and Joseph G. Conti, *The Truth About Tolerance: Pluralism, Diversity, and the Culture Wars* (Downers Grove, IL: InterVarsity Press, 2005), 139.

6. Kelly Monroe, ed., *Finding God at Harvard: Spiritual Journeys of Christian Thinkers* (Grand Rapids: Zondervan, 1996), 17, italics added.

7. See George Yancey, *Hostile Environment: Understanding and Responding to Anti-Christian Bias* (Downers Grove, IL: InterVarsity Press, 2015). See also Yancey, "What Christianophobia Looks Like in America," *Christianity Today*, March 27, 2015, http://

www.christianitytoday.com/ct/2015/march-web-only/what-christianophobia-looks
-like-in-america.html?start=1.

8. Kirsten Powers, *The Silencing: How the Left Is Killing Free Speech* (Washington, DC: Regnery, 2015), Kindle loc. 198–211.

9. The immediate context is Jesus's disciples knowing what to say when they are persecuted. The timeless principle we derive from this is that God's Spirit is with all Christians and will help them know what to say when facing tough situations.

10. Movies such as *Easy A* come to mind.

CHAPTER 9: How to Read the Bible

1. Howard G. Hendricks and William Hendricks, *Living by the Book* (Chicago: Moody Publishers, 1991), 30.

2. I owe a great debt to Howard Hendricks (affectionately called "Prof" by his students) for his lifetime of faithful service to God and the teaching of God's Word. I was fortunate to have Hendricks as a teacher in seminary, and his passion for helping his students dig into God's Word is a large reason you are reading this chapter. Thanks, Prof!

3. Roy B. Zuck, *Basic Bible Interpretation* (Wheaton, IL: Victor, 1991), 74–75.

4. This does not mean that we cannot experience doubts about the reliability of the Bible or other such questions. For more on that see chapter 10, "Can I Trust the Bible?," and chapter 20, "Dealing with Doubt."

5. J. Scott Duvall and J. Daniel Hays, *Grasping God's Word: A Hands-On Approach to Reading, Interpreting, and Applying the Bible*, 2nd ed. (Grand Rapids: Zondervan, 2005), 95.

6. My discussion relies upon the approach developed in Hendricks and Hendricks, *Living by the Book*.

7. Ibid., 39.

8. David S. Dockery and George H. Guthrie, *The Holman Guide to Interpreting the Bible* (Nashville: B&H Publishers, 2004), 49.

9. Just because people approach the Bible with sound principles of interpretation does not mean that everyone will agree. In fact, godly people disagree all the time, and that is OK. Each of us needs to, with intellectual honesty and integrity, do our best to understand a passage as a skilled worker (2 Tim. 2:15). But we also need to extend charity to those with whom we disagree. See chapter 3, "Getting Theological," for more about the levels of agreement and disagreement Christians can have.

10. More will be said about the important discipline of devotional/meditative reading in chapter 29, "Becoming More Like Jesus." See Richard J. Foster, *Celebration of Discipline: The Path to Spiritual Growth*, 25th anniversary ed. (San Francisco: HarperSanFrancisco, 1998), and Donald S. Whitney, *Spiritual Disciplines for the Christian Life* (Colorado Springs: NavPress, 1991).

11. These questions are taken from Hendricks and Hendricks, *Living by the Book*, 308. Also, you may want to purchase a *Life Application Study Bible* in your favorite translation; they do a phenomenal job of applying God's Word to our lives.

12. Hendricks and Hendricks, *Living by the Book*, 293. A related question is, "Do I have to rightly interpret a passage before God can use His Word in my life?" While what I am about to say could be misconstrued, I am going to say it anyway because I think it's true. Can God encourage me in reading His Word even if I am not "studying it"? Absolutely!

There are many times when the Holy Spirit has taken a passage and impressed something on my heart to encourage me that the biblical author never intended. However, the more I read the Bible, the more my *interpretations* tend to coincide with the actual meaning of the passage. The point of saying this is not to diminish the importance of the careful study of a passage to determine its meaning; rather, I say this only to honestly describe an experience that is common to most everyone who has ever picked up a Bible. Can God teach us something or encourage us even if we have misinterpreted the text? I sure hope so! Now this is not the way to determine the authoritative meaning of a text. But God in His grace causes His Spirit to help us in spite of our inadequacy or error. People throughout church history have been encouraged by some pretty fantastical interpretations that would have received an "F" in Bible 101. Again, God's grace. However, our goal is to be like the worker who skillfully seeks to handle God's Word accurately (2 Tim. 2:15). To parrot Paul in Romans 6:1, should bad interpretation increase so that God's grace can abound all the more? May it never be!

13. Duvall and Hays, *Grasping God's Word*, 210.

CHAPTER 10: Can I Trust the Bible?

1. Darrell L. Bock, *Can I Trust the Bible? Defending the Bible's Reliability*, RZIM Critical Questions Series (Norcross, GA: RZIM, 2001), 52.

2. Robert Saucy, *Scripture: Its Power, Authority, and Relevance* (Nashville: Word, 2001), 78.

3. David S. Dockery, *Christian Scripture: An Evangelical Perspective on Inspiration, Authority, and Interpretation* (Nashville: B&H Publishing, 1995), 64.

4. God may have providentially arranged it this way on purpose so we would worship Him—the God of the Bible—instead of the original documents themselves. Just a thought. It is probably better that we don't have the originals.

5. This illustration is from Bruce K. Waltke, "Old Testament Textual Criticism," in *Foundations for Biblical Interpretation: A Complete Library of Tools and Resources*, eds. David S. Dockery, Kenneth A. Matthews, and Robert B. Sloan (Nashville: B&H Publishing, 1994), 158–59.

6. If you want to set your watch, go to http://tycho.usno.navy.mil/.

7. This is not to say that scholars in a PhD seminar don't debate different theories surrounding the literary composition and textual traditions of Homer. However, I can guarantee you this: there are no #1 best sellers entitled *Misquoting Homer*. But *Misquoting Jesus*—a book on textual criticism of the Bible that takes a rather skeptical view—*did* become a best seller.

8. Gleason L. Archer, *A Survey of Old Testament Introduction*, rev. and exp. ed. (Chicago: Moody Publishers, 1994), 27.

9. Every now and again a well-meaning scribe would add words of clarification to the text, but these difficulties are resolved due to the large number of texts we have to compare with one another through a process called textual criticism.

10. See Paul D. Wegner, *The Journey from Texts to Translations: The Origin and Development of the Bible* (Grand Rapids: Baker, 1999), 171–75.

11. "Thus we have a consistent level of good, fact-based correlations right through from circa 2000 B.C. (with earlier roots) down to 400 B.C. In terms of general reliability . . . the Old Testament comes out remarkably well, so long as its writings and writers are treated fairly and evenhandedly, in line with independent data, open to all." From K. A.

Kitchen, *On the Reliability of the Old Testament* (Grand Rapids: Eerdmans, 2003), 500. This book contains a lot of great information and analysis, but it is challenging to read.

12. Archer, *A Survey of Old Testament Introduction*, 29.

13. Wegner, *The Journey from Texts to Translations*, 165.

14. Ibid., 101, italics added.

15. Waltke, "Old Testament Textual Criticism," 157–58.

16. Bock, *Can I Trust the Bible?*, 52.

17. This discussion comes from J. Ed Komoszewski, M. James Sawyer, and Daniel B. Wallace, *Reinventing Jesus: How Contemporary Skeptics Miss the Real Jesus and Mislead Popular Culture* (Grand Rapids: Kregel, 2006), 66–73.

18. Norman L. Geisler, *Baker Encyclopedia of Christian Apologetics* (Grand Rapids: Baker, 1999), 533.

19. *Jesus: Fact or Fiction*, directed by Peter Sykes (Orlando, FL: Inspirational Films, 2004). See also the Center for the Study of New Testament Manuscripts at www.csntm.org.

20. See Colin J. Hemer and Conrad H. Gempf, *The Book of Acts in the Setting of Hellenistic History* (Tübingen: Mohr, 1989).

21. See Sean McDowell, *The Fate of the Apostles: Examining the Martyrdom Accounts of the Closest Followers of Jesus* (Burlington: Ashgate, 2015).

22. This is known as the criterion of embarrassment.

23. Paul Copan, *How Do You Know You're Not Wrong? Responding to Objections That Leave Christians Speechless* (Grand Rapids: Baker, 2005), 230. This is an excellent summary chapter on the canon of Scripture.

24. Ibid., 226–30.

25. Douglas Stuart, "Inerrancy and Textual Criticism," in *Inerrancy and Common Sense*, eds. Roger R. Nicole and J. Ramsey Michaels (Grand Rapids: Baker, 1980), 115–16.

26. Jesus subtly affirmed the Old Testament canon by His reference in Matthew 23:35. He was quoting from Genesis (i.e., Abel), the first book of the Hebrew Scriptures, all the way to 2 Chronicles (i.e., Zechariah), which is the last book of the Hebrew Scriptures. Our English Bible arranges the thirty-nine books of the Old Testament differently than the Hebrew Bible does. Not only did Jesus affirm the authority of the Bible, but Peter also called Paul's writings Scripture (2 Peter 3:16). Paul views Luke and Deuteronomy as equally authoritative by quoting them in the same verse (1 Tim. 5:18).

CHAPTER 11: Knowing Versus Showing Your Faith

1. William Lane Craig, quoted in Steven B. Cowan, *Five Views on Apologetics* (Grand Rapids: Zondervan, 2000), 28.

2. William Lane Craig, *Reasonable Faith: Christian Truth and Apologetics*, rev. ed. (Wheaton, IL: Crossway, 1994), 17–50. Also discussed in Cowan, *Five Views on Apologetics*, 26–55. My discussion is based on the content of these pages.

3. Alvin Plantinga, "The Foundations of Theism: A Reply," *Faith and Philosophy* 3, no. 3 (1986): 310.

4. Gary R. Habermas, *The Historical Jesus: Ancient Evidence for the Life of Christ* (Joplin, MO: College Press, 1996).

5. This is what we see happening in the New Testament. For example, the apostles in the book of Acts are often reasoning with and attempting to persuade unbelievers

concerning the truthfulness of Christianity (17:2–4, 17; 18:4; 19:8). For more see Craig J. Hazen, "Defending the Defense of the Faith," in *To Everyone an Answer: A Case for the Christian Worldview*, eds. Francis J. Beckwith, William Lane Craig, and J. P. Moreland (Downers Grove, IL: InterVarsity Press, 2004).

6. See Avery Dulles, *A History of Apologetics* (San Francisco: Ignatius, 2005).

CHAPTER 12: No Apologies Needed

1. Dallas Willard, *The Divine Conspiracy: Rediscovering Our Hidden Life in God* (San Francisco: HarperSanFrancisco, 1997), 92.

2. William Lane Craig, *Reasonable Faith: Christian Truth and Apologetics*, rev. ed. (Wheaton, IL: Crossway, 1994), 50.

3. To see how every generation of Christians has risen to the challenge to defend Christianity, see Avery Dulles, *A History of Apologetics* (San Francisco: Ignatius, 2005).

4. You can no more love a person into the kingdom of God than argue them in—yet both may be means that the Holy Spirit uses in drawing that individual to Christ.

5. Francis Beckwith, William Lane Craig, and J. P. Moreland, *To Everyone an Answer: A Case for the Christian Worldview* (Downers Grove, IL: InterVarsity Press, 2004), 22.

CHAPTER 13: The Existence of God

1. Thomas Nagel, *The Last Word* (New York: Oxford University Press, 1997), 130.

2. Augustine, quoted in Tony Lane, *A Concise History of Christian Thought*, rev. ed. (Grand Rapids: Baker, 2006), 51.

3. G. W. Leibniz, "The Principles of Nature and of Grace, Based on Reason," in *Leibniz Selections*, ed. Philip P. Wiener, The Modern Student's Library (New York: Scribner, 1951), 527.

4. Pew Research Center, "The Future of World Religions: Population Growth Projections, 2010–2050," April 2, 2015, http://www.pewforum.org/2015/04/02/religious-projections -2010-2050/.

5. Kenneth R. Samples, *Without a Doubt: Answering the 20 Toughest Faith Questions* (Grand Rapids: Baker, 2004), 21.

6. This is called the Kalam cosmological argument.

7. To read the whole interview online, see Biola University, Biola News and Communications at http://digitalcommons.liberty.edu/cgi/viewcontent.cgi?article=1336 &context=lts_fac_pubs. See also Associated Press, "There Is a God, Leading Atheist Concludes," NBCNews.com, December 9, 2004, http://www.nbcnews.com/id/6688917 /ns/world_news/t/there-god-leading-atheist-concludes/#.WCue_eErJZp.

8. For example, even if carbon-based life were possible on Jupiter, an observer could not discover anything about the solar system or universe from its surface. Earth struck the jackpot on carbon-based life and the ability to make observations. See Guillermo Gonzalez and Jay Wesley Richards, *The Privileged Planet: How Our Place in the Cosmos Is Designed for Discovery* (Washington, DC: Regnery, 2004).

9. See Erik Melaxas, "Eugenics and Not-So Ancient History," *BreakPoint*, September 15, 2014, http://www.thepointradio.org/bpcommentaries/entry/13/26063.

10. There are attempts, but they all seem to have to use theistic motivations to find a natural explanation for evil and objective morality. See Chad Meister and James K. Dew, *God*

and Evil: The Case for God in a World Filled with Pain (Downers Grove, IL: InterVarsity Press, 2013).

11. C. S. Lewis, *Mere Christianity* (New York: Simon & Schuster, 1996), 119–22.

CHAPTER 14: Do All Roads Lead to God?

1. Ravi Zacharias, quoted in Norman L. Geisler and Paul K. Hoffman, *Why I Am a Christian: Leading Thinkers Explain Why They Believe* (Grand Rapids: Baker, 2001), 268.

2. Pew Forum on Religion and Public Life, "U.S. Religious Landscape Survey: Summary of Key Findings," June 2008, http://www.pewforum.org/files/2008/06/report2religious -landscape-study-key-findings.pdf.

3. Some may dispute this, and there are even statements in the Second Vatican Ecumenical Council that are much more inclusive. My point here is that the New Testament seems pretty clear on this issue. So unless we do violence to the New Testament in the name of political correctness and misplaced compassion, then Christianity is a form of particularism.

4. Like all of these chapters, there is no way to explore every issue or deal with every objection. I have tried to pick a handful of the important ones that you are likely to ask yourself or be asked by others. To dig deeper, consult the resources listed at the end of the chapter.

5. William Lane Craig, *Hard Questions, Real Answers* (Wheaton, IL: Crossway, 2003), 150–51.

6. Ibid., 151.

7. Expounding and then arguing against this view (e.g., John Hick) would take me well beyond the purpose of this book. However, Christians have adequately addressed it. See Harold A. Netland, *Encountering Religious Pluralism: The Challenge to Christian Faith and Mission* (Downers Grove, IL: InterVarsity Press, 2001). Also there is an excellent— but more technical—treatment of these issues by Philip L. Quinn and Kevin Meeker, eds., *The Philosophical Challenge of Religious Diversity* (New York: Oxford University Press, 2000).

8. Alvin Plantinga, "Pluralism," in *The Philosophical Challenge of Religious Diversity,* 179.

9. Ibid., 175–77.

10. Plantinga, quoted in Paul Copan, *True for You, but Not for Me: Overcoming Objections to Christian Faith* (Minneapolis: Bethany House, 1998), 85.

11. For example, see David Garrison, *A Wind in the House of Islam: How God Is Drawing Muslims Around the World to Faith in Jesus Christ* (Monument, CO: WIGTake Resources, 2014).

12. If someone is not constrained by biblical teaching, then the only boundaries are his creativity.

13. God's normative plan for reaching the nations is through missionaries and the sharing of the gospel. But God can and often does use other ways to assist in the gospel's proclamation around the globe: people dream dreams of Christ or have visions of missionaries coming to their village. But this should not be seen as diminishing the motivation to go into the mission field. See Pauline Selby, *Persian Springs: Four Iranians See Jesus* (Godalming, UK: Highland Christian Books, 2003). Also, check out the amazing stories of what is going on with the *Jesus* film at the Jesus Film Project, http:// www.jesusfilm.org.

14. Some suggest that 1 Peter 3:18–22 speaks of Christ proclaiming the gospel to the "spirits now in prison." However, this is an exegetical stretch because the Greek words used suggest that Christ is proclaiming victory not offering the gospel.

15. A philosophical objection is sometimes raised: If God perfectly foreknows the future and knew that so many people would reject Him thus condemning themselves to hell, then why did He create this world? The problem? A good God wouldn't do that. All that is needed to undercut this objection is a *possible* scenario. It is at least *possible* that God in His providence so arranged the world that those whom God knew would accept Him were placed in the path of the gospel as it went forth, while those whom He knew would not—no matter what the circumstances—never heard the gospel. Whether this is true or not, who knows! But it is philosophically plausible and fits nicely with the picture found in Acts 17:24–28. See Craig, *Hard Questions, Real Answers*, 156–65. Regarding the challenging question of what happens to babies when they die, see John MacArthur, *Safe in the Arms of God: Truth from Heaven About the Death of a Child* (Nashville: Thomas Nelson, 2003).

16. William Lane Craig, "No Other Name: A Middle Knowledge Perspective on the Exclusivity of Salvation through Christ," in *The Philosophical Challenge of Religious Diversity*, 52.

17. For sample conversations on this topic with different kinds of people, see under "What About Those Who Have Never Heard" in chapter 4 of Randy Newman, *Questioning Evangelism: Engaging People's Hearts the Way Jesus Did*, 2nd ed. (Grand Rapids: Kregel, 2017).

18. James W. Sire, *Why Good Arguments Often Fail: Making a More Persuasive Case for Christ* (Downers Grove, IL: InterVarsity Press, 2006), 58–60.

CHAPTER 15: The Problem of Evil and Suffering

1. David Hume, *Dialogues Concerning Natural Religion*, ed. Richard H. Popkin (Indianapolis: Hackett, 1998), 63.

2. William Lane Craig, *Hard Questions, Real Answers* (Wheaton, IL: Crossway, 2003), 112.

3. See Cornelius Plantinga, *Not the Way It's Supposed to Be: A Breviary of Sin* (Grand Rapids: Eerdmans, 1995).

4. While these numbers are disputed (like all numbers), there is no denying the atrocities and the millions who died under his hand.

5. Of course there are other forms of theism, but we are concerned here with the Christian variety. For more details concerning the worldviews, see James W. Sire, *The Universe Next Door: A Basic Worldview Catalog*, 4th ed. (Downers Grove, IL: InterVarsity Press, 2004).

6. Some have said that if the theist has a problem of evil, the atheist has a problem of good. I think this is an important observation. From where does our common intuition of good come?

7. Recently, however, due to the weight of the problem of evil, some theologians have begun to revise classical attributes of God in order to get God "off the hook" for evil. This is unnecessary and unhelpful, not to mention it's a departure from orthodoxy. See William Lane Craig, *What Does God Know?* (Norcross, GA: RZIM, 2002), and Bruce A. Ware, *God's Lesser Glory: The Diminished God of Open Theism* (Wheaton, IL: Crossway, 2000).

8. Augustine called evil a "privation of the good" in *The City of God*, trans. Henry Bettenson (New York: Penguin, 2003), 454.

9. I am grateful to my friend Mike Good for his insight on this section.

10. I am appreciative for William Lane Craig's work in this area. I had the privilege of taking a class from him in which we discussed these various objections to Christian theism. My discussion has been enhanced by his insights. For more philosophical defenses and theodicies, see William Lane Craig, *Philosophy of Religion: A Reader and Guide* (Edinburgh: Edinburgh University Press, 2002), 303–425.

11. Alvin Plantinga, *God, Freedom, and Evil* (Grand Rapids: Eerdmans, 1977), 30.

12. Craig, *Hard Questions, Real Answers*, 90–91.

13. See the helpful and honest discussion in chapters 5 and 6 of Randy Newman, *Questioning Evangelism: Engaging People's Hearts the Way Jesus Did*, 2nd ed. (Grand Rapids: Kregel, 2017).

14. I heard him say this in a lecture.

15. For why the dying and rising gods of pagan religions are not parallel to Christianity, see chapter 17 of Sean McDowell and Jonathan Morrow, *Is God Just a Human Invention? And Seventeen Other Questions Raised by the New Atheists* (Grand Rapids: Kregel, 2011). See also my podcast, "Was Jesus Invented and Borrowed from Pagan Mythology?," JonathanMorrow.org, http://www.jonathanmorrow.org/was-jesus-invented-and -borrowed-from-pagan-mythology-podcast/.

16. Alister E. McGrath, *The Mystery of the Cross* (Grand Rapids: Zondervan, 1988), 159, italics added.

17. Dr. Doug Blount introduced this perspective about Job to me in a class, and I have found it extremely helpful. Also, I owe the explication of this truth about Jesus and Lazarus to pastor Tommy Nelson of Denton Bible Church.

18. C. S. Lewis, *The Problem of Pain* (New York: HarperSanFrancisco, 2001), 91.

CHAPTER 16: Thirty-One Flavors of Jesus

1. Ben Witherington, *The Gospel Code: Novel Claims About Jesus, Mary Magdalene, and Da Vinci* (Downers Grove, IL: InterVarsity Press, 2004), 1.

2. Scot McKnight, "Who Is Jesus? An Introduction to Jesus Studies," in *Jesus Under Fire: Modern Scholarship Reinvents the Historical Jesus*, eds. Michael J. Wilkins and J. P. Moreland (Grand Rapids: Zondervan, 1995), 68.

3. The Jesus Seminar is a small group of New Testament scholars who have been meeting since 1985, seeking to decide, by vote, what little recorded in the Gospels was actually spoken by Jesus.

4. See, for example, Bart D. Ehrman, "What DO We Really Know About Jesus?," *Newsweek*, December 10, 2012, http://www.newsweek.com/what-do-we-really -know-about-jesus-63427. For a response to these kinds of objections, see my book *Questioning the Bible: 11 Major Challenges to the Bible's Authority* (Chicago: Moody Publishers, 2014).

5. For a short, accessible book answering these claims, check out Darrell L. Bock, *Breaking the Da Vinci Code: Answers to the Questions Everyone's Asking* (Nashville: Thomas Nelson, 2004). What made Dan Brown's book more than "fiction" was the claim printed on the title page that the descriptions of artwork, architecture, documents, and secret rituals were accurate.

6. This refers to the documents found in 1945 called the Nag Hammadi codices.

7. Bart D. Ehrman, *Lost Scriptures: Books that Did Not Make It into the New Testament* (Oxford: Oxford University Press, 2003).

8. Ibid., 58.

9. Ibid., italics added.

10. Ibid., 28, italics added. These sayings are from the Coptic Gospel of Thomas.

11. One high-profile proponent of this is Elaine Pagels; see *The Gnostic Gospels* (New York: Random House, 2004). For interaction with these and other claims, see Darrell L. Bock, *The Missing Gospels: Unearthing the Truth Behind Alternative Christianities* (Nashville: Thomas Nelson, 2006).

12. Since I am trying to introduce this topic, I didn't mention that *some* of the other sayings recorded in the Coptic Gospel of Thomas could be part of a list of sayings circulating at the time of the writing of the New Testament, and some sound like statements found in the some of the gospels. For more on issues like this, see Bock, *The Missing Gospels*.

13. I had the privilege of taking a class from Dr. Bock as well as listening to several lectures given on various occasions concerning who Jesus claimed to be.

14. See chapter 4 of Michael R. Licona, *The Resurrection of Jesus: A New Historiographical Approach* (Downers Grove, IL: InterVarsity Press, 2010).

15. See Michael F. Bird et al., *How God Became Jesus: The Real Origins of Belief in Jesus' Divine Nature—A Response to Bart Ehrman* (Grand Rapids: Zondervan, 2014).

16. C. S. Lewis, *Mere Christianity* (New York: Simon & Schuster, 1996), 56.

CHAPTER 17: Did Jesus Rise from the Dead?

1. George Ladd, quoted in Paul Copan, ed., *Will the Real Jesus Please Stand Up? A Debate Between William Lane Craig and John Dominic Crossan* (Grand Rapids: Baker, 1998), 24.

2. J. P. Moreland, *Scaling the Secular City: A Defense of Christianity* (Grand Rapids: Baker, 1987), 171–72.

3. William Lane Craig, "Did Jesus Rise from the Dead?" in *Jesus Under Fire: Modern Scholarship Reinvents the Historical Jesus*, eds. Michael J. Wilkins and J. P. Moreland (Grand Rapids: Zondervan, 1995), 166.

4. Craig J. Hazen, "Defending the Defense of the Faith," in *To Everyone an Answer: A Case for the Christian Worldview*, eds. Francis J. Beckwith, William Lane Craig, and J. P. Moreland (Downers Grove, IL: InterVarsity Press, 2004), 43–44.

5. Much of what I say here is a summary of Gary R. Habermas and Michael R. Licona, *The Case for the Resurrection of Jesus* (Grand Rapids: Kregel, 2004).

6. Ibid., 48.

7. Technically, there are 4 + 1 facts. The first "4" are accepted by virtually every scholar while the last "1" enjoys very wide support among scholars (about 75 percent according to Habermas and Licona, ibid., 70).

8. Paul Barnett, *Is the New Testament Reliable?* 2nd ed. (Downers Grove, IL: InterVarsity Press, 2003), 188.

9. Tacitus, *The Annals* 15.44, trans. Alfred John Church and William Jackson Brodribb, *The Internet Classics Archive*, Massachusetts Institute of Technology, http://classics.mit .edu/Tacitus/annals.11.xv.html. For other non-Christian sources, see Josephus, Lucian, Mara Bar-Serapion, and the Talmud.

10. See Paul Barnett, *The Birth of Christianity: The First Twenty Years* (Grand Rapids: Eerdmans, 2005).

11. Habermas and Licona, *The Case for the Resurrection of Jesus*, 51.

12. Ibid., 59.

13. Craig, "Did Jesus Rise from the Dead?" 151.

14. I do not have time to go into them here, but you can see the other explanations and why they fail in Habermas and Licona, *The Case for the Resurrection of Jesus*, 84–150.

CHAPTER 18: **Science Rules!**

1. Ian Barbour, quoted in J. P. Moreland, *Christianity and the Nature of Science: A Philosophical Investigation* (Grand Rapids: Baker, 1989), 59.

2. Alexander Rosenberg, *The Philosophy of Science: A Contemporary Introduction*, 2nd ed., Routledge Contemporary Introductions to Philosophy (New York: Routledge, 2005), 10–11.

3. George Marsden, paraphrased in Del Ratzsch, *Science and Its Limits: The Natural Sciences in Christian Perspective*, 2nd ed. (Downers Grove, IL: InterVarsity Press, 2000), 159.

4. This is not to say there aren't other authorities; see the new moral code in David Kinnaman and Gabe Lyons, *Good Faith: Being a Christian When Society Thinks You're Irrelevant and Extreme* (Grand Rapids: Baker, 2016), 56–59. But when push comes to shove, when people want certainty or knowledge on a question, they leverage science and empirical research as "real proof."

5. C. John Collins, *Science and Faith: Friends or Foes?* (Wheaton, IL: Crossway, 2003), 29.

6. Moreland, *Christianity and the Nature of Science*, 33.

7. Ibid., 140.

8. There are actually "weak" and "strong" forms of scientism. For an explanation and critique, see Garrett J. DeWeese and J. P. Moreland, *Philosophy Made Slightly Less Difficult: A Beginner's Guide to Life's Big Questions* (Downers Grove, IL: InterVarsity Press, 2005), 134–38.

9. J. P. Moreland, *Scaling the Secular City: A Defense of Christianity* (Grand Rapids: Baker, 1987), 197.

10. DeWeese and Moreland, *Philosophy Made Slightly Less Difficult*, 136.

11. Ibid., 136–37.

12. Paul Copan, *How Do You Know You're Not Wrong? Responding to Objections That Leave Christians Speechless* (Grand Rapids: Baker, 2005), 83. It is often charged that this kind of thinking is a "science stopper." But properly employed, I don't think this charge fits. See Alvin Plantinga, "Should Methodological Naturalism Constrain Science?" in *Science: Christian Perspectives for the New Millennium*, eds. Scott Luley, Paul Copan, and Stan W. Wallace (Norcross, GA: RZIM, 2003).

13. Ratzsch, *Science and Its Limits*, 93.

14. Ibid., 94.

15. That is, they will be known a priori, not a posteriori.

16. This discussion and these quotations are from J. P. Moreland and William Lane Craig, *Philosophical Foundations for a Christian Worldview* (Downers Grove, IL: InterVarsity Press, 2003), 350–58.

17. For more on the doctrine of creation and the interpretation of Genesis, see J. P. Moreland and John Mark Reynolds, eds., *Three Views on Creation and Evolution* (Grand Rapids: Zondervan, 2010), and David G. Hagopian, ed., *The Genesis Debate: Three Views on the Days of Creation* (Mission Viejo, CA: Crux, 2001).

18. Ratzsch, *Science and Its Limits*, 140.

CHAPTER 19: Designed or Not Designed?

1. Thomas Nagel, *Mind and Cosmos: Why the Materialist Neo-Darwinian Conception of Nature Is Almost Certainly False* (New York: Oxford University Press, 2012), 5–6.

2. Charles Darwin, *On the Origin of the Species*, Barnes & Noble Classics (New York: Fine Creative Media, 2003), 12.

3. William A. Dembski, *The Design Revolution: Answering the Toughest Questions About Intelligent Design* (Downers Grove, IL: InterVarsity Press, 2004), 45.

4. Richard Dawkins, *The Blind Watchmaker: Why the Evidence of Evolution Reveals a Universe Without Design* (New York: W. W. Norton, 1996), 1.

5. Because Darwin's core idea of natural selection as the "designer" of biological life is still the driving engine of evolutionary thought, the term *neo-Darwinism* captures its essence. The modern addition of population genetics is the heart of what is "new." Other terms you may encounter are *modern synthesis, evolutionary synthesis, neo-Darwinian synthesis, evo-devo,* or *evolutionary biology.* Because the term *evolution* is so slippery, it is important to focus on the most central contrast. Is natural selection acting on genetic mutations sufficient to create all the diversity and complexity of life we observe?

6. Phillip E. Johnson, *Darwin on Trial*, 2nd ed. (Downers Grove, IL: InterVarsity Press, 1993), 103–4.

7. Robert Shapiro, *Origins: A Skeptic's Guide to the Creation of Life on Earth* (New York: Summit, 1986); see also Fazale Rana and Hugh Ross, *Origins of Life: Biblical and Evolutionary Models Face Off* (Colorado Springs: NavPress, 2004).

8. Obviously, I cannot argue for this claim. I must merely assert it here. I encourage you to avail yourself of the resources at the end of the chapter.

9. Jonathan Wells, *Icons of Evolution: Science or Myth? Why Much of What We Teach About Evolution Is Wrong* (Washington, DC: Regnery, 2000), 8.

10. Dembski, *The Design Revolution*, 139. For a more rigorous discussion of this, see Dembski, *No Free Lunch: Why Specified Complexity Cannot Be Purchased Without Intelligence* (Oxford: Rowman & Littlefield, 2006).

11. Michael Ruse, *Can a Darwinian Be a Christian? The Relationship Between Science and Religion* (Cambridge: Cambridge University Press, 2004), 73.

12. One of the leading philosophers of mind, Jaegwon Kim, is honestly trying to supply one. But he has to either assume physicalism is true (or borrow some explanatory power from nonphysicalist theories) or so modify the notion of consciousness that it no longer resembles the robust notion everyone seems to experience. See Jaegwon Kim, *Physicalism, or Something Near Enough* (Princeton: Princeton University Press, 2005).

13. "A Scientific Dissent from Darwinism," The Discovery Institute, http://www.discovery.org/scripts/viewDB/filesDB-download.php?command=download&id=660. For a documented history of ID over the last fifteen years, see the excellent work by Thomas

Woodward, *Doubts About Darwin: A History of Intelligent Design* (Grand Rapids: Baker, 2003).

14. I include philosophers as well, because it is actually impossible to separate scientific inquiry from philosophical assumptions.

15. The examples are many, but see Barbara Forrest and Paul R. Gross, *Creationism's Trojan Horse: The Wedge of Intelligent Design* (New York: Oxford University Press, 2007).

16. Dembski, *The Design Revolution*, 45.

17. We could also talk about cryptology or the SETI project (search for extraterrestrial intelligence—regardless of what you think about this, these scientists are assuming that intelligence can be recognized, like a series of prime numbers 1, 3, 13, etc. See the movie *Contact*, directed by Robert Zemeckis [Burbank, CA: Warner Home Video, 1997]). So if scientists know what does and doesn't count as intelligence, then why the hesitance to apply that understanding to what they observe in biology?

18. William A. Dembski, "Explaining Specified Complexity," Metanexus Institute, September 13, 1999, http://www.metanexus.net/essay/explaining-specified-complexity.

19. Michael J. Behe, *Darwin's Black Box: The Biochemical Challenge to Evolution* (New York: Simon & Schuster, 1996).

20. Dembski, *The Design Revolution*, 36.

21. Charles Darwin, quoted in Lee Strobel, *The Case for Faith: A Journalist Investigates the Toughest Objections to Christianity* (Grand Rapids: Zondervan, 2000), 92, italics added.

22. See Michael J. Behe, *The Edge of Evolution: The Search for the Limits of Darwinism* (New York: Free Press, 2007).

23. This powerful evidence was part of what ultimately changed atheist Antony Flew's mind. See Antony Flew and Roy Abraham Varghese, *There Is a God: How the World's Most Notorious Atheist Changed His Mind* (San Francisco: HarperOne, 2007).

24. For interpretations on the days of Genesis 1, see David G. Hagopian, ed., *The Genesis Debate: Three Views on the Days of Creation* (Mission Viejo, CA: Crux, 2001), and also J. Daryl Charles, *Reading Genesis 1–2: An Evangelical Conversation* (Peabody, MA: Hendrickson, 2013).

25. For a robust defense of this claim, see Francis Beckwith, William Lane Craig, and J. P. Moreland, *To Everyone an Answer: A Case for the Christian Worldview* (Downers Grove, IL: InterVarsity Press, 2004).

26. Dawkins, *The Blind Watchmaker*, 6.

CHAPTER 20: **Dealing with Doubt**

1. Os Guinness, *God in the Dark: The Assurance of Faith Beyond a Shadow of Doubt* (Wheaton, IL: Crossway, 1996), 26. This is the best book you can buy on doubt in my opinion.

2. C. S. Lewis, *Mere Christianity* (New York: Simon & Schuster, 1996), 125.

3. The chapters on knowing versus showing Christianity to be true (chapter 11) and being blinded by faith (chapter 4) will help round out the discussion in this chapter.

4. Gary Habermas estimates that upward of 70 percent of the doubt that people encounter stems from unruly emotions. Only about 10 percent arises from factual doubt. I have heard him speak on this topic on several occasions and am grateful for his willingness to interact with such a neglected topic. This section is largely based on what Habermas

covers in his lectures and books, *Dealing with Doubt* (Chicago: Moody Publishers, 1990) and *The Thomas Factor: Using Your Doubts to Draw Closer to God* (Nashville: B&H Publishing, 1999). It is excellent material, and I have personally benefited from it (also see GaryHabermas.com).

5. Guinness, *God in the Dark*, 125–26.

6. Habermas, *Dealing with Doubt*, available at www.garyhabermas.com/books/dealing _with_ doubt/dealing_with_doubt.htm.

7. Dallas Willard, *Renovation of the Heart: Putting on the Character of Christ* (Colorado Springs: NavPress, 2002), 96.

8. See William Backus and Marie Chapian, *Telling Yourself the Truth* (Minneapolis: Bethany House, 2000).

9. As quoted in Guinness, *God in the Dark*, 143.

CHAPTER 21: Good News to Share

1. Douglas M. Cecil, *The 7 Principles of an Evangelistic Life* (Chicago: Moody Publishers, 2003), 35.

2. Baptism is sometimes taught as a requirement for salvation. I think this is false (see 1 Cor. 1:17), but many times people minimize the significance of baptism. I think the best way to conceive of the relationship between baptism and salvation is to say that baptism is not essential for salvation, nor is it optional. The New Testament expects those who trust Jesus to obediently follow Him in baptism as identification with the Christian community and as a picture of dying and rising with Christ (Rom. 6:3–4).

3. Now people can suppress and resist the work of the Spirit in their hearts. This seems to be what is going on in a passage like Acts 7:51: "You stiff-necked people, with uncircumcised hearts and ears! You are just like your fathers: You always resist the Holy Spirit!"

4. Cecil, *The 7 Principles of an Evangelistic Life*, 77.

5. See John R. W. Stott, *The Cross of Christ* (Downers Grove, IL: InterVarsity Press, 2012).

6. You can find historical evidence for the resurrection in chapter 17.

7. Cecil, *The 7 Principles of an Evangelistic Life*, 82. For more on faith, see chapter 4, "Blinded by Faith?"

8. Technically speaking, there is no sinner's prayer in the Bible. But a person desiring to trust Christ can take this step of faith by praying out loud with you. So while they are not magic words, they are a useful way to express a decision to accept Christ. We place our faith in Christ with our hearts (i.e., the center of our being). Two great passages on assurance of salvation in Christ are John 5:24 and 1 John 5:13. After a person trusts Christ it is imperative to follow up with them and get them connected to a body of believers to encourage their decision. If you led them to Christ, then make sure they have a Bible to start reading so they can meet with God.

9. Darrell Bock, "What's the Good News? For Us—and Creation," *Christianity Today*, February 7, 2000, http://www.christianitytoday.com/ct/2000/february7/40.47.html.

10. Dallas Willard, *The Divine Conspiracy: Rediscovering Our Hidden Life in God* (San Francisco: HarperSanFrancisco, 1997), 58.

11. Sometimes the question arises as to how aggressive versus relational we should be in sharing Christ. While this takes discernment, I think both are needed. I like Doug

Cecil's approach: "It appears that *the closer my relationship with an individual, the more relational my strategy should be. The more casual the relationship that I have with an individual, the more aggressive in my strategy I have to be.*" The rest of this section is helpful as well, Cecil, *The 7 Principles of an Evangelistic Life*, 137.

12. Randy Newman, *Questioning Evangelism: Engaging People's Hearts the Way Jesus Did*, 2nd ed. (Grand Rapids: Kregel, 2017), and *Corner Conversations: Engaging Dialogues About God and Life* (Grand Rapids: Kregel, 2006).

13. Gregory P. Koukl, "Applying Apologetics to Everyday Life," in *To Everyone an Answer: A Case for the Christian Worldview*, eds. Francis Beckwith, William Lane Craig, and J. P. Moreland (Downers Grove, IL: InterVarsity Press, 2004).

14. Now you shouldn't go looking to challenge professors just to see if you can. Be respectful. Also be careful; they may "take you behind the woodshed" . . . intellectually speaking.

15. William Lane Craig, *Reasonable Faith: Christian Truth and Apologetics*, rev. ed. (Wheaton, IL: Crossway, 1994), 50.

CHAPTER 22: To the Ends of the Earth

1. Statistics are available from the Joshua Project at www.joshuaproject.net.

2. See DC Talk and Voice of the Martyrs, *Jesus Freaks: Stories of Those Who Stood for Jesus, The Ultimate Jesus Freaks* (Tulsa: Albury, 1999).

3. This story was taken from the Jesus Film Project at www.jesusfilm.org/progress/africa .html?type=regular&id=230 (accessed March 24, 2007).

CHAPTER 23: Getting to Know You

1. T. S. Eliot, *Four Quartets* (New York: Houghton Mifflin Harcourt, 2014), 59.

2. The section on identity is based on the Center of Christian Leadership at Dallas Theological Seminary, *Identity: Investigating Who I Am*, Transforming Life Series (Colorado Springs: NavPress, 2004).

3. There is much confusion today about gender identity. Ideally and biblically speaking, our gender is intended to correspond to our biological sex (male or female). However, in a physiologically and psychologically fallen and broken world (see Gen. 3), people sometimes experience confusion along gender identity developmental pathways. For more, see Mark A. Yarhouse's work, *Understanding Gender Dysphoria: Navigating Transgender Issues in a Changing Culture* (Downers Grove, IL: InterVarsity Press, 2015), and *Understanding Sexual Identity: A Resource for Youth Ministry* (Grand Rapids: Zondervan, 2013).

4. Spiritual-gift tests are helpful, but I think the best way to discover your gifts is to start serving in your local church according to your passions and the needs of the body. Then take it from there.

5. This section on the four *h*'s and the following questions are taken from the Center of Christian Leadership at Dallas Theological Seminary, *Community: Discovering Who We Are Together*, Transforming Life Series (Colorado Springs: NavPress, 2004). I have had the privilege of walking through this material with small groups both in seminaries and in local churches. Every time people have made significant discoveries about themselves to the extent of expressing to others who they were in the redemptive power of God's authorship of their lives.

CHAPTER 24: Here's to Your Health

1. Henry de Bracton, quoted in *The New Dictionary of Cultural Literacy*, 3rd ed., ed. E. D. Hirsch Jr. et al. (Boston: Houghton Mifflin Harcourt, 2002).
2. See Chip Ingram, *The Invisible War: What Every Believer Needs to Know About Satan, Demons, and Spiritual Warfare* (Grand Rapids: Baker, 2015).
3. See, for example, the honest story of J. P. Moreland in Moreland and Klaus Issler, *The Lost Virtue of Happiness: Discovering the Disciplines of the Good Life* (Colorado Springs: NavPress, 2006), 155–78.
4. I am not saying we need to overdiagnose anxiety disorders or depression (i.e., see them behind every bad day). My point is only that they are real, they are nothing to be ashamed of, and you are not alone.
5. I am indebted to Matt Getz for some of his insights on this chapter. We collaborated on organizing some of this material for a student-training seminar.

CHAPTER 25: Sticks and Stones

1. Biblically understood, the heart expresses the sum total of the intellect, emotions, and will (Prov. 4:23). But it is still desperately sick until glory (Jer. 17:9).
2. Dallas Willard, *Renovation of the Heart: Putting on the Character of Christ* (Colorado Springs: NavPress, 2002), 14.
3. This is a phrase used in "The Resolution of Conflict" from Tommy Nelson, *The Book of Romance: What Solomon Says About Love, Sex, and Intimacy* (Nashville: Thomas Nelson, 2007), 132–51. These principles have saved us a lot of heartache in marriage. But we are still growing!
4. Ken Sande, *The Peacemaker: A Biblical Guide to Resolving Personal Conflict*, rev. and updated ed. (Grand Rapids: Baker, 2004), 263. This is an excellent book. See also the student edition.
5. The following section, "The Peacemaker's Pledge," is taken directly from Sande, *The Peacemaker*, 259–61. Used by permission.

CHAPTER 26: Has the Church Lost Her Mind?

1. W. Jay Wood, *Epistemology: Becoming Intellectually Virtuous* (Downers Grove, IL: InterVarsity Press, 1998), 17.
2. William Lane Craig, *Hard Questions, Real Answers* (Wheaton, IL: Crossway, 2003), 13.
3. Ravi Zacharias, *Recapture the Wonder* (Nashville: Integrity, 2003), 153.
4. This is the title of a talk that J. P. Moreland delivered at the Set Forth Your Case apologetics conference in Atlanta in 2003.
5. Os Guinness, *Fit Bodies, Fat Minds: Why Evangelicals Don't Think and What to Do About It* (Grand Rapids: Baker, 1994), 8.
6. J. P. Moreland, "Philosophical Apologetics, the Church, and Contemporary Culture," *Journal of the Evangelical Theological Society* 39, no. 1 (1996): 140.
7. Douglas Groothuis, "Jesus: Philosopher and Apologist," *Christian Research Journal* 25, no. 2 (2003): 51.
8. Ibid., 52. For more on this, see Douglas R. Groothuis, *On Jesus* (Belmont, CA: Wadsworth, 2003).

9. J. P. Moreland and David M. Ciocchi, eds., *Christian Perspectives on Being Human: A Multidisciplinary Approach to Integration* (Grand Rapids: Baker, 1993), 8.

10. Mark A. Noll, *The Scandal of the Evangelical Mind* (Grand Rapids: Eerdmans, 1994), 79–80.

11. This is a saying that I heard Ben Witherington use in a talk one time that made me laugh.

CHAPTER 27: Overcoming Syllabus Shock

1. Despair, Inc., "Procrastination," http://despair.com/viewall.html (accessed December 3, 2007).

2. Now, this is coming from a true night owl. So if you are a morning person, disregard and have at those 8 a.m. classes!

3. Peter Drucker, quoted in Greg McKeown, *Essentialism: The Disciplined Pursuit of Less* (New York: Crown Business, 2014), 13.

CHAPTER 28: Show Me the Money

1. John D. Rockefeller, quoted in Randy Alcorn, *The Treasure Principle: Discovering the Secret of Joyful Giving* (Sisters, OR: Multnomah, 2001), 52.

2. Is having money bad? Is it more "spiritual" to be poor? Our answers to these kinds of questions need to be informed by the teaching of the Bible. What is condemned is the love of money, not money itself. Many times people are blessed financially so that they might be a blessing to others. Whether they are being good stewards with what God has provided or not is between them and the Lord—and the accountability of the body of Christ. But we need to be careful not to judge people too quickly, for God knows their heart. Explore these and other important questions further in Gene Getz, *Rich in Every Way: Everything God Says About Money and Possessions* (New York: Rosen, 2010).

3. Alcorn, *The Treasure Principle*, 25.

4. At the end of 2015, the average US household had about $90,000 of debt, with $15,762 of that being credit card debt. See "Household Debt Surpasses $90,000," *The Huffington Post*, May 23, 2016, http://www.huffingtonpost.com/moneytips/household-debt-surpasses-_b_10060954.html.

CHAPTER 29: Becoming More Like Jesus

1. J. P. Moreland and Klaus Issler, *The Lost Virtue of Happiness: Discovering the Disciplines of the Good Life* (Colorado Springs: NavPress, 2006), 29.

2. Gordon D. Fee, *Paul, the Spirit, and the People of God* (Peabody, MA: Hendrickson, 1996), 183.

3. James Emery White, *You Can Experience . . . a Spiritual Life* (Nashville: Thomas Nelson, 1999), 30.

4. Klaus Issler, *Wasting Time with God: A Christian Spirituality of Friendship with God* (Downers Grove, IL: InterVarsity Press, 2001), 26.

5. Dallas Willard, quoted in Michael Wilkins, *In His Image: Reflecting Christ in Everyday Life* (Colorado Springs: NavPress, 1997), 59.

6. These are summarized from Kenneth Boa, *That I May Know God: Pathways to Spiritual*

Formation (Sisters, OR: Multnomah, 1998), 81–87. Excellent guides to how to practice the various disciplines are Richard J. Foster, *Celebration of Discipline: The Path to Spiritual Growth* (New York: HarperCollins, 2009); Dallas Willard, *The Spirit of the Disciplines: Understanding How God Changes Lives* (New York: HarperCollins, 2009); and Donald S. Whitney, *Spiritual Disciplines for the Christian Life* (Carol Stream, IL: Tyndale House, 2014).

7. The following subsections are taken from the very helpful guide by Kenneth Boa, *Sacred Readings: A Journal* (Colorado Springs: NavPress, 2000).

8. Other good translations for Bible study are the English Standard Version, Holman Christian Standard Bible, and New International Version. Many people enjoy *The Message* for an informal change of pace.

9. Some have found it helpful to pick different categories to pray for according to what day of the week it is (e.g., Monday—pray for family, Tuesday—pray for friends, Wednesday—pray for a country in the world, etc.).

CHAPTER 30: Discovering the Will of God

1. While all Christians do not agree, I think the New Testament strongly suggests that God has an individual will for our lives. This can be inferred from passages like Romans 12:1–8, 1 Corinthians 12:4–7, Ephesians 2:10, and 1 Peter 4:10. God has created a work for us to do and has gifted us to function in unique ways in the body of Christ. There is both freedom in decision-making and God's leading in specific areas. See M. Blaine Smith, *Knowing God's Will: Finding Guidance for Personal Decisions*, 2nd ed. (Downers Grove, IL: InterVarsity Press, 1991), 228–39. For an overview of this debate, see Garry Friesen and J. Robin Maxson, *Decision Making and the Will of God: A Biblical Alternative to the Traditional View* (New York: Crown, 2009).

2. Charles R. Swindoll, *The Mystery of God's Will: What Does He Want for Me?* (Nashville: Word, 1999), 30.

3. Be sure to read chapter 41 in this book, "A Christian View of Alcohol," so that you don't misunderstand what I am saying about a conviction.

4. Haddon W. Robinson, *Decision-Making by the Book: How to Choose Wisely in an Age of Options* (Wheaton, IL: Victor, 1991), 126–27.

5. Andy Stanley, *The Principle of the Path: How to Get from Where You Are to Where You Want to Be* (Nashville: Thomas Nelson, 2008), 73.

6. Dallas Willard, *Hearing God: Developing a Conversational Relationship with God* (Downers Grove, IL: InterVarsity Press, 1999), 28.

7. Henry T. Blackaby and Claude V. King, *Experiencing God: How to Live the Full Adventure of Knowing and Doing the Will of God* (Nashville: B&H Publishing, 1994), 117–27.

8. Since God's Spirit is our Helper and Counselor, I don't find it unreasonable that He would lead us by internal means at times in life (see John 14–17).

9. Does God still speak today? Absolutely! Is God speaking new Scripture? No! Nothing more is needed; the Bible is complete and sufficient. So any word from the Lord or vision or dream (God clearly still uses these mediums here in America and around the world) needs to be tested against Scripture. And if God leads you to tell someone something, then do so tentatively in a spirit of obedience. God may lead you individually in a certain way, but this is not binding for the community of Christians

and does not carry the same authority as Scripture. Now admittedly, this is sometimes messy. But the experiences of Christians throughout history testify to God's leading.

10. Andy Stanley, *The Best Question Ever: A Revolutionary Approach to Decision Making* (Sisters, OR: Multnomah, 2004), 60.

CHAPTER 31: When Someone You Love Dies

1. In chapter 15, I talk more about how God works even through death and evil. Death does not have the final word. This chapter is not an apologetic but more of a testimony.

2. This reality is brought before me powerfully every time I listen to Andrew Peterson's song "After the Last Tear Falls." Visit www.andrew-peterson.com to check it out. Two other songs of his that have especially ministered to me as I have reflected on the grieving process are "The Silence of God" and "No More Faith."

CHAPTER 32: Gentlemen, Become Who You Were Born to Be

1. Maureen Dowd, *Are Men Necessary? When Sexes Collide* (New York: Penguin, 2005).

2. "'Are Men Necessary?' *Times* Columnist Maureen Dowd Raises Ruckus with New Book," CNN.com, November 15, 2005, www.cnn.com/2005/SHOWBIZ/books/11/15/dowd .men.necessary/index.htmlm.

3. "The Extent of Fatherlessness," National Center for Fathering, http://www.fathers.com /statistics-and-research/the-extent-of-fatherlessness/ (accessed November 14, 2016).

4. "Unmarried Childbearing," Centers for Disease Control and Prevention, June 13, 2016, http://www.cdc.gov/nchs/fastats/unmarried-childbearing.htm.

5. Louis Jacobson, "CNN's Don Lemon Says More Than 72 Percent of African-American Births Are Out of Wedlock," Politifact, July 29 2013, http://www.politifact.com/truth -o-meter/statements/2013/jul/29/don-lemon/cnns-don-lemon-says-more-72-percent -african-americ/.

6. "Fatherless Epidemic," National Center for Fathering, 2015, http://fathers.com/wp39 /wp-content/uploads/2015/05/fatherlessInfographic.png (accessed November 14, 2016).

7. William Bennett, "Why Men Are in Trouble," CNN.com, October 4, 2011, http://www .cnn.com/2011/10/04/opinion/bennett-men-in-trouble/.

8. Jonathan Wells, "Why Are Men Less Happy Than Women?" *The Telegraph*, February 12, 2016, http://www.telegraph.co.uk/men/thinking-man/why-are-men-less-happy-than -women/.

9. This chapter has been heavily influenced by the Men's Fraternity *The Quest for Authentic Manhood* curriculum by Robert Lewis at AuthenticManhood.com, as well as Lewis's *Raising a Modern-Day Knight: A Father's Role in Guiding His Son to Authentic Manhood* (Carol Stream, IL: Tyndale House, 2011).

10. Lewis, *Raising a Modern-Day Knight*, 60.

11. It is impossible to condense the insights of a twenty-four-week study into a single page, so I will be frustratingly brief. I would encourage you to see if there is a Men's Fraternity near you and to read the books mentioned at the end of the chapter. See also the video study *33 The Series* available at AuthenticManhood.com. *33 The Series* is an updated and enhanced study on authentic manhood that includes the core content of Robert Lewis's teaching from *The Quest for Authentic Manhood* as well as many new insights. I

would also recommend the *Stepping Up* video study by Dennis Rainey and Family Life at http://www.familylife.com/steppingup.

12. Lewis, *Raising a Modern-Day Knight*, 56.

13. Ibid., 57.

14. Ibid., 69–70.

15. Winston Churchill, quoted in Dennis Rainey, *Stepping Up: A Call to Courageous Manhood* (Little Rock: FamilyLife, 2011), 24.

CHAPTER 33: Ladies, Pursue Real Beauty

1. Michelle Graham, *Wanting to Be Her: Body Image Secrets Victoria Won't Tell You* (Downers Grove, IL: InterVarsity Press, 2009).

2. For more on the context of this book, see Tommy Nelson, *The Book of Romance: What Solomon Says About Love, Sex, and Intimacy* (Nashville: Thomas Nelson, 2007).

3. Bruce K. Waltke, *The Book of Proverbs: Chapters 15–31* (Grand Rapids: Eerdmans, 2005), 535.

4. Ibid.

5. This passage is set within the context of a believing wife married to an unbelieving husband. It seeks to show her how she ought to live with him so as to lead him to Christ. However, the principle of true beauty—which God highly values—is clearly transferable to women in general.

6. It is not as though the physical is bad and the spiritual is good. No, the point here is that the heart is the overall direction of a person, and it spills out into all of life. Your heart is essentially who you are.

7. This definition is taken from the "Fathers and Daughters" session of the Men's Fraternity *The Quest for Authentic Manhood* curriculum by Robert Lewis at www.mensfraternity.com. *The New Eve* by Robert Lewis and Jeremy Howard (Nashville: B&H Publishing, 2008) explores this definition in further detail.

8. Now, I am not saying that a woman must be married or have a family to be significant. There are those who remain single who dedicate themselves solely to the work of the Lord (see 1 Cor. 7:32–35). Others through a fallen world suffer divorce, are widowed, or are unable to have children. I am not for one instant diminishing the value and expression of femininity that these women live out. Yet, for the majority of women, being a wife and mother are core expressions of their calling as women (Titus 2:3–5).

9. Nowhere does the Bible say that a woman should never work (in a career sense) or seek to express her gifts and talents outside the home.

10. I want to make sure I am not misunderstood here. This emphatic statement is intended to encourage future moms who are called to stay at home and nurture the next generation (which is plenty!). This is hugely important and needed—whether the world thinks so or not. I also am not diminishing the importance or role of singleness. See Tim Keller, "A Theology of Singleness," Vimeo video, 31:50, posted by "Redeemer Video," 2014, https://vimeo.com/88162694 (accessed November 15, 2016).

11. Lydia Saad, "Children a Key Factor in Women's Desire to Work Outside the Home," Gallup, October 7, 2015, http://www.gallup.com/poll/186050/children-key-factor-women-desire-work-outside-home.aspx.

CHAPTER 34: The Dating Game

1. Henry Cloud and John Townsend, *Boundaries in Dating: Making Dating Work* (Grand Rapids: Zondervan, 2000), 51.
2. Much of my thinking on these topics has been shaped by Tommy Nelson's *Song of Solomon* study (https://www.rightnow.org/Content/Speaker/1188). Much of what follows is my summary of major points he makes or my reflection on this material. I am thankful to God for men like Tommy Nelson who are not afraid to preach the truth to our generation. For this material in book form, see Tommy Nelson, *The Book of Romance: What Solomon Says About Love, Sex, and Intimacy* (Nashville: Thomas Nelson, 2007).
3. The Christian life is not about what we have to say no to; rather, it is about what we get to say yes to. The biblical ideal of sexual intimacy between a husband and wife far outweighs the hollow imitation of premarital sex.

CHAPTER 35: Sex, Sex, Sex

1. Lauren F. Winner, *Real Sex: The Naked Truth About Chastity* (Grand Rapids: Brazos, 2006), 38.
2. Joe S. McIlhaney and Freda McKissic Bush, *Hooked: New Science on How Casual Sex Is Affecting Our Children* (Chicago: Moody Publishers, 2008), 19.
3. David Kinnaman and Gabe Lyons, *Good Faith: Being a Christian When Society Thinks You're Irrelevant and Extreme* (Grand Rapids: Baker, 2016), 58.
4. Tommy Nelson, *The Book of Romance: What Solomon Says About Love, Sex, and Intimacy* (Nashville: Thomas Nelson, 1998), 87.
5. Much of what I will say on this topic has been influenced by this wonderful study. There are DVDs and other online materials available at https://www.rightnow.org/Content/Speaker/1188. I recommend the student edition, but any of them are good.
6. For a biblical theology of marriage and family, see Andreas J. Köstenberger and David W. Jones, *God, Marriage, and Family: Rebuilding the Biblical Foundation* (Wheaton, IL: Crossway, 2010).
7. Leland Ryken et al., *Dictionary of Biblical Imagery* (Downers Grove, IL: InterVarsity Press, 1998), 806–7.
8. This image is borrowed from Tommy Nelson.
9. For a sobering look at the effects of sexual immorality, read Solomon's description of a young man's run-in with an adulterous woman (Prov. 7). I did not even mention the horrors of sexually transmitted diseases, but these should also deter you from premarital sex. Your physical health and ability to have children one day are literally at stake.
10. Glenn T. Stanton, *The Ring Makes All the Difference: The Hidden Consequences of Cohabitation and the Strong Benefits of Marriage* (Chicago: Moody Publishers, 2011), 11.
11. Ibid., 117.
12. McIlhaney and Bush, *Hooked*, 105.

CHAPTER 36: A Call to Purity

1. William Goldman, *The Ghost and the Darkness*, directed by Stephen Hopkins (Hollywood, CA: Paramount Pictures, 1996). For a powerful depiction of the enemy

scheming to destroy us, read C. S. Lewis's *Screwtape Letters* (New York: HarperCollins, 2001).

2. See the groundbreaking study *The Porn Phenomenon* by the Barna Group and the Josh McDowell Ministry at https://barna-resources.myshopify.com/products/porn -phenomenon.

3. This is the basis of the Internet accountability software I use and would recommend you to install as well: Covenant Eyes at www.covenanteyes.com.

4. On the devastating cultural effects of pornography, Luke Gilkerson writes, "Porn's effects don't stop with individuals and couples—it impacts society itself. Porn shapes the sexual expectations of teens. Porn has become the norm on college campuses. Porn brings about real harms to the women who are involved in the industry. Worse yet, porn fuels a thirst for other forms of commercial sex, including sex trafficking." See Gilkerson, "Effects of Porn Addiction and Other Online Dangers," Covenant Eyes, October 2, 2013, http://www.covenanteyes.com/2013/10/02/effects-of-porn -addiction/#, and also Chrissy Gordon, "Key Findings in Landmark Pornography Study Released," Josh McDowell Ministry, January 19, 2016, http://www.josh.org/key-findings -in-landmark-pornography-study-released/.

5. A common struggle for young men and women—but especially men—is masturbation. Is it a sin? Christians of good will handle this differently. But the answer to this question hinges on what God's design for sex really is. Tim Challies has a helpful two-part series worth reading as you think this through. Here are some of his discerning comments on self-centered sex: "By now I think it should be clear that masturbation is a sin—one that ought to be repented of and one that Christians need to fight against. Sadly, though, for many young Christians, it becomes an issue that begins to define their spiritual state. Some people feel such guilt for this act that they begin to question their salvation and begin to see themselves only through the lens of this sin. There is no doubt that this is a serious sin, but it should not be given so much prominence that people can see nothing past it. Josh Harris writes wisely, 'When we inflate the importance of this act, we'll either overlook the many evidences of God's work in us or we'll ignore other more serious expressions of lust that God wants us to address.'" See Tim Challies, "Self-Centered Sex," Challies.com, January 24–25, 2007, http://www.challies.com/articles/self-centered-sex -part-1 and http://www.challies.com/articles/self-centered-sex-part-2.

6. Chrissy Gordon, "Key Findings in Landmark Pornography Study Released," Josh McDowell Ministry, January 19, 2016, http://www.josh.org/key-findings-in-landmark -pornography-study-released/.

7. I am not denying that we are positionally pure before God in Christ, only that our experience of God and fellowship with Him can be affected by sin.

CHAPTER 37: Christianity, Homosexuality, and the Bible

1. Caleb Kaltenbach, *Messy Grace: How a Pastor with Gay Parents Learned to Love Others Without Sacrificing Conviction* (Colorado Springs: WaterBrook Press, 2015), 95.

2. Preston M. Sprinkle, *People to Be Loved: Why Homosexuality Is Not Just an Issue* (Grand Rapids: Zondervan, 2015), 123.

3. Ryan T. Anderson, *Truth Overruled: The Future of Marriage and Religious Freedom* (Washington, DC: Regnery, 2015), 4.

4. See Eugene H. Peterson, *A Long Obedience in the Same Direction: Discipleship in an Instant Society* (Downers Grove, IL: InterVarsity Press, 2012).

5. New Atheists like Richard Dawkins in his book *The God Delusion* (Boston: Houghton Mifflin Harcourt, 2008) would be an example of this.

6. This approach is advocated by people like Matthew Vines, *God and the Gay Christian* (New York: Crown, 2014), and Lisa Miller, "Gay Marriage: Our Mutual Joy," *Newsweek*, December 5, 2008, http://www.newsweek.com/gay-marriage-our-mutual-joy-83287.

7. See Kevin DeYoung, *What Does the Bible Really Teach About Homosexuality?* (Wheaton, IL: Crossway, 2015), 74–75.

8. Ibid., 59–67, for more discussion and lexical documentation.

9. Christopher Yuan, "Why 'God and the Gay Christian' Is Wrong About the Bible and Same-Sex Relationships," *Christianity Today*, June 9, 2014, http://www.christianitytoday .com/ct/2014/june-web-only/why-matthew-vines-is-wrong-about-bible-same-sex -relationshi.html. See also the personal reflections of Rosaria Butterfield, "Love Your Neighbor Enough to Speak Truth," The Gospel Coalition, October 31, 2016, https:// www.thegospelcoalition.org/article/love-your-neighbor-enough-to-speak-truth, and Wesley Hill's personal reflections and analysis in "Nicholas Wolterstorff's Cheap Shots," *First Things*, November 1, 2016, https://www.firstthings.com/web-exclusives/2016/11 /nicholas-wolterstorffs-cheap-shots.

10. Kaltenbach, *Messy Grace*, 70.

11. Wesley Hill, *Washed and Waiting: Reflections on Christian Faithfulness and Homosexuality* (Grand Rapids: Zondervan, 2010), 150.

12. Peter Hubbard, *Love into Light: The Gospel, the Homosexual and the Church* (Greenville, SC: Ambassador International, 2013), Kindle loc. 2594.

13. Anderson, *Truth Overruled*, 12.

14. See, for example, the new family structures study by University of Texas sociologist Mark Regnerus at http://www.familystructurestudies.com/.

15. For more on why religious liberty is not bigotry, see Ben R. Crenshaw, "'Shut Up, Bigot!' Civil Rights and Same-Sex Marriage," *Public Discourse*, The Witherspoon Institute, April 14, 2016, http://www.thepublicdiscourse.com/2016/04/16749/.

16. Gary J. Gates, "How Many People are Lesbian, Gay, Bisexual, and Transgender?" The Williams Institute, eScholarship University of California, April 1, 2011, https:// escholarship.org/uc/item/09h684x2#page-1.

17. Mark Mittelberg, *The Questions Christians Hope No One Will Ask* (Carol Stream, IL: Tyndale House, 2010), 216.

18. Alan Shlemon, "Are Homosexuals Born That Way?" *Stand to Reason* (blog), February 23, 2012, http://str.typepad.com/weblog/2012/02/are-homosexuals-born-that-way .html#_edn2. The APA research can be found at http://www.apa.org/helpcenter/sexual -orientation.aspx#sthash.HEv0FkH8.dpuf.

19. Simon LeVay, quoted in David Nimmons, "Sex and the Brain," *Discover*, March 1, 1994, http://discovermagazine.com/1994/mar/sexandthebrain346/?searchterm=levay.

20. "Additional 'Gay Gene' Studies," American Family Association of Pennsylvania, http:// afaofpa.org/resources/additional-gay-gene-studies/ (accessed November 15, 2016).

21. See video testimonials at http://voices-of-change.org/.

22. Alan Shlemon, "Can Gay People Change? Is It Psychologically Harmful to Make Them Try?" ThinkChristainly.org, March 7, 2012, http://www.thinkchristianly.org/can-gay -people-change-is-it-psychologically-harmful-to-make-them-try/. For more on this, see Stanton L. Jones and Mark A. Yarhouse, *Ex-Gays? A Longitudinal Study of Religiously Mediated Change in Sexual Orientation* (Downers Grove, IL: InterVarsity Press, 2007).
23. Greg Koukl, *Tactics: A Game Plan for Discussing Your Christian Convictions* (Grand Rapids: Zondervan, 2009), 78.

CHAPTER 38: Unplugged and Offline

1. Dallas Willard, *The Spirit of the Disciplines: Understanding How God Changes Lives*, 2nd ed. (San Francisco: HarperSanFrancisco, 1999), 163.
2. Donald S. Whitney, *Simplify Your Spiritual Life: Spiritual Disciplines for the Overwhelmed* (Colorado Springs: NavPress, 2003), 164.
3. Sherry Turkle, "Connected, but Alone?" Technology, Entertainment, and Design, April 2012, https://www.ted.com/talks/sherry_turkle_alone_together?language=en.
4. See Sherry Turkle, *Alone Together: Why We Expect More from Technology and Less from Each Other* (New York: Basic Books, 2011), as well as Carolyn Gregoire, "Why Loneliness Is a Growing Public Health Concern—And What We Can Do About It," *The Huffington Post*, March 21, 2015, http://www.huffingtonpost.com/2015/03/21/science -loneliness_n_6864066.html, and Maria Konnikova, "How Facebook Makes Us Unhappy," *The New Yorker*, September 10, 2013, http://www.newyorker.com/tech /elements/how-facebook-makes-us-unhappy.

CHAPTER 39: Compassionately Engage Your World

1. Thomas R. Schreiner, *Paul, Apostle of God's Glory in Christ: A Pauline Theology* (Downers Grove, IL: InterVarsity Press, 2001), 451.
2. A thought-provoking work that calls the church to good works is Ronald J. Sider, *Good News and Good Works: A Theology for the Whole Gospel* (Grand Rapids: Baker, 1999).
3. One church's story can be found in Robert Lewis and Rob Wilkins, *The Church of Irresistible Influence: Bridge-Building Stories to Help Reach Your Community* (Grand Rapids: Zondervan, 2002).
4. For the impact of Christianity lived out in culture throughout history, see the excellent book by Alvin J. Schmidt, *How Christianity Changed the World* (Grand Rapids: Zondervan, 2009).
5. Francis A. Schaeffer, *True Spirituality: How to Live for Jesus Moment by Moment*, 30th anniversary ed. (Wheaton, IL: Tyndale House, 2001), 158.
6. I am grateful for Dr. Scott Rae's ethics class in graduate school in which we talked about justice and its relationship to God and His people.
7. Sider, *Good News and Good Works*, 163.
8. In Ronald J. Sider and Diane Knippers, eds., *Toward an Evangelical Public Policy: Political Strategies for the Health of the Nation* (Grand Rapids: Baker, 2005), 366. The entire well-written statement is also available at http://nae.net/for-the-health-of -the-nation/.
9. See International Justice Mission at www.ijm.org.
10. It is estimated that fifty-six million abortions occur annually worldwide. See the

worldwide induced abortion fact sheet published by the World Health Organization and Guttmacher Institute at https://www.guttmacher.org/fact-sheet/induced-abortion -worldwide.

11. Schmidt, *How Christianity Changed the World*, 277.

12. See Living Water International at https://water.cc/.

13. Stephen Monsma and Mark Rodgers, "In the Arena: Practical Issues in Concrete Political Engagement," in *Toward an Evangelical Public Policy*, 333.

14. Scott B. Rae, *Moral Choices: An Introduction to Ethics*, 2nd ed. (Grand Rapids: Zondervan, 2000), 123–28.

15. J. Budziszewski, *How to Stay Christian in College* (Colorado Springs: NavPress, 2004), 116.

16. Michael Bauman, "Legislating Morality," in *To Everyone an Answer: A Case for the Christian Worldview*, eds. Francis J. Beckwith, William Lane Craig, and J. P. Moreland (Downers Grove, IL: InterVarsity Press, 2004), 254–55, italics added.

CHAPTER 40: Watching Movies with Eyes Wide Open

1. Brian Godawa, *Hollywood Worldviews: Watching Films with Wisdom and Discernment* (Downers Grove, IL: InterVarsity Press, 2002), 178.

2. Please note that my intention is not to be insensitive toward anyone who struggles with eating disorders. I am using Godawa's categories for illustration purposes as they relate to media.

3. Godawa, *Hollywood Worldviews*, 21. Used by permission of InterVarsity Press, P.O. Box 1400, Downers Grove, IL 60515, USA. www.ivpress.com.

4. This is what has been so damaging about books and movies like *Fifty Shades of Grey*. Some are calling this "mommy porn." But the dehumanizing effects are just as heinous.

5. Rebecca Adams, "It's Not Just Girls. Boys Struggle with Body Image, Too," *The Huffington Post*, September 17, 2014, http://www.huffingtonpost.com/2014/09/17/body -image-boys_n_5637975.html.

6. For a fuller discussion of these themes, see Godawa, *Hollywood Worldviews*, 187–208. By way of summary, the Bible deals honestly and redemptively with evil, violence, and sexuality—it is not gratuitous in its descriptions to be shocking or disturbing for its own sake. Moreover, "humankind's depravity is not emphasized more than our redemptive potential. Sin is a manifestation of the need for redemption, not an object of obsessive focus" (ibid., 202). For example there is a horrible depiction of where sin leads in Judges 19, but what you don't get is *Saw VII* or *The Purge: Election Year*. (I have not seen these movies, nor do I recommend you to, but the previews were more than telling.)

7. I am borrowing the title of this chapter from Godawa, *Hollywood Worldviews*, 177.

CHAPTER 41: A Christian View of Alcohol

1. "Facts on College Student Drinking," StopAlcoholAbuse.org, Interagency Coordinating Committee on the Prevention of Underage Drinking, https://www.stopalcoholabuse.gov /townHallMeetings/pdf/tipsresources/5486_UADPEI_College_Drinking_Fact_Sheet _FINAL_4-2016.pdf (accessed November 15, 2016). See also "College Drinking," National Institute on Alcohol Abuse and Alcoholism, December 2015, https://www.niaaa.nih.gov /alcohol-health/special-populations-co-occurring-disorders/college-drinking.

2. Daniel B. Wallace, "The Bible and Alcohol," Bible.org, June 21, 2004, www.bible.org /page.asp?page_id=988.

3. Walter Bauer, *A Greek-English Lexicon of the New Testament and Other Early Christian Literature*, 3rd ed. (Chicago: University of Chicago Press, 2000), 499.

4. Leland Ryken et al., *Dictionary of Biblical Imagery* (Downers Grove, IL: InterVarsity Press, 1998), 953.

5. R. V. Pierard, "Drinking of Alcohol," in *Evangelical Dictionary of Theology*, ed. Walter A. Elwell (Grand Rapids: Baker, 2001), 42.

6. For those of you attending a Christian school, you probably signed a contract that you would not drink alcohol while enrolled at school. Even if you are twenty-one and can legally drink, you need to fulfill this obligation and abstain. It is a matter of personal integrity before the Lord. If you find the temptation to have a drink too strong, then this may indicate a larger problem.

7. He is finally free of this because he is now in the presence of the Lord.

8. For more on these consequences, see "College Drinking," NIAAA, https://www.niaaa .nih.gov/alcohol-health /special-populations-co-occurring-disorders/college-drinking.

9. See "DWI: Driving While Intexticated," TextingAndDrivingSafety.com, 2012, http:// www.textinganddrivingsafety.com/texting-and-driving-stats (accessed November 15, 2016).

10. I want to thank Mike Good for his invaluable comments on this particular chapter.

11. Sydney Lupkin, "77 Percent of American Teens Now Believe It's Safe to Smoke Weed," Vice News, January 27, 2016, https://news.vice.com/article/77-percent-of-american -teens-now-believe-its-totally-safe-to-smoke-weed.

12. Joe Carter, "Is Recreational Marijuana Use a Sin?," The Gospel Coalition, January 6, 2014, https://www.thegospelcoalition.org/article/is-recreational-marijuana-use-a-sin.

13. For more about these studies, see "Regular Marijuana Use by Teens Continues to Be a Concern," National Institutes of Health, December 19, 2012, https://www.nih.gov/news -events/news-releases/regular-marijuana-use-teens-continues-be-concern; Kirsten Weir, "Marijuana and the Developing Brain," American Psychological Association, November 2015, http://www.apa.org/monitor/2015/11/marijuana-brain.aspx; and Krista M. Lisdahl et al., "Dare to Delay? The Impacts of Adolescent Alcohol and Marijuana Use Onset on Cognition, Brain Structure, and Function," *Frontiers in Psychiatry*, July 1, 2013, http://journal.frontiersin.org/article/10.3389/fpsyt.2013.00053/full.

14. John Stonestreet, "Marijuana Madness: The Negative Effects of Weed," BreakPoint, October 26, 2015, http://www.breakpoint.org/bpcommentaries/entry/13/28363. See also Sushrut Jangi, "Can We Please Stop Pretending Marijuana Is Harmless?," *The Boston Globe*, October 8, 2015, https://www.bostonglobe.com/magazine/2015/10/08/can -please-stop-pretending-marijuana-harmless/MneQebFPWg79ifTAXc1PkM/story .html. To be clear, what I am not talking about is the use of medicinal marijuana by people suffering from cancer to ease symptoms and improve their quality of life during and after treatments. This is very different from recreational marijuana.

CHAPTER 42: Ethics in a Brave New World

1. Scott B. Rae, *Moral Choices: An Introduction to Ethics*, 2nd ed. (Grand Rapids: Zondervan, 2000), 12.

2. Paul Chamberlain, *Talking About Good and Bad Without Getting Ugly: A Guide to Moral Persuasion* (Downers Grove, IL: InterVarsity Press, 2005), 39.

3. Quote traditionally attributed to Edmund Burke, an eighteenth-century British statesman, though no source with this exact wording has ever been located.

4. In a controversial story, a deaf couple genetically screened for and succeeded in having a deaf child. They took a healthy child who was not deaf and made the child deaf according to their preferences!

5. This is especially the case for evangelicals. See J. Daryl Charles, *The Unformed Conscience of Evangelicalism: Recovering the Church's Moral Vision* (Downers Grove, IL: InterVarsity Press, 2002).

6. If you are looking for a great place to start, buy a copy of *Moral Choices: An Introduction to Ethics* by Scott Rae (Grand Rapids: Zondervan, 2009) and work through it.

7. Francis J. Beckwith, *Abortion and the Sanctity of Human Life* (Joplin, MO: College Press, 2000), 70.

8. For the dire implications of physician-assisted suicide, see John Stonestreet, "Vote Against Assisted Suicide in Colorado," *USA Today*, October 18, 2016, http://www.usatoday.com/story/opinion/2016/10/18/suicide-colorado-prop-106-euthanasia-column/91964372/.

9. Beckwith, *Abortion and the Sanctity of Human Life*, 72.

10. Francis J. Beckwith, "What Does It Mean to Be Human?," *Christian Research Journal* (2003): 19.

11. Beckwith, *Abortion and the Sanctity of Human Life*, 74–75.

12. The SLED acrostic was developed by Stephen Schwarz and popularized by Scott Klusendorf, *The Case for Life: Equipping Christians to Engage the Culture* (Wheaton, IL: Crossway, 2009).

CHAPTER 43: Beyond the Horizon

1. Os Guinness, *The Call: Finding and Fulfilling the Central Purpose of Your Life* (Nashville: Thomas Nelson, 1998), 4.

2. Greg Ogden, *Unfinished Business: Returning the Ministry to the People of God*, rev. ed. (Grand Rapids: Zondervan, 2003), 259.

3. C. S. Lewis, *Mere Christianity* (New York: Simon & Schuster, 1996), 121.

4. William Carey, quoted in Beverly Hyles, *Life, as Viewed from the Goldfish Bowl* (Murfreesboro, TN: Sword of the Lord Publishers, 2000), 160.

5. Check out Dave Barnes at www.davebarnes.com.

6. Gordon T. Smith, *Courage and Calling: Embracing Your God-Given Potential* (Downers Grove, IL: InterVarsity Press, 2011).

7. This is a question that shaped many of the decisions that William Lane Craig and his wife, Jan, made. It is a good one because it zeroes in on what you are passionate about and strips away a really bad reason for not doing what God is calling you to do—money!

8. Guinness, *The Call*, 51.

9. Tom Schulman, *Dead Poets Society*. Directed by Peter Weir (Burbank, CA: Buena Vista Home Entertainment, 1989), italics added.

10. Mitch Albom, *Tuesdays with Morrie: An Old Man, a Young Man, and Life's Greatest Lesson*, 1st ed. (New York: Doubleday, 1997).

POSTSCRIPT: What I've Learned Thus Far

1. C. S. Lewis, *Mere Christianity* (New York: Simon & Schuster, 1996), 119.

APPENDIX A: A Devotional Reading Plan for Your First Semester

1. These questions are taken from Howard G. Hendricks and William Hendricks, *Living by the Book* (Chicago: Moody Publishers, 1991), 308.

APPENDIX B: Christian Versus Secular Colleges: Pros and Cons

1. See for example "Three Spiritual Journeys of Millennials," Barna Group, June 3, 2013, https://www.barna.com/research/three-spiritual-journeys-of-millennials/; also Christian Smith and Melinda Lundquist Denton, *Soul Searching: The Religious and Spiritual Lives of American Teenagers* (Oxford: Oxford University Press, 2005); Christian Smith and Patricia Snell, *Souls in Transition: The Religious and Spiritual Lives of Emerging Adults* (Oxford: Oxford University Press, 2009); and David Kinnaman, *You Lost Me: Why Young Christians Are Leaving Church . . . and Rethinking Faith* (Grand Rapids: Baker, 2011).

APPENDIX C: Resources for Philosophy

1. C. S. Lewis, *The Weight of Glory* (San Francisco: HarperSanFrancisco, 2001), 58.

About the Author

JONATHAN MORROW (DMIN, MDIV, MA) BLOGS AT JONATHANMORROW.ORG. He is the author of *Welcome to College: A Christ-Follower's Guide for the Journey*, *Questioning the Bible: 11 Major Challenges to the Bible's Authority*, *Think Christianly: Looking at the Intersection of Faith and Culture*, and *Is God Just a Human Invention? And Seventeen Other Questions Raised by the New Atheists* (coauthored with Sean McDowell). He has contributed the chapter "Introducing Spiritual Formation" to *Foundations of Spiritual Formation: A Community Approach to Becoming Like Christ* and the chapter "How to Question the Bible in a Post-Christian Culture" to *A New Kind of Apologist*. Jonathan also contributed several articles to the *Apologetics Study Bible for Students* and has written for Leadership Journal Online (of *Christianity Today*) and *The Stream*. He graduated with an MDiv and an MA in philosophy of religion and ethics from the Talbot School of Theology at Biola University. Jonathan is currently the director of cultural engagement and immersion at Impact 360 Institute where he trains high school and college students in Christian worldview, apologetics, and leadership, and he serves as an adjunct professor of apologetics at Biola University. His books have been featured on shows like *FamilyLife Today*, *Stand to Reason*, *BreakPoint*, *In the Market with Janet Parshall*, *Janet Mefferd Live*, *Building Relationships* with Dr. Gary Chapman, and *Apologetics 315*. He and his wife have been married for sixteen years and have three children.

—PARENTS—
READY TO HELP **YOUR TEENAGER** BUILD A **LASTING FAITH?**

Many Christian parents worry their teenagers will walk away from their faith in college. **Jonathan Morrow,** author of **Welcome to College,** has developed a clear and actionable plan that helps parents give their teenagers a faith that lasts.

Whether your kids go to public school, private school, or homeschool—they can build a confident faith. As their parents, you are the most important guide for them along the way.

While you can't control the choices your teenager will ultimately make, you can be confident that you've invested in the most important areas of life during their formative years.

Don't wait until graduation day to begin thinking about what they need to live well.

Start today at
5ThingsEveryTeenagerNeeds.com

The question of God is up for public debate. How should Christians respond?

The New Atheists want you to question your faith. So do authors Sean McDowell and Jonathan Morrow. The truth about God is too important not to be seriously investigated and honestly discussed.

With bonus material from nineteen scientists, apologists, and philosophers, McDowell and Morrow accessibly yet rigorously examine the challenges of the New Atheists, including:

- Are Science and Christianity at Odds?
- Is Faith Irrational?
- Is Religion Dangerous?
- Are Miracles Possible?
- Is Hell a Divine Torture Chamber?
- Why Jesus Instead of the Flying Spaghetti Monster?

Kregel
Publications
www.kregel.com

FINISHED?

Find more resources to
help you on your journey
at WelcometoCollege.tv!